The Well-Crafted Argument
Across the Curriculum

The Well-Crafted Argument
Across the Curriculum

Fred D. White *Santa Clara University*

Simone J. Billings *Santa Clara University*

WADSWORTH
CENGAGE Learning

Australia • Brazil • Japan • Korea • Mexico • Singapore • Spain • United Kingdom • United States

WADSWORTH
CENGAGE Learning·

The Well-Crafted Argument: Across the Curriculum
Fred D. White and
Simone J. Billings

Senior Publisher: Lyn Uhl

Executive Editor: Monica Eckman

Acquisitions Editor: Margaret Leslie

Assistant Editor: Amy Haines

Editorial Assistant: Danielle Warchol

Media Editor: Janine Tangney

Marketing Manager: Stacey Purviance

Marketing Coordinator: Brittany Blais

Marketing Communications Manager: Linda Yip

Design Direction, Production Management, and Composition: PreMediaGlobal

Manufacturing Planner: Betsy Donaghey

Rights Acquisition Specialist: Shalice Shah-Caldwell

Cover Image: Getty Images (Royalty free)

For product information and technology assistance, contact us at
Cengage Learning Customer & Sales Support, 1-800-354-9706

For permission to use material from this text or product, submit all requests online at **www.cengage.com/permissions**. Further permissions questions can be emailed to **permissionrequest@cengage.com**.

Library of Congress Control Number: 2011938550

ISBN-13: 978-1-133-05047-6

ISBN-10: 1-133-05047-6

Wadsworth
20 Channel Center Street
Boston, MA 02210
USA

Cengage Learning is a leading provider of customized learning solutions with office locations around the globe, including Singapore, the United Kingdom, Australia, Mexico, Brazil and Japan. Locate your local office at: **international.cengage.com/region**

Cengage Learning products are represented in Canada by Nelson Education, Ltd.

For your course and learning solutions, visit **www.cengage.com**.

Purchase any of our products at your local college store or at our preferred online store **www.cengagebrain.com**.

Instructors: Please visit **login.cengage.com** and log in to access instructor-specific resources.

Brief Contents

Contents

2 Methods of Critical Reading   58

7 Argument across the Disciplines   214

8 Researching Your Argument   272

9 Documenting Your Sources: MLA and APA Styles   301

Preface

The ability to plan and write a well-crafted argument has always been highly prized, but never more so than in these times of rapid scientific and technological development and social change. Mastery of argumentative writing brings tremendous advantages in every academic discipline, in the workplace, and in life generally. It can also provide the satisfaction that comes with thoughtful, self-expression and effective, responsible communication. For these reasons, because we wish to help students contribute their well-thought-out ideas to resolve issues of the present and of the future and to be taken seriously, we wrote *The Well-Crafted Argument: Writing across the Curriculum.*

Features

Over the years we have used a number of argumentation textbooks in our courses. Time after time, we found that these books left out much that was essential—or put in too much that was not essential—in helping students to master argumentative writing. This textbook is distinctive because it contains the following resources for mastering argumentative discourse:

- **A thorough discussion of critical reading strategies of both written and visual texts.** Critical reading skills are necessary for enabling students to understand and evaluate arguments, perform successful peer critiquing, and then draft and revise their own arguments.

- **An introduction to the three principal methods of argument.** Separate chapters are devoted to instruction in Classical (Aristotelian), Toulmin, and Rogerian methods of constructing arguments. Similarities and differences among the three methods are also discussed.

- **Extensive use of student essays to represent the range of argumentative writing.** Student argumentative essays from several disciplines are included to illustrate different topics and strategies and form the basis for discussions of their strengths and weaknesses, and for exercises and writing projects related to those essays.

- **A focus on the writing process as it applies to argumentative writing.** Chapter 1, The Nature and Process of Argument, and other chapters, consider the writing process—gathering ideas, drafting, and revising—in the context of structuring and writing effective arguments.

- **Comprehensive instruction in conducting research for purposes of argument.** Chapter 8, Researching Your Argument, guides students in locating and using print, database, and Internet resources, using effective search strategies, and understanding as well as avoiding plagiarism. This chapter also introduces students to interviewing, conducting surveys, and designing questionnaires as ways of obtaining information. Chapter 9, Documenting Your Sources, presents up to date MLA and APA citation styles, with examples.

- **A chapter devoted to writing in the disciplines.** Argumentative discourse is essential in all disciplines. This chapter introduces students to the protocols of arguing a thesis in the fine arts, literature, the natural sciences, the social sciences, business, and industry/technology.

The Well-Crafted Argument Website

The Well-Crafted Argument has a companion website at <www.cengage.com/english/white/argumentacrossthecurriculum>. For instructors, resources include sample syllabi, interviews with student writers, sample student essays, useful links, and handouts. The Instructor's Manual is also available for download on this site, for use in either electronic or print form. This manual can help you maximize your class preparation efforts. Included are teaching tips, writing prompts, and suggested answers for exercises. The student website provides valuable course resources, including an extensive library of interactive exercises and animations that cover grammar, diction, mechanics, punctuation, research, and writing concepts, as well as a library of student papers and interviews with student writers.

The Well-Crafted Argument CourseReader

CourseReader: Composition is a fully customizable online reader which provides access to hundreds of readings, audio, and video selections from multiple disciplines. This easy to use solution allows you to select exactly the content you need for your courses, and is loaded with convenient pedagogical features like highlighting, printing, note taking, and audio downloads. YOU have the freedom to assign individualized content at an affordable price. The CourseReader: Composition is the perfect complement to any class.

Acknowledgments

We wish to thank Santa Clara University and our current and former department chairs John Hawley, Phyllis Brown, and the late Richard Osberg, for their enthusiastic support of this project. We are also grateful to our colleagues Terry Malik, Jeff Zorn, and Aparajita Nanda for their feedback. To our spouses Terry M. Weyna and William R. Billings, we express our deepest gratitude for their inspiration, patience, understanding, and caring. We extend a special thank you to Devorah Harris, who expressed enthusiasm for the book from the very beginning.

Throughout the development of this text, many of our colleagues have been extremely helpful with their suggestions and generous with their time. We gratefully acknowledge the assistance of the following reviewers:

Gail Henderson, *Baton Rouge Community College*, Ashley Lauro, *James Madison University*, Sheila Mable, *Southern New Hampshire University*, Bryan Moore, *Arkansas State University*, Carol Narigon, *Wright State University*, Logan M. Oliver, *Mid-South Community College*, Katherine Rocca, *Old Dominion University*, and Dixie Shaw-Tilmon, *University of Texas at San Antonio*.

We also wish to thank our students at Santa Clara University and at other academic institutions. Their help has been essential to the creation of this text, and we have learned a great deal from them. We owe a special debt of gratitude to the talented student writers who have given us permission to include their work: Nikolay Balbyshev, Gaby Caceres, Quentin Clark, Melissa Conlin, Joseph Forte, Powell Fraser, Chris Garber, Daniela Gibson, Patrick Green, Kate Guarente, Scott Klausner, Yung Le, Jillian Lenahan, Daniel Neal, Regina Patzelt, Kareem Raad, Kelly Ryan, Nathan Salha, Lauren Silk, Kiley Strong, and Sara Vakulskas.

Finally, we thank the remarkable staff of Cengage Learning editors: Margaret Leslie and Amy Haines. We are also deeply grateful for the superb job of copyediting and book production of The Well-Crafted Argument: Writing across the Curriculum, coordinated by Marcia Youngman and PreMediaGlobal.

We have made a special effort to present this challenging and complex material in an engaging, stimulating fashion, and we welcome feedback on how this textbook can continue to be improved in the future. We invite ou to email us with any questions or suggestions you might have.

Fred D. White <fwhite@scu.edu>
Simone J. Billings <sbillings@scu.edu>
Santa Clara University

Authors' Choice CourseReader for *The Well-Crafted Argument: Across the Curriculum*

The authors have hand-picked the following reading selections in **CourseReader: Argument** to correlate with this edition. These selections are intended as a time-saving starting point for instructors to modify as they see fit. Learn more at www.cengage.com/coursereader and speak to your Cengage Learning Representative about pricing options.

Nathan Seppa, "Not just a high: scientists test medicinal marijuana against ms, inflammation and cancer"

Shahla Sherkat, "Telling the Stories of Iranian Women's Lives: 'Anyone Who Did Research on Women's Issues Benefitted from Hundreds of Articles, Stories and Interviews that Were Featured in Zanan'"

Mike Shields, "Homing Device: Mobile Marketers Can Find You Anywhere: And Everywhere. Will Their Quest for Big Bucks Infringe on People's Privacy?"

Vanessa Silberman, "Inside Shock Art"

Mano Singham, "The New War Between Science and Religion"

Emily Sohn, "Anorexia May Have a Biological Basis"

Deborah Tannen, "I'm Sorry, I'm Not Apologizing"

Deborah Tannen, "You're Wearing That? Exploring the Delicate and Explosive Mother-Daughter Relationship"

Alice Walker, "Lest We Forget: An Open Letter to My Sisters Who Are Brave"

Cathy Young, "Common Sense is Needed in Marijuana Policy"

The Well-Crafted Argument
Across the Curriculum

1 | The Nature and Process of Argument

Give me the liberty to know, to utter, and to argue freely according to conscience, above all liberties.
—John Milton

CONSIDERING THE DISCIPLINES

Students sometimes sign up for a course in argument because friends have told them they'd do well in it since they like to argue over every little thing with their friends. But being argumentative (in the sense of quarrelsome) is not the same as constructing well-thought-out formal arguments. When one of the authors of this textbook (Billings) disagrees with her spouse on, say, how best to spend an income tax refund, her goal is not "to win" the argument but to convince him that her plan makes the most sense out of several possible plans. To argue effectively one must focus on the issue, not how to "defeat your opponent." This chapter introduces you to fundamental concepts of argument and its importance to all fields of study. As the disagreement with a spouse indicates, skill in argument can benefit you personally, but it can also benefit you in engineering and economics as well as in English and education. Regardless of your field, you'll find material in this chapter applicable. Specific topics include a formal definition of argument; the reasons for argument; basic argument structure; and the rhetorical rhombus that situates the communication act in the context of the audience, the topic, the writer, and the purpose of the communication.

The freedom to think for ourselves and the freedom to present and defend our views rank among the most precious rights that we as individuals possess, as the great poet and essayist John Milton knew. The more we know about argument—what it involves, how a strong argument is constructed, and what a weak argument lacks—the more likely we are to benefit from this liberty.

Why Argue?

All of us find occasions to argue every day. Sometimes we argue just to make conversation. We argue casually with friends about which restaurant serves the best food, which movies are the most entertaining, or which automobile performs the best or most reliably for the money. Sometimes we engage in arguments presented in the media, taking positions on topics debated in newspapers and magazines, or on television, radio, and the Internet. And sometimes we argue in a more analytical manner on issues we have thought a lot about, such as which political party is most sympathetic to education reform, whether the Internet is a reliable research tool, or how we might solve a particular problem. When more is at stake, as in this last type of argument, the chances are greater that we will fail to be persuaded by what we hear or read or become frustrated by our own failure to persuade. We often fail to persuade because we lack evidence to back up our claims or because the evidence we do have is inadequate.

In other words, while casual arguments often consist of little more than exchanges of opinions or unsupported generalizations, more formal arguments are expected to include evidence in support of generalizations if they are to succeed in making strong points, solving real problems, or changing minds.

What Is an Argument?

People sometimes say that *everything* is an argument. That is quite true in the sense that whatever is communicated represents an individual point of view, one compelling enough to be accepted by the audience. Thus, if you're writing on a seemingly neutral *topic*, such as a day in the life of an emergency room nurse, you are implicitly arguing that your portrayal of the nurse is accurate and that nurses play a vital role in emergency rooms.

But *argument* as we use the term in this textbook is more explicitly an effort to change readers' minds about an issue. Thus, we would generally call a day-in-the-life article mainly explanatory or reportorial writing. However, if your aim is to show that people often have the wrong idea about the role or importance of hospital nurses, you would be engaged in argumentative writing.

An argument must possess three basic ingredients to be successful. First, it must contain as much *relevant information* about the issue as possible. Second, it must present *convincing evidence* that enables the audience to accept the writer's or speaker's claim. The more controversial the claim, the more compelling the evidence must be. Third, it must lay out a *pattern of reasoning*. That is, it must logically progress from thesis to support of thesis to conclusion. Before we examine these three elements, though, let us consider a formal definition of argument.

A Formal Definition of Argument

An argument is a form of discourse in which the writer or speaker tries to persuade an audience to accept, reject, or think a certain way about a problem that cannot be solved by scientific or mathematical reasoning alone. The assertion that the circumference of a circle is a product of its diameter times pi is not arguable because the assertion cannot be disputed; it is a universally accepted mathematical fact. At the other extreme, asserting an unsubstantiated opinion is not stating an argument; it is only announcing a stance on a particular issue. For example, someone in a casual conversation who asserts that public flogging of robbers would be a more effective deterrent than jailing them is voicing an opinion, not presenting an argument. If you respond by saying "Yeah, probably," or "No way—that would contribute to a culture of violence," you are also stating an opinion. If you respond instead by requesting evidence, such as statistics that show a correlation between public punishment and crime rate, you are helping to shape the conversation into a true argument. It is useful to keep in mind that the word *argument* is derived from the Latin word *arguere,* to clarify or prove.

A good argument is not casual. It takes considerable time and effort to prepare. It not only presents evidence to back up its claim but also acknowledges the existence of other claims about the issue before committing to the claim that corresponds most closely to the arguer's convictions. A good argument also guides the audience through a logical, step-by-step line of reasoning from thesis to conclusion. In short, a good argument uses an argumentative structure.

Amplifying the Definition

Let us now amplify our definition of argument: An argument is a form of discourse in which the writer or speaker presents a *pattern of reasoning,* reinforced by detailed evidence and refutation of challenging claims, that tries to persuade the audience to accept the claim. Let us take a close look at each of the elements in this definition.

"… a pattern of reasoning …"   This element requires that a good argument disclose its train of thought in a logical progression that leads the reader or listener from thesis to support of thesis to conclusion. It also implies that any unfamiliar terms or concepts are carefully defined or explained, and that enough background information is provided to enable readers or listeners to understand the larger *context* (interacting background elements) contributing to the argument. For example, to make the claim that gas-guzzling sports utility vehicles (SUVs) are selling better than fuel-efficient subcompacts does not qualify as an argument because no context for the claim is given. Readers or listeners would ask, "So what?" But if the assertion is placed in the context of an urgent problem—for example, that the enormous popularity of SUVs is rapidly increasing gasoline consumption nationally, which in turn is leading to greater dependence on foreign oil—then a valid argument is established.

"… reinforced by detailed evidence …"   In a formal argument, any assertion must be backed up with specific, compelling evidence that is accurate, timely, relevant, and sufficient. Such evidence can be data derived from surveys, experiments, observations, and firsthand field investigations (statistical evidence), or from expert opinion (authoritative evidence).

"… that tries to persuade the audience to accept the claim."   This last element of the definition brings to mind the ultimate aim of any argument: to convince the audience that the arguer's point of view is a sensible one, worthy of serious consideration if not outright acceptance. To accomplish this aim, arguers often

reinforce their evidence with what are known as *appeals*—appeals to authority and traditional values, to feelings, and to reason. In an ideal world, evidence (the hard facts) alone would be enough to persuade audiences to accept the truth of a claim, but in reality, more persuasive force often is needed and appeals are drawn in.

What Is an Arguable Thesis?

As we noted in our formal definition of *argument*, statements of fact are not arguable because they are beyond dispute. One cannot challenge the fact that Homer's *Iliad* is about the Trojan War; however, one can challenge the assertion (or claim) that the Trojan War actually occurred. Now, merely to assert that you don't believe the Trojan War occurred would be expressing your *opinion*, but it is not yet an arguable thesis. Consider what is necessary for this opinion to qualify for both criteria.

For an opinion to become a thesis, it must be presented as *a problem capable of being investigated*—for example, "Judging from the latest archaeological evidence, I wish to argue that the fabled Trojan War did not occur." Moreover, the thesis must be counterarguable. In other words, it should at least be conceivable that the evidence used to support the thesis could be interpreted differently, or that new evidence could negate the old or at least lead to a very different interpretation of the old. We now have a thesis because (1) we have characterized the subject matter as a problem (i.e., experts have been trying to determine for a long time whether the Trojan War occurred), (2) it is capable of being investigated at least through archaeological evidence (and perhaps through other forms of evidence as well— accounts by contemporary historians, for example), and (3) the thesis is refutable.

The next step is to ensure that the argument to be presented is substantive. Merely referring to "archaeological evidence" will not do because it is too generalized; it's like the advertising phrase "Doctors everywhere recommend . . ." or "A million satisfied customers prove. . . ." To make the thesis substantive, reference to evidence needs to be more specific: "Archaeological evidence from the latest excavations in Turkey suggest that the fabled Trojan War did not occur."

"Wait," you say. "Doesn't evidence from excavations qualify as 'fact' and therefore beyond dispute?" No. Facts are self-evident: The square root of 144 will always equal 12, no matter who does the calculating. Archaeological findings are subject to interpretation. One archeologist will study newly discovered artifacts and construct one historical scenario; another archaeologist will study the same artifacts yet construct a completely different scenario. That's because the evidence uncovered (a potsherd, a sculpture fragment, etc.) does not shed enough light on the historical event being investigated.

Using Evidence in Argument

Argumentative writing uses two kinds of evidence: indisputable (or factual) and disputable. The first kind refers to matters of public record that anyone can verify. No one is going to dispute the fact that the earth revolves around the sun every 365.25 days, say, or that the state of California was admitted to the Union on September 9, 1850. How such facts are applied is another matter, but the facts themselves are beyond dispute.

But what about disputable evidence? Imagine that a friend's room is filled with art books and reproductions of paintings. If someone asks about this friend's interests, you would reply, "Art!" without hesitation, and cite as evidence the books and paintings. But that evidence is disputable: The books and paintings could belong to a roommate, could be a mere inheritance, or could represent a former interest only recently abandoned.

Just the fact that evidence is disputable, however, does not mean it is unreliable. Such evidence often represents the closest one can get to the truth. Will banning handguns prevent tragedies like the Columbine school shootings? One researcher might discover statistical evidence of a correlation between banning guns and reduced crime; yet another researcher could find evidence of a contrary correlation. Different parts of the country or the world, different years, different times of year, different age groups—all represent constantly changing variables that can affect such a correlation. The more aware you are of the possible ways in which evidence may be disputed, the less likely you are to reach facile or premature conclusions.

Exercise 1.1

1. Consulting an unabridged dictionary, prepare a critical summary of the terms *argument*, *debate*, *dispute*, and *quarrel*. In what ways do the definitions differ? Where do they overlap, and how do you account for the overlap?

2. Supplement these definitions with examples, drawing from your own experiences.

3. Which of the following assertions could be developed into a formal argument, and which could not? Explain your reasons.

   a. A clear link has been established between secondhand cigarette smoke and lung cancer.

   b. The Surgeon General has determined that smoking is a health hazard.

   c. Studying a foreign language gives children a greater command of their native language.

   d. The more video games children play, the less likely their abstract reasoning skills are to develop properly.

4. List the topics of recent disputes you have had with friends or family. Under each topic, note the claims asserted by each side, followed by any support that had been attempted for each. Next, go back over these topics and list additional support you would give to one or more of these claims if you had been asked to elaborate on them in a more formal manner.

5. Discuss the kinds of evidence writers would want to use to resolve the following controversial assumptions. What problems with definitions might arise in some of these claims?

   a. Adults are safer drivers than teenagers.

   b. The many species of birds that still inhabit the Everglades suggest that this ecosystem is not as endangered as environmentalists say it is.

   c. The greater number of violent shows you watch, the more likely you are to commit acts of violence.

   d. Male smokers are three times more likely to become impotent than male nonsmokers.

   e. Obscene books should be banned from public school libraries.

Communicating with a Purpose

Before we turn to the writing of effective arguments, consider the elements in an act of communication. Any communication act consists of the *writer* or *speaker*, an *audience*, and the *subject* being communicated. This is known as the *Aristotelian* or *Communication Triangle*, as shown in Figure 1.1.

The Aristotelian Triangle reminds us that the act of writing, virtually by definition, involves writing about something to someone—that writing never occurs in a vacuum.

Any act of communication involves a writer or speaker conveying a particular viewpoint to a particular audience in a particular way. We have all had the experience of describing something one way to one person and quite another way to someone else. For example, we might discuss a romantic relationship one way with a friend, quite another way with a parent, and yet another way with a minister, rabbi, or psychologist. The writer or speaker, subject, and audience all shape the communication.

FIGURE 1.1
_____

The Aristotelian or
Communication Triangle

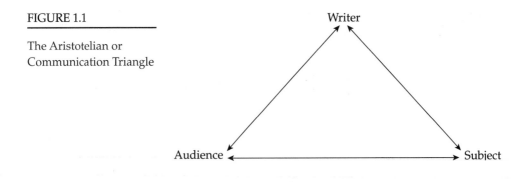

A fourth major element that shapes communication is *purpose.* There are three basic kinds of communication, each with a different purpose:

1. *Referential* or *expository:* communication that primarily aims to inform and explain;

2. *Expressive:* communication that primarily aims to stimulate the imagination, create mood or "atmosphere," and evoke feelings; and

3. *Argumentative:* communication that primarily aims to help skeptical readers or listeners make up their minds about a debatable issue.

These three modes of communication are not mutually exclusive. For instance, writers of arguments must take time to inform readers about the facts underlying a problem. They also must try to make such explanations interesting— perhaps by dramatically re-creating a moment of discovery or by describing the beauty of an observed phenomenon. But argumentative writing does have a distinct purpose, which is to present, support, or challenge a debatable proposition (such as a conflict in ethical behavior or policymaking). Such views cannot be proven with experiments or made compelling through descriptive writing alone.

To incorporate this element of purpose, we can transform Aristotle's triangle into a square or, to be a bit more alliterative (to help remember it better), into a *rhetorical rhombus* (see Figure 1.2). Simple as this diagram may seem, it calls to mind a subtle interconnection among the elements; that is, any one element is indispensable to the other three. Thus, the writer's way of seeing the world is made significant by the fact that he or she has a particular purpose for writing; a subject is enriched by the way in which it is made relevant to a particular audience; and so on.

Let us examine each element of the rhetorical rhombus separately, in depth, as it pertains to the writing of effective arguments. Once you establish that your primary purpose is not expository (to inform) or expressive (to evoke feelings) but rather argumentative (to persuade your audience to agree with your claim), you will want to consider purpose in that context.

FIGURE 1.2

Rhetorical Rhombus

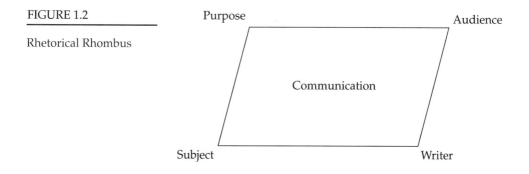

Purpose in an Argumentative Context

The purpose of your argument is the reason *why* you want your audience to agree with your claim and take whatever action is necessary to carry it out. Often, the purpose for wanting to communicate anything is complex. For example, if your claim is that wolf-hunting must be stopped (say, by passing laws that prohibit wolf-hunting), your purpose might consist of the following:

- The facts make it clear to you that wolves are rapidly becoming an endangored species.

- You are convinced that such species endangerment poses a serious threat to the environment.

- You love wolves, and it distresses you to see these beautiful, intelligent animals slaughtered by those who cannot appreciate them.

Purpose, then, is the motivational force that imbues the mere potential for communication with the desire to communicate. In a required writing course, however, purpose becomes even more complicated. Unlike working writers, whose purpose for writing a given piece is intrinsically related to the subject, student writers are often motivated by extrinsic matters, such as getting a good grade on the assignment or in the course. While there is nothing wrong with this kind of motivation, it does not quite constitute a bona fide purpose for writing about a given topic.

It is preferable, however, to adopt a professional sense of purpose toward your subject matter. The best way to accomplish this involved, engaged stance is to role-play. *Become* the writer you would like to be. Instead of thinking of yourself as a student in a composition course, think of yourself as an expert in the field about which you are writing—one who genuinely cares about the topics at hand enough to want your audience to understand them and appreciate them the way you do.

Audience in an Argumentative Context

The people at whom you aim your argument can significantly influence the way you present that argument. For example, two arguments supporting the prohibition of wolf-hunting, one aimed at legislators and the other aimed at hunters, would differ greatly from each other. If you were addressing an audience of legislators, you would want to focus on the need for laws that would better protect the environment. If you were addressing an audience of hunters, you would want to explain why it is in the hunters' best interest to stop hunting wolves. You could argue that damage to the habitat would ultimately cause the wolves to die out.

Audience also affects the writing and reading of arguments, in that some arguments may be classified as academic (or scholarly) and others as nonacademic (or popular). Academic arguments are written for fellow scholars affiliated with higher education, although some scholars are "independent"—that is, they are not employed by a college or university yet pursue similar research projects. The purpose of such writing is knowledge-sharing or idea-sharing; academic arguers say, in effect, "Here is what fellow researchers have determined thus far about the issue at hand; now, here are my views on the matter." A research paper is the student version of the professional scholarly article, in which the scholar carefully and explicitly articulates a claim and provides support for that claim.

Types of Academic Arguments As college students, you are probably experiencing several different audiences for arguments. In a literature course, you are asked to write papers in which you argue for what you consider to be an important theme in a poem, work of fiction, or play. This type of argumentation is known as *literary criticism*. The evidence you would gather for such an argument would consist of specific passages from the literary work in question (and possibly other works by the same author as well), relevant information about the author's life and times, and commentary from other scholars.

In a science course, you learn to write *scientific papers* in which you analyze, say, the properties of newly observed phenomena, or *laboratory reports* in which you accurately describe and interpret the results of physics, chemistry, or psychology experiments. "The Perils of Obedience," is Stanley Milgram's reworking of his original psychological experiment into an article for lay readers.

Another type of academic argument is the *ethnographic study*, common to sociology and anthropology. The ethnographer closely observes the behavior of individuals of a particular community or group, and derives inferences from what has been observed.

One of the most common types of academic writing is the *position paper*, in which you take a stance on a debatable issue, making sure that you represent each challenging view as fairly as possible before demonstrating the limitations of those views and proceeding to support your own view. "Two Languages Are Better Than One," by Wayne Thomas and Virginia Collier, is one of several position papers that appear in this textbook.

Your history courses present you with the opportunity to conduct a *historical inquiry* into a particular period or event. New archaeological discoveries or lost documents brought to light can profoundly change the way a historical event or even an entire period is interpreted.

Students as well as professionals in the fields of engineering, business administration (management, finance, marketing), and law all must produce documents that have an argumentative component: A *proposal* describes a work in progress, often to receive approval for its completion; a *feasibility study* demonstrates the need for a new program or facility; and a *progress report* chronicles, as the name implies, the progress that has been made on a given project. Of course, many of these forms of academic writing exist outside the academy. Magazines publish literary criticism, specialized companies submit proposals to large manufacturers or agencies, and so on.

TABLE 1.1   **Distinction between Academic and Nonacademic Arguments**

Academic Arguments	Nonacademic Arguments
Specialized (i.e., discipline-specific), precise language	Nonspecialized, less precise but more accessible language
Formal or semiformal tone	Less formal, more personal tone
All primary and secondary sources explicitly cited and documented, using standard formats (MLA, APA, etc.)	Sources are acknowledged informally, without footnoting
Contributions by other scholars in the field are discussed formally and in detail	Contributions by other writers in the field are discussed briefly
Scholarly audience	General audience

Nonacademic Arguments   On the other hand, nonacademic arguments focus more on reporting the "gist" of new developments or controversies. While academic arguments examine issues in depth and use specialized language to ensure precision, nonacademic arguments tend to gloss over the technicalities and use nonspecialized language, which is less accurate but more accessible to the general public. The chief distinguishing features between academic and nonacademic arguments are outlined in Table 1.1.

The more aware you are of your target audience's needs and existing biases, the greater the likelihood that you will address their particular concerns about the topic and, in turn, persuade them to accept your *thesis*. To heighten your audience awareness, ask yourself these questions:

1. What do my readers most likely already know about the issue? Most likely do not know?

2. How might the issue affect my readers personally?

3. What would happen to my argument if my conclusions or recommendations are accepted? If they are not accepted?

4. Why might readers not accept my conclusions or recommendations?

Note that this last question leads you to think about counterarguments and how you might respond to them. See "Refutation" in Chapter 3, pages 110–111.

Writer in an Argumentative Context

How, you may wonder, is the writer a variable in the communication, aside from the obvious fact that the writer is the one who presents the argument (the "Communication" that lies at the center of the rhetorical rhombus and is its very reason for being)? Actually, the writer can assume one of many roles, depending on the target audience. Say, for example, that you are trying to convince a friend to lend you $500 to use as a down payment for a summer trip to Europe. Your role here is that of trustworthy friend. If instead you are trying to convince your bank to lend you that same $500, your role becomes that of client or applicant. You are likely to use different language and different support in making your argument to the bank's loan officer than to your friend. Similarly, writers often are obliged to play different roles, depending on the particular needs of different audiences.

Subject in an Argumentative Context

The subject refers to what the argument (the text) is about. Although the subject remains identifiably constant, a writer might shift the *focus* of a subject to accommodate a particular audience or situation. For example, to convince your friend to lend you $500 for the down payment on that European trip (your argument's subject), you might focus on how the friend could come with you to make for an even more rewarding trip. To convince the bank, you might shift the focus to emphasize future job security and the likelihood of your paying back the loan.

As you study the Classical, Toulmin, and Rogerian models of argument in the chapters that follow, think about how the rhetorical rhombus applies to each and about how different models place different emphasis on **p**urpose, **a**udience, **w**riter, or **s**ubject (PAWS).

The Process of Composing an Argument

Unlike cooking, which follows a rather fixed sequence of steps, writing arguments (or essays of any kind) is mainly a dynamic, recursive process rather than a linear one. That is, you can start anywhere and return to any stage at any time. You can *brainstorm* for additional ideas, rework the organizational scheme, wad up and rewrite part of the existing draft, or walk over to the library or log on to the Internet to conduct additional research—and you can do any of these activities whenever you feel the need. Some writers simply do not feel comfortable composing in a linear fashion; some like to compose their endings first, or "flesh out" particular points of an argument as they leap to mind, and then organize them into a coherent sequence later on. Some writers need to map out their ideas in clusters, write outlines, or simply let loose their spontaneous flow of associations via freewriting.

Freewriting to Generate Ideas Rapidly

As you may recall from your earlier composition studies, freewriting is a good way to generate material for an argument. Start writing without any advance planning. Your goal is to let your thoughts run loose on the page; do not concern yourself with organization, sentence structure, word choice, or relevancy to the topic of your argument. You might surprise yourself with how much you already know!

There are two kinds of freewriting: unfocused and focused. In *unfocused freewriting*, let your pen move across the page, recording whatever comes to mind. Try not to pause. In the following example, a student, Janis, engages in some unfocused freewriting to stir up ideas about a subject for her argument. She is thinking spontaneously with a pencil, you might say, making no effort to develop a thesis:

> Let's see, I'm supposed to write an argument that would per-
> suade first-year college students what would be the best major
> in preparation for a particular career. Well, I'm undeclared
> myself, but want to study law after I graduate, so maybe I
> could do a comparative analysis of three or four majors that
> would seem to offer the best preparation for law school (hey,
> this could help me make up my own mind). Poli sci seems like
> an obvious possibility, since lawyers need to have a basic
> knowledge of the way governments work, the nature of public
> policy, how laws are passed. . . . Also, English, because lawyers
> need strong communication skills and need to acquire the kind
> of deep insight into the human heart that great works of
> literature offer. . . . Then I might talk to law students as
> well as professors in the four different majors—and maybe
> even practicing attorneys to find out what they majored in
> as undergraduates, and why. Hey, my aunt is a lawyer! I could
> talk to her.

Janis knows that she likely will discard most, if not all, of her freewriting; her goal was not to whip out a rough draft or even test out a topic, but to help her mind tease out ideas and associations that otherwise might have remained buried. The goal of freewriting is greater than overcoming not knowing what to say; it includes becoming more receptive to what is possible.

In *focused freewriting*, you write spontaneously as well, but attempt something resembling an actual draft of the essay. Your goal is to generate as much as you know about the topic. It is an excellent way of discovering gaps in knowledge.

Immersing Yourself in the Subject

Imagine spending twenty minutes or so freewriting and getting down on paper everything that comes to mind; you produce several scraggly pages in longhand, or neater ones on a computer. You read them over, highlighting with a marker or with your computer's highlighting tool what seems most relevant and useful. Then, you ask yourself these questions: What seems to be the dominant or recurrent trend? What more do I need to know about my topic to write persuasively about it? What kinds of evidence do I need to back up my thesis, however tentative it may be at this stage? In taking these steps, you are preparing to immerse yourself in your subject.

Having relevant information available is important to all writers. Once you know what more you need, you can start looking for information. On the

Internet, an enormous quantity of information can be accessed quickly, so it is a good place to begin your research. A strong search engine like Google, Dogpile, or Yahoo! can bring material from any subject onto your screen in seconds. On the other hand, a large percentage of Internet sources are superficial, dated, or not very relevant to your needs. Balance your Internet research by examining a variety of reliable print sources, such as books, articles, encyclopedias (general as well as subject-specific), handbooks, and specialized dictionaries. For more information about using sources, see Chapter 8, Researching Your Argument.

Your goal in reading and researching should be to learn all you possibly can about your topic. Familiarize yourself with the differing views experts have about it. Talk to experts. As a college student, you are surrounded by them; get in the habit of contacting professors who can give you timely and in-depth information about your topic or suggest material to read. Read and explore as many sources as possible. In other words, immerse yourself in the subject matter of your argument. This involvement will show in your writing and will give the finished paper added depth and vigor.

Using Listing and Clustering

Like freewriting, listing and clustering tap into writers' natural inclination to take a mental inventory of what they already know about a topic as well as to discover what they do not know about it. To list, jot down as quickly as you can ideas (or idea fragments) or names of people, places, events, or objects. One student prepared the following list as a prelude to writing about the increasing problem of childhood obesity:

```
Fast-food chains aggressively target their products to
preteen kids.
TV commercials give wrong impressions.
Parents too busy to cook.
Hamburgers often loaded with mayonnaise.
Burgers, fries, milk shakes, ice cream loaded with fat.
Parents not paying close enough attention to their kids' diets.
```

You can use lists to make notes to yourself or to ask questions the moment they occur to you:

```
Check how many calories are in a typical fast-food burger.
How much fat content in a bag of fries?
What do nutritionists and pediatricians say about the increas-
ing obesity problem?
Find out how often kids eat fast food, on the average.
How can kids learn more about this problem in school?
```

FIGURE 1.3   Student Cluster Diagram

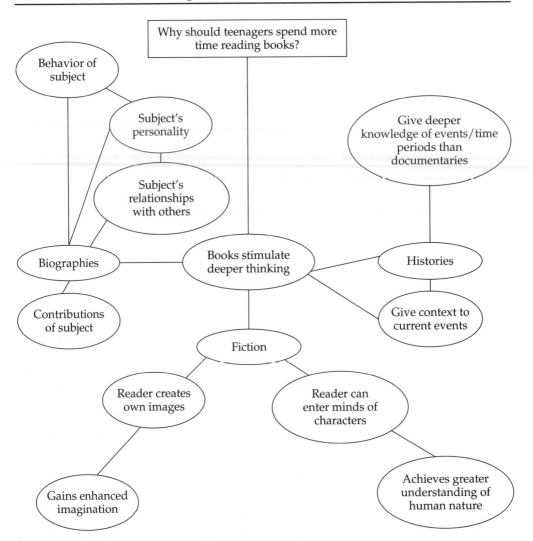

Clustering helps writers take an inventory of what they know, but it also helps them discover relationships among the ideas they list by seeing how the cluster bubbles connect. This discovery helps writers organize their ideas more efficiently when they begin outlining or drafting their arguments.

To cluster an idea for an argumentative essay, take a sheet of paper and write down words or phrases; at the same time, keep similar words and phrases close together and draw large circles around them to form "clusters." Next, draw lines between bubbles that seem to go together. Figure 1.3 shows how one student clustered her thoughts for an argumentative essay on why teenagers should spend more time reading books.

◎/◎ Exercise 1.2

1. Your science instructor asks you to evaluate the benefits and dangers of vitamin C. Using the Internet, locate information that both supports and challenges claims about the benefits and dangers of this vitamin. Keep a record of the websites that you visit.

2. List things you might say in a paper arguing for or against the benefits or dangers of vitamin C.

3. Having gathered potentially useful information about vitamin C and listed things you might want to include in your argument, do a focused freewrite. Do not pause or organize your thoughts or choice of words and phrases. Write rapidly until you have filled at least two handwritten pages.

Using Appeals in Argument

To argue successfully, a person does not rely solely on facts; facts need to be explained, be placed into a particular context (that is, related to the problem being argued), or have their importance validated. Successful writers of argument often demonstrate the importance of these facts so as to persuade their audience that the facts are important. For such demonstration, these arguers turn to strategies of *persuasion* known as appeals.

The ancient Greek philosopher Aristotle in his *Rhetoric* identifies three kinds of appeals:

1. *Ethical:* the appeal to tradition, authority, and ethical and moral behavior, which Aristotle terms *ethos*;

2. *Emotional:* the appeal to feelings and basic human needs, such as security, love, belonging, and health and well-being, which Aristotle terms *pathos*; and

3. *Rational:* the appeal to reason and logic, which Aristotle terms *logos*.

As Figure 1.4 shows, these three appeals correspond to Aristotle's three modes of communication, Writer, Audience, and Subject (see Figure 1.1). In other words, Ethos (character, values, trusted authority) is the attribute of a responsible Writer. Similarly, Pathos (emotion, compassion) suggests appealing to the needs and desires of the public—that is, of the Audience. Finally, Logos (reason) corresponds to the factual, rational truth-content of the Subject.

How do appeals reinforce evidence? Say that a writer wishes to argue that if acid rain fallout continues to increase, agriculture in a certain region will be

FIGURE 1.4

Aristotelian Appeals,
in Correspondence
with the Elements
of Communication

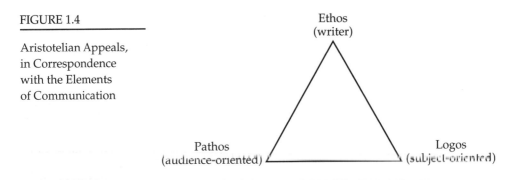

threatened. To argue this claim convincingly, a writer first needs to bring in in-disputable facts—those derived from scientific experiments. These facts would suggest a correlation between increased acidity and rainfall, and decreased crop yield. Note that the correlation may be disputable, but it still constitutes valid evidence.

Use of appeals can enhance the persuasive force of the thesis. The writer above, for example, might use one or more of the following appeals:

- An ethical appeal that introduces the testimony of an expert, such as a farmer whose crops have been affected or an industrial chemist who has a professional understanding of the way in which acidity in rainfall reacts with soil nutrients.

- An emotional appeal that discusses the basic human need for uncontaminated food or justifies the fear of cancer many people will have if the situation is not corrected.

- A rational appeal that emphasizes the logical and inevitable consequences of what happens to soil and crops when acid rainfall goes untreated.

Appeals such as these go a long way toward reinforcing the evidence and strengthening the writer's argument.

Combining appeals in a given argument can be especially effective. In the following excerpt from *The Souls of Black Folk* (1903), the educator and pioneer sociologist W. E. B. Du Bois (1868–1963)—the first African American to earn a Ph.D. from Harvard University—calls attention to the living conditions of black people in the post–Civil War South, specifically in Dougherty County, Georgia. Note how Du Bois appeals to both reason and emotion in order to convince read-ers of the injustice of such living conditions:

> Above all, the cabins are crowded. We have come to associate crowding with homes in cities almost exclusively. This is primarily because we have so lit-tle accurate knowledge of country life. Here in Dougherty County one may find families of eight and ten occupying one or two rooms, and for every

ten rooms of house accommodation for the Negroes there are twenty-five persons. The worst tenement abominations of New York do not have above twenty-two persons for every ten rooms. Of course, one small, close room in a city, without a yard, is in many respects worse than the larger single country room. In other respects it is better; it has glass windows, a decent chimney, and a trustworthy floor. The single great advantage of the Negro peasant is that he may spend most of his life outside his hovel, in the open fields.

There are four chief causes of these wretched homes: First, long custom born of slavery has assigned such homes to Negroes; white laborers would be offered better accommodations, and might, for that and similar reasons, give better work. Secondly, the Negroes, used to such accommodations, do not as a rule demand better; they do not know what better houses mean. Thirdly, the landlords as a class have not yet come to realize that it is a good business investment to raise the standard of living among labor by slow and judicious methods; that a Negro laborer who demands three rooms and fifty cents a day would give more efficient work and leave a larger profit than a discouraged toiler herding his family in one room and working for thirty cents. Lastly, among such conditions of life there are few incentives to make the laborer become a better farmer. If he is ambitious, he moves to town or tries other labor; as a tenant-farmer his outlook is almost hopeless, and following it as a makeshift, he takes the house that is given him without protest.

First, Du Bois appeals to reason by providing "accurate" information about country life to reverse the assumption that crowding occurs only in city life; he also appeals to reason by examining the "four chief causes" of such housing. But appealing to reason is not enough: It is important to address the heart as well as the mind. Hence, Du Bois appeals to emotion by referring to the urban tenements as "abominations," adding that they are less extreme than the country housing situation, and by calling the prospects for tenant-farmers "almost hopeless."

In the following passage, from "Civil Disobedience" (originally delivered as a lecture to his fellow townspeople in 1848), we see Henry David Thoreau using all three appeals—ethical, emotional, and rational—in his effort to convince his audience, although the ethical appeal dominates:

Under a government which imprisons any unjustly, the true place for a just man is also a prison. The proper place to-day, the only place which Massachusetts has provided for her freer and less desponding spirits, is in her prisons, to be put out and locked out of the State by her own act, as they have already put themselves out by their principles. It is there that the fugitive slave, and the Mexican prisoner on parole, and the Indian come to plead the wrongs of his race, should find them; on that separate, but more free and honorable ground, where the State places those who are not *with* her but *against* her,—the only house in a slave-state in which a free man can abide with honor. If any think that their influence would be lost there, and their voices no longer afflict the ear of the State, that they would not be as an enemy within its walls, they do not know by how much truth is stronger than error, nor how much more eloquently and effectively he can combat injustice who has experienced a little in his own person. Cast your whole vote, not a strip of paper merely, but your whole influence. A minority is powerless while it conforms to the majority; it is not even a minority then; but it is irresistible when it clogs by its whole weight. If the alternative is to keep all just men in prison, or give up war and slavery, the State will not hesitate which to choose. If a thousand men were not to pay their tax-bills this year, that would not be a violent and bloody measure, as it would be to pay them, and enable the State to commit violence and shed innocent blood. This is, in fact, the definition of a peaceable revolution, if any such is possible. If the tax-gatherer, or any other public officer, asks me, as one has done, "But what shall I do?" my answer is, "If you really wish to do any thing, resign your office." When the subject has refused allegiance, and the officer has resigned his office, then the revolution is accomplished. But even suppose blood should flow. Is there not a sort of blood shed when the conscience is wounded? Through this wound a man's real manhood and immortality flow out, and he bleeds to an everlasting death. I see this blood flowing now.

I have contemplated the imprisonment of the offender, rather than the seizure of his goods,—though both will serve the same purpose,—because they who assert the purest right, and consequently are most dangerous to a corrupt State, commonly have not spent much time in accumulating property. To such the State renders comparatively small service, and a slight tax is wont to appear exorbitant, particularly if they are obliged to earn it by special labor with their hands. If there were one who lived wholly without the use of money, the State itself would hesitate to demand it of him. But the rich man—not to make any invidious comparison—is always sold to the institution which makes him rich. Absolutely speaking, the more money, the less virtue; for money comes between a man and his objects, and obtains them for him; and it was certainly no great virtue to obtain it. It puts to rest many questions which he would otherwise be taxed to answer; while the only new question which it puts is the hard but superfluous one, how to spend it. Thus his moral ground is taken from under his feet. The opportunities of living are diminished in proportion as what are called the "means" are increased. The best thing a man can do for his culture when he is rich is to endeavour to carry out those schemes which he entertained when he was poor. Christ answered the Herodians according to their condition. "Show me the tribute-money," said he;—and one took a penny out of his pocket;—If you use money which has the image of Caesar on it, and which he has made current and valuable, that is, *if you are men of the State*, and gladly enjoy the advantages of Caesar's government, then pay him back some of his own when he demands it; "Render therefore to Caesar that which is Caesar's, and to God those things which are God's,"—leaving them no wiser than before as to which was which; for they did not wish to know.

When I converse with the freest of my neighbors, I perceive that, whatever they may say about the magnitude and seriousness of the question, and their regard for the public tranquility, the long and the short of the matter is, that they cannot spare the protection of the existing government, and they dread the consequences of disobedience to it to their property and families. For my own part, I should not like to think that I ever rely on the protection of the State. But, if I deny the authority of the State when it presents its tax-bill, it will soon take and waste all my property, and so harass me and my children without end. This is hard. This makes it impossible for a man to live honestly and at the same time comfortably in outward respects. It will not be worth the while to accumulate property; that would be sure to go again. You must hire or squat somewhere, and raise but a small crop, and eat that soon. You must live within yourself, and depend upon yourself, always tucked up and ready for a start, and not have many affairs. A man may grow rich in Turkey even, if he will be in all respects a good subject of the Turkish government. Confucius said,—"If a State is governed by the principles of reason, poverty and misery are subjects of shame; if a State is not governed by the principles of reason, riches and honors are the subjects of shame." No: until I want the protection of Massachusetts to be extended to me in some distant southern port, where my liberty is endangered, or until I am bent solely on building up an estate at home by peaceful enterprise, I can afford to refuse allegiance to Massachusetts, and her right to my property and life. It costs me less in every sense to incur the penalty of disobedience to the State, than it would to obey. I should feel as if I were worth less in that case.

Thoreau's appeal to ethics is revealed in his allusions to the injustice of the State, to what constitutes proper and honorable behavior when the State has exercised unethical judgment. He also appeals to ethics by invoking Christ's example regarding Roman tribute-money.

We can detect Thoreau's subtle appeal to emotion in at least two ways: by presenting seemingly nonviolent acts such as taxation as acts of violence that can "shed innocent blood" as easily as cannons and by presenting the State as harassing its citizens rather than protecting them whenever those citizens dare to challenge the State's authority.

Finally, Thoreau appeals to reason by tracing the logical consequences of a tax bill: "it will . . . waste all my property and so harass me and my children, which in turn makes it no longer worth the while to accumulate property."

◎/◎   Exercise 1.3

1. What types of appeals would be most appropriate for persuading readers of the following assumptions?

   a. Reading stories to children greatly enhances their mental skills as well as their emotional stability.

   b. All work and no play makes Jill a dull girl.

   c. Severer penalties should be imposed on those who abuse animals.

   d. Safety should be anyone's top priority when purchasing a family car.

   e. This painting is definitely a Picasso because an art historian from Yale authenticated it as such.

2. Determine the appeals at work in each of the following passages. What words or images show the appeals at work?

   a. My mistress was . . . a kind and tender-hearted woman, and in the simplicity of her soul she commenced, when I first went to live with her, to treat me as she supposed one human being ought to treat another. In entering upon the duties of a slaveholder, she did not seem to perceive that I [was] mere chattel, and that for her to treat me as a human being was not only wrong, but dangerously so. Slavery proved as injurious to her as it did to me. When I went there, she was a pious, warm, and tender-hearted woman. There was no sorrow or suffering for which she had not a tear. She had bread for the hungry, clothes for the naked, and comfort for every mourner that came within her reach. Slavery soon proved its ability to divest her of these heavenly qualities. Under its influence, the tender heart became stone, and the lamblike disposition gave way to one of tiger-like fierceness. The first step in her downward course was in her ceasing to instruct me. . . . Nothing seemed to make her more angry than to see me with a newspaper. —Frederick Douglass, *The Narrative of the Life of Frederick Douglass, an American Slave* (1845) ch. 7.

   b. Most films and television shows are produced by men for men. Their main purposes are to show white males triumphant, to teach gender roles, and to cater to men's delight in male predation and victimization, especially young, pretty, near-naked women with highly developed breasts and buttocks (parts that are usually the locus of attack). Like the men of the proto-Nazi German Freikorps that waged between the wars, shooting women between the legs because they carried grenades there (!), American men's most satisfying target is women's sexuality, the area of men's greatest fear. Pornography is a systemic abuse of women because the establishment colludes in this male sadism toward women, which fits its purposes. Case in point: the Indian government, which does censor films for political content, *forbids scenes of lovemaking or kissing but allows rape;* indeed, a rape scene has been "all but requisite" in Indian films for some years, writes Anita Pratap.—Marilyn French, *The War Against Women* (New York: Ballantine, 1992) 175.

c. There is no single way to read well, though there is a prime reason why we should read. Information is endlessly available to us; where shall wisdom be found? If you are fortunate, you encounter a particular teacher who can help, yet finally you are alone, going on without further *mediation*. Reading well is one of the great pleasures that solitude can afford you, because it is, at least in my experience, the most healing of pleasures. It returns you to otherness, whether in yourself or in friends, or in those who may become friends. Imaginative literature is otherness, and as such alleviates loneliness. We read not only because we cannot know enough people, but because friendship is so vulnerable, so likely to diminish or disappear, overcome by space, time, imperfect sympathies, and all the sorrows of familial and passional life. —Harold Bloom, *How to Read and Why* (New York: Scribner, 2000) 19.

3. Read the magazine ads on pages 23–24, plus those in the color pages, and consider the images they use. Then answer these questions:

    a. What are the basic arguments of the magazine ads?

    b. What appeals can you identify in them?

    c. Is there more than one appeal in a given ad?

Organizing the Argument

All writing must be organized or structured. Whether you are relating an experience (*narration*), or explaining an idea or process (*exposition* or *explanation*), or defending a thesis (*argumentation*), you must structure your writing to communicate best with an audience.

Organizing your writing means that you do the following:

1. Introduce the topic (the situation in a narrative; the subject matter to be explained in an exposition or explanation; the problem in an argument).

2. Present the particulars of the situation (the sequencing of incidents in a narrative; elements of a phenomenon in an exposition or explanation; the nature of the problem, followed by the body of evidence, in an argument).

3. Conclude (the outcome in a narrative; the "whole picture" in an explanation; the interpretation, assessment, and recommendations, if appropriate, in an argument).

How you meet these three organizational requirements in an argument depends on the type of model you adopt: the Classical (or Aristotelian/Ciceronian), the Toulmin, or the Rogerian. The chapters that follow examine each model in depth, but for now you merely need to be aware of each one's distinguishing organizational features.

In the *Classical model*, the organizational scheme is predetermined. One begins with an introduction that establishes the problem and states the thesis; next, one analyzes the evidence and refutes opposing views in light of the evidence collected; finally, one draws conclusions and provides recommendations.

In the *Toulmin model* (named for the philosopher Steven Toulmin), truth is not absolute but value dependent. Accordingly, the logic content of the arguments is scrutinized for its underlying values. Evidence does not operate in a vacuum, but must be tested according to the values (called *warrants*) of the arguer. These values always come into play during the argument, meaning that no one argues for timeless, eternal truths.

In the *Rogerian model* (named for the psychologist Carl Rogers), one shifts emphasis to the social act of negotiating difference through argument. Truth is not only value based, it must be negotiated cooperatively if argument is to have any constructive social function.

Drafting the Argument

There are several ways to compose a draft. One way of drafting (and, alas, too common) is to put off the task until the day or night before it is due and then to dash off a single draft and proofread it hastily. In general, this is the least productive way of writing. The best writers tend to revise *most* often, not least often.

Another way of drafting is to use an outline as a template. By elaborating on each section of the outline, the drafter takes an important step toward substantive *development* of the essay. The subsequent rethinking of the argument and the additional research that results becomes more apparent using this method.

A third way is to produce a *discovery draft*, which is like freewriting in its spontaneity and in its goal of getting down on paper as much as possible about the topic. However, discovery drafters do have a rudimentary sense of structure and purpose in mind. They believe that, to some extent at least, the things they want to say will fall into place through the very act of writing, and if not, they can rearrange, revise, and edit once they have a rough draft in hand.

Whichever drafting method you choose, allow yourself enough time to reread the draft two or three times and to make marginal notations about possible changes. Mark up a printout of your draft with reminders of what else to include, questions that might help you identify and gather additional evidence, and ideas for changes that will strengthen your argument.

Common Problems in Composing an Argument and Ways to Resolve Them

Most writing projects seem more like obstacle courses than walks through the park. The obstacles also can be difficult to anticipate because they usually arise from the particular demands of the subject at hand. That said, here are

GOD, I'M STARVING!

GOD, SO AM I.

The **CATHOLIC** ✚ **CHARITIES** OF THE ARCHDIOCESE OF CHICAGO

☐ Yes, I would like to make a donation to Catholic Charities of Chicago. My donation is $ _____
☐ Please send me more information on wills and estate planning.

Name: _____
Address: _____
City: _____ State: _____
Zip Code: _____

Send to: Rev. Edwin M. Conway, Administrator, Catholic Charities, 126 N. Desplaines St., Chicago, Illinois 60606

"Starving." So easy to say when you sit down to satisfy your appetite. But it's an empty, hopeless reality for many. Please. Send a check now; leave a bequest in your will later . . . your willpower can work miracles.

At Catholic Charities, 98.8¢ of each dollar goes to help the needy through 189 services at 96 locations. We helped over a half a million people last year. People of all faiths. The homeless, addicted, abused . . . and hungry. Victims of unfortunate circumstances who need our help.

Next time you feel "starved," consider those who really are, and help.

Write Rev. Edwin M. Conway, Administrator, 126 N. Desplaines, Chicago, IL 60606, or call 236-5172.

PHOTO: BILL EMRICH

Catholic Charities, Chicago

five common problems that arise during drafting, along with suggestions for resolving them:

1. *The basis for the argument—the problem—has not been clearly or fully articulated.* Let the initial response to a problem be your starting point for laying the foundation, not the foundation itself. Angry that your local library has cut its hours? Use that as the catalyst for framing the problem of public-library closures in your area, describing the underlying causes, and explaining why the problem deserves urgent attention.

2. *The thesis is not sufficiently forceful or urgent.* If you are arguing that your school needs to improve its health-care services, be sure that you are able to pinpoint specific improvements and why they are needed.

3. *The evidence to support your claim is faulty or missing.* For your claim to be convincing, you must present compelling evidence to support it. How can you determine what constitutes compelling evidence? Check to see that the evidence is relevant, current, sufficient (in other words, not just an isolated, atypical case), and accurate.

4. *The appeal(s) to emotion, logic, and/or authority (laws, customs, etc.) ought to be used to greater advantage.* Appeals provide the dimension of persuasion to an argument. To convince readers of our views, go beyond detached logic to stir their hearts, their minds, their souls.

5. *Opportunities to represent and refute challenging views have been overlooked, ignored, or slighted.* Develop the habit of "testing" your thesis by imagining how it could be refuted; by doing so, you will be better prepared to locate counterarguments. Keep in mind, too, that some counterarguments may be so compelling that you'll want to at least modify your original thesis.

Composing Openings

Openings can be difficult to write because they usually lay out the terrain for the whole argument. Nobody likes to spend a lot of time writing an introduction, only to realize later that it has to be scrapped because the claim or approach has shifted during drafting. But no rule says that you must write your opening first. You can postpone writing the full opening until you have written part of the body of the paper or until you have a firm sense of your paper's shape.

Openings serve two purposes: to introduce the topic and the background information needed to understand or appreciate the topic's seriousness, and to state the thesis.

Consider the following types of openings. Keep in mind that one type can overlap the other (for example, startling openings can be partly anecdotal).

- **Occasional opening.** An occasional opening refers to a current event or local incident and uses it as the occasion for writing the essay. "In light of the current crisis in Addis Ababa. . . ."

- **Startling opening.** A startling opening grabs the attention of readers with unexpected information. "While you are reading this sentence, fifty people will die of cigarette-related illnesses in this country."

- **Anecdotal opening.** An anecdotal opening uses a brief story to engage the reader's attention quickly. An article arguing that some of the most dangerous toxins are found in the home might begin with an anecdote about a toddler lifting an opened bottle of nail polish remover to his lips just as his mother enters the room.

- **Analytical opening.** An analytical opening launches immediately into a critical discussion of the issue. An argument on the effects of alcohol on the body might open with an explanation of how alcohol damages certain bodily functions.

What makes one opening more appropriate than another? When choosing, consider the four interconnected elements of communication discussed earlier in the rhetorical rhombus. You may find that your subject lends itself more to an analytical opening. Or perhaps the writer's personal experience with the issue leads to an anecdotal opening. Or your purpose to shock readers into accepting the urgency of the matter suggests a startling opening. Maybe the kind of audience you are targeting (impatient to learn the facts? uncertain about the relevance of the topic?) justifies the use of an occasional opening.

Therefore, weigh the purpose of your argument, the kinds of readers you are targeting, and the nature of the subject matter.

◎/◎ Exercise 1.4

Discuss the rhetorical techniques used in each of the following openings:

1. The opening to an argument about the potential significance of discovering life elsewhere in the universe, by a professor of natural history:

   The recent discovery of abundant water on Mars, albeit in the form of permafrost, has raised hopes for finding traces of life there. The Red Planet has long been a favorite location for those speculating about extraterrestrial life, especially since the 1890s, when H. G. Wells wrote *The War of the Worlds* and the American astronomer Percival Lowell claimed that he could see artificial canals etched into the planet's parched surface. Today, of course, scientists expect to find no more than simple bacteria dwelling deep underground, if even that. Still, the discovery of just a single bacterium somewhere beyond Earth would force us to revise our understanding of who we are and where we fit into the cosmic scheme of things, throwing us into a deep spiritual identity crisis that would be every bit as dramatic as the one Copernicus brought about in the early 1500s, when he asserted that Earth was not at the center of the universe. —Paul Davies, "E.T. and God," *Atlantic Monthly* Sept. 2003:112.

2. The opening to an argument about the merits of urban public schools, by a newspaper columnist:

   I was terrified. It felt as if I were shoving my precious 4-year-old into a leaky canoe and pushing him off into croc-infested waters. My friends acted as if they thought I was crazy. I was enrolling my little boy in a mob scene, sending him off to a place as dangerous as it was crowded. Didn't I see the newspaper that showed students crammed into shower-stall study halls or watch the television report where box-cutter-wielding delinquents were barely contained by exhausted security guards? Hadn't I read Jonathan Kozol? My tow-headed treasure was poised at the edge of the blackboard jungle, a place where the stairwells were as dangerous as the banks of the Amazon. It was 10 years ago, and I was sending my son off to kindergarten in the infamous New York City public school system. —Susan Cheever, "Thriving in City's Schools—Until 9th Grade?" *Newsday* 12 Nov. 2003:32.

3. The opening to an argument about how best to curtail obesity among young people, by two medical researchers:

   Obesity in children has tripled in the past 20 years. A staggering 50 percent of adolescents in some minority populations are overweight. There is an epidemic of type 2 (formerly "adult onset") diabetes in children. Heart attacks may become a disease of young adults. In response to this public health crisis, federal and state officials are seeking ways to protect children from the ravages of poor diet and physical inactivity. National legislation on the prevention and treatment of obesity is being considered. California and Texas are working to remove snack foods from schools. There are proposals for the regulation of food advertising to children. —Kelly D. Brownell and David S. Ludwig. "Fighting Obesity and the Food Lobby," *Washington Post* 9 June 2002.

Composing the Body of the Argument

If you think of your argument's opening as the promise you make to your readers about what you are going to do, then the body of the argument is the fulfillment of that promise. Here you deliver the goods that comprise the subject node of the rhetorical rhombus: the detailed support—facts, examples, illustrations—as well as the emotional, logical, and ethical appeals that collectively demonstrate to your readers that the claim you set forth in your introduction is valid.

Let's consider the development strategy of a famous argument, "Allegory of the Cave." In this famous allegory from *The Republic*, Plato aims to convince his audience of the difference between appearance (or illusion) and reality. After introducing his statement of purpose to his pupil Glaucon—"Let me show in a figure how far our nature is enlightened or unenlightened"—Plato first describes the setting of the cave (or underground den) and the condition of the prisoners: They are chained so that they see only the shadows that are cast on the walls, and they can hear voices but are unable to determine who is speaking because they cannot turn their heads toward the actual source. Plato is now ready to elaborate on his thesis, which is in two parts: (1) Even though, when released, the prisoners would be temporarily blinded by the actual light (from the fire in the cave and then, even more so, after being dragged against their will outside the cave, from the light of the sun), their eyes would eventually grow accustomed to the true reality of things; that is, "the journey upwards [represents] the ascent of the soul into the intellectual world." (2) It is not enough to take the journey upwards; once accomplished, one should return to the cave to acquire a clearer judgment of the quality of life down there and to persuade the prisoners that a better life exists above.

How should you proceed in writing out the body of your argument? First, check that the sequence you developed in your outline includes everything you want to say about the issue. Jot down additional notes in the margins if necessary. If you have completed a freewrite or rough draft, now is the time to retrieve those pages and decide what to keep. You may already have more of the draft of your argument completed than you realize!

Many writers find it productive to move back and forth from draft to outline. The outline gives a bird's-eye view of the whole scheme; the draft concentrates on the minutiae of point-by-point discussion and exemplification.

Composing Conclusions

A good conclusion enables readers to grasp the full impact of the argument. If the introduction states the claim and the body argues for the validity of the claim by citing evidence for it, the conclusion encapsulates all those points of evidence, leaving readers with a renewed sense of the argument's validity.

To write an effective conclusion, then, aim for conciseness: capture in just one or two paragraphs the gist of your argument. Conclusions of short papers need not be long and could be just three to four sentences.

What might you do in a conclusion? Here are three possibilities:

1. Reflect back on the paper.

   - Return to the image or analogy or anecdote you discussed in the introduction and provide a frame for the piece.

   - Restate the thesis to underscore the argument of your essay.

   - Summarize your main points if the argument is complex or the paper is longer than six pages.

2. Broaden the scope beyond your paper.

   - Forecast the future if your main points should prove to be true.

   - Point out the implications of the ideas presented.

   - Exhort your readers to action.

3. Reinforce your readers' emotional involvement in the matter at hand. Keep in mind that "emotional involvement" can refer to feelings of security, hope, happiness, self-confidence, optimism, or overall well-being.

   - Introduce or reintroduce in a different way appropriate rational, ethical, or emotional appeals.

   - Aim for conciseness. Less is more when it comes to striking an emotional chord with readers.

◎/◎   Exercise 1.5

Discuss the strengths and/or weaknesses in the body and conclusion of the following essay, in which the author argues that video games are doing a better job than schools of teaching kids to think.

High Score Education | James Paul Gee

The US spends almost $50 billion each year on education, so why aren't kids learning? Forty percent of students lack basic reading skills, and their academic performance is dismal compared with that of their foreign counterparts. In response to this crisis, schools are skilling-and-drilling their way "back to basics," moving toward mechanical instruction methods that rely on line-by-line scripting for teachers and endless multiple-choice testing. Consequently, kids aren't learning how to think anymore—they're learning how to memorize. This might be an ideal recipe for the future Babbitts of the world, but it won't produce the kind of agile, analytical minds that will lead the high tech global age. Fortunately, we've got *Grand Theft Auto: Vice City* and *Deus Ex* for that.

After school, kids are devouring new information, concepts, and skills every day, and, like it or not, they're doing it controller in hand, plastered to the TV. The fact is, when kids play videogames they can experience a much more powerful form of learning than when they're in the classroom. Learning isn't about memorizing isolated facts. It's about connecting and manipulating them. Doubt it? Just ask anyone who's beaten *Legend of Zelda* or solved *Morrowind*.

The phenomenon of the videogame as an agent of mental training is largely unstudied; more often, games are denigrated for being violent or they're just plain ignored. They shouldn't be. Young gamers today aren't training to be gun-toting carjackers. They're learning how to learn. In *Pikmin*, children manage an army of plantlike aliens and strategize to solve problems. In *Metal Gear Solid 2*, players move stealthily through virtual environments and carry out intricate missions. Even in the notorious *Vice City*, players craft a persona, build a history, and shape a virtual world. In strategy games like *WarCraft III* and *Age of Mythology*, they learn to micromanage an array of elements while simultaneously balancing short- and long-term goals.

That sounds like something for their résumés.

The secret of a videogame as a teaching machine isn't its immersive 3-D graphics, but its underlying architecture. Each level dances around the outer limits of the player's abilities, seeking at every point to be hard enough to be just doable. In cognitive science, this is referred to as the regime of competence principle, which results in a feeling of simultaneous pleasure and frustration—a sensation as familiar to gamers as sore thumbs. Cognitive scientist Andy diSessa has argued that the best instruction hovers at the boundary of a student's competence. Most schools, however, seek to avoid invoking feelings of both pleasure and frustration, blind to the fact that these emotions can be extremely useful when it comes to teaching kids.

Source: James Paul Gee, "High Score Education: Games, Not School, Are Teaching Kids to Think," *Wired* May 2003: 91–92. Reprinted by permission of the author.

Also, good videogames incorporate the principle of expertise. They tend to encourage players to achieve total mastery of one level, only to challenge and undo that mastery in the next, forcing kids to adapt and evolve. This carefully choreographed dialectic has been identified by learning theorists as the best way to achieve expertise in any field. This doesn't happen much in our routine-driven schools, where "good" students are often just good at "doing school."

How did videogames become such successful models of effective learning? Game coders aren't trained as cognitive scientists. It's a simple case of free-market economics: If a title doesn't teach players how to play it well, it won't sell well. Game companies don't rake in $6.9 billion a year by dumbing down the material—aficionados condemn short and easy games like *Half Life: Blue Shift* and *Devil May Cry 2*. Designers respond by making harder and more complex games that require mastery of sophisticated worlds and as many as 50 to 100 hours to complete. Schools, meanwhile, respond with more tests, more drills, and more rigidity. They're in the cognitive-science dark ages.

We don't often think about videogames as relevant to education reform, but maybe we should. Game designers don't often think of themselves as learning theorists. Maybe they should. Kids often say it doesn't feel like learning when they're gaming—they're much too focused on playing. If kids were to say that about a science lesson, our country's education problems would be solved. ◎/◎

Revising the Argument: A Form of Reevaluation

You have written a draft of your argument, using one of the above methods. Now it is time to revise. "I love the flowers of afterthought," the novelist Bernard Malamud once said. The wonderful thing about writing is that you do not need "to get it right the first time." In fact, you can try as many times as you wish, which is not the case with speaking. Malamud, you will notice, is commenting on the opportunity that revision provides to writers: the opportunity to say it better—more clearly, effectively, or convincingly. And for most writers, the very best "flowers" of thought occur only *after* they have written something down.

In revising argumentative essays, attend closely to the ways you have presented the problem, stated your claims, reported the evidence and testimony, represented the challenging views, drawn inferences, and reached reasonable conclusions. What follows is a closer look at each of these steps.

- **Presenting the problem.** Unless you capture the exact nature and full complexity of the problem you are examining, your entire argument is built on a shaky foundation. To determine whether the problem is represented well, question whether the introduction suits the audience and subject (recall the PAWS rhombus) and whether you establish sufficient ethos and pathos for readers to care to read on and to trust you, the writer.

- **Stating the claim.** Just as the problem must be stated clearly, so must the assertions that presumably solve the problem. Ask yourself whether your claim is realistic, practical, and sensible in light of the nature of the problem and the circumstances underlying it.

- **Reporting the evidence.** Facts and statistics—the raw data that comprise evidence—do not carry much meaning outside of a context of discussion. In presenting evidence in support of a thesis, the writer aims to communicate the significance of those facts and figures, not simply to drop them on the page. The writer also aims to present facts and figures in a way that readers can easily absorb, ideally in a visual configuration of some kind, such as an attractively designed chart or graph. When revising your discussion of evidence, ask yourself whether you interpret the data accurately, relate one cluster of data to another clearly enough (through visual representation of the data), and establish your ethos as a careful researcher and thinker on the issue.

- **Refuting challenging views.** When revising refutations, make sure that your writing represents the claims and evidence of the other side as fairly as possible. If you argue from a Rogerian perspective, think of establishing common ground with the audience in terms of shared values (warrants) or of cooperating to reach shared goals. Resist the temptation to omit parts of a challenging perspective because you are not sure about how to refute it. Also, double-check the reliability of your refutation: Does it reveal the limitations or falsity of the challenging view?

- **Drawing inferences and conclusions.** How do you interpret your findings? How clearly do your underlying warrants emerge? Should you give more attention to them? How willing will your readers be to cooperate with you, based on your interpretation of the findings? What else can you say to ensure their cooperation—assuming that you would find such cooperation desirable?

The Pulitzer Prize–winning journalist and teacher of writing Donald Murray, in *The Craft of Revision*, 5th ed. (2004), identifies three cardinal virtues of revision:

1. Revision allows one to identify problems to be solved.

2. Revision enables writers to explore the topic more deeply to arrive at new insights into the topic.

3. Revision enhances the brain's capacity for recall and patterning.

Reading to Revise

Reading well, especially in the context of writing, provides you with a wider perspective of your subject and of the many divergent views that give it depth and richness. As a well-read writer, you are in the position of integrating the ideas of different authors into your own views on the subject. Reading and reflecting critically on what you have read also help you to revise more successfully because they force you to get into the habit of reading your own writing as if it were someone else's. The advantage to beginning your project well in advance of the due date is that you will have the time to do such a critical reading of your drafts.

Using Your Reading Skills in Peer-Critiquing Workshops

You may be given the opportunity to respond critically to other students' drafts. Always read the draft as carefully as you would any published argument. Consider the following criteria as you read the first draft of a peer.

- **Purpose-related issues.** Is the purpose of the draft apparent? Stated clearly enough? Is the thesis (claim) well-stated? Directly related to the purpose?

- **Content-related issues.** Is the scope of the topic sufficiently limited? Does the writer provide enough background information? Provide enough evidence in support of the claim? Provide enough examples and illustrations to support the evidence? Represent challenging views fully and fairly before pointing out their flaws? Are the writer's interpretive and concluding remarks thorough? Does the writer offer clear recommendations, if appropriate?

- **Issues relating to style and format.** Is the writing concise? Easy to read? Are the sentences coherent, well-constructed, varied? Is the level of usage consistent and appropriate for the intended audience? Is the word choice accurate? Are unfamiliar terms defined? Does the writer use subheadings and visual aids where appropriate? Follow proper documentation format? For a discussion of the way incorporating visuals can enhance your argument, see "Visual Aids as Tools for Argumentative Writing," beginning on page 34.

Types of Revision Tasks

Revising an argument involves a lot more than just "fixing things up;" it also involves re-*seeing* the entire draft from a fresh perspective, checking to make sure that each assertion is fully discussed and that the discussion follows a logical sequence. Here are some different types of revision strategies:

Holistic Revision   F. Scott Fitzgerald liked to speak of "revising from spirit"—that is, revising from scratch after realizing that the first draft is on the wrong track or just does not seem to "click" in your mind. This kind of holistic revision—of revision as re-seeing—makes it more likely that new energy and insights will be infused into the argument. For this kind of revision to work best, you often need to set aside (though not necessarily "scrap") the original draft and start afresh.

Content Revision   When revising for content, you examine your ideas in greater depth than you did during the earlier draft. Typically, you gather more information or return to the original information to process it more efficiently. You may discover that you have underdeveloped an idea, so you would need to provide specific detail to support your claim. Usually, such revisions can be "pasted into" the original draft.

Organizational Revision   Writers often revise to strengthen the structure of their argument. When you revise for organization, pay close attention to the logical progression of your ideas. An argument can be made more effective, for example, by saving the most compelling point for last. As for moving coherently and smoothly from one point to the next, make sure you include transitional markers such as "on the other hand," "nevertheless," "in spite of," "according to," "however," and so on. Strive for the best possible order of ideas, not just the order in which the ideas occurred to you. When an argument unfolds logically, you create what is casually referred to as *flow*. The smoother the flow, the more likely your readers are to follow along and comprehend your argument.

Stylistic Revision   When revising to improve your style, pay attention to the way you sound on paper—to the manner in which you convey your ideas. Stylistic problems include inconsistency in tone of voice (too informal here, excessively formal there), lack of sentence and paragraph variety and emphasis, and use of jargon.

One of the pleasures of writing is projecting something of your individual personality and your own manner of emphasizing ideas, of relating one point to another, and of making colorful or dramatic comparisons. As Sidney Cox writes, "What you mean is never what anyone else means, exactly. And the only thing that makes you more than a drop in the common bucket, a particle in the universal hourglass, is the interplay of your specialness with your commonness" (*Indirections*, 1981:19).

One way to become more adept at constructing sentences and paragraphs is to play around with them. Take any paragraph, your own or someone else's from a magazine article, and rewrite it in different ways, discovering what is possible. You can sense a personality behind Cox's tone of voice, can you not? Look at his syntax, his peculiar word choice. But the point is, if *you* were the one asserting Cox's point, you would have done so in your own manner. For example, you might have expressed the point like this:

> People communicate ideas differently because each person sees the world differently. Each person uses language differently. At the same time, all of us who belong to the same culture share a common language. It is a writer's special blending of his or her individual voice with a commonplace voice that makes for a memorable writing style.

In this "revised" passage, the voice has become less conversational and more impersonal. The syntax and word choice seem more formal, which create the impression that the author is speaking to a large audience rather than to a single person.

Proofreading   One of our students once referred to proofreading as *prof-reading*—making sure the essay is ready for the prof's critical eye. Some students mistakenly equate proofreading with copyediting or even with revision in general, but proofreading refers to a very careful line-by-line scrutiny of the semifinal draft to make sure that no errors of any kind are present. The term *proofreading* comes from the profession of printing; a proof is an initial printing of a document that is used for correcting any mistakes. Most desk dictionaries list common standardized proofreaders' marks, or symbols and abbreviations that professional compositors use to indicate changes. You already know some of them: the caret (^) to indicate insertion of a word or letter; the abbreviation *lc*, which means change to lowercase (a diagonal line drawn through a capital letter means the same thing). Proofreading is not reading in the usual sense. If you try to proofread by reading normally, you will miss things. An ideal way to proofread is slowly and orally.

Visual Aids as Tools for Argumentative Writing

Our eyes "are the monopolists of our senses," asserts the poet-naturalist Diane Ackerman in *A Natural History of the Senses* (Random House, 1990), so it's no surprise, as she also points out, that "our language is steeped in visual imagery" (229, 230). Visual elements—photographs, drawings, charts, and diagrams—contribute much to the comprehension of ideas by stimulating the audience's imagination—"imagination" in the sense of being able to see, to image, in the mind's eye, a concrete representation of the ideas being discussed in the text. Keep in mind, however, that abstract ideas are not automatically "improved" by translating them into visuals. Visuals need to be selected with care. It is perfectly all right, often preferable—even in this visual age—to write text-only documents. Most books and articles (even in popular magazines, aside from an introductory visual) continue to be written that way. That said, images used judiciously help readers assimilate information and add persuasive force to an argument.

> In the following article, "Tribal Relations," Steven Waldman and John C. Green argue that instead of religion versus secularism being the major determining factor for the way Americans vote, many more factors are involved. As you read the article, consider the role that the visual elements play in conveying the author's premise.

Tribal Relations

How Americans really sort out on cultural and religious issues—and what it means for our politics

Steven Waldman
and John C. Green

Many Americans, when they think about values and politics, focus on the "religious right"—conservatives led by James Dobson, Jerry Falwell, and Pat Robertson, and interested mostly in cultural issues, such as abortion and same-sex marriage. So on election night in 2004, when exit polls found that the No. 1 priority cited by voters was "moral values," many jumped to the conclusion that these voters and their agenda had propelled George W. Bush back into the White House.

Soon it became clear that the "values vote" had been exaggerated. Only one-fifth of the respondents listed moral values as the primary basis for their vote. Nearly four out of five listed one of several foreign-policy, economic, or other domestic concerns. And the same polls showed Americans to have social views that would make conservative Christians weep: 60 percent said gays should be allowed either to legally marry or to form civil unions, and 55 percent believed that abortion should be legal in all or most cases.

Religion and values undoubtedly play a large role in our politics. But their impact is often misunderstood. In the most simplistic renderings values come in only two varieties: those held by the religious right and those held by everybody else. During the 2004 campaign we began to map out a very different topology of religion, values, and politics in America, based on survey data gathered by the Ray C. Bliss Institute at the University of Akron in collaboration with the Pew Forum on Religion & Public Life. We combined measures of religious affiliation, behavior, and belief to see how values cluster within the voting public. The resulting picture—which we initially described on the faith-and-spirituality Web site Beliefnet.com and have continued to refine—reveals not two monolithic and mutually antagonistic camps but, rather, twelve coherent blocs with overlapping interests and values. We call these groups the twelve tribes of American politics.

The chart on page 38 shows the twelve tribes and their politics in 2004—Republican tribes in [black], Democratic in [gray], and swing in [dark gray]. The tribes have been placed on a two-way grid that reflects their positions on cultural and economic issues. The cultural issues include abortion, stem-cell research, and gay rights. The economic issues include social-welfare programs and the scope of the federal government. Foreign-policy issues are left off the grid for simplicity's sake, but we will mention them where relevant.

Source: Steven Waldman and John C. Green. "Tribal Relations," *The Atlantic Monthly* Jan.-Feb. 2006.

A brief review of the political habits and migratory patterns of the twelve tribes shows both the complex relationship between values and voting in the United States and the striking degree of compatibility in the values of most Americans. It reveals the role actually played by moral values in the 2004 election, and helps illuminate how the clash of values is likely to influence politics and law in the future.

The Republican Tribes

The fervor and coherence of the Republican base, especially the base of social conservatives, attracted a lot of attention in 2004—and compared with the Democratic base, it is cohesive on moral issues. But it's not monolithic. The Republican base sorts into three related tribes that agree on many issues but place different emphasis on each.

The **religious right**, consisting of traditional evangelical Protestants, accounted for 12.6 percent of the electorate and the core of the moral-values voters in 2004. Almost 90 percent of these voted for Bush. This cohort is as Republican as Republican gets: no group is more conservative on moral values, economic issues, or foreign policy. Contrary to popular belief, the religious right is not growing quickly; its size barely changed from 2000 to 2004.

Heartland culture warriors stand arm-in-arm with the religious right on most moral issues and are nearly as numerous (11.4 percent of the electorate). They are traditional Christians outside the evangelical community, the most prominent being Bush (a traditional United Methodist). Culture warriors are neither as religiously orthodox nor as politically conservative as the religious right, but they were nonetheless energized by same-sex marriage and other high-profile moral issues in 2004. Seventy-two percent voted for Bush in that election.

Heartland culture warriors did not exist as a distinct political group twenty years ago. They are the product of a convulsive theological restructuring—one that has pushed moral values further into the political limelight. Whereas denomination used to predict political affiliation (Catholics were Democrats; Episcopalians were Republicans), religious beliefs and practices are now more important. Congregations and denominations have split over issues such as the inerrancy of the Bible, the role of women, and sexual morality. In recent decades theological conservatives from different denominations—Catholic, Protestant, Mormon—have found one another. In some cases they've formed caucuses within their churches. In others they've switched to more-congenial congregations. One consequence is that they've coalesced on Election Day, voting for candidates who fit their beliefs rather than their churches' historic loyalties.

Moderate evangelicals (10.8 percent of the electorate) make up the final solidly Republican tribe. The less traditional members of evangelical churches, they are culturally conservative but moderate on economic issues, favoring a larger government and aid to the poor. Bush received 64 percent of this tribe's vote, up from 60 percent in 2000.

Moderate evangelicals are much less absolutist than their religious-right cousins: for example, they favor restricting rather than banning abortion, and support some gay rights but not same-sex marriage. As much as anything, they like Bush's personal faith. If you want a Rosetta stone for Bush's evangelical appeal, watch *George Bush: Faith in the White House*, a 2004 documentary that was shown at many church-based Republican campaign events and barely mentions gays or abortion. Rather, it emphasizes that Bush once was lost—a drunk and a ne'er-do-well—but found his faith and was saved; that he was persecuted (by the media) for his faith; that his faith gave him strength and moral clarity; and, most controversial, that he was called by God to the office. These themes resonated deeply among evangelicals.

The three red tribes make up about 35 percent of the electorate, and although their members don't vote exclusively on the basis of cultural issues, values are certainly a key ingredient in the glue that holds the three together. Most of these voters desire a measure of religious expression in public life and a person of faith in the White House. But their positions on such hot-button issues as abortion, gay rights, and stem-cell research are not uniform. Should a future presidential election offer two obviously pious candidates, the Republican "values" base may show itself to be less cohesive than it now appears—and moderate evangelicals in particular could conceivably begin to defect.

The Democratic Tribes

While much hay was made of the "religion gap" in 2004—the tendency of weekly worship attendees to vote Republican—Democrats have religious constituencies too. Indeed, though Democrats may attend church less frequently, many have rich devotional lives, and a surprising number hold conservative cultural views.

A deep-blue **religious left** is almost exactly the same size as the religious right but receives much less attention. John Kerry is perhaps one representative of this group, which draws members from many Christian denominations and is a product of the same theological restructuring that created the heartland culture warriors. Members of the religious left espouse a progressive theology (agreeing, for instance, that "all the world's great religions are equally true") and are very liberal on cultural issues such as abortion and gay marriage. About a quarter attend church weekly. The religious left is somewhat liberal on economic policy and decidedly to the left on foreign policy. Its stances on both moral values and the Iraq War—but especially the latter—have pushed it further into the Democratic camp. Seventy percent backed Kerry in 2004; 51 percent had backed Gore in 2000. The religious left was the largest—and the fastest-growing—single tribe in the Kerry coalition.

Spiritual but not religious voters, who made up 5.3 percent of the electorate in 2004, are also increasing in number. These are people with no religious affiliation who nonetheless believe in God or the soul. It might be tempting to imagine the members of this tribe as aging flower children or their cultural heirs—and indeed, these voters are liberal on both economic issues and foreign policy. But they actually lean slightly to the right on abortion and gay rights. In 2004 their votes were based on economics and the war, so Kerry won more than three-fifths of them.

www.jasonschneider.com

Black Protestants (9.6 percent of the electorate) are the most traditionally religious of the Democratic tribes, and the most culturally conservative as well—in fact, on moral-values issues they are remarkably similar to the hard-right heartland culture warriors. Whereas many Democrats worried about the intermingling of Bush's faith and his politics, 50 percent of African-Americans said his faith had too little impact on his policymaking. Bush made modest gains among black Protestants in Ohio and other battleground states, and those gains contributed to his re-election. But this tribe was also the most liberal on economic and foreign-policy issues, and more than four-fifths voted for Kerry.

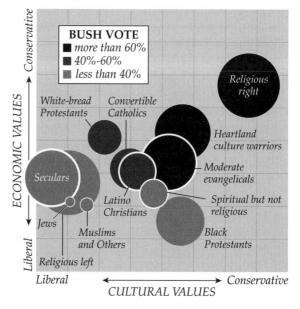

Jews and **Muslims and Others** make up a small part of the electorate—1.9 percent and 2.7 percent, respectively—but the latter group is growing. Members of non-Christian faiths tend to be liberal on cultural issues, and moral values may have helped Kerry a bit with these constituencies, but like many of the blue tribes, they favor the Democratic Party mostly because of its economic and foreign-policy stances.

Non-religious Americans, or **seculars** (10.7 percent of the electorate), are largely responsible for the common view that Democrats are less religious than Republicans—and deeply divided from them on most cultural issues. Seculars are the most culturally liberal of the twelve tribes, and also liberal on economics and foreign policy. Many seculars are especially irritated by Bush's religious expression, and most dislike any commingling of religion and public life. Seculars pose a political dilemma for the Democratic Party: Attempts to energize them based on moral issues would antagonize not only the red tribes and many swing voters but also many blue tribes. Yet attempts to play to more-mainstream American views may turn them off, depressing their turnout.

Indeed, while the blue tribes are fairly well united on economic and foreign-policy issues, they're all over the map on cultural issues. Because the Democratic coalition includes highly religious tribes, non-religious tribes, and everything in between, talking about values can be perilous. Go strongly progay, and one will alienate black Protestants and the spiritual but not religious. Go anti-abortion, and one will lose seculars and the religious left. So Democrats tend to elevate one particular moral value—tolerance—above all others. The merits of tolerance aside, it is part of what keeps the coalition together. But it leaves the Democrats open to attack for lacking a strong moral identity.

The Swing Tribes

Three tribes were up for grabs in 2004 and are still on the move politically. Bush won two of them, and could not have been re-elected without them.

White-bread Protestants (8.1 percent of the electorate) are the most Republican of the purple tribes. They come from the once dominant mainstream Protestant churches that were the backbone of the Republican coalition from William McKinley to Gerald Ford. By now their more traditional coreligionists have joined the heartland culture warriors, and their most liberal brethren the religious left.

In 2004 Bush won just under three-fifths of this tribe. He held those voters because of his views on tax cuts (they tend to be affluent and laissez-faire) and terrorism. But white-bread Protestants are closer to the Democrats on moral issues: for instance, a majority are pro-choice. From a historical perspective Kerry did well among this group—perhaps a harbinger of further Democratic gains.

Convertible Catholics (seven percent of the electorate) are the moderate remnant of the non-Latino Catholic vote. Bush won 55 percent of them in 2004. If Kerry, who is Catholic, had done as well with them as the Southern Baptist Al Gore did in 2000, he probably would have won Ohio and the national election.

Convertible Catholics are true moderates. Both the Democrat Maria Shriver and her Republican husband Arnold Schwarzenegger are good examples. Few believe in papal infallibility, but they are less likely than liberals to say that "all the world's great religions are equally true." They are conflicted on abortion and the scope of government, but strongly favor increased spending to help the poor. Many favor a multilateral foreign policy—except when it comes to the war on terrorism, about which they agree with the president. Scholars describe them as "cross-pressured"—in other words, squishy. They feel that neither party represents them well.

Bush pursued convertible Catholics aggressively in 2004 with shrewd appeals to social stability (backing traditional marriage), concern for the poor (faith-based initiatives), and toughness on terrorism. Al-Qaeda was more important than abortion to his success with this tribe.

Latino Christians are the final swing tribe. They went 55 percent for Kerry in 2004, but Bush made large inroads: he'd won only 28 percent of them in 2000. Values played a large part in this swing—but not primarily because of any Latino Catholic affinity for Republican stances on hot-button cultural issues. Latino Catholics, although they tend to be pro-life, voted for Kerry by more than two to one, largely because of their liberal economic views. Bush did best among Latino Protestants, many of whom come from a Pentecostal tradition that stresses conservative values and an emotional, spirit-filled worship experience. Bush's personal history was appealing to them, as were his efforts to reach out to evangelical churches and religious voters.

As one might expect, the purple tribes lean in different directions on different issues. But where they lean least—or, more precisely, where they vote their leanings least—is on moral issues. They are generally religious, but care little for the culture wars. Their values are largely in line with the legal status quo, and they usually vote based on economic and foreign-policy concerns— at least so long as they don't see either party as seeking a revolution (one way or the other) in personal freedom or the separation of church and state.

Given the beliefs and attitudes of the twelve tribes, what can we say about the future of moral values in politics?

Perhaps the most important lesson is that the size and beliefs of the moderate tribes—the "moral middle," comprising the swing tribes and even a few of the tribes within each party's base—strictly limit how much public policy can actually change after an election. Nothing illustrates that better than the behavior of the Bush administration in the White House. Republican control of all three branches of the federal government is the realization of a religious-right dream. Yet Bush, whatever he said on the campaign trail, has done little to advance the religious right's agenda.

In the 2004 election the official Republican policy, as stated in the party's platform, was to support a constitutional amendment banning abortion. The Republicans also championed Bush's support for an amendment banning gay marriage. Since the election, however, Bush has been silent on both issues. He has not proposed any major restrictions on abortion—nor have the Republican leaders who control both houses of Congress—and has limited his public remarks to criticisms of "partial-birth" abortion and general comments about the "culture of life." He has given not one major speech advocating an amendment to ban gay marriage; in fact, he has dramatically reduced his emphasis on this issue. Bush made a few well-publicized comments expressing openness to the teaching of intelligent design in public schools, but he subsequently pushed no legislation to encourage that goal.

In the past when we've asked religious conservatives privately why they tolerated Bush's doing so little on the cultural issues that were so important during the election, they have responded, in effect, "We need to keep our eye on the ball." The "ball" is the Supreme Court. Religious conservatives believe that permissive judges are the root of much evil in America, and consequently they have allowed Bush enormous latitude as long as they thought he would deliver on judicial nominees.

But he hasn't really—at least not obviously. Conservatives reacted so harshly to the Harriet Miers nomination because neither Miers nor John Roberts was prepared to side with them openly on crucial sexual and moral issues. Had Roberts and Miers replaced Rehnquist and O'Connor, the Court would probably not have shifted much to the right; in fact, it might have shifted a bit to the *left*.

Even the Samuel Alito nomination is telling on this point. Religious conservatives were thrilled with the choice and yet went along with the White House strategy of obscuring rather than clarifying Alito's views on abortion. Alito may yet turn out to be a hero to religious conservatives, but surely it pained them to see him courting Democrats and moderate Republicans by asserting his respect for *Roe* v. *Wade*.

President Bush and his political tacticians are fully aware that they won the election in part by appealing to convertible Catholics, Latinos, moderate evangelicals, and white-bread Protestants. These tribes simply do not support most of the agenda of the religious right. Of course, this is not to say that our laws and cultural norms are forever frozen—far from it. For instance, polls suggest public support for some blurring of the church-state divide: many Americans think that God has been ejected too forcefully from the public square. And to judge from the slow drift of public opinion since the 1980s toward expanding gay rights, it's quite possible that government at all levels will eventually become more supportive of gay unions and even gay marriage. But such changes depend on support from the center—and for the most part our nation's current laws and policies on issues of moral values reflect majority opinion quite well.

None of this means, however, that our elections are likely to become any less fractious. In fact, we believe that the culture wars will increase in intensity during the next few election campaigns, even as the government continues to serve the broad cultural center.

There are two reasons for this view. First, although the poles are not demographically dominant, they have grown somewhat as heartland culture warriors and the religious left have each coalesced into a coherent voting bloc that can be cultivated politically. The secular and moderate-evangelical blocs are also growing. Second, both parties have strong tactical incentives to turn up the rhetorical volume in soliciting support from these tribes during campaigns.

This is especially true for the Republicans. Using moral values to rally the base has become a central tenet of Republican strategy. Because of the investments the party has made in building social-conservative networks and cultivating relationships with them, it would be extremely difficult to abandon this strategy in the short term.

Instead the Republicans may be compelled to intensify their strategy. The personal nature of George Bush's connection to evangelicals is unusual. Someone who lacks that "I once was lost but now am found" narrative may need a harder-edged stand on cultural issues to connect with social conservatives. And the state of other issues behind the Bush coalition, such as foreign policy and the economy, may also necessitate further emphasis on values.

Perhaps this is why Senate Majority Leader Bill Frist took on the Terri Schiavo case, and why the would-be presidential nominee Mitt Romney—who starts with the double disadvantage of being a Mormon and a resident of Massachusetts—has taken the lead in opposing gay marriage. It may also explain why the Republican Senator Sam Brownback so publicly questioned the nomination of Harriet Miers.

But most of the specific issues emphasized by the Republicans are likely to be symbolic, and much of their language carefully coded so as not to alienate the swing tribes. Above all, the Republicans will try to paint themselves as the party of faith. One of the most striking outcomes of the 2004 election is that the Democrats were tagged as "anti-religion." A Pew Forum poll last summer showed that only 29 percent of the public—compared with 40 percent in the summer of 2004—saw the Democrats as "friendly" toward religion.

It is hard to appeal even to blue tribes if one is perceived as hostile to faith in general. Surely the Republicans, having opened this wound, will want to make it bleed some more. Yet if the conservative values agenda is advanced too far, Democrats and liberal interest groups may go on the attack, and Republicans will find themselves at a distinct electoral disadvantage. For instance, if religious conservatives prevail in their efforts to allow teaching of intelligent design in public schools, we can expect that liberals will push hard for reversals. And the center—including convertible Catholics, Latinos, and especially white-bread Protestants—may start to get twitchy if Republicans are perceived as "anti-progress." God is popular, but so is education, because most voters consider it crucial to the future economic prospects of their children.

In politics as in physics, every action produces a reaction, so continued pushing by conservatives will no doubt lead to pushing back by liberals. Cultural conflict will remain a staple of American politics for the foreseeable future. But concerns that the nation may become subject to the cultural views of either party's poles are alarmist—as is the view that at any one time half the nation is oppressed by the federal government's cultural agenda. The gap between the rhetoric and the reality of American cultural division is unlikely to shrink anytime soon. And it's that gap that is perhaps the most fundamental feature of our cultural politics today. ◎⁄◎

Before discussing the two visuals (a drawing and a chart) that accompany the article, let's consider its typography. Instead of unbroken, uniform type (tedious to readers of articles and book-length nonfiction, although not a problem for fiction readers), the writers divide their text into sections and subsections to allow for more efficient assimilation of the material. In "Tribal Relations," consider the use of the boldfaced headings and subheadings that, respectively, divide the article into three main components, each representing the major-party tribes plus the swing tribes, and then subdivide each of these into segments based on individual tribes (for example, the "heartland culture warriors" and the "moderate evangelicals" that constitute the Republican tribes). Note how segmenting the article this way serves a dual purpose: (1) It enables the reader to know at a glance what facet of the subject matter is going to be examined in detail, and (2) it reinforces the overall coherence of the article—in this case, the way the authors have classified the "tribes" of American politics. These simple forms of document design do much to help organize the article and make it visually attractive.

Turning now to the two visuals: What do they contribute to the piece? Let's start with the fanciful drawing of a man wearing a maze of religious symbols around his neck. Is this just a bit of frivolity, or does the illustration reinforce the authors' views on the subject? Notice the particular icons dangling from the man's neck. Some of them reflect particular religions; others, like the Mercedes-Benz icon, do not. Then why are they even depicted? Perhaps the artist and/ or author wants to create an image of "values complexity"—that American voters possibly bring a great deal more than what they themselves are consciously aware of to the polls.

The second image appears to be more explicitly purposeful. It is a chart consisting of circles of varying sizes depicting the degree of influence of particular criteria on the Bush vote of 2004. The bigger the circle, the greater the influence. One might speculate on the choice of a field of circles rather than, say, a bar graph. Perhaps it serves to allude wryly to the election-year party conventions during which balloons are dropped from the ceiling—a bit of playfulness that may not contribute to the argument other than to suggest the spiritedness of the voters, regardless of political affiliation.

Using Visual Aids as a Heuristic Device for Generating Content

Images often can tell stories or embody arguments. You can learn to read an image for its story or argumentative content by considering what the image implies as well as what it depicts explicitly. In the Florida's Natural orange juice ad (see Color Advertisement B), for example, the advertiser attempts to convince you of the freshness and naturalness of the product by depicting physical (i.e., instantaneous) contact between the orchard grower and you, the consumer. The gloved hand of the former also implies that the processes involved in transporting the product from orchard to supermarket adheres to sanitation regulations. The ad copy then reinforces what the image already depicts by noting that the producers own the land on which the oranges are grown. Less conspicuous, but likely to register subconsciously, is the similarity in color between the sleeve of the orchard grower and the sleeve of the consumer—suggesting kinship (and therefore trustworthiness).

Using Visual Aids as an Organizing Tool

As with text, visuals can be given a logical or thematic sequence. Think of visuals used to accompany a procedural document, such as how to assemble a bookcase. Each visual would give the assembler an idea of what the bookcase would look like at each stage of the assembly. Or consider how the organization of an article that examines, say, the effects of drought on crops can be reinforced by a series of photographs. Or how the organization of an article that correlates fields of study with salaries of graduates can be reinforced by a series of color-coded line or bar graphs, one for each field of study.

Using Visual Aids as Evidence

One very common example of a set of visuals used as evidence—or at least purported evidence—is the "before" and "after" images of individuals following a diet or exercise regimen. Of course such photographic evidence can always be manipulated: How much time elapsed between images? What other factors besides the diet or exercise regimen might have contributed to the weight loss? Were the images "Photoshopped" in any way? Readers should be skeptical about the reliability of such photographic evidence unless the article addresses it explicitly.

A more important use of photographs as evidence occurs in scientific and medical documents. Images can provide visual evidence of, say, the destruction of the Brazilian rain forests, the devastation caused by earthquakes, or the physiological consequences of malnutrition.

Color Advertisement A

Color Advertisement B

Looks fast standing still.
That's called truth in packaging.

Color Advertisement C

Color Advertisement D

Chapter Summary

An argument is a form of discourse in which a writer or speaker tries to persuade an audience to accept, reject, or think a certain way about a problem that cannot be solved by scientific or mathematical reasoning alone. To argue well, a writer uses the three appeals of ethos, pathos, and logos—personal values and ethics, feelings, and logical reasoning—to supplement the facts themselves. The rhetorical rhombus reminds us that every communication act involves targeting a particular audience, whose particular needs and expectations regarding the subject must be met by the writer, and that every act of communication must have a clear, often urgent purpose for establishing communication in the first place.

Good argumentative writing is carefully structured. The three models of argumentative structure—Classical, Toulmin, and Rogerian—represent three different views about the nature and purpose of argument. *Classical argument* follows a predetermined structure consisting of an introduction and statement of the problem, presentation of evidence, refutation of opposing views, and a conclusion derived from the evidence presented. *Toulmin argument*, growing out of the practicalities of political and legal debate, emphasizes the context-dependency of argument and the arguer's underlying values associated with the data the arguer brings forth to support a claim. *Rogerian argument*, growing out of modern humanistic psychology, emphasizes the need for human cooperation when viewpoints differ; hence, a basic assumption underlying the Rogerian argument is that a common ground can be found between the arguing parties, no matter how irreconcilable their differences may seem to be.

Composing arguments is a dynamic process that involves generating ideas, organizing the argument, drafting, revising, editing, and proofreading. These phases of composing overlap and are recursive. Understanding the composing process also means being aware of using different strategies for different parts of the argument, such as openings and conclusions. One final and vitally important phase in the composing process is acquiring feedback from peers. Feedback on first drafts is usually immensely valuable in helping writers think more deeply about the purpose, audience, and subject of their arguments.

Checklist

1. Do I clearly understand the four elements of the rhetorical rhombus—purpose, audience, writer, and subject—that comprise the communication act? How each element interacts with the others?

2. Do I understand how the three appeals of ethos, pathos, and logos function in argumentative writing?

3. Do I understand the nature of evidence? Of refutation?

4. Am I familiar with the strategies that comprise the composing process?

5. Have I prepared an outline to prompt me in my drafting?

6. Am I familiar with the different kinds of revision?

7. Have I learned to proofread my drafts carefully?

8. Do I know the definitions of Classical, Toulmin, and Rogerian arguments?

Writing Projects

1. Conduct an informal survey of students' study habits by talking to your fellow students. How many of them "cram" for exams or write their papers immediately before the assignment is due? What specific strategies do students use when they study? (For example, do they make marginal glosses in their books? Write notes on index cards? Make flash cards? Get together with other students in regular study groups?) Can you correlate methods or habits of study to levels of academic success? Write an essay in which you argue for or against such a correlation, using the responses you have gathered.

2. Write an essay on the role that argumentative writing can play in helping people who disagree about a given issue to arrive at better understanding— or at least at a greater willingness to cooperate. What likely obstacles must initially be overcome?

3. Keep a "writing process log" the next time you write an argument. Describe in detail everything you do when prewriting, composing each draft, revising, and proofreading. Next, evaluate the log. Which facets of the composing process were most useful? Which were least useful?

4. Compose four possible openings, each a different type (occasional, anecdotal, startling, analytical) for your next argument-writing assignment. Which opening seems most appropriate for your essay, and why?

5. Prepare an outline (Classical, Toulmin, or Rogerian) for an essay taking a position on one of the following topics:

   a. All bicyclists should (should not) be required by law to wear helmets.

   b. This college should (should not) sponsor formal skateboarding competitions.

   c. More courses or programs in multicultural awareness need (do not need) to be offered at this college.

6. Locate four or five editorial cartoons on a single, timely subject. Write an essay in which you analyze their different strategies for satirizing the subject.

7. Read the following essay on editorial cartoons by Herb Block, himself an editorial cartoonist for *The Washington Post*. Write an essay of your own in which you agree or disagree with Block's assertion that "I don't believe there should be any sacred cows." In your support or rebuttal, consider the case in early 2006 in which a series of Danish editorial cartoons satirizing the prophet Mohammed generated outrage among Islamic communities worldwide.

The Cartoon | Herb Block

In one of Charles Schulz's *Peanuts* strips, Lucy announces that she's going to be a political cartoonist "lashing out with my crayon." Just as Charlie Brown asks the subject of her work, she strikes the paper with such a bold stroke that it snaps her crayon in half. "I'm lashing out," she says, "at the people who make these stupid crayons."

I don't believe in the Lucy method of deciding first to "lash out" and then picking a convenient target. But as a person with definite opinions, she might have done well to stick with cartooning anyhow.

A wide range of work comes under the heading of editorial or political cartooning today, including gag cartoons on current topics. I enjoy many of these and usually put some fun into my work. But I still feel that the political cartoon should have a view to express, that it should have some purpose beyond the chuckle. So what I'm talking about here is the cartoon as an opinion medium.

Herblock painting McCarthy, Nixon, Reagan, and Clinton. "The Cartoon," © 1977, 2000 by Herbert Block. Cartoons appear courtesy of the Herb Block Foundation.

The political cartoon is not a news story and not an oil portrait. It's essentially a means for poking fun, for puncturing pomposity.

Cartooning is an irreverent form of expression, and one particularly suited to scoffing at the high and the mighty. If the prime role of a free press is to serve as critic of government, cartooning is often the cutting edge of that criticism.

We seldom do cartoons about public officials that say: "Congratulations on keeping your hands out of the public till," or "It was awfully nice of you to tell

"What—us tell fibs of some kind?" "The Cartoon," © 1977, 2000 by Herbert Block. Cartoons appear courtesy of the Herb Block Foundation.

Source: Herb Block, "The Cartoon," © 1977, 2000. Cartoons appear courtesy of the Herb Block Foundation.

the truth yesterday." Public officials are *supposed* to keep their hands out of the till and to tell the truth. With only one shot a day, cartoons are generally drawn about officials we feel are *not* serving the public interest. And we usually support the "good guys" by directing our efforts at their opponents.

For people who think political cartoons are inclined to be negative, a good explanation is in the story of the school teacher who asked the children in her class to give examples of their kindness to birds and animals. One boy told of how he had taken in a kitten on a cold night and fed it. A girl told of how she had found an injured bird and cared for it. When the teacher asked the next boy if he could give an example of his kindness to nature's creatures, he said, "Yes ma'am. One time I kicked a boy for kicking a dog."

In our line of work, we frequently show our love for our fellow men by kicking big boys who kick underdogs. In opposing corruption, suppression of rights and abuse of government office, the political cartoon has always served as a special prod—a reminder to public servants that they ARE public servants.

That is the relationship of the cartoonist to government, and I think the job is best performed by judging officials on their public records and not on the basis of their cozy confidences.

As for the cartoonist's relationship to the rest of the newspaper, that depends on the individual cartoonist and the paper. The editorial page cartoon in the *Washington Post* is a signed expression of personal opinion. In this respect, it is like a column or other signed article—as distinguished from the editorials, which express the policy of the newspaper itself.

Other newspapers operate differently. On some, the cartoon is drawn to accompany an editorial. The cartoonist may sit in on a daily conference, where the content of editorials and cartoons is worked out. Or he may be given copies of the editorials before publication.

A completely different arrangement is followed when the cartoonist simply sends in his work, sometimes from another city. Still other variations include cartoonists submitting sketches (one or several) for editorial approval.

I draw my cartoons at the *Washington Post*, but don't submit sketches or sit in on editorial conferences. And I don't see the editorials in advance. This is for much the same reason that I don't read "idea letters." I like to start from scratch, thinking about what to say, without having to "unthink" other ideas first.

Fiddler. "The Cartoon," © 1977, 2000 by Herbert Block. Cartoons appear courtesy of the Herb Block Foundation.

That's something like the old business of trying *not* to think of an elephant for five minutes. It's easier if nobody has mentioned an elephant at all.

In my case, the actual work process is more methodical than inspirational—despite the apparent aimlessness of strolls out of the office, chats with friends, shuffling papers, lining up drawing materials and other diversions that may or may not have to do with creativity. It's methodical compared to the popular impression that "getting an idea" consists of waiting for a cartoon light bulb to flash on overhead.

The day's work begins with reading the newspapers, usually starting the night before with the first edition of the *Washington Post*, and making notes on possible subjects. I also flip on the radio or TV for late news developments. This practice began when I was just about to turn in a finished cartoon one day, only to learn that a major story had broken and kept the newsroom people too busy to tell me about it. The quick return to the drawing board to produce a new cartoon in minutes was an experience I wouldn't want to repeat. And with broadcast reports on the hour or even the half hour, I now occasionally pass along late-breaking news to others.

Unless there is one subject of overriding importance or timeliness on a particular day, or some special outrage, I generally try to narrow down the list of subjects to two or three. Next comes the business of thinking about what it is that needs to be said—and then getting the comment into graphic form, which involves drawing several rough sketches.

It is hard to say just when a thought turns into a cartoon. In writing or speaking, we all use phrases that lend themselves to visual images. Where you might say that a politician is in trouble up to his neck, a drawing might show him as a plumber in a flooded basement or a boy at the dike with his chin just above the water line. On one occasion when a public figure obviously was not telling the truth, I did a sketch of him speaking, with a tongue that was shaped exactly like a table fork. These are pretty simple examples, but they may provide some clue to how concepts develop into drawings.

"Speak softly and carry a big stick." "The Cartoon," © 1977, 2000 by Herbert Block. Cartoons appear courtesy of the Herb Block Foundation.

It may not sound very exciting or "cartoony," but to me the basic idea is the same as it ought to be with a written opinion—to try to say the right thing. Putting the thought into a picture comes second. Caricature also figures in the cartoons. But the total cartoon is more important than just fun with faces and figures.

I mention this because it is a common conversational gambit to ask cartoonists if they're having a good time with some well-known face. And when media people are doing articles on a new political personality, they often phone cartoonists to ask what it is about the politician's features that grabs them. Some even ask which candidate you would like to see elected on the basis of "drawability." That's like asking a writer what person he wants elected on the basis of whether the candidate's name lends itself to puns.

I have not yet yielded to the temptation to answer such questions by saying I liked Ronald Reagan's right ear lobe or Jimmy Carter's left nostril. Actually, anyone can be caricatured. And if a cartoonist needed a public figure with Dumbo-the-Elephant ears a Jimmy Durante nose, he'd have to be pretty hard up for ideas *and* drawing.

From time to time the question of cartoon fairness comes up—with some practitioners asserting that they are not supposed to be fair. This is a view I don't share. Caricature itself is sometimes cited as being unfair because it plays on physical characteristics. But like any form of satire, caricature employs exaggeration—clearly recognized as such. Also the portrayal of a person is often part of the opinion. For example, President George Bush was associated with words like "Read my lips" and "The vision thing." Emphasizing his overhanging upper lip and squinty eyes expressed a view identifying him with his words. I think fairness depends on the cartoon—on whether the view is based on actual statements, actions or inactions.

Questions of fairness are not confined to pictures. Some broadcasters and columnists regularly earn championship belts for fighting straw men. (Those "liberals" want the government to take all your money and run your lives in Washington. Those "conservatives" want to see your kids starve to death.) Incidentally I would like to see a better word than "conservative" for some who are not eager to conserve basic rights or the environment.

A columnist who opposes political campaign funding reform—based on his interpretation of the First Amendment—wrote a piece in which he pointed out that we spend more on potato chips than on political campaigns. But if true, the purchase and consumption of potato chips, whatever

Arms payoff for hostage release. "The Cartoon," © 1977, 2000 by Herbert Block. Cartoons appear courtesy of the Herb Block Foundation.

they do to our diets, can hardly be compared to the purchase and corruption of public offices. I'd guess the columnist who reached for that statistical irrelevance probably regards cartoons for campaign funding reform as "gross caricatures."

But back to the drawing board and the sketches—a series of "roughs" may approach a subject from different angles or may be variations on a theme. This is where other people come into the picture—or, more accurately, where I bring the pictures to other people. By showing sketches to a few colleagues on the paper, I often find out which sketch expresses a thought most clearly. The purpose of these trial runs is not only to get individual reactions, but also to get out any bugs that might be in the cartoon ideas.

One of the advantages of working at the *Washington Post* is the access to information about government and assorted news items. Reporters, researchers and other staff members are available—with special knowledge about subjects they have dealt with. They also know where to find answers to questions about who said what or exactly what happened when. And computers now make it possible to recall statements and records of all kinds.

A sketch on arms programs or military costs, for example, is one I'd particularly want to discuss with the Pentagon correspondent. A writer covering the courts can tell me if I've missed anything in a decision. Capitol Hill writers, familiar with the exact status of congressional bills, can tell if a sketch on a piece of legislation is well-timed. Staff members may also have information that helps me decide which cartoon is the best bet for that day. Such help—not "ideas for cartoons," but background information and relevant facts—is of enormous value.

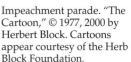

I'm a deadline pusher, and one reason the finished cartoon is usually a last-gasp down-to-the-wire effort is because of the time spent on sketches. I work on them as long as possible. And after deciding on one, I send a Xerox copy of it to the editor's office.

Impeachment parade. "The Cartoon," © 1977, 2000 by Herbert Block. Cartoons appear courtesy of the Herb Block Foundation.

Other cartoonists—as well as other papers—prefer different arrangements. One cartoonist told me he had tried for years to get the kind of freedom I have on the *Post*. When he finally got it, he found the decision-making to be a burden. He went back to asking an editor to make the daily choice.

I enjoy the freedom to express my own ideas in my own way. And this is also consistent with the *Washington Post* policy expressed by the late publisher, Eugene Meyer, who said he believed in getting people who knew what they were doing and then letting them do it.

One of the things that has made the *Washington Post* great is the fact that it *does* provide for differing views instead of offering a set of written and drawn opinions all bearing the stamp of a single person. Over the years, there have been differences between the cartoons and the editorials on issues, on emphasis and on performances of individual public figures.

In 1952, for example, the *Washington Post* endorsed Gen. Dwight Eisenhower for president before either major party had made nominations. The cartoons expressed my unhappiness with the campaign conducted by Eisenhower and his choice for vice president, Richard Nixon—and expressed my clear preference for candidate Adlai Stevenson.

About 1965, with a different editor and a different publisher, the cartoons focused more and more on President Johnson's "credibility gap" and his escalation of the war in Vietnam, while the editorials generally supported the president and his Vietnam policy. Even on this extremely divisive issue, the editor and I respected each other's views.

Later, the cartoons and editorials diverged on other subjects. For example, in the 1970s I did a series of cartoons opposing the confirmation of Clement Haynsworth to the Supreme Court—a view not shared in the editorials. But we were in agreement in opposing the next nominee—G. Harold Carswell.

During the Clinton administration I did not share in the *Post's* approval of the expansion of the North American Treaty Organization (NATO) after the collapse of the Soviet Union. And the cartoons hardly matched the editorials on Independent Counsel Kenneth Starr—which acknowledged that he had made mistakes in the probe of President Clinton's relationships but saw him as a victim of a vicious organized attack.

On important issues involving civil rights and civil liberties the editorials and cartoons have been in general agreement. There was no possible doubt about the stands they shared on the attempted censorship involved in the publication of the Pentagon Papers on Vietnam or the culmination of the Nixon scandals in Watergate. And they have both been involved in the long continuous battles for campaign finance reform and gun controls and tobacco industry curbs.

But even where the general viewpoints have been the same, there have been times when I knew a publisher or editor would have preferred my using a different approach. During the Watergate disclosures, I did a "naked Nixon." This might have seemed like *lèse majesté* to an editor but was *au naturel* for a cartoonist.

I've often summed up the role of the cartoonist as that of the boy in the Hans Christian Andersen story who says the emperor has no clothes on. And that seemed to be just what was called for during this phase of the "imperial presidency."

What a written piece can do more easily than a cartoon is to comment on a subject that requires giving background information. Wordiness can be awkward in a cartoon—though sometimes needed to explain an issue or provide dialogue. But a cartoon at times can say something that might be harder to put into words. The one of Nixon hanging between the tapes comments not only on his situation at the time, but on his veracity and honesty—without using any words other than his own.

As for a comparison of words and pictures—each has its role. Each is capable of saying something necessary or something irrelevant—of reaching a right conclusion or a wrong one.

A cartoon does not tell everything about a subject. It's not supposed to. No written piece tells everything either. As far as words are concerned, there is no safety in numbers. The test of a written or drawn commentary is whether it gets at an essential truth.

As for subject matter, I don't believe there should be any sacred cows. But there's no obligation for the cartoonist to deal with a topic unless he feels there is a point that needs to be made. Regardless of Lucy's view, the object is not to "lash out" just because the means is at hand.

There is no shortage of subjects for opinions. I don't long for public misfortunes or official crooks to provide "material for cartoons." Hard as it may be for some people to believe—I don't miss malefactors when they are gone from pub-

Source: Nixon hanging between the tapes. "The Cartoon," © 1977, 2000 by Herbert Block. Cartoons appers courtesy of the Herb Block Foundation.

lic life. There are more things amiss than you can shake a crayon at.

If the time should come when political figures and all the rest of us sprout angel wings, there will still be different views on the proper whiteness and fluffiness of the wings, as well as flaps over their flapping, speed and altitude. And there will still be something funny about a halo that's worn slightly askew.

When that happy heaven-on-earth day comes, I'd still like to be drawing cartoons. I wouldn't want to see any head angel throwing his weight around. ◎/◎

2 | Methods of Critical Reading

A reader must learn to read.
—Alberto Manguel

CONSIDERING THE DISCIPLINES

Most of us learned to read English so long ago that we don't even think about adjusting our reading to different texts—poetry, fiction, nonfiction, web pages. Sometimes, though, we may need to become more conscious of just how we read when we are reading for different purposes, just as we might watch a movie differently if we knew we were going to be quizzed about the movie afterwards rather than talking about our favorite parts with our friends. Especially when we read texts to see how we might incorporate ideas into our own arguments or to see how our own arguments are developing, we may benefit from thinking consciously about different methods of critical reading. Regardless of academic discipline, critical reading skills are necessary for determining the strength or weakness of an argument. The strategies this chapter presents can be adapted to your reading of a text in the social sciences as well as a newspaper, from an art exhibit to a web page, and you will learn from doing a critical reading of texts within your field what its conventions generally entail. Reading critically involves the following interdisciplinary skills:

- Previewing an argument for its basic premise, method of argument, and use of evidence
- Analyzing the argument to determine its logical and ethical foundations
- Being open-minded in order to evaluate the writer's premise as fairly as possible

---

Reading and writing are intimately related modes of thinking—so intertwined that you really cannot do one without doing the other. Just as writers determine how to approach their subjects by considering their purpose and their readers, so too do readers determine how to approach *their* purpose for reading by considering how to approach the subject, often working along similar lines to those intended by the author.

Reading as the Construction of Meaning

Some researchers refer to the symbiotic relationship between reading and writing as the *construction of meaning*. That is, readers must process meaning from those symbols on the page that, by themselves, possess no intrinsic meaning.

Topic	Perspective 1 (neutral outsider)	Perspective 2 (offensive)	Perspective 3 (defensive)
Value of Exit Tests	To weigh pros vs. cons to pass a fair judgment	I've always been held back by these biased tests!	Tests have always enabled me to show how much I know!

TABLE 2.1 **Sample Perspectives from Which We Read**

As readers, we also construct meaning beyond what we see on the page before us. For example, when we read through a draft of an argument to revise and edit it, we monitor our sense of direction, the development of the ideas, the coherence (that is, the logical progression of ideas), the clarity, and the larger concerns of persuasiveness and originality.

All of these activities are context-dependent. As the example in Table 2.1 reveals, reading strategies that work well, say, in drafting an essay that objectively analyzes the strengths and weakness of a high school exit test may not work when drafting a more subjective essay on why the school should retain or abandon such tests. In the first essay, you need to read for such elements as logical progression of ideas, thorough support of assertions, and fair representation of challenging or alternative views. In the second essay, aware that you are presenting an individual preference, you need to keep an eye out for sufficiently clear (if not always logical) reasons behind your preferences.

Thus, whenever we read, we do a great deal more than simply absorb words like a sponge. In reading others' work, we sometimes think to ourselves, "If I had written this essay, I'd have made this introduction much shorter and put in more examples in the third paragraph—I barely understood it, after all!" Such thinking is comparable to what we do as we revise our own work, so clearly we are reading another's text from the writer's perspective.

We might also "revise" another's writing when someone asks us about a book or article we've read: "What is Adrian Nicole LeBlanc's *Random Family* about?" In summarizing that contemporary work of creative nonfiction, we would use our own words to shorten a three-hundred-page work to one or two paragraphs. In fact, while you are reading such a text, you are summarizing it to yourself—during the actual reading or during breaks between readings. Thus, to understand a text means, in a sense, to rewrite the author's ideas so that we blend them with our own ideas. Such rewriting is built into the very nature of reading. We cannot truly comprehend a text without doing so.

Active versus Passive Reading

In the sense that to read means processing written language to understand it, all reading is "active." But some forms of reading represent a greater challenge to the comprehension process than others. A letter from a loved one may be processed relatively swiftly and efficiently, almost as a photograph would, whereas a demanding legal or technical document of the same length may need to be processed in a much more methodical manner.

When we read primarily for pleasure—whether a novel, a work of nonfiction, or a friend's email—we are concerned primarily about content: What is going to happen to the characters in the novel? What is the author's premise in the work of nonfiction? What fun activities did the friend experience in London over the summer?

But when we read for a purpose besides (or in addition to) pleasure, we need to think more consciously of our reading process so that we can make necessary modifications. Such reading is task-oriented: to find out certain information, to summarize the work, to analyze the structure of the work, to assess the merits of the argument, to determine how the information coincides with our position on the issue.

You can adopt certain strategies to become a more active reader. It may seem strange to think of a "strategy" of reading. The only strategy that leaps to mind is moving our eyes across the page from left to right and top to bottom (for readers of most Western languages). But from a psychological and linguistic perspective, we are pulling off complex feats of cognition. At the simplest level, we are doing any or all of the following, more or less simultaneously:

- *Linking* one part of a sentence with another, for example, linking a subordinate clause to a main clause or nouns and verbs to their respective adjectival or adverbial modifiers, or linking the data in a visual aid such as a graph or diagram to the discussion of those data in the body of the argument. Visuals themselves possess components that need to be linked together when they are read. Imagine a pie chart that breaks down someone's college-related expenses for a given month. The reader links each slice of the chart with the others, reflecting on proportions. If 40 percent of the pie is given over to the cost of meals, for example, the reader may agree or disagree with your claim that food costs on this campus are disproportionate relative to food costs on other college campuses.

- *Tracking* the constantly shifting parameters of meaning from word to word, phrase to phrase, sentence to sentence, paragraph to paragraph

- *Relating* any given sentence or paragraph to a premise or theme, whether implied or explicitly stated

Those are just some of the *basic* strategies. As students of writing, you read not just for understanding but for insight into the way in which an author organizes and develops an argument. This type of active reader needs to do the following:

1. Determine the *framework* of the author's argument. What are the claim, data, and warrant?

2. Evaluate the *data* (evidence) presented. Are they accurate? Sufficient? Appropriate? Relevant?

3. Evaluate the author's *organizational strategy.* Why does the author bring in X before Y and after W? Is the sequence beyond dispute, or is there no clear rhetorical purpose behind the sequence? Should the author have arranged things differently?

4. Speculate on the *significance* of what is being argued. What are the short- and long-term consequences of the author's views? If the author argues that student athletes are treated unfairly in the classroom, for example, and uses compelling evidence to back up that claim, then the significance of the argument is that it could persuade classroom teachers to be more flexible, say, in permitting student athletes to miss class to participate in out-of-town athletic competitions.

5. Analyze the *logic* of the argument. Has the writer inadvertently committed any of the logical fallacies covered later on in Chapter 6? Each of these cognitive acts works together to comprise active reading. Passive reading, by contrast, means reading without reflecting or "talking back" to the text— that is, without forming questions that can and should be asked of an author who is trying to communicate with us.

Exercise 2.1

1. Assess your reading process. What kinds of material do you read actively? Passively? What about the material encourages one mode of reading rather than another?

2. Select a short piece such as a magazine feature or editorial on a social or political issue and discuss it in terms of the four concerns of an active reader (framework, data, organizational strategy, and significance).

3. Read a short piece for coherence alone. Explain how the author "glues" sentences and paragraphs together to make them interrelate clearly and meaningfully.

Reading as a Writer of Arguments

Chapter 1 describes the role that supporting data and expert opinion play in building your argument. As you read to find sources of support for your argument, use the following strategies: previewing, in-depth reading, and postreading.

Previewing

Imagine Bob, a first-year student, trying to study for a political science quiz the next day. He's having trouble reading the textbook chapter being tested. It seems like more pages than he has time or inclination to absorb. So he finds his classmate Julie in the library and tells her he's having trouble motivating himself to do all that reading. Julie, who's already read the chapter, encourages him by saying, "Oh, Bob, the chapter essentially covers only four points about the economic conditions on the Greek islands comprising Santorini." Relieved that the chapter highlights only four main points, Bob returns to his room motivated to read but also with a sense of how to read the chapter productively. Julie has given him a *preview* of what to expect. Previewing is typically a two-stage process: (1) prereading, and (2) skimming.

Anything worth reading typically requires several readings, so you approach this previewing stage knowing that you will read the assignment more thoroughly later on.

To read as critical thinkers and writers, you must read to ensure that you

- understand the content and progression of the story or argument,
- can determine the rhetorical strategy (for example, the validity and significance of the claim, the data, and the warrant), and
- are able to incorporate the author's views into your own.

Prereading You preread the text to determine its central purpose and approach. You may do this at the beginning of the term when, standing in line to purchase your textbook, you peruse the table of contents and the introductions to each of the chapters. You also preread when you read the topic sentences of the paragraphs in the introduction. (The topic sentence usually is the first, second, or last sentence.)

To preread an article or chapter from a work of nonfiction, you can rely on the structure that writers in the Western tradition have used for centuries and handed down to the modern college composition course:

- Introduction
- Thesis statement
- Topic sentences
- Transitional paragraphs
- Conclusion

Remember that the purpose of prereading is not to understand the whole piece but to identify the key points of the piece so that when you do read it in its entirety, you already have a clear sense of its framework.

After reading the introduction in full, read the topic sentences of the body paragraphs. These tend to be in one of three spots: first, last, or second. Topic sentences most frequently appear as the first sentences of the paragraphs, just where you have been taught to put them. But they also may occur as the last sentence in the paragraph when the writer has organized the content of the paragraph by presenting his or her evidence before the claim. And the topic sentence sometimes is the second sentence of the paragraph (the third most frequent position) when the first sentence is transitional, linking the paragraph before to the one that follows. In these cases, you will read both the transitional sentences and the topic sentences. You may need to read a bit of the article or essay to gain a sense of the writer's style—that is, where he or she tends to position the topic sentence.

Here is an example of a paragraph in which the topic sentence appears at the very end, a technique that this particular author, Carl Sagan, uses quite commonly in his writing. This selection is from Sagan's *The Demon-Haunted World: Science as a Candle in the Dark* (1995):

> What do we actually see when we look up at the Moon with the naked eye? We make out a configuration of irregular bright and dark markings—not a close representation of any familiar object. But, almost irresistibly, our eyes connect the markings, emphasizing some, ignoring others. We seek a pattern, and we find one. In world myth and folklore, many images are seen: a woman weaving, stands of laurel trees, an elephant jumping off a cliff, a girl with a basket on her back, a rabbit, . . . a woman pounding tapa cloth, a four-eyed jaguar. People of one culture have trouble understanding how such bizarre things could be seen by the people of another.

The pattern Sagan uses in this paragraph is this: He opens with a question, gives a string of examples to illustrate the basis of the question, and then answers the question, that is, posits the topic sentence. Such rhetorical patterning provides a coherence that enables readers to follow the strands of a complex discussion.

The final step in prereading is paying close attention to concluding paragraph or paragraphs of the argument. Writers often summarize their main points here. They may also point out implications of the ideas or perhaps let readers know what steps they should take. To return to the chapter from *The Demon-Haunted World* that focuses on the difficulty of observing nature objectively, we arrive at Sagan's conclusion:

> By and large, scientists' minds are open when exploring new worlds. If we [scientists] knew beforehand what we'd find, it would be unnecessary to go [there]. In future missions to Mars or to the other fascinating worlds in our neck of the cosmic woods, surprises—even some of mythic proportions—are possible, maybe even likely. But we humans have a talent for deceiving ourselves. Skepticism must be a component of the explorer's toolkit, or we will lose our way. There are wonders enough out there without our inventing any.

Sagan not only stresses his central idea about the need to maintain objectivity in the search for truth, but also assures us that the search for truth will reward us with discoveries every bit as wondrous as anything we could concoct.

By following a pattern of prereading, you may not yet fully understand the text, but at this stage you are just trying to provide yourself with an overview. You are also giving yourself a sense of how much energy you will need to invest before reading the piece fully.

Skim-Reading   At this stage, read the article in full, including the parts you have preread. But read swiftly, keeping alert for the key words in each sentence. To skim well, take advantage of your peripheral vision: You do not have to look directly at a word to see it; your eyes notice it just by looking in its general vicinity. Also, you already have an idea of the general parts of the article, and you are fleshing out those generalizations via the specifics that the writer provides. This enables you to grasp more readily the writer's logical progression of ideas and use of evidence.

By the time you reach the conclusion, you should feel more comfortable with whatever the author is summarizing or exhorting readers to do.

If the piece you are reading is printed in columns, you probably will make your eyes stop once every line, approximately following a pattern indicated by the *x*'s in the passage that follows:

X
As you read these two columns,
                  X
you'll notice that there are *x*'s above
     X
the typed lines, one to the left on the
            X
first line and then one to the right on
    X
the second line. The *x*'s continue to
              X
alternate down the columns. Fixing
      X
your eyes on those *x*'s, you can see
     X
the words written below them—not
       X
just the words directly below the *x*'s
             X
but the words before and after those
      X
as well. If you were looking just for
            X
a particular date, such as June 20,
    X
2000, then you would be looking just
              X
for that particular configuration of

X
numbers. Looking somewhat above
          X
the lines rather than directly at
    X
the words on the lines helps you
            X
not to read the words but more
X
to focus on the particular pattern of
          X
words or numbers that you are
      X
looking for. (The date of June 20,
            X
2000, was chosen because that's the
    X
wedding date of two British friends,
            X
Dave and Jenny.) You see how you
X
could systematically skim for just
              X
the two occasions of a date-like
    X
configuration. Essentially, that's
  X
skimming.

When skimming a page with visuals, return to the visual after skimming the text. First look for connections between the text and the visual; then, look for points of comparison and contrasts within the visual itself—for example, in a multiple-bar graph that shows changes in use of coal versus oil for heating in three different decades in the United States (represented by three different-colored bars), you want to notice the degree of difference between coal and oil, and whether such a difference is significant in arguing, say, that the United States has been doing a good job in becoming less oil-dependent from one decade to the next.

In-Depth Reading

The previewing strategies detail methods that you can follow if you wish to locate specific, brief information or to quickly scope out the gist of a piece. As a writer of arguments, you read for other reasons as well:

- *Summarizing* to demonstrate an ability and willingness to present another's ideas in a fair, unbiased way (see "Writing a Summary," pages 66–67)

- *Analyzing* the structure of the piece to understand precisely the logic the writer uses, to determine whether the writer omits some important causal or temporal element, or whether the writer fairly and accurately represents all major viewpoints regarding the issue

- *Assessing* the strengths and weaknesses of the argument and determining the extent to which the writer's position influences your own

- *Annotating* in the margins to maintain an ongoing critical-response dialogue with the author as you are reading (see "Reading with a Pencil," page 71)

Postreading

You follow the full reading with a postreading. Essentially, you read the same parts of the piece that you read for the preread. The purpose of a postread is to reinforce the framework of the whole in your mind and to distinguish between details and main points of a piece. In a postread, you cement in your mind the structure and logic of the piece by going back over it and reviewing its contents. During the postread, follow these steps:

1. Ask yourself, "What is the most important thing I learned from this piece, and where is it most clearly expressed?" At this stage, not any earlier, you begin to mark the text. Highlight this passage with a marker and make a marginal note briefly summarizing the passage in your own words. Summarizing helps you reinforce what you have read.

2. Now ask, "What evidence does the author use that supports the claim most convincingly?" Highlight and annotate this passage as well.

3. Finally, ask, "What concluding insight does the author leave me with?" Again, highlight and then annotate this segment of text in your own words.

Once you get into the habit of previewing, in-depth reading, and postreading articles and essays, you will find it an efficient and satisfying process.

◎/◎   Exercise 2.2

1. Choose an article from your campus newspaper. First, preview the article and jot down what you remember immediately afterward. Next, read the article in depth and jot down new things you had not obtained during the preread. Finally, postread the article, and answer the questions posed in the three steps above.

2. Preview an article in one of your favorite magazines. Write down all the information you obtain from this preview reading. Next, read the article as you normally would and write down any information you had not obtained from the prereading. Write a brief assessment of the value of prereading based on this experience.

Writing a Summary

One of the most effective ways of reinforcing your comprehension of a piece is to write a formal *summary* of it shortly after you read it. As you already know, a summary is a concise but accurate rephrasing, primarily in your own words, of the premise of a work. Writing summaries of works you read is a valuable exercise for three reasons:

1. To summarize is to demonstrate (to yourself and to others) the degree to which you understand the piece as the author means it to be understood— realizing, of course, that there is no way of knowing whether one's understanding of an argument corresponds *exactly* to what the author has in mind. Unfortunately, readers sometimes praise or criticize a work based on a misreading or a misunderstanding of what the author is trying to convey. Writing a concise summary of the thesis statement and the principal support statements can help you avoid that problem.

2. Writing a summary helps you better integrate into your knowledge base what you have learned from the piece.

3. Summaries of related articles and books serve as an important resource for a research paper. You may be reading many different sources on a given topic. Summarizing each one immediately after reading the work helps you to internalize the material better and keep various sources straight in your mind. Sometimes, you will use these summaries when preparing an annotated bibliography.

Typically, a summary is about one-fourth the length of the original, but a special type of summary is referred to as an *abstract*. Abstracts of books are generally a single page long, and those of articles, a single paragraph. Volumes of abstracts, such as *Resources in Education* (which summarizes thousands of articles on education collected in a vast *database* known as ERIC) and *Chemical Abstracts* (which maintains a similar service for articles on chemistry), are located in your school library and often online.

Writing a summary returns you to the skeletal outline of your essay, where you are better able to isolate the key points. The procedure of summarizing is relatively simple in principle, but in practice it can be tricky. Some pieces are more difficult to summarize than others, depending on whether the key ideas are presented explicitly or implicitly. Here are the steps you should take:

1. Determine the thesis of the essay, rephrase it in your own words, and make that the opening sentence of your summary.

2. Locate the supporting statements. Sometimes these are the topic sentences of each paragraph, but some writers are inventive with paragraph structure. Rephrase the supporting statements in your own words.

3. Write a concluding sentence, paraphrasing the author's own conclusion if possible.

Read the following short argument at least twice. During the second reading, underline key passages and make marginal notations as needed. Next, write a summary of the article. After completing your summary, compare it with the summary that follows the article.

Death to the Classics!
Is it time to update the reading list? | Melissa Slager

To be, or not to be.

That is the question—not only asked by Hamlet, but increasingly asked about the de facto reading list that has enshrined him in high school English classes for decades.

Teach only these time-tested classics—your Shakespeare, Dickens and Hawthorne? Or take up arms against tradition and bring in some new blood—your Cisneros, Tan and Hosseini? And what exactly makes up "the canon," anyway?

Source: Melissa Slager, "Death to the Classics! Is it time to update the reading list?" from Encarta.msn.com. Used by permission.

These are questions that draw plenty of slings and arrows. And that may be because there is no right answer, says David Kipen, director of literature for national reading initiatives with the National Endowment for the Arts.

"A canon is a useful thing until you start treating it like one," Kipen says, "and then it becomes slightly dangerous."

Ye Olde Canon

There appears to be nothing dangerous, however, about William Shakespeare. The English bard has dominated high school reading lists, unquestioned, for decades, and there's still no sign of the curtain falling.

Shakespeare isn't going anywhere," says Carol Jago, a past president of the National Council of Teachers of English.

In many schools, neither are other old standbys—*To Kill a Mockingbird*, *The Great Gatsby* and *Of Mice and Men*, to name a few. For teachers such as Diane Bahrenburg, a Vermont Teacher of the Year at Colchester High School, the syllabus of must-teach titles also includes Homer's *Odyssey* and Dante Alighieri's *Inferno*. To most people's minds, these are what make up "the canon." They are the classics, and there are good reasons for teaching them.

"They're the foundation of so much of the rest of literature—it's our base," Bahrenburg says.

The New Canon

But that base has been slowly shifting alongside cultural and educational fads. While the 1980s saw a movement to preserve cultural heritage by teaching foundational Western classics, the 1990s ushered in an era of multiculturalism to depict the women and minorities frequently left out.

In many ways, the reading list is merely expanding to include the faces that have appeared on the literary map since the Calvin Coolidge administration. Among these so-called modern classics, for example, are *Their Eyes Were Watching God* by Zora Neale Hurston, a black woman, and *Bless Me, Ultima* by Chicano author Rudolfo Anaya.

Today, with video games and TV crowding out reading habits, there's a move to put just about any book in kids' hands—so long as they're reading it.

As a result, many 19th-century texts, such as Dickens' *Great Expectations*, are disappearing completely from classrooms, deemed "too long, too hard" for attention-deficit teenagers of the 21st century. "Teachers are giving up," Jago says.

A Quasi Canon

Researcher Sandra Stotsky of the University of Arkansas says this trend to get teens to read, no matter what's between the covers, reveals a different kind of canon altogether—one where Harry Potter supplants Macbeth.

"The (traditional) canon is being taught in some schools, in some places, in some grades. But it's like the tail of an emaciated dog," she says.

She points to a 2007 study of 162,000 high school students who took on-line quizzes on books they'd read during the school year through a program called Accelerated Reader.

To Kill a Mockingbird was the most-read book, reflecting its continuing popularity among teachers. But also cracking the top 20 were all seven books in J.K. Rowling's *Harry Potter* series, as well as Stephenie Meyer's vampire-romance hit, *Twilight*.

Likely, these best-sellers are self-selected books that students read to earn extra class credit and are probably not assigned by teachers. But it's no less horrifying, Stotsky says.

"This has turned out to be a disaster," she says. "Most of what these kids are reading is at an arrested intellectual level. That's not what you want."

The Coming Canon

And yet, at times, what the kids choose is exactly the direction you should head, some teachers say.

At Billings Senior High School, teachers are required to teach a core curriculum that includes all the usual suspects, from *The Old Man and the Sea* to *Macbeth*. Beyond that, teachers are allowed to add works of their choosing.

For Steve Gardiner, a Montana Teacher of the Year, that means letting students pick their own books during "sustained silent reading." He sees kids pull everything from Stephenie Meyer to John Steinbeck out of their backpacks. He also sees a lot of nonfiction—something fiction-heavy English departments often overlook.

"We're very good about teaching poetry and fiction, and not so good about teaching nonfiction. And a lot of kids want nonfiction—that's how their minds work," Gardiner says.

There also are lessons in the protagonists students choose to follow, characters that tend to be brooding teenagers rather than brooding adults, says Kylene Beers, president of the National Council of Teachers of English.

"Because the characters are still in childhood, there's this inclination to still be interested [in and] worried about [them], and [to] develop an empathetic bond," Beers says. "That's what really moves a kid through a book. It's sometimes hard to develop that bond with Daisy in *The Great Gatsby*."

Beers and colleague Robert Probst conducted a survey in 2008 of about 1,200 teachers, asking them what they assign their students. She was disappointed to find that only about one-quarter of teachers assigned books from the young adult market with regularity, books such as Walter

Dean Myers' *Fallen Angels*, a 1988 novel published by Scholastic about the Vietnam War.

"To me, that's the bravest teacher," Beers says.

Seeking a Story, a Fight

But what follows this expansion? Should graphic novels also be added to the canon? Cell-phone serials? English professor Mark Bauerlein of Emory University says the background college freshmen bring to class is already helter-skelter.

"You can't refer to a core set of texts anymore and expect that all students have read it," he says.

Bauerlein, author of *The Dumbest Generation*, blames the unclear goals of the politically correct and a dumbed-down digital culture. But he adds that the solution doesn't necessarily mean a classics-only catholicon.

"The important thing is this: Students need to leave a classroom with a deep sense of a tradition—whatever that tradition is. They need to walk out of class with a story," he says.

And, from there, refrain from setting it in concrete.

This thing we call a canon is really this "endlessly elastic, flexible, argument-worthy thing," says Kipen of the National Endowment for the Arts.

Kipen directs the NEA's Big Read, which seeks to tie readers together from across the country like one gigantic book club. None of the three books in his "personal pantheon"—Alan Paton's *Cry, the Beloved Country*, Charles Dickens' *Bleak House*, and Thomas Pynchon's *Gravity's Rainbow*—have yet made that list.

"Is this a canon—these three books? Are my three books better than your three books? I don't know," Kipen says. "All I know is I want to fight about it with you." ◎/◎

One Possible Summary

Despite the endurance of canonical works of literature like Homer's *Iliad* and *Odyssey*, Shakespeare's plays, and modern works like Harper Lee's *To Kill a Mockingbird*, the traditional canon has been slowly eroding since the 1980s in an effort get today's students to become more committed readers. Some teachers feel that it's more important *that* students read than what they read. But for Emory University professor Mark Bauerlein, the most important thing is that students need to acquire a sense of tradition.

◎/◎   Exercise 2.3

1. Do an in-depth reading of the article you preread for the second item in Exercise 2.2. How does the prereading help you to absorb the discussion as you encountered it in the in-depth reading?

2. Write a summary of Martin Luther King, Jr.'s, essay, "Letter from Birmingham Jail," found on pages 161–174.

3. After everyone in class has written a summary of the King essay, compare the summaries in small groups. How do they differ? How are they alike? How do you know? What accounts for the similarities among the summaries? What accounts for the dissimilarities? Are the differences and similarities significant? In what way?

4. Consider the differences and similarities found in question 3 above to see whether they account for greater accuracy of some summaries.

5. Explain the relationship between summary writing and reading comprehension.

Reading with a Pencil

To help you pay special attention to key ideas during a postreading, write marginal comments, underline text, or use visual icons such as asterisks, checkmarks, or arrows. Such annotations, or *marginalia*, enhance your involvement with the reading material and reinforce understanding. (*Note:* Of course, if you are reading library books or books belonging to someone else, do not put a mark of any kind in them. Instead, jot your notes down in a journal.) If you are not in the habit of writing in the margins or in journals, it is a valuable habit to cultivate. Here are some types of marginalia to try:

• **Glosses**: One-sentence summaries of what each paragraph is about.

• **Comparisons**: Notes to yourself reinforcing correspondences you notice. Say you want to compare a passage with something you have read earlier in the piece or in a different piece. The abbreviation *cf.* (Latin for "compare") is most often used; it means compare and/or contrast this passage with such-and-such a passage on such-and-such a page.

• **Questions or reactions**: Spur-of-the-moment concerns you have about an assertion, the validity of the data or other kinds of evidence, or something the author overlooks or overstates.

• **Icons**: These are your own personal symbols—asterisks, wavy lines, checkmarks, bullets, smiley faces, and so on—that instantly convey to you on re-reading whether the passage marked is problematic or especially noteworthy.

Let us take a look at one possible way of annotating a piece. Study the example that follows.

Say No to Trash | Samuel Lipman

In canceling the Robert Mapplethorpe exhibition last week, Washington's Corcoran Gallery did more than refuse to show a few raunchy photographs of what the press, unable to print them, primly called "explicit homoerotic and violent images." Because the exhibition was supported in part by public funds from the Congressionally embattled National Endowment for the Arts, the Corcoran doubtless considered financial self-interest in arriving at its decision. One hopes those responsible are aware that in saying no to Mapplethorpe, they were exercising the right to say no to an entire theory of art.

Why is the NEA "Congressionally embattled"?

Or maybe they were saying no to work that offended the most viewers.

This theory assumes, to quote an official of the neighboring Hirshhorn Museum, that art "often deals with extremities of the human condition. It is not to be expected that, when it does that, everyone is going to be pleased or happy with it." The criterion of art thus becomes its ability to outrage, to (in the Hirshhorn official's words) "really touch raw nerves."

Graffiti also outrages many. Should graffiti be considered art too?

Despite its occasional usefulness, this theory ignores the vast corpus of great art that elevates, enlightens, consoles and encourages our lives. The shock appeal of art is questionable when it encompasses only such fripperies as displaying inane texts on electronic signboards in the fashion of Jenny Holzer; it becomes vastly more deleterious when it advances, as Mapplethorpe does, gross images of sexual profligacy, sadomasochism and the bestial treatment of human beings.

I don't know what "immediately injurious" means.

In a free society, it is neither possible nor desirable to go very far in prohibiting the private activities that inspire this outré art. People have always had their private pleasures, and as long as these pleasures remain private, confined to consenting adults, and not immediately injurious, the public weal remains undisturbed. But now we are told that what has been private must be made public. We are told that it is the true function of art to accommodate us to feelings and action that we—and societies and nations before us—have found objectionable and even appalling.

Source: Samuel Lipman, "Say No to Trash." Originally published in *The New York Times,* 23 June 1989. © 1989. Reprinted by permission of Jeaneane Dowis Lipman.

In evaluating art, the viewer's role is thus only to ap- 5
prove. We are told that whatever the content of art, its very
status as art entitles it to immunity from restraint. There
are certainly those who will claim that the Mapplethorpe
photographs are art, and therefore to be criticized, if at
all, solely on aesthetic, never on moral, grounds. Are we
to believe that the moral neutrality with which we are
urged to view this art is shared by its proponents? Can it,
rather, be possible that it is the very content so many find
objectionable that recommends the art to its highly vocal
backers?

Can any work of art ever be morally neutral?

A key concern: exposure of erotic art to children.

Further, there are those who would have us believe
that because we are not compelled to witness what we as
individuals find morally unacceptable, we cannot refuse
to make it available for others. Taking this position not
only ignores our responsibility for others; it ignores the
dreadful changes made in our own lives, and the lives of
our children, by the availability of this decadence everywhere, from high art to popular culture.

It is undeniable that there is a large market for the
hitherto forbidden. Upscale magazines trumpet the most
shocking manifestations of what passes for new art. A
rampant media culture profits hugely from the pleasing,
and the lowering, of every taste.

Just as it is neither possible nor desirable to do much
about regulating private sexual behavior, little can be
done legally about the moral outrages of culture, either
high or popular. But we can say no, and not only to our
own participation as individuals in this trash. We can
decline to make it available to the public through the use of
our private facilities and funds; this, the Corcoran, acting
as a private institution, has now done.

Much "great art of the past" was shocking in its day.

There is still more to be done. Acting on our behalf
as citizens, our Government agencies—in particular the
National Endowment for the Arts—can redirect their energies away from being the validators of the latest fancies
to hit the art market. Instead, public art support might
more fully concentrate on what it does so well: the cham-
pioning of the great art of the past, its regeneration in the
present and its transmission to the future. This would
mean saying yes to civilization. It is a policy change that
deserves our prompt attention. One hopes that the Corcoran, by saying no to Robert Mapplethorpe, has begun
the process. ◎∕◎

◎/◎   Exercise 2.4

1. Your instructor will distribute a short article for everyone in class to annotate. Then, share your manner of annotating. What useful methods of annotation do you learn from other classmates?

2. Clip a relatively short newspaper story, paste or photocopy it on a sheet of paper, leaving very wide margins, and then annotate the article fully.

Reading Visuals in Argument

You might be thinking, "Who needs to be shown how to read a visual? All you need to do is look at it!" Well, that might be true for the consumer—in fact, advertisers *hope* that consumers will simply look at their images so that the hidden persuasive appeals can work their alchemy. As writers of argument, however, you need to read visuals critically, just as you would read any book or article critically. But how does one read an image critically? Graphs and charts are virtually self-explanatory; their captions in effect tell you how to read them, so let's set this type of visual aside for the moment and focus instead on photographs and drawings.

As simple and unified as a photograph or drawing might be, it generates several different kinds of relationships: external, internal (that is, the interplay of particular visual elements within the whole image), and rhetorical (that is, what the different elements in the visual communicate or seem to communicate to the audience).

External Relationships

- The relationship of the visual to the text surrounding it and/or to the text referring to it

- The relationship of the visual to other visuals in the article, if any

Internal Relationships

- The interplay of figure and ground

The terms "figure" and "ground" refer to the object of focus (the figure), which dominates the photograph or drawing, and what is in the background. In a visual, everything in an image establishes a relationship of some sort with everything else, simply by its presence.

Before deciding on including a particular visual for your article, ask yourself these two questions:

1. Do the figure and ground elements interconnect in ways that enhance the purpose of the image? Study David Plowden's photograph, "The Hand of Man on America." Notice how the foreground objects interact with the

background object, the Statue of Liberty. One of the many ironies of this image is that the Statue of Liberty not only dominates the image, even though it's in the background (the telephoto lens used to take the photograph makes it appear larger than it would otherwise), but it also embodies the implicit conflict between the precious liberties it symbolizes and the ways in which those liberties are sometimes abused by environmentally damaging technology and industry.

2. Do all the objects in the foreground or background serve a unifying purpose? Are there extraneous elements in the ground that could prove to be distracting? Test the criterion of unity on Plowden's photograph. Can anything be deleted from the image without diminishing its impact? The cranes in the background? No; they, along with the telephone poles and the piles of refuse, contribute to the ironic contrast between the dark images of abuse and the bright image of liberty.

Visuals need not be specifically connected to an argument in order to be useful to that argument. Consider the role played by the visuals in the following piece about the relevance of traditional Jesuit liberal arts courses to modern-day students. What implicit point is being made by the photograph of the students playing tug-of-war? How do the portraits of the saints relate to the photograph? To the premise of the article?

David Plowden

Philosophers, Theologians, Postmodern Students: Why They Need Each Other | J. Joseph Feeney, S.J.

In November 2001, *Newsweek* interviewed a Princeton undergrad about his education, and with palpable regret he said "he had been taught how to deconstruct and dissect, but never to construct and decide." Reading his comment, I acutely felt his sense of loss, and wondered whether a similar loss affects undergrads at Jesuit universities. This issue of *Conversations* prompts me to ask how much our professors of philosophy, theology, and religious studies help students to "construct," to "decide," and even to *affirm*—specifically, to affirm *meaning* and *faith*. I write, then, to propose a dialogue with philosophers and theologians about our students.

A number of my own students, I find, are "postmodern"—skeptical about truth, emotionally wary, prone to parody. Since 1993 I've taught "Modernism and Postmodernism" at Saint Joseph's University (we study literature, music, art, and architecture, but not formal theory), and for their final essay I ask if they are modernist, postmodern, traditional, or some mix of these. Such a personal essay first baffles, then entrances them, as they discover aspects of themselves they never noticed. Probing their own lives, they tell me about themselves (I am always touched and honored by their trust in me, and a fair number call themselves postmodern in whole or in part. Thus allowed to know them, I find it my role as, well, professor of postmodernism, to raise this issue with my colleagues in philosophy and theology, I offer, then, a three-part invitation to dialogue: (I) What is postmodernism? (II) What do my recent students (Fall, 2006) say about themselves? (III) What kind of dialogue do I propose?

I

The word "postmodern" resists easy definition. Some dictionaries just omit the word, others focus on philosophy or architecture. The New Oxford American Dictionary (2001) is more encompassing, defining postmodernism as

> *A late 20th-century style and concept in the arts, architecture, and criticism that . . . has at its heart a general distrust of grand theories and ideologies as well as a problematic relationship with any notion of "art." Typical features include a deliberate mixing of different artistic styles and media [and] the self-conscious use of earlier styles and media [and] the self-conscious use of earlier styles and conventions . . .*

Source: J. Joseph Feeney, S. J. "Philosophers, Theologians, Postmodern Students: Why They Need Each Other," *Conversations on Jesuit Higher Education*, No. 32 (Fall 2007): 22–24. Reprinted by permission.

In my own teaching, I begin postmodernism with a 1967 essay from *The Atlantic Monthly* where the novelist John Barth asserts that traditional art forms are tired, used-up, worn out, and can be used only "with ironic intent" as a wry comment on, or parody of, the past. As postmodernism develops, such suspicion of the past affects attitudes and convictions, and both art *and* life seem worn out, random, incoherent, meaningless. With little depth or stability, postmodern works glitter with surface verve: bright colors, bizarre collages, playful contradictions, references to their own artifice. For example, John Fowles' novel *The French Lieutenant's Woman* (1969) parodies Victorian prose, mixes past/present and fiction/reality, and has three endings. In Jeff Koons' sculpture "Three Ball 50/50 Tank" (1985) three basketballs just float on water in a glass tank. Boundaries are pushed, freedom reigns. No longer able to be surprised or shocked, postmodernists grow cool and detached, their dulled emotions relieved by laughter and parody. I must say, though, that I find postmodern works fun to read, see, hear, and teach. But such freedom has its cost: like that Princeton student, people "deconstruct and dissect" but find it hard to "construct and decide."

In the recent *Postmodernism: A Very Short Introduction* (2002), Christopher Butler of Oxford University reviews both theory and practice, finding the "party" of postmodernists "not particularly united in doctrine" yet "certain of its uncertainty." "A deep irrationalism [lies] at the heart of postmodernism," he writes, and "a kind of despair about the Enlightenment-derived public functions of reason." Yet, he concludes, "I believe that the period of its greatest influence is now over."

II

But postmodernism is not over for our students—the fragile, lovely people who sit before us in our classrooms. Many live with the emotions dulled, trust and meaning limited, religious faith lost. Let me quote (with permission, for which I thank them) two of my postmodern students from last fall. One writes,

> *Life is completely random. Life is chaos. By acknowledging this simple truth I can elevate myself above the bullshit and find some meaning in life, and by that I mean I can make life mean to me virtually whatever I want. . . . I can choose to interpret my life and the world around me in whatever way I see fit. That is a great power.*

About belief, he continues.

> *Who knows if there is indeed a god or a Christ? If there is, I am not concerned. . . . I would be satisfied with death as a complete non-entity. I do not want to waste my time puzzling over who created me and why I was put on the Earth . . . Polytheism is just as acceptable as monotheism, and atheism is just as feasible as Wicca. . . . I say simply that God is whoever you wish him to be; live freely.*

Public Domain

A second student describes his own stance:

> *I think the postmodern world has given me my sense of humor—nothing is too ridiculous, and offensive (usually) equals funny. . . . I don't take things seriously anymore. . . . I cannot find any attachment for characters in a television program or movie—they are not real and there's no sense in feeling emotion for them. . . . I became so cynical. And sometimes that cynicism bothers me. . . . I just don't care about the outside world anymore. . . . I am critical of everything—that way I don't get attached to something.*

And about belief:

> *I don't believe in God or any religion, in fact, I believe in nothing. I see a chaotic world around me; I can't even begin to try to explain my consciousness. I've given up trying to search for answers—how the world was created, what is right and what is wrong, is there an afterlife?*

He concludes, "What's next? I don't know, I would love to see what I am like 5 or 10 years from now—it's as big a mystery to me as it is to anyone else."

These are the students, the postmodern students, who sit before us at Jesuit universities. Not all students, of course, are postmodern. Many have strong faith; indeed, a current research project at UCLA on "Spirituality in Higher Education" finds undergraduates far more spiritual than is widely believed, though the students say they are ignored when they seek spiritual help from their colleges. Yet others have lost their faith in high school or in college, and a number, like the second student above, have lost their ability to feel:

> *I think the news media have had a profound impact on my worldview. How can I allow myself to feel emotion when watching the video of the World Trade Center fall to the ground? Just like every other American, I will never forget that day but I don't think I was ever sad. I came home from school early that day, I remember my seeing sadness in my mom's eyes. I watched the news and then I went outside and played football with my friends. Sure, I felt sorry for the victims, but it was a gorgeous September day and I wasn't going to allow some outside event to govern my happiness. . . . I've seen that footage hundreds of times since then—I'd be in a state of clinical depression if I allowed myself to be sad. I have to cut it all off and feel numb.*

What can I, a professor of English, say to such students? How can our professors of philosophy and theology help them, and help me? To seek an answer I propose a dialogue of professors which I hope to begin here.

III

As we work to help our students, who might enter this dialogue? First, those who teach literature, philosophy, and theology—and of course our students, chaired perhaps by the dean of arts and sciences. Later, psychologists, sociologists, historians, campus ministry, student life, and the counseling center can well join in.

The basic issue is the plight of our students: are they, like the Princeton undergrad, taught *only* to "deconstruct and dissect" and not "to construct and decide"? Do we teach *only* information without offering meaning and faith—as if they were graduate students and not undergrads? The key word, I note, is "offer": we do not proselytize or browbeat, but we can surely offer, even advocate, certain stances, for we dare not stand by as students flounder. We who teach literature, philosophy,

Culver Pictures, Inc./SuperStock

Archive Photos/Hulton Archive/Getty Images

and theology, must offer more: this is the *magis* of a Jesuit education. And students deserve this educational "more," with a careful *balance* on our part: (1) we teach our fields with intellectual integrity and (2) with academic freedom, (3) in Jesuit institutions, committed to faith (a triune God, Jesus as the poor Christ). (4) to justice (prophecy, service, the poor), (5) to the Catholic Church (with ecumenical consciousness), and (6) to each individual student. To help our students, I suggest, we professors need a dialogue on academic and religious cura personalis.

About what might we talk? About how best to offer our students—postmodernists and all the others—a worldview that questions *and* affirms. Literature offers them a rich humanism, philosophy, meaning and synthesis; theology, a belief that is intellectual, centrist-Catholic, ecumenical. Outside the classroom, campus ministry, service-learning, and semester-break trips offer their own invitations. To end, I return to my title: Why do philosophers, theologians, and postmodern students need each other? So philosophers can offer meaning, so theologians can offer belief, so students can discover—and affirm—both meaning and belief. We don't want our students to be like that disappointed Princeton undergrad in *Newsweek*. ◎/◎

To give another example of the way visuals can reinforce a point of view, consider the full-color inserted ad for I Am Biotech, part of a public information project produced by the Biotechnology Industry Organization (BIO). What do the visual elements contribute to the assertions that appear in the advertising copy?

The first image, that of a parent (or medical professional?) holding a child presumably suffering from some form of cancer (suggested by her lack of hair) reinforces the idea that biotechnology research is people-centered, compassionate, implicitly refuting the idea that such research is excessively clinical, and indifferent to the human element. The second image, that of specimen tubes being organized by a researcher, comes closer to the commonplace image of "scientific research"—which in its own way is generally regarded as a source of progress and hope. Note how the designer of the ad cleverly links the two images together, as if to say, "Scientific research is never separate from human caring and compassion." Thus, even before readers take in the information presented in the ad copy, they are predisposed to the implied thesis that biotech research works on behalf of people, and is not merely research for its own sake.

◎/◎   Exercise 2.5

Write an analysis of the compositional technique of one of your favorite photographs or paintings. Pay attention to the interplay of foreground objects with background objects, and the way each object in the image contributes to a central idea.

◎/◎   **Exercise 2.6**

Consider the advertisements in Chapter 1. In each case, decide whether the appeal is basically visual or basically verbal—that is, whether the photographs or the words are most important to the impact of the ad. Why do you think as you do?

Becoming a Highly Motivated Reader

People read for many reasons: to be entertained; to be informed of global, local, and job-related events; to enhance their general knowledge of fields such as history, science and technology, commerce, politics, social developments, and the arts; and to improve their personal lives and health.

You, however, have an additional reason to read: to become a better writer. To realize this goal, you must become not only an alert, active reader but a highly motivated one as well.

To acquire a sense of the rich possibilities of argumentative writing, begin to read (if you don't already) any or all of the following material:

- Newspaper editorials and op-ed pieces (familiarize yourself not only with the editorial section of your local newspaper but with those of the *New York Times* and the *Washington Post* as well)

- Essays that appear in magazines and journals noted for high-quality commentary on important issues, such as *Newsweek, Time, Harper's Magazine*, the *Atlantic Monthly*, and the *New York Review of Books*

- Books that take strong stands on current, intensely debated issues, such as John Mueller's *Overblown: How Politicians and the Terrorism Industry Inflate National Security Threats, and Why We Believe Them* (Free Press, 2006) or Victoria de Grazia's analysis of the influence of the United States on Europe after World War II, *Irresistible Empire: American's Advance through Twentieth-Century Europe* (Belknap Press/Harvard University Press, 2006)

You likely are already a motivated reader, or else you could not have made it into college. Your goal now is to capitalize on your already strong reading skills by reading even more widely and avidly. Here are a few suggestions to consider:

1. Begin by thinking of each reading experience—each opportunity to scrutinize an argument—as a chance to recruit more brain cells. It is said that we use only 10 percent of our brain capacity, so there's no danger in running out of cells!

2. Think of each reading experience as yet another opportunity to study a talented writer's craft, an important step toward helping you develop your own craft.

3. Select books for reading that you have intended to read but "never got around to." Do not be overly ambitious; you do not want to disappoint yourself. It is not necessary to give yourself page quotas (for example, a hundred pages a night); that has a way of backfiring when you have an already busy schedule. The key is to read *regularly*, every day, at the same time, just as you might with exercising, so that reading becomes a habit. And be patient with yourself: It sometimes takes a while for a habit to take hold. After about three or four weeks of "forcing" yourself to read, say, one hour of non-course-required reading every morning, the ritual will become so ingrained that it will feel as natural (and as enjoyable) as eating.

4. Finally, take the time to keep a reading journal. This does not have to be elaborate. After each reading session, take about fifteen minutes to jot down your reflections on or reactions to the reading you have just finished. In addition to reinforcing your comprehension of the material and your insights into it, the journal will serve as a logbook of your reading experiences.

Once again, it is impossible to overemphasize the importance of reading to learning, to the life of the mind, and to what it means to be educated in this complex, information-driven, competitive world. Reading is truly your ticket to the treasures of knowledge and understanding.

◎/◎ Exercise 2.7

1. Write a reading autobiography in which you describe your childhood and early adolescent reading experiences and tastes. Note how your tastes in and habits of reading have changed over the years.

2. Keep a record of your reading activities over the next four weeks. Record the time you spend reading each day. List everything you read, but only after you finish reading it (individual chapters can count as separate pieces). Divide the material into "required" and "nonrequired" reading. Do an "active reader" critique of each work (refer back to the list on page 60). At the end of the fourth week, evaluate your reading. Did your motivation to read improve? When? Did your reading become more efficient? Be as honest with yourself as you can.

3. If you consider yourself a slow or inefficient reader, make a special effort to improve. If it takes you longer than an hour to read fifty pages of a book, you are probably subvocalizing (sounding out one word at a time in your head, as if you were reading aloud). Practice reading *clusters* of words and be sure your pacing is swift and smooth, not jerky. Check to see whether your campus offers classes in speed reading or efficient reading.

4. Keep a reading improvement log. Each day for the next four weeks, record the number of pages you read in a given time (say, half an hour). Do not sacrifice your comprehension as you work on improving your efficiency. The more efficient your reading process, the more your comprehension should improve.

Reading Responsibly

To read arguments responsibly is to engage in a three-step procedure:

1. Read to learn the author's position on the issue.

2. Reread to understand fully that position.

3. Reread to compare and contrast the author's views with the views of others.

Every time we read or listen to someone's views about an issue, we may feel prematurely inclined to agree or disagree. Remaining neutral is sometimes difficult, especially if the writer or speaker presents his or her ideas with passion, eloquence, and wit. As a responsible reader, you do not need to maintain neutrality permanently, only to delay judgment. Before judging an issue, regard any argument as but one perspective, and assume that many perspectives must be considered before a fair judgment can be made.

Reading well is like listening well. Good readers give writers the benefit of the doubt, at least momentarily, and respect the author's point of view, believing it worthy of serious attention (unless the author demonstrates negligence, such as distorting another author's views). But disagreement should never be confused with contentiousness, even if the author comes across as adversarial. You will comprehend and subsequently respond more successfully if you read the argument attentively, if you assume that the writer has considered the argument's assertions with great care, and if you are willing to give the writer the benefit of any doubts, at least for the time being. Once you have read the argument and reflected on it, go over it again, making sure you have understood everything. Then, before you do a third reading, place the writer's point of view in the context of others' views. The third reading is the critical one in which you ask questions of every assertion, questions that reflect the larger conversation produced by other essays.

◎/◎ Exercise 2.8

1. Make a list of five or six books you plan to read during the semester, including books for class. After each title, briefly state your reason for wanting to read the book.

2. Keep a reader's log for each book you read. Each entry might include the following information:

- Author, title, publication data, and number of pages in the book
- Dates you began and finished the book
- Your reason for wanting to read the book
- The most important things you learned from the book
- Any criticisms or questions you have of the book

3. Use active reading strategies to read the following editorial on the need to combat global warming. *Preread* the editorial to get a sense of its premise and key points. *Skim* it straight through without critical questioning, allowing the author to present his case without interruption, so to speak. Then *read* the essay in depth, paying close attention to the way in which the writer develops the argument. Finally, *postread* it to reinforce full comprehension, making notes in the margins as recommended above.

High Noon

Global warming is here. It is moving as fast as scientists had feared. If it is not checked, children born today may live to see massive shifting and destruction of the ecosystems we know now. They may witness the proliferation of violent storms, floods, and droughts that cause terrible losses of human life.

The good news is that we are not helpless. We can still curb the greenhouse trend. Our next, best chance will come November 13–24 in the Netherlands, when the nations of the world negotiate again over the terms of the global warming treaty called the Kyoto Protocol. If we lose this chance, we may lose momentum for the entire protocol, and with it five or more years of precious time. But if we win a strong treaty in the Netherlands, it will start real movement on the long road to change.

Evidence and Damage

Like trackers on the trail of a grizzly, scientists read the presence of global warming in certain large-scale, planet-wide events. Over the last century, the surface of the planet heated up by about one degree Fahrenheit. More rain and snow began falling worldwide, an increase of 1 percent over all the continents. The oceans rose 6–8 inches. If these numbers applied to local weather, they would be trivial. As planetary averages, they are momentous. The past decade was the warmest in at least a thousand years. A graph of average global temperatures since the year 1000 shows a precipitous rise that starts at about the time of the Industrial Revolution and shoots upward to our own time.

The results may be profound and unpredictable. In altering the climate of the planet, we are playing with a vastly complicated system we barely understand. As Columbia University scientist Wallace Broecker has said, climate is an angry beast, and we are poking it with sticks.

We may already be feeling its anger. Of course, weather happens in spurts,   5 with or without global warming. It is impossible to know whether this storm or that drought was an ordinary event, say the effect of a little extra moisture carried over the West Coast by El Niño, or whether it was a flick of the tail of the global warming beast.

What is certain is that the kinds of catastrophes global warming will cause are already happening all over the world. Hundreds of people died in exceptionally high monsoon floods in India and Bangladesh this fall. Three dozen died last month in mud slides in the Alps; the floodwaters rushing out of the mountains were said to have raised one lake to its highest point in 160 years. A heat wave last year across much of this country claimed 271 lives. Penguins in the Antarctic are finding it harder and harder to find food for their chicks, as the shrimplike krill they eat grow scarcer in warmer waters. Disease-bearing mosquitoes have moved to altitudes and longitudes they usually never reach: malaria has come to the Kenyan highlands; the West Nile virus thrives in New York City.

If global warming continues unchecked, the next hundred years will be a century of dislocations. Ecosystems cannot simply pick up and move north. Many will break apart as temperatures shift too far and too fast for all their plants and animals to follow. Others, such as alpine tundra, will die out in many places because they have nowhere to go.

According to some climate models, by the year 2100 the southern tip of Florida may be under water and much of the Everglades may be drowned. Vermont may be too warm for sugar maples; wide swaths of the forests of the Southeast may become savannah; droughts may be frequent on the Great Plains. Meanwhile, according to the UN's Intergovernmental Panel on Climate Change, heat-related human deaths will double in many large cities around the world and tropical diseases will spread. Deaths from malaria alone may rise by more than a million a year.

Problem and Solution

There is no scientific question about the cause of global warming. Carbon dioxide and other "greenhouse gases" in the atmosphere trap heat. For millennia, the planet's temperature has moved in lockstep with the concentration of carbon dioxide in the atmosphere. Humans have now increased that concentration by 30 percent since the pre-industrial era, principally by burning oil, coal, and other fossil fuels. Today we have the highest atmospheric carbon concentration since the evolution of Homo sapiens.

The United States is the world's biggest greenhouse gas polluter. We   10
have only 5 percent of the world's population, but we produce more than
20 percent of its greenhouse gases. In the face of climate chaos, we continue
to increase our pollution. Power plants are the fastest-growing source of U.S.
carbon dioxide emissions, primarily because we are increasing the output
from old, inefficient coal plants, many of which don't meet current standards.
Cars are another major and growing source.

To stop piling up carbon dioxide, we need to shift to cutting-edge technologies for energy efficiency and for renewable energy from the sun, wind,
and geothermal sources. Prosperity doesn't require fossil fuels. According to
the American Council for an Energy-Efficient Economy, U.S. carbon intensity
(carbon emissions per unit of gross domestic product) has been cut almost in
half since 1970. Even during 1997–1999—at the height of an economic boom
and with the subsidies and policies that reinforce fossil fuel use still deeply
entrenched—the United States achieved a steep decline in carbon intensity,
partly through the use of advanced efficiency technologies.

Just tightening up national fuel economy standards would eliminate
450 million tons of carbon dioxide per year by 2010.

As the biggest polluter, the United States should take the lead in dealing
with global warming. Instead, for most of the past decade, we have obstructed
progress. One reason is obvious: the enormously powerful and wealthy fossil
fuel lobby, whose campaign contributions subvert the relationship between
Congress and the public.

As a result, the Kyoto Protocol is far weaker than it should be. Though
many other industrialized countries had pushed for deep cuts in greenhouse
gas pollution, U.S. intransigence kept the final agreement conservative. The
protocol requires the industrialized nations to reduce their greenhouse gas
emissions only 5 percent below 1990 levels by 2012. But for the moment, the
protocol is our best hope for nationwide and global progress.

What happens in the Netherlands will be critical in making the Kyoto
Protocol work, because the rules on exactly how countries can meet their tar-
gets have yet to be written. Three issues stand out:

- The protocol allows a country to meet part of its target by buying greenhouse
  gas "credits" from nations that emit less than their quota. The negotiators at
  the Netherlands must make sure that any credits traded represent real pollution cuts, not just paper-pushing.

- The protocol needs strong rules on enforcement. Countries that fail to act and
  countries with slipshod accounting cannot be permitted to undermine the
  effort.

- Growing trees absorb carbon, and the protocol allows a nation to meet
  some of its target by planting trees. The negotiators must make sure that
  the rules do not permit countries either to raze ancient forests and replant
  (which releases more carbon than it takes up) or to start counting all the

plantings they would have undertaken anyway as new, climate-friendly tactics.

The United States must push to eliminate all of these carbon loopholes. If we get a good treaty, it could be the impetus we need to start modernizing our power plants, vehicles, factories, and buildings. Study after study has shown that these steps will create thousands of new jobs and reduce consumers' energy bills. And, for the sake of future generations, it is our responsibility to change our ways.

We have an enormous job to do. It's time to roll up our sleeves and get to work.

To support a strong U.S. position in the Netherlands, contact Undersecretary Frank Loy, State Department Building, 2201 C Street, N.W., Washington, D.C. 20520; phone 202-647-6240; fax 202-647-0753. For more information as the negotiations proceed, see the global warming homepage. ◎/◎

1. Write a one-paragraph summary of the article to ensure that you accurately understand the author's premise and line of reasoning. What is the most important insight you gain from this editorial? What do you most agree with? Least agree with?

2. How does the editorial compare with other commentary on global warming, such as Al Gore's book and film, *An Inconvenient Truth* (2006)? Do a subject or keyword search using your library's online catalog or your Internet search engine, or consult one of the periodical indexes in your library's reference room, such as the *Environmental Index* or the *Reader's Guide to Periodical Literature*. Keep in mind the simple but easily overlooked fact that a single argument is but one voice in a multitudinous conversation. As John Stuart Mill wisely states, "He who knows only his own side of a case knows little." Before you can fully understand the complexities of an issue, let alone take a stance on it, you must become thoroughly familiar with the ongoing conversation, not just with one or two isolated voices.

3. If you had the opportunity to address this topic in an essay of your own, what would be your thesis? How would you defend it? Is there anything missing from the editorialist's argument that should be included? Why do you suppose he omitted it? Out of ignorance? His wish to hide a persuasive contrary view? His assumption that it is irrelevant? Do you find anything in the writer's treatment of the topic that seems especially illuminating or, on the contrary, misleading or confusing?

4. Rewrite the opening paragraph of the editorial. What expectations does your paragraph set up for your readers? How do they differ, if at all, from the expectation the editorialist sets up with his original opening?

5. Consider the author's style, identifying as many stylistic elements as you can. Examples include use of metaphor, manner of incorporating or alluding to outside sources, manner of emphasizing a point, devices used to connect one idea with another, orchestration of sentence patterns, choices

of words and phrases, manner of integrating outside sources, overall read-ability, and concision. What about his style most delights you? Annoys you? What would you do differently and why?

6. Describe the author's concluding paragraphs. Suggest an alternative con-clusion for the editorial.

7. Locate up-to-date information about the Kyoto Protocol. How justifiable is the editorialist's faith in this treaty? How would you rewrite the editorial, if at all, in light of your findings?

Active Reading as Shared Reading

Most of the reading you do is in solitude. However, a significant chunk of learning takes place in social contexts such as classrooms or college learn-ing assistance centers, book discussion groups, or student-coordinated study groups. Whenever possible, arrange to have an in-depth discussion of an as-signed essay with another classmate or friend, ideally with two or three other classmates or friends. Here is how to make your reading discussion group most productive:

1. After the group reads the piece once, have each person go through it again, following the annotating suggestions given in "Reading with a Pencil," page 71.

2. Discuss each writer's strategies identified by the group.

3. Discuss the strengths and weaknesses of the argument, keeping tabs on any common ground that is mentioned (see the discussion of Rogerian argu-ment in Chapter 5).

4. Also keep tabs on any outside sources mentioned by group members. If at all possible, everyone in the group should consult these sources before trying to reach a consensus (see next point below).

5. Attempt to reach consensus, despite differences of opinion. What unified position statement can your group produce that fairly represents the view (by now quite likely modified) of each individual member?

◎/◎   Exercise 2.9

1. Reflect on your private reading experience in relation to your public one. What does each reading context contribute toward your understanding and enjoyment of the text? Draw from actual reading experiences that included both a private and a public phase.

2. Does reading with others increase or decrease your comprehension of the text? What do you think accounts for this difference?

Using the Modes of Argument as a Schema for Analysis

To analyze the logic and merits of an argument, first determine which of the predominant general patterns of argument introduced in Chapter 1 and discussed in detail in Chapters 3 through 5—Classical, Toulmin, Rogerian—the argument fits into.

- If the piece follows the Classical (Aristotelian) model, you might ask: Is the intended audience uninformed or well informed on the issue?

- If the piece follows the Toulmin model, you might ask: Are the warrants on solid or shaky ground? Do they need to be made more explicit?

- If the piece follows the Rogerian model, you might ask: Is the tone sufficiently conciliatory to reduce the possibility of reader hostility?

The Importance of Open-Mindedness When Reading

One of the most important attributes that an education affords, along with self-discipline and attentiveness, is open-mindedness—the willingness to suspend judgment until one considers as many differing viewpoints as possible.

Learning to be truly open-minded takes effort. Everyone has deeply rooted beliefs, some of which even border on superstition. When these beliefs are challenged for whatever reasons, no matter how logical the reasons offered are, we resist—sometimes against our own better judgment. Beliefs often operate outside the realm of intellectual control and are entwined with our values and emotions. If, for example, someone in your family earns his or her livelihood in the Pacific Northwest logging industry, you may find it difficult to sympathize with environmentalists who advocate putting an end to logging in that region, even though a part of you wishes to preserve any species threatened with extinction due to continued deforestation.

Being predisposed toward a certain viewpoint is to be expected. Rare is the individual who goes through life with a neutral attitude toward all controversial issues. But one can be predisposed toward a certain view or value system and still be open-minded. For example, you might be highly skeptical of the existence of extraterrestrial creatures yet be willing to suspend that skepticism to give a writer a fair chance at trying to change your mind. Your willingness to be open-minded may increase, of course, if the author is a scientist or if the body of evidence presented has been shared with the entire scientific community for independent evaluations.

Sometimes we feel defensive when a long-held conviction is suddenly challenged. We may wish to guard the sanctity of that conviction so jealously that we may delude ourselves into thinking that we're being open-minded when we're not. When Galileo made his astronomical discoveries of the lunar craters and the moons of Jupiter known in 1610, he was promptly accused of heresy. We may think, from our enlightened perspective at the dawn of the twenty-first century, that the church was narrow-minded and intolerant, neglecting to realize that at the dawn of the seventeenth century, modern science had not yet come into being. Most people's conception of "the heavens" was literally that: The night sky was a window to Heaven. And celestial (that is, heavenly) objects like planets, stars, and the moon all occupied divine niches in that Heaven; they were called the *crystal spheres*. Galileo's modest telescopic observations revolutionized our conception of the universe, but it did not happen overnight, particularly because Galileo recanted his "heresy"—or, rather, was persuaded to recant by the threat of execution. We know that Galileo never wavered in his convictions because, even while under house arrest, he continued to write about his discoveries.

The moral of Galileo's story, and the stories of many other daring thinkers throughout history, is that open-mindedness is precious, despite its difficulties. Take a few steps to ensure that you will not judge an argument prematurely or unfairly:

1. Identify and perhaps write down in your notebook the specific nature of the resistance you experience toward the author's point of view. Is it that you're a Republican reading a Democrat's evaluation of a Republican presidential administration? A strict vegetarian or vegan and animal-rights activist reading an article about the importance of preserving the cattle industry? An evolutionist reading an article by a creationist questioning the validity of the hominid fossil record? Consciously identifying your predisposition helps you approach neutrality and open-mindedness.

2. Allow yourself to accept the author's premise at least temporarily. What are the consequences of doing so? Are there any reasonable facets to the argument? Can you establish some kind of common ground with the author? Does the author perhaps expose weaknesses in the viewpoint that you would advocate?

◎/◎   Exercise 2.10

Read the excerpt from Galileo's "Letter to the Grand Duchess Christina," which illustrates a famous example of reading (in this case the Bible) with an open mind.

Letter to the Grand Duchess Christina | Galileo Galilei

. . . The reason produced for condemning the opinion that the earth moves and the sun stands still is that in many places in the Bible one may read that the sun moves and the earth stands still. Since the Bible cannot err, it follows as a necessary consequence that anyone takes an erroneous and heretical position who maintains that the sun is inherently motionless and the earth movable.

With regard to this argument, I think in the first place that it is very pious to say and prudent to affirm that the holy Bible can never speak untruth—whenever its true meaning is understood. But I believe nobody will deny that it is often very abstruse, and may say things which are quite different from what its bare words signify. Hence in expounding the Bible if one were always to confine oneself to the unadorned grammatical meaning, one might fall into error. Not only contradictions and propositions far from true might thus be made to appear in the Bible, but even grave heresies and follies. Thus it would be necessary to assign to God feet, hands, and eyes, as well as corporeal and human affections, such as anger, repentance, hatred, and sometimes even the forgetting of things past and ignorance of those to come. These propositions uttered by the Holy Ghost were set down in that manner by the sacred scribes in order to accommodate them to the capacities of the common people, who are rude and unlearned. For the sake of those who deserve to be separated from the herd, it is necessary that wise expositors should produce the true senses of such passages, together with the special reasons for which they were set down in these words. This doctrine is so widespread and so definite with all theologians that it would be superfluous to adduce evidence for it.

Hence I think that I may reasonably conclude that whenever the Bible has occasion to speak of any physical conclusion (especially those which are very abstruse and hard to understand), the rule has been observed of avoiding confusion in the minds of the common people which would render them contumacious toward the higher mysteries. Now the Bible, merely to condescend to popular capacity, has not hesitated to obscure some very important pronouncements, attributing to God himself some qualities extremely remote from (and even contrary to) His essence. Who, then, would positively declare that this principle has been set aside, and the Bible has confined itself rigorously to the bare and restricted sense of its words, when speaking but

---

Source: Galileo Galilei, "Letter to the Grand Duchess Christina," from DISCOVERIES AND OPINIONS OF GALILEO by Galileo Galilei, translated by Stillman Drake, copyright © 1957 by Stillman Drake. Used by permission of Doubleday, a division of Random House, Inc.

Galileo (1564–1642) is here shown lecturing on the Copernican or heliocentric (sun-centered) theory of the solar system. He helped to confirm this theory, with detailed telescopic observations of the movements of Venus, the moons of Jupiter, and sunspots.

Bettmann/CORBIS

casually of the earth, of water, of the sun, or of any other created thing? Especially in view of the fact that these things in no way concern the primary purpose of the sacred writings, which is the service of God and the salvation of souls—matters infinitely beyond the comprehension of the common people.

This being granted, I think that in discussions of physical problems we ought to begin not from the authority of scriptural passages, but from sense-experiences and necessary demonstrations; for the holy Bible and the phenomena of nature proceed alike from the divine Word, the former as the dictate of the Holy Ghost and the latter as the observant executrix of God's commands. It is necessary for the Bible, in order to be accommodated to the understanding of every man, to speak many things which appear to differ from the absolute truth so far as the bare meaning of the words is concerned. But Nature, on the other hand, is inexorable and immutable; she never transgresses the laws imposed upon her, or cares a whit whether her abstruse reasons and methods of operation are understandable to men. For that reason it appears that nothing physical which sense-experience sets before our eyes, or which necessary demonstrations prove to us, ought to be called in question (much less condemned) upon the testimony of biblical passages which may have some different meaning beneath their words. For the Bible is not chained in every expression to conditions as strict as those which govern all physical effects; nor is God any less excellently revealed in Nature's actions than in the sacred statements of the Bible. Perhaps this is what Tertullian meant by these words:

"We conclude that God is known first through Nature, and then again, more particularly, by doctrine; by Nature in His works, and by doctrine in His revealed word."[1]

From this I do not mean to infer that we need not have an extraordinary esteem for the passages of holy Scripture. On the contrary, having arrived at any certainties in physics, we ought to utilize these as the most appropriate aids in the true exposition of the Bible and in the investigation of those meanings which are necessarily contained therein, for these must be concordant with demonstrated truths. I should judge that the authority of the Bible was designed to persuade men of those articles and propositions which, surpassing all human reasoning, could not be made credible by science, or by any other means than through the very mouth of the Holy Spirit.

Yet even in those propositions which are not matters of faith, this authority ought to be preferred over that of all human writings which are supported only by bare assertions or probable arguments, and not set forth in a demonstrative way. This I hold to be necessary and proper to the same extent that divine wisdom surpasses all human judgment and conjecture.

But I do not feel obliged to believe that that same God who has endowed us with senses, reason, and intellect has intended to forgo their use and by some other means to give us knowledge which we can attain by them. He would not require us to deny sense and reason in physical matters which are set before our eyes and minds by direct experience or necessary demonstrations. This must be especially true in those sciences of which but the faintest trace (and that consisting of conclusions) is to be found in the Bible. Of astronomy, for instance, so little is found that none of the planets except Venus are so much as mentioned, and this only once or twice under the name of "Lucifer." If the sacred scribes had had any intention of teaching people certain arrangements and motions of the heavenly bodies, or had they wished us to derive such knowledge from the Bible, then in my opinion they would not have spoken of these matters so sparingly in comparison with the infinite number of admirable conclusions which are demonstrated in that science. Far from pretending to teach us the constitution and motions of the heavens and the stars, with their shapes, magnitudes, and distances, the authors of the Bible intentionally forbore to speak of these things, though all were quite well known to them. Such is the opinion of the holiest and most learned Fathers, and in St. Augustine we find the following words:

"It is likewise commonly asked what we may believe about the form and shape of the heavens according to the Scriptures, for many contend much about these matters. But with superior prudence our authors have forborne to speak of this, as in no way furthering the student with respect to a blessed life—and, more important still, as taking up much of that time which should be spent in holy exercises. What is it to me whether heaven, like a sphere, surrounds the earth on all sides as a mass balanced in the center of the universe, or whether like a dish it merely covers and overcasts the earth? Belief in Scripture is urged rather for the reason we have often mentioned; that is, in order that no one, through ignorance of divine passages, finding anything in our Bibles or hearing anything cited from them of such a nature as may seem to oppose manifest conclusions, should be induced to suspect their truth when they teach, relate, and deliver more profitable matters. Hence let it be said briefly, touching the form of heaven, that our authors knew the truth but the Holy Spirit did not desire that men should learn things that are useful to no one for salvation."[2]

The same disregard of these sacred authors toward beliefs about the phe-   10
nomena of the celestial bodies is repeated to us by St. Augustine in his next chapter. On the question whether we are to believe that the heaven moves or stands still, he writes thus:

"Some of the brethren raise a question concerning the motion of heaven, whether it is fixed or moved. If it is moved, they say, how is it a firmament? If it stands still, how do these stars which are held fixed in it go round from east to west, the more northerly performing shorter circuits near the pole, so that heaven (if there is another pole unknown to us) may seem to revolve upon some axis, or (if there is no other pole) may be thought to move as a discus? To these men I reply that it would require many subtle and profound reasonings to find out which of these things is actually so; but to undertake this and discuss it is consistent neither with my leisure nor with the duty of those whom I desire to instruct in essential matters more directly conducing to their salvation and to the benefit of the holy Church."[3]

From these things it follows as a necessary consequence that, since the Holy Ghost did not intend to teach us whether heaven moves or stands still, whether its shape is spherical or like a discus or extended in a plane, nor whether the earth is located at its center or off to one side, then so much the less was it intended to settle for us any other conclusion of the same kind. And the motion or rest of the earth and the sun is so closely linked with the things just named, that without a determination of the one, neither side can be taken in the other matters. Now if the Holy Spirit has purposely neglected to teach us propositions of this sort as irrelevant to the highest goal (that is, to our salvation), how can anyone affirm that it is obligatory to take sides on them, and that one belief is required by faith, while the other side is erroneous? Can an opinion be heretical and yet have no concern with the salvation of souls? Can the Holy Ghost be asserted not to have intended teaching us something that does concern our salvation? I would say here something that was heard from an ecclesiastic of the most eminent degree: "That the intention of the Holy Ghost is to teach us how one goes to heaven, not how heaven goes."[4]

But let us again consider the degree to which necessary demonstrations and sense experiences ought to be respected in physical conclusions, and the authority they have enjoyed at the hands of holy and learned theologians. From among a hundred attestations I have selected the following:

"We must also take heed, in handling the doctrine of Moses, that we altogether avoid saying positively and confidently anything which contradicts manifest experiences and the reasoning of philosophy or the other sciences. For since every truth is in agreement with all other truth, the truth of Holy Writ cannot be contrary to the solid reasons and experiences of human knowledge."[5]

And in St. Augustine we read: "If anyone shall set the authority of Holy Writ against clear and manifest reason, he who does this knows not what he has undertaken; for he opposes to the truth not the meaning of the Bible, which is beyond his comprehension, but rather his own interpretation; not what is in the Bible, but what he has found in himself and imagines to be there."[6]

This granted, and it being true that two truths cannot contradict one another, it is the function of wise expositors to seek out the true senses of scriptural texts. These will unquestionably accord with the physical conclusions which manifest sense and necessary demonstrations have previously made certain to us. Now the Bible, as has been remarked, admits in many places expositions that are remote from the signification of the words for reasons we have already given. Moreover, we are unable to affirm that all interpreters of the Bible speak by divine inspiration, for if that were so there would exist no differences between them about the sense of a given passage. Hence I should think it would be the part of prudence not to permit anyone to usurp scriptural texts and force them in some way to maintain any physical conclusion to be true, when at some future time the senses and demonstrative or necessary reasons may show the contrary. Who indeed will set bounds to human ingenuity? Who will assert that everything in the universe capable of being perceived is already discovered and known? Let us rather confess quite truly that "Those truths which we know are very few in comparison with those which we do not know." . . . ◎/◎

Notes

1. *Adversus Marcionem*, ii, 18.
2. *De Genesi ad literam*, ii, 9. Galileo has noted also: "The same is to be read in Peter the Lombard, master of opinions."
3. *Ibid.*, ii, 10.
4. A marginal note by Galileo assigns this epigram to Cardinal Baronius (1538–1607). Baronius visited Padua with Cardinal Bellarmine in 1598, and Galileo probably met him at that time.
5. Pererius on Genesis, near the beginning.
6. In the seventh letter to Marcellinus.

1. How convincing is Galileo's effort to reconcile Scripture with his findings?

2. Describe Galileo's attitude toward his audience. To what degree does his manner of supporting his assertions reflect this attitude?

3. How does Galileo connect his different points together? What is his central thesis? Do all of his points relate clearly to this thesis?

4. Why do you suppose Galileo chose to present his argument to a noble-woman and in the form of a letter? Does the letter itself provide any clues?

Chapter Summary

Reading and writing are interconnected modes of thinking. We critically read our own writing (for sense of direction, development of ideas, coherence, clarity, persuasive force, and so on) as well as the writing of others. We construct meaning (a kind of internal writing) when we read in depth—that is, we read actively rather than passively whenever we read critically. To read effectively also means to read in stages: previewing (prereading and skim-reading) to grasp the central purpose of the piece; in-depth reading to understand the content, progression, and rhetorical strategies at work in the piece; and postreading to reinforce the framework of the whole argument. To read effectively also means to respond spontaneously with a pencil, writing marginal glosses, comparisons, and questions in the margins. Finally, reading effectively means to read with an open mind, in a highly motivated manner, as if you are interacting with the author on paper, attempting to reconcile your views with the author's.

Checklist

1. Have I read the assigned essays, as well as the drafts of my fellow students, in three stages: first previewing, then reading in depth, and then postreading?

2. When reading in depth, do I determine the framework of the argument? Evaluate the data presented? Evaluate the author's organizational strategy? Speculate on the significance of what is being argued?

3. Do I understand what it means to read responsibly? Open-mindedly?

4. Have I considered including visuals that would enhance the reading experience and reinforce the key ideas of my argument?

Writing Projects

1. Write a critical response to one of the following quotations about reading.

    a. "To write down one's impressions of Hamlet as one reads it year after year would be virtually to record one's own autobiography, for as we know more of life, Shakespeare comments on what we know." (Virginia Woolf)

    b. "We read often with as much talent as we write." (Ralph Waldo Emerson)

    c. "The greatest part of a writer's time is spent in reading." (Samuel Johnson, as quoted by James Boswell)

    d. "To read well . . . is a noble exercise. . . . It requires a training such as the athletes underwent, the steady intention almost of the whole life to this object." (Henry David Thoreau)

    e. "A reasoning passion." (how the French novelist Colette described her experience of reading Victor Hugo's *Les Miserables*)

2. Write an essay in which you propose ways of improving one's reading strategies. You may want to discuss these strategies in relation to particular types of reading materials.

3. Find a print, television, or radio advertisement for an Internet dating service. Write an essay evaluating how convincingly the ad argues for the effectiveness of the service in securing a romantic relationship with someone. Add to your argument by visiting the websites of various Internet dating services, including the one featured in the ad. What assurances do they give? How reliable are they? What hard evidence can you bring to bear on your point of view? Finally, incorporate two or three appropriate visual aids (photographs, a graph or a chart summarizing statistical data, etc.) into your argument.

3 | Using the Classical Model in Your Arguments

> We need the capacity effectively to urge contradictory
> positions . . . not so that we may adopt either of the
> two (it is quite wrong to persuade men to evil), but
> that we should be aware how the case stands and be
> able, if our adversary deploys his arguments unjustly,
> to refute them.
> —Aristotle

CONSIDERING THE DISCIPLINES

The art of fashioning and presenting a strong, convincing argument has concerned rhetoricians for 2500 years. In the ancient world teachers of rhetoric (Aristotle among them) instructed individuals planning to enter any profession—whether it be law, politics, education, or civil service—to master the art of persuasion by adhering to a pre-determined structure, known as the classical model. Today, we see that model at work in today's law courts. Case in point: Public Defender A and District Attorney B, working on the same case (e.g. grand theft) must share all the evidence they discover about the case involving Defendant C. Judge D and the jury of twelve men and women will decide on the basis of how the Public Defender and the District Attorney argue whether Defendant C is guilty or not guilty and, if guilty, what punishment C deserves. How can the same facts (evidence) lead to the different conclusions that the Public Defender and the District Attorney will argue? Even if you do not plan to pursue a career in law, after reading this chapter you will begin to see that this approach to argument is used in different fields, sometimes so varied as psychology, history, and art history. Some examples in this chapter illustrate Classical Argument in the arts and in environmental science. As this chapter will make clear, a strong argument relies as much on its structure as its content.

Rhetoric, or the art of using language persuasively, has a long history. The work of ancient rhetoricians such as Plato, Aristotle, Quintilian, and Cicero has influenced Western education and literature for nearly two thousand years, shaping public discourse and public life. Though rooted in the past, rhetoric plays an integral role in today's judicial, political, religious, and educational institutions.

Argument in the Ancient World

In the ancient world, rhetoric was taught as oratory (public speaking) and was basic preparation for students entering law, politics, and teaching. Students learned how to communicate a point of view clearly and convincingly. There were three categories of argumentative oratory in the ancient world, corresponding to three different functions. Two of these functions were professional or quasi-professional, such as presenting lectures and debates emulating professional situations; one function was political (*deliberative*), such as deliberating over military and civic policies; the other was legal (*forensic*), such as courtroom prosecution or defense motions. The third category of oratory—celebratory (*epideictic*)—generally falls outside the scope of argument. This kind of oratory was used in eulogies, commendations, dedications, and so on. Early rhetoricians, itinerant teachers known as *Sophists*, emphasized the pragmatic skills to be developed in winning an argument. Later, the Platonic school gained ascendancy, valuing philosophical reasoning over mere "training." Plato's student, Aristotle, achieved a sort of middle ground between the idealistic truth-seeking of his mentor and the mercenary pragmatism of the Sophists by viewing rhetoric as the art of finding the best available means of persuasion in a given case— that is, by applying the rigors of philosophical reasoning to actual problems.

Another important element of ancient rhetoric was its system of topic development. For ancient orators, topics were preestablished "modes of thought" regionalized in the mind (the word *topic* comes from the Greek *topos*, meaning "place") to aid the memory when speaking. The first topic, logically enough, is definition, followed by comparison, temporal/causal connection, circumstance (for example, what is capable or incapable of happening), and testimony (use of authority, laws, or concrete examples to establish authenticity).

In addition to the ancients' everyday uses of argument in law, politics, religion, athletics, and the military, oratorical competitions were held. Individuals or teams would argue an issue, and an impartial judge would determine the winner based on each argument's strengths (much like what happens in debate tournaments today). Debating, we might say, is the "sport" side of argument—a show of argumentative skill for its own sake and valuable for the development of such skill.

The Classical Model of Argument

The Classical model for structuring an argument is both simple and versatile. First, here is a look at it in outline form:

I. Introduction

    A. Lead-in

    B. Overview of the situation

    C. Background

II. Position statement (thesis)

III. Appeals (ethos, pathos, logos) and evidence

    A. Appeals: to ethics, character, authority (ethos); to emotions (pathos); to reason (logos)

    B. Evidence: citing of statistics, results, findings, examples, laws, relevant passages from authoritative texts

IV. Refutation (often presented simultaneously with the evidence)

V. Conclusion (peroration)

    A. Highlights of key points presented (if appropriate)

    B. Recommendations (if appropriate)

    C. Illuminating restatement of thesis

Argument structure was given its fullest examination by the Roman rhetorician Quintilian, who not only described the five parts of a discourse—the introduction, the statement of facts relating to the issue, the evidence, the refutation of challenging views, and the conclusion—but stressed the importance of exercising judgment in using them. Rhetorical arrangement, after all, is an art, not a rote computer program. Hence, not all introductions are alike in scope or tone; in fact, the orator may sometimes dispense with an introduction altogether—as when someone wants to hear only "the bottom line." Similarly, the orator may want to refute opposing views before presenting the evidence. The orator may also decide whether the evidence should be strictly factual— that is, appeal exclusively to reason—or should include ethical and emotional appeals as well.

FIGURE 3.1

Aristotle (384–322 B.C.E.) wrote the *Rhetoric*. It was the first systematic study of argument and reasoning for practical purposes— political, judicial, and ceremonial.

Organizing Your Argument Using the Classical Model

The Classical argument introduces the problem and states the thesis; it next presents background information in the form of a narrative. It then presents the evidence in support of the thesis, including refutation of opposing views. Finally, it reaches a conclusion.

Consider the case of physicians John Guillebaud and Pip Hayes, who have set out to structure an article that argues for increased availability of, and more accurate information about, contraceptives to better control unsustainable population growth. First they present the facts (e.g., that the world's population increases by 1.5 million every week); next they challenge the conventional wisdom about how population should be controlled; then they advance their own argument regarding noncoercive methods of increasing contraceptive use. Quite likely, the authors used a set of guiding questions similar to the following to help structure their argument:

1. What is my reason for writing the paper?
2. What is the best way to introduce the problem, given my evidence and audience?
3. What wrong assumptions need to be identified and refuted?
4. How can I make my stance on the issue most persuasive?
5. How will my readers most likely react to my assertions? Negatively? Indifferently? Skeptically? Enthusiastically? How can I deal with these reactions in advance? (For example, if the audience is likely to be skeptical, what might I say to remove their skepticism?

◎/◎   Exercise 3.1

Read Guillebaud's and Hayes's article on "Population Growth and Climate Change," and then answer the questions that follow.

Population Growth and Climate Change

Universal access to family planning should be the priority   John Guillebaud and Pip Hayes

Lead-in
Overview

The world's population now exceeds 6700 million, and humankind's consumption of fossil fuels, fresh water, crops, fish, and forests exceeds supply. These facts are connected. The annual increase in population of about

79 million means that every week an extra 1.5 million people need food and somewhere to live. This amounts to a huge new city each week, somewhere, which destroys wildlife habitats and augments world fossil fuel consumption. Every person born adds to greenhouse gas emissions, and escaping poverty is impossible without these emissions increasing.

Thesis

Resourcing contraception therefore helps to combat climate change, although it is not a substitute for high emitters reducing their per capita emissions. In 1798 Malthus predicted that as the population increased expo nentially, shortfalls in food supply would be unavoidable. A sevenfold increase in the population has led, 210 years later, to unprecedented food shortages, escalating prices, and riots. Until these events Borlaug's "green revolution" had seemingly proved Malthus wrong. Yet fertilizers, pesticides, tractors, and transport are dependent on fossil fuels, which apart from being in short supply, exacerbate climate change.

Statistical evidence

Last year's [2006] parliamentary hearings concluded that the United Nation's millennium development goals, including millennium development goal number 1—to eradicate extreme poverty and hunger—"will be difficult or impossible to achieve without a renewed focus on, and investment in, family planning." The number of people now living on less than $2 (£1; €1.3) a day is about 2 billion, which is equal to the world's total population when Oxfam was founded in 1942.

Historical background info

It is often assumed that "any quantitative concern for population must be intrinsically coercive." India in the 1970s polluted the whole concept by adopting coercive means for population "control." China stands similarly accused. But why consider infringing human rights when around half of pregnancies worldwide are unplanned? Moreover, numerous countries as varied as Costa Rica, Iran, Korea, Sri Lanka, and Thailand halved their total fertility rates primarily through meeting women's unmet fertility needs and choices.

Refutation of challenging views

Conventional economic wisdom says that couples in resource-poor settings actively plan to have many children to compensate for high child mortality, to provide labor, and to care for parents as they age. Often with cultural and religious endorsement, those factors enhance the post-hoc acceptance of large families. But

Additional refutation

economists overlook the fact that, everywhere, potentially fertile intercourse is more frequent than the minimum needed for intentional conceptions. Thus, having a large rather than a small family is less of a planned decision than an automatic outcome of human sexuality. Something active needs to be done to separate sex from conception—namely, contraception. But access to contraception is often difficult. Barriers to access for women intrude through lack of empowerment and abuse of their rights by husbands, partners, or mothers-in-law, or from religious authorities or, regrettably, even contraceptive providers.

Appeal to logic (logos)

The evidence is clear within a wide variety of settings that—despite no increase in per capita wealth or other presumed essentials—demand for contraception increases when it becomes available, accessible, and accompanied by correct information about its appropriateness and safety; when barriers are removed; and when the principles of marketing are applied. This is consistent with normal consumer behavior.

Evidence (case in-point)

In Iran, where the total fertility rate ("average family size") declined from 5.5 to 2 (replacement level) in just 15 years, all couples must learn about family planning before marriage, and contraception is endorsed by the pronouncements of religious leader. The Population Media Centre uses serial radio dramas or "soaps." Audiences learn from decisions that their favorite characters make—such as allowing wives to use contraception to achieve smaller and healthier families. In Rwanda, 57 percent of new attendees at family planning clinics named the radio drama *Rwanda's Brighter Future* as their reason for attending.

Appeal to compassion (pathos)

As doctors, we must help to eradicate the many myths and non-evidence-based medical rules that often deny women access to family planning. We should advocate for it to be supplied only wisely and compassionately, and for increased investment, which is currently just 10 percent of that recommended at the UN's Population Conference in Cairo.

Appeal to compassion (ethos)

The Optimum Population Trust calculates that "each new UK birth will be responsible for 160 times more greenhouse gas emissions . . . than a new birth in Ethiopia." Should UK doctors break a deafening silence here? "Population" and "family planning" seem taboo words and were notably absent from two *British Medical Journal* editorials on climate

Conclusion

change. Although we endorse everything that those editorials recommended, isn't contraception the medical profession's prime contribution for all countries?

Unplanned pregnancy, especially in teenagers, is a problem for the planet, as well as the individual concerned. But what about planned pregnancies? Should we now explain to UK couples who plan a family that stopping at two children, or at least having one less child than first intended, is the simplest and biggest contribution anyone can make to leaving a habitable planet for our grandchildren? We must not put pressure on people, but by providing information on the population and the environment, and appropriate contraception for everyone (and by their own example), doctors should help to bring family size into the arena of environmental ethics, analogous to avoiding patio heaters and high carbon cars. ◎/◎

1. How convincingly do Guillebaud and Hayes support their thesis? What additional evidence, if any, do you think should be included?

2. Comment on the (a) usefulness, (b) relevance, and (c) thoroughness of the statistics the authors have cited.

3. Identify any Aristotelian appeals the authors have used; how effective and appropriate are they?

4. Evaluate the effectiveness of the authors' refutation of challenging views.

5. Comment on the overall structure of the piece. How well does it adhere to Classical argument structure? How might the authors have strengthened their argument?

Elements of a Classical Argument in Action

Now let us examine each element in detail and see how it operates in a particular argument. Keep in mind that outlines serve to remind writers of the basic strategy for developing a sound argument; they should not be followed slavishly as if they were some unalterable blueprint for constructing a house.

Introduction   A good introduction accomplishes three things:

1. It presents the topic of inquiry or the problem requiring attention, and perhaps briefly states the thesis.

2. It establishes a clear context for the problem.

3. It engages the reader's attention and desire to get "the whole picture."

Consider the following introduction to an argument against the use of school vouchers, a system whereby the state promises to pay parents a percentage of tuition for attending a quality school of the parents' choice:

> Most Americans believe that improving our system of education should be a top priority for government at the local, state, and Federal levels. Legislators, school boards, education professionals, parent groups and community organizations are attempting to implement innovative ideas to rescue children from failing school systems, particularly in inner-city neighborhoods. Many such groups champion voucher programs. The standard program proposed in dozens of states across the country would distribute monetary vouchers (typically valued between $2,500–$5,000) to parents of school-age children, usually in troubled inner-city school districts. Parents could then use the vouchers towards the cost of tuition at private schools—including those dedicated to religious indoctrination.
>
> Superficially, school vouchers might seem a relatively benign way to increase the options poor parents have for educating their children. In fact, vouchers pose a serious threat to values that are vital to the health of American democracy. These programs subvert the constitutional principle of separation of church and state and threaten to undermine our system of public education. You will be able to judge for yourself when you read the article in its entirety later in this chapter.

How well do these two paragraphs meet the criteria for a strong introduction to an argument? First, the author (an anonymous writer for the Anti-Defamation League) introduces the problem: the need to improve our educational system and the fact that vouchers are considered to be a promising solution for that problem. The second paragraph presents the thesis: Vouchers are a bad idea. Finally, the author engages the reader's attention by using strong, dramatic language to convey a sense of urgency to the matter: Vouchers "pose a serious threat to values that are vital to the health of American democracy" and "subvert the constitutional principle of separation of church and state." Such language not only piques interest but heightens anticipation: How is this writer going to convince me that such an assertion makes sense? You will be able to judge for yourself when you read the article in its entirety later in this chapter.

Appeals and Evidence   At the heart of any Classical argument is the evidence, reinforced by the persuasive appeals (see pages 4–5) that will ideally demonstrate, beyond doubt, the validity and reasonableness of the thesis. To be persuasive—that is, to change the minds of readers who otherwise would reject your thesis—facts and appeals must be conveyed in a way that allows readers to see the path by which they lead directly to the thesis.

Let us consider the way in which the three appeals are applied to the argument on school vouchers.

1. *Ethos* (the appeal to ethics, character, valid authority). When the school vouchers author argues that a voucher program would undermine the ideals on which this country was founded, he or she is evoking the appeal of ethos: It would be unethical, or a sign of bad character, to undermine what are considered the fundamental ideals of American democracy and liberty. It should be taken for granted, the author implies, that the authority of the U.S. Constitution must always be upheld.

2. *Pathos* (the appeal to emotion, compassion, sympathy). By alluding to "a serious threat" that vouchers pose to American values, the author is evoking the appeal of pathos—specifically, the fear of what might happen if states violated the U.S. Constitution.

3. *Logos* (the appeal to logic, to sound, reason-based decision making). Note how the author sets up a logical connection between separation of church and state and the American system of public education: If the former is violated, the integrity of the latter is threatened. This is an example of the appeal to logic and reason: There is a logical connection to be made between A and B.

Appeals go a long way toward persuading readers, but strong evidence is also needed. Two kinds of evidence are appropriate to Classical argumentative writing—direct and indirect. *Direct evidence* consists of data from surveys, scientific experiments, and cases-in-point—phenomena that clearly point to a causal agency ("where there's smoke, there's fire"). Facts represent evidence that anyone can check firsthand at any time. *Indirect evidence* consists of formal analytical and mathematical reasoning. Here, the author takes the reader through a step-by-step analysis of causes that lead to inevitable effects.

Reinforcing Aristotelian Appeals with Visuals

Good argumentative writing makes its claims convincing by appealing to readers' emotions, values, and reason (as Aristotelian appeals demand), as well as by providing "hard" evidence through data—and even hard data should be "warranted" on a platform of values as the Toulmin method of argument demands (see Chapter 4).

Using Visuals to Reinforce Ethical Appeals

Many of the public service ads published by humanist and religious organizations to help raise public consciousness demonstrate how visuals can appeal to

one's sense of ethics. The UNICEF ad below, for example, dramatically illustrates the unethical practice of child-labor exploitation in sweatshops.

Using Visuals to Reinforce Emotional Appeals

Sometimes, raising reader consciousness needs to be reinforced with an emotional jolt appealing to our deepest psychological needs: safety, love, youth, tradition (for example, family, custom), longevity, strength or power, or compassion. Here are some examples:

- **Security, freedom from fear**. Say you wanted to incorporate visuals for an essay on the seriousness of domestic violence. You might consider using the following photograph of a run-down city block with the words "It's safer here" (superimposed on the street) "than here" (superimposed beneath an upstairs window).

- **Strength, power**. If you plan to write an essay on the ways in which the armed forces help develop leadership skills, you may want to consider matching expectations (as reflected in the U.S. Army ad on page 109) against actualities.

THAN HERE.

IT'S SAFER HERE

For many women and children, there is no more dangerous place to be than home.
Call **1.877.868.4JOE** or go to **www.joetorre.org** to help make home safe again.

JOE TORRE
Safe At Home
FOUNDATION

Joe Torre Safe At Home−Æ Foundation

Digital Vision/Getty Images

- **Appeal to youth**. For an essay arguing that keeping in shape will keep you youthful, you might incorporate an image similar to this photograph of two runners.

- **Appeal to compassion.** World events that affect large numbers of people may generate strong feelings of compassion. These emotions can be stirred up for years to come by using evocative imagery. This memorial of American flags, shown on page 110, marked the first anniversary of 9/11. The layout of the flags, resembling a graveyard, presents a powerful and moving visual reminder of those who lost their lives on that day in 2001.

Using Visuals to Reinforce Logical Appeals

In argumentative writing, it is frequently necessary to provide hard data such as statistics or findings from surveys or experiments to support a claim. Using charts, graphs, and tables to capture in images what you analyze in the body

Norma Jean Gargasz/Alamy

of your argument aids in comprehension and in turn makes your claim more convincing. If you happen to be writing about population growth, for example, and wanted not only to support your claim that the world population has grown exponentially in recent history but also to convey the fact as dramatically as possible, you might choose to use this graph:

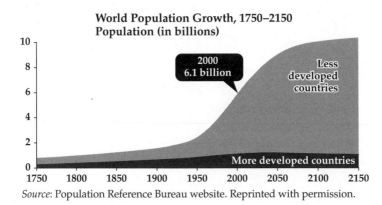

Source: Population Reference Bureau website. Reprinted with permission.

Note how the data are laid out in a way that emphasizes the relationship between the variables on each axis—in this case, the quantity variable on the horizontal (x) axis and the temporal variable on the vertical (y) axis. What would take readers thirty seconds or more to read in a paragraph-long explanation can be perceived—and understood with greater clarity—in just two or three seconds via the graph. By the way, there's no reason why you need to restrict yourself to just a line graph. You can, for example, combine drawings and graphs into what are known as pictographs, as in the following example:

The 10 most frequently performed surgeries

Arteriography and angiocardiography: 2.1 million

Cardiac catheterizations: 1.3 million

Endoscopy of small intestine: 1.1 million

Computerized axial tomography (CAT scans): 828,000

Diagnostic ultrasound: 813,000

Balloon angioplasty of coronary artery: 664,000

Reduction of fracture: 667,000

Hysterectomy: 617,000

Insertion of coronary artery stents: 615,000

Endoscopy of large intestine: 596,000

> During 2004, 45 million procedures were performed on hospital inpatients in the United States. Here are the 2004 figures for the ten most frequently performed procedures in non-Federal short-stay hospitals.

Combining the Appeals

Most arguments combine all three appeals. Here is a case in point: Imagine that your instructor has assigned the class to investigate the issue of the arts funding in public-school education. As state educational budgets are cut back, school boards tend to target arts programs—music, dance, theater, applied arts-and-crafts classes in painting or illustration, and so on—for elimination. Your task is to write an argument defending or challenging a decision to eliminate an arts program. What kinds of appeals might you use to persuade readers to accept your point of view? What kind of visual will you select or design that would reinforce those appeals?

To get the research ball rolling, your instructor shows you the ad on page 113 by an organization called Americans for the Arts.

First, take a few moments to contemplate the ad, noticing how the visual elements interact with the text in order to enhance the persuasive force of the message. For example, you notice how the image of the box of graham crackers is labeled, absurdly, "Martha Grahams"; directly on the other side of the first column of text is a larger image of Martha Graham herself in a classic dance pose—one of her skills being that of using dance to tell a story. The caption wittily recontextualizes the original aim of that photograph: "Ms. Graham told stories using movement. Here, she tells us how sad it is that kids aren't getting enough art." The third image, positioned within the second column of text and below the Martha Graham photo, is the schematic of the human brain. Perhaps you will incorporate the ad into your argument.

The next step, you decide, is to access the Americans for the Arts website, http://www.AmericansForTheArts.org.

Here you discover a wealth of links to information resources, field services, events, and ways to become involved with their cause. Here you will find the support data you need to make your claim convincing. You will also find testimonials from parents and teachers describing the impact of an arts education on children's success in and out of school.

Visuals can be effective in argumentative writing because they seem to demonstrate something irrefutable about the nature of what is being represented. As Susan Sontag says in her book-length essay *On Photography* (Delta, 1977), "Photographed images do not seem to be statements about the world so much as pieces of it" (4). That is why they so effectively convey evidence, despite the fact that photographs can be faked or misrepresented.

No matter what type of evidence is used, it must be tested for its relevance, accuracy, thoroughness, and timeliness.

- **Relevance.** The evidence must relate directly to the claims being made. If an argument claims that high school teachers tend subtly to discourage young women from pursuing careers in science or engineering, but then cites instances of that problem only from colleges or private schools, critics would argue that the evidence is not relevant to the claim.

- **Accuracy.** Inaccurate evidence is worse than useless: It can deceive—and even harm. Facts and figures must always be double-checked. Experts or passages from texts must be quoted or paraphrased accurately. Accuracy also requires a degree of precision relevant to what is being argued. It may be acceptable to say "water was brought to a boil" in reference to a recipe, but when describing a chemical experiment involving a water temperature to a precise fraction of a degree, such a statement would be problematic.

- **Thoroughness.** The evidence must cover every facet or implication of the claim. If a writer claims that teenagers in the United States have fewer traffic accidents today than they did ten years ago but then cites accident statistics

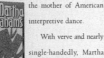

from only three states, readers rightly would argue that the evidence could be made more thorough by including statistics from all fifty states.

- **Timeliness.** The evidence must be appropriately recent. If a writer argues that teenagers are safer drivers "today" but presents statistics from 1995, then one rightly could argue that the evidence needs to be updated.

Refutation   Closely associated with evidence is refutation, or referring to opposing views and then rebutting them. Refuting viewpoints that challenge our own is seldom easy; quite often, it is the most difficult stage in writing an effective argument. To refute effectively, we must assume that the challengers are equally convinced of their views. We may be tempted to trivialize or misrepresent an adversarial point by leaving out certain information or giving a faulty interpretation. Disagreements tend to be rooted in deeply personal values and beliefs, so we instinctively try to protect these beliefs. They have worked for us, have stabilized our sense of the world, have helped us cope. Any challenges are avoided. Yet unless we have the courage to permit these beliefs to be challenged, perhaps modified, maybe even abandoned, learning and personal growth cannot take place.

Knowledge consists not of disembodied facts but of negotiated ideas. What we know we have assimilated from innumerable points of view. The health of our own ideas depends on a steady influx of fresh viewpoints, just as a body of water must be continuously replenished to avoid becoming stagnant. Such receptivity to new ideas requires courage, of course. It is never easy to say of those who argue against us, "Maybe there is some validity to these challenging views; maybe I should adopt some of them."

If after a careful and critical analysis of opponents' arguments we still hold to our overall stance and, in fact, have found flaws in theirs, we are ready to refute them. The aim of refutation is to demonstrate the limitations or errors of challenging views. It is not necessary to establish a distinct boundary between evidence and refutation, since evidence may be brought in as part of the refutation process. Notice that in the body of the article on school vouchers (reprinted on pages 111–115), the author refutes the pro-voucher argument by first stating the opposition's rationale and then showing why that rationale is in error:

> Proponents of vouchers argue that these programs would allow poor students to attend good schools previously only available to the middle class. The facts tell a different story. A $2,500 voucher supplement may make the difference for some families. . . . But voucher programs offer nothing of value to families who cannot come up with the rest of the money to cover tuition costs.

The refutation is clearly articulated, but is it convincing? Skeptics probably would demand that the anti-vouchers author supply more in the way of evidence to substantiate the claim that vouchers undermine the integrity of American public schools.

How thorough is the evidence in support of the Anti-Defamation League's thesis that vouchers are harmful? The author brings in important facts that appear to demonstrate the unconstitutionality of vouchers, such as the Supreme Court's quoting of the Establishment Clause or its striking down "education programs that allow parents of parochial school students to recover a portion of their educational expenses from the state." However, much of the argument relies on speculation. There is no way of knowing for sure that the Supreme Court would judge vouchers to be unconstitutional, nor is there any way of knowing for sure that voucher programs "would force citizens—Christians, Jews, Muslims and atheists—to pay for the religious indoctrination of schoolchildren."

Effective argument depends on not only the kinds of evidence used but also the degree to which that evidence resolves the stated problem.

Conclusion   The minimal task of a conclusion is to provide a final wisdom about the thesis just argued. Some conclusions summarize the key points of the argument, a strategy that can be much appreciated in a long and complicated argument but may be unnecessary otherwise. Quite often, such summary statements are followed by recommendations for what actions to take. Other conclusions are more speculative: Instead of recommending what should be done, they focus on what *might* be done. And still other conclusions are more open-ended, offering not summative statements but questions for the readers to consider.

The Anti-Defamation League writer on school vouchers does not present as full-fledged a conclusion as he or she does an introduction. Is the conclusion sufficient?

> School voucher programs undermine two great American traditions: universal public education and the separation of church and state. Instead of embracing vouchers, communities across the country should dedicate themselves to finding solutions that will be available to every American schoolchild and that take into account the important legacy of the First Amendment.

The author succinctly restates the problem and leaves the reader with the provocative suggestion found in the concluding sentence. But what sort of solution will solve that complex problem? The author brings the readers no closer to a real solution.

◎/◎   **Exercise 3.2**

Read the complete text of "School Vouchers: The Wrong Choice for Public Education." Then answer the questions that follow.

School Vouchers
The Wrong Choice for Public Education | Anti-Defamation League

Most Americans believe that improving our system of education should be a top priority for government at the local, state and Federal levels. Legislators, school boards, education professionals, parent groups and community organizations are attempting to implement innovative ideas to rescue children from failing school systems, particularly in inner-city neighborhoods.

Many such groups champion voucher programs. The standard program proposed in dozens of states across the country would distribute monetary vouchers (typically valued between $2,500–$5,000) to parents of school-age children, usually in troubled inner-city school districts. Parents could then use the vouchers towards the cost of tuition at private schools—including those dedicated to religious indoctrination.

Superficially, school vouchers might seem a relatively benign way to increase the options poor parents have for educating their children. In fact, vouchers pose a serious threat to values that are vital to the health of American democracy. These programs subvert the constitutional principle of separation of church and state and threaten to undermine our system of public education.

Vouchers Are Constitutionally Suspect

Proponents of vouchers are asking Americans to do something contrary to the very ideals upon which this country was founded. Thomas Jefferson, one of the architects of religious freedom in America, said, "To compel a man to furnish contributions of money for the propagation of opinions which he disbelieves . . . is sinful and tyrannical." Yet voucher programs would do just that; they would force citizens—Christians, Jews, Muslims and atheists—to pay for the religious indoctrination of schoolchildren at schools with narrow parochial agendas. In many areas, 80 percent of vouchers would be used in schools whose central mission is religious training. In most such schools, religion permeates the classroom, the lunchroom, even the football practice field. Channeling public money to these institutions flies in the face of the constitutional mandate of separation of church and state.

While the Supreme Court has upheld school vouchers in the *Zelman* v. *Simmons-Harris* case, vouchers have not been given a green light by the Court beyond the narrow facts of this case. Indeed, Cleveland's voucher program was upheld in a close (5–4) ruling that required a voucher program to (among other things):

- be a part of a much wider program of multiple educational options, such as magnet schools and after-school tutorial assistance,

- offer parents a real choice between religious and non-religious education (perhaps even providing incentives for non-religious education),

- not only address private schools, but to ensure that benefits go to schools regardless of whether they are public or private, religious or not.

This decision also does not disturb the bedrock constitutional idea that no government program may be designed to advance religious institutions over non-religious institutions. Finally, and of critical importance, many state constitutions provide for a higher wall of separation between church and state— and thus voucher programs will likely have a hard time surviving litigation in state courts.

Thus, other states will likely have a very hard time reproducing the very   5
narrow set of circumstances found in the Cleveland program.

Vouchers Undermine Public Schools

Implementation of voucher programs sends a clear message that we are
giving up on public education. Undoubtedly, vouchers would help some students. But the glory of the American system of public education is that it is for
all children, regardless of their religion, their academic talents or their ability
to pay a fee. This policy of inclusiveness has made public schools the backbone of American democracy.

Private schools are allowed to discriminate on a variety of grounds. These
institutions regularly reject applicants because of low achievement, discipline
problems, and sometimes for no reason at all. Further, some private schools
promote agendas antithetical to the American ideal. Under a system of vouchers, it may be difficult to prevent schools run by extremist groups like the
Nation of Islam or the Ku Klux Klan from receiving public funds to subsidize
their racist and anti-Semitic agendas. Indeed, the proud legacy of *Brown* v.
Board of Education may be tossed away as tax dollars are siphoned off to deliberately segregated schools.

Proponents of vouchers argue that these programs would allow poor students to attend good schools previously only available to the middle class.
The facts tell a different story. A $2,500 voucher supplement may make the
difference for some families, giving them just enough to cover the tuition at a
private school (with some schools charging over $10,000 per year, they would
still have to pay several thousand dollars). But voucher programs offer nothing of value to families who cannot come up with the rest of the money to
cover tuition costs.

In many cases, voucher programs will offer students the choice between
attending their current public school or attending a school run by the local
church. Not all students benefit from a religious school atmosphere—even
when the religion being taught is their own. For these students, voucher programs offer only one option: to remain in a public school that is likely to dete-
riorate even further.

As our country becomes increasingly diverse, the public school system   10
stands out as an institution that unifies Americans. Under voucher programs, our educational system—and our country—would become even more
Balkanized than it already is. With the help of taxpayers' dollars, private
schools would be filled with well-to-do and middle-class students and a
handful of the best, most motivated students from inner cities. Some public
schools would be left with fewer dollars to teach the poorest of the poor and
other students who, for one reason or another, were not private school material.
Such a scenario can hardly benefit public education.

Finally, as an empirical matter, reports on the effectiveness of voucher
programs have been mixed. Initial reports on Cleveland's voucher program,

published by the American Federation of Teachers, suggest that it has been less effective than proponents argue. Milwaukee's program has resulted in a huge budget shortfall, leaving the public schools scrambling for funds. While some studies suggest that vouchers are good for public schools, there is, as yet, little evidence that they ultimately improve the quality of public education for those who need it most.

Vouchers Are Not Universally Popular

When offered the opportunity to vote on voucher-like programs, the public has consistently rejected them; voters in 19 states have rejected such proposals in referendum ballots. In the November 1998 election, for example, Colorado voters rejected a proposed constitutional amendment that would have allowed parochial schools to receive public funds through a complicated tuition tax-credit scheme. Indeed, voters have rejected all but one of the tuition voucher proposals put to the ballot since the first such vote over 30 years ago.

Voucher proposals have also made little progress in legislatures across the country. While 20 states have introduced voucher bills, only two have been put into law. Congress has considered several voucher plans for the District of Columbia, but none has been enacted.

A recent poll conducted by the Joint Center for Political and Economic Studies demonstrates that support for vouchers has declined over the last year. Published in October 1998, the poll revealed that support for school vouchers declined from 57.3 percent to 48.1 percent among blacks, and from 47 to 41.3 percent among whites. Overall, 50.2 percent of Americans now oppose voucher programs; only 42 percent support them.

Conclusion

School voucher programs undermine two great American traditions: universal   15
public education and the separation of church and state. Instead of embracing vouchers, communities across the country should dedicate themselves to finding solutions that will be available to every American schoolchild and that take into account the important legacy of the First Amendment.

1. Suggest one or more alternative ways in which the Anti-Defamation League author might have structured the essay, keeping within the general framework of Classical organizational strategy. What may gain or lose emphasis as a result of the reordering?

2. Evaluate the author's use of facts and appeals. What additional facts and appeals, if any, might have been appropriate?

3. How convincing is the author's argument that school vouchers are constitutionally suspect?

◎/◎   **Exercise 3.3**

Read "Why School Vouchers Can Help Inner-City Children," an argument by Kurt L. Schmoke, Mayor of Baltimore, in support of school vouchers. Then answer the questions that follow.

Why School Vouchers Can Help Inner-City Children | The Honorable Kurt L. Schmoke

I have been a strong supporter of public education during my tenure as mayor. In 1987 I said that it was my goal as mayor to one day have Baltimore be known as "The City That Reads." In doing that I underscored my commitment to improving all levels of education and getting people in our city focused on lifelong learning.

The state of Baltimore's economy was one of a variety of reasons for this commitment. Thirty years before I came into office, the largest private employer in Baltimore was the Bethlehem Steel Corporation's Sparrow's Point Plant. When I entered into office, however, the largest private employer in Baltimore was the Johns Hopkins University and Medical Center.

This transition meant that though there were jobs available, they would require a level of education that was higher than that which our children's parents and grandparents had to attain. It was clear to me that a commitment to improving literacy and understanding that education is a lifelong process was vitally important to our city.

With this knowledge in mind, I worked to improve our library system and our community college. Additionally, we created a Literacy Corporation to combat illiteracy in our city. In fact, President Bush presented Baltimore with the National Literacy Award in 1992.

In addition to my public responsibility for the Baltimore educational system, I also have a strong private interest in our city's schools. I have two children who are graduates of city public high schools. In fact, both of my children have at some point while growing up attended both public and private schools, so I have been able to observe my own children in different educational environments.

What I've found as a result of my experiences in pursuing a better-educated Baltimore, and a better-educated family, is a major void in current school reform efforts. I believe that the issues of competition and accountability are all too often ignored in efforts to improve public education.

Source: Kurt L. Schmoke, "Why School Vouchers Can Help Inner-City Children," *Civic Bulletin* No. 20 Aug. 1999. Reprinted by permission of The Manhattan Institute.

My years of experience in education have led me to be in favor of school choice: quite simply, I believe in giving parents more choice about where to educate their children. My support of school choice is founded in the common sense premise that no parent should be forced to send a child to a poorly performing school.

Unfortunately, however, countless parents, especially in the inner cities, are now forced to do just that. Parents in middle- and upper-class communities have long practiced school choice. They made sure that their children attended schools where they would get the best possible education. There is no reason why this option should be closed to low-income parents.

The consequences of this unfairness are not at all difficult to grasp. As one perceptive observer of urban education has written "Education used to be the poor child's ticket out of the slums. Now it's part of the system that traps people in the underclass."

This was part of the thinking behind what people in Baltimore call my   10
conversion to school choice. It did not happen overnight. It evolved slowly. My belief in school choice grew out of my experiences and, yes, my *frustrations* in trying to improve Baltimore's public schools over the last twelve years.

Under my watch as mayor we have tried all sorts of programs to reform the schools. Looking back, some of these programs showed promise, and some of our schools did demonstrate that they were doing a good job of educating our children.

Our successes, however, were still the exceptions, not the norm. I feared that, unless we took drastic action, this pattern would only continue. I considered school choice to be an innovation strong enough to change the course of what was widely recognized as an ailing system.

Why school choice? Two reasons: excellence and accountability. Parents want academic *excellence* for their children. They also want to know that there is someone in their child's school who is *accountable* for achieving those high academic standards.

In most cities in this nation, however, if your child is zoned into a school that is not performing well academically, and where teachers and administrators don't see themselves as being responsible for academic performance, parents have no recourse. Parents can only send their child to that school and hope for the best.

Under a school choice plan, a parent would have options. There would   15
be consequences for a school's poor performance. Parents could pull their children out of poorly performing schools and enroll them someplace else. If exercising this option leads to a mass exodus from certain underachieving schools, schools will learn this painful lesson: schools will either improve, or close due to declining enrollments.

Any corporation that tolerated mediocre performance among its employees, unresponsiveness to the complaints of its customers, and the promotion of a large number of failed products, would not survive in the marketplace very long. What is true of corporations should also be true of poorly performing and poorly run schools.

These are some of the ideas that I expressed when I first came out in support of school choice in a speech at Johns Hopkins University in March of 1996, not as a panacea, but as another way to improve public education. Though I thought my remarks were relatively benign, the speech sparked a great deal of controversy.

One of my own aides even joked that he wanted to see my voter registration card to see if I was still a Democrat. Well, I am still a Democrat and I have no plans to change my political affiliation. I, nonetheless, believe that the Democratic Party should reevaluate its position on school choice issues.

In actuality, choice should not be included in partisan rhetoric. School choice should be about giving our nation's children the best possible educational foundation.

The same week as my speech at Johns Hopkins, I appointed a task force   20 to explore the idea of school choice. I asked the task force to consider the pros and cons of school choice programs in all their variations, including programs such as the system implemented in Los Angeles where parents and students have the freedom to choose any school in the public system. I also asked that they investigate private school voucher plans such as the program in Milwaukee, as well as charter and magnet schools.

The task force released a report in that year which recommended that the Baltimore school system expand magnet schools and initiate a system-wide open enrollment program as a way to provide more educational options for parents and their children.

In my view, the task force unfortunately stopped short of endorsing publicly funded vouchers as a way to achieve the goal of school choice. The group, however, did leave open the door for reconsideration of the voucher issue later on. Meanwhile, the Baltimore city public school system has now implemented a variation of the school choice idea through what is called the New Schools Initiative.

These "New Schools" are very similar to charter schools. They are publicly funded schools that are planned and operated by parents or institutions or other non-traditional sponsors.

I recently spoke at Coppin State University for commencement. Coppin State is an historically black college in Baltimore that started out as a teacher training school. Today, under one of the New School Initiatives, Coppin is managing an elementary school in its home neighborhood drawing on its teaching and research to improve that school.

Now, three years after that Hopkins speech, I continue to believe that   25 choice holds the greatest hope for instilling excellence and accountability in the nation's public schools.

At that time, as a Democrat and an African-American mayor, I was considered a maverick, or worse, for expressing that idea. No longer. A ground-swell of support for choice is rising all over the nation, including from some unlikely quarters. Certainly, there's no greater proof of this than the tremendous response to the Children's Scholarship Fund funded by Wal-Mart heir John Walton and financier Ted Forstmann.

Under this program, the parents of some 1.25 million low-income children across the country applied for partial scholarships to help their children attend private and parochial schools. Civil rights pioneer and former mayor of Atlanta Andrew Young wrote these words in a nationally syndicated newspaper column shortly after the results of the scholarship drive were announced: "1.25 million cries for help, voiced by poor, largely minority families, seeking something most Americans take for granted. A decent education for their children."

In that column, Young described the collective cry for help as "a moment of moral awakening" that promises to be just as pivotal in America's civil rights struggle as Rosa Park's refusal to give up her bus seat in Montgomery, Alabama more than 40 years ago.

Such moments of moral awakening, Young observed, force us to reevaluate our beliefs and finally to take action. In Baltimore, that particular scholarship program attracted twenty thousand applicants. This represents an astonishing 44 percent of city children who were eligible.

The conclusions that can be drawn from these figures are unmistakable.   30
The *Baltimore Sun* education editor wrote, "We know now that there's a pent-up demand for school choice in the city. And we know that poor parents do care about the education of their children."

In fact, some low-income African-American parents in our city have shown they care so much that they will even go so far as to look *halfway around the world* in order to find a good school for their children. The school which I refer to is called Baraka, which means blessings in Swahili. It's located in rural Kenya, 10,000 miles and eight time zones from inner-city Baltimore. And it's funded by a Baltimore-based foundation, The Abell Foundation. The Foundation recruits and selects at-risk seventh- and eighth-grade boys from the Baltimore city public schools to participate in this bold education experiment.

The kids chosen for this program are generally headed for serious trouble. It is safe to assume that many of the boys in the Baraka program would have ended up incarcerated, or worse, had they not been selected.

Baraka School is going to begin its fourth year of operation in the fall. With 30 graduates to date, the school is having remarkable success in boosting the academic achievement of these at-risk youngsters and truly turning around their lives.

Because of the persistent resistance to school choice by some Maryland politicians, however, the State Education Department has refused to fund the Baraka School project. I do not speak of any extra funding here. I am only talking about taking the state's cost of educating each Baraka student, which would normally have gone to the school that they had been assigned to had they remained in the public system, and allowing it to be used to educate the students in this alternative environment.

The state has absolutely refused. Were it not for the support of the Foun-   35
dation, the Baraka School, which has done such an excellent job for these young men, would have closed.

So, despite greater acceptance of school choice it's certainly premature to declare victory in the public opinion contest. Indeed, criticisms of school choice are as strident as ever and I am sure you have heard the more familiar ones.

Some say that school choice, especially vouchers, will weaken public education. My response is that choice can only strengthen public education by introducing competition and accountability into the mix. Others claim that school choice is undemocratic. My response to them is that choice is in keeping with the aspirations for freedom that formed the core of American democracy. As former Delaware Governor Pete Du Pont once wrote, "It's about the liberty to choose what's best for your children." All of us should have that choice.

Some say that school choice is elitist, or even racist. The truth is that black low-income children are among the prime victims of the nation's failing public schools. African-American parents know this all too well. This is why they have been so open to the idea of school choice.

A recent national poll released by the Joint Center for Political and Economic Studies found a trend toward growing support of tuition vouchers among African-American parents.

Another common criticism of school choice, and especially vouchers, 40 is that it violates the principle of separation of church and state. A properly structured voucher program is no more a violation of the principle of separation of church and state than is the GI Bill. This program allowed military veterans to use government dollars to attend any university of their choice, public or private, religious or secular.

I am convinced that with time, and through open dialogue, critics of school choice will come to see this movement for what it is: part of an emerging new civil rights battle for the millennium, the battle for education equity. We need to give poor children the same right that children from more affluent households have long enjoyed. The right to an education that will prepare them to make a meaningful contribution to society. It is that simple.

In speaking of battles, and in closing, I remind you of those few words of wisdom from Victor Hugo: "Greater than the tread of Mighty Armies, is an Idea whose Time has Come . . ." As we look to the future, evidence is increasingly compelling, that school choice is such an idea. ◎/◎

1. Compare Schmoke's method of arguing his thesis with the Anti-Defamation League's method. Is one method more effective than the other? Why or why not?

2. Critique the essay in terms of (a) the effectiveness of its introduction; (b) the strength of its evidence and appeals; (c) the strength of its refutations; and (d) its conclusion.

3. Prepare an outline of your own essay on school vouchers. What will be your thesis? What kind of evidence will you present? How will you refute challenging views?

FIGURE 3.1   Classical Model Flowchart

What *issue* am I going to investigate? [Example: The issue of visual arts education in U.S. public schools.]

↓

What is my *thesis*? [Example: Acquiring basic skills in painting, illustrating, and sculpting is as important as acquiring basic math and reading skills.]

↓

What *evidence* can I use to support my thesis convincingly? [Example: Timely published reports by properly credentialed experts (such as educational psychologists) that explain why acquiring visual arts related skills are as important as math and reading skills.]

↓

What are the opposing views that I must acknowledge and *refute*? [Example: The argument that math and reading skills must take priority over visual arts skills in today's world overlooks the fact that creative thinking is just as important as analytical thinking.]

↓

In light of my evidence and refutation of opposing views, what are my *recommendations* for resolving the problem? [Example: We must find ways to integrate math and reading with painting and illustrating.]

↓

What are my *concluding reflections*?

↓

Using the above information, what can I say in my opening paragraph that would best *introduce* my argument and engage my reader's attention?

Chapter Summary

The Classical model of argument dates back to ancient Greece and Rome, and it is still used. In effect, the Classical model presents a template, a preestablished structure for framing an argument. It includes these elements:

- An introduction, which presents the claim to be argued and gives necessary background information

- A body of collected data or evidence and appeals, which together attempt to persuade the audience that the claim is convincing, and acknowledgment and refutation of challenging views

- A conclusion, which may summarize key points, reflect on implications and consequences, or make recommendations (if appropriate)
- In addition, the content of an argument was generated by modes of thought or topics, which included definition, comparison, temporal/causal connection, circumstance, and testimony.

Argument in the ancient world was conducted mainly through oratory, the art of speechmaking. Training for a profession in which argument was part of the job included being trained in the rhetorical strategies needed for giving speeches in that profession. Hence, aspiring politicians were trained in deliberative oratory, aspiring lawyers in forensic oratory. Everyone involved in public life was probably trained in celebratory oratory, which was used for honoring individuals and events.

Checklist

1. Does my paper include the elements of Classical argument structure in proper sequence?
2. Does my introduction clearly present my thesis and necessary background information?
3. Have I acknowledged and accurately presented challenging views? Have I refuted them thoroughly?
4. Does my conclusion summarize the key points of my argument, present insightful interpretations, or make appropriate predictions or recommendations?

Writing Projects

1. Using the Classical model of argument structure, write a three-page position paper on one of the following topics:

   a. Students should (should not) be required to take fewer core courses and allowed to take more electives.

   b. First-year composition courses should (should not) be an elective instead of a requirement.

   c. The college bookstore's buyback policy should (should not) be reformed.

2. Using the Classical model of argument, write an essay defending or challenging the value or usefulness of an existing law, policy, or program, such as the electoral college, the National Endowment for the Arts, the banning of prayer from public schools, or the minimum drinking age.

4

The Toulmin Model of Argument

Rationality has to be understood in terms of formal argumentation.
—Stephen Toulmin

CONSIDERING THE DISCIPLINES

Arguing effectively on any subject across the curriculum can lead to more civil discourse, not just in professional circumstances but in everyday life. Viewpoints need to be based not only on facts (scientific, historical, legal, etc., depending on the discipline you're working in) but also on values and ethical principles to be plausible—and to be taken seriously by those whose views differ from yours. The philosopher of science Stephen Toulmin (1922–2009) gave classical argument a modern reworking by calling attention to the ethical underpinnings of supporting a claim with particular kinds of evidence. To put it another way: facts do not usually speak for themselves. This chapter introduces the Toulmin method: using data to best authenticate a claim, introducing assurances (warrants) that reinforce the grounds (or data), and determining the soundness of the assurances (warrants).

Stephen Toulmin (1922–2009), an English philosopher of science and the history of ideas, developed a system of argument that has proven useful and influential in the modern world of complex rhetorical situations. Toulmin's model of argument is systematic in its reasoning; at the same time, it demands that this reasoning be scrutinized for its ethical underpinnings. It is not enough to present a claim and try to "prove" it with evidence. The arguer must also examine the evidence itself to scrutinize the assumptions we make about the evidence, and even to ensure that *those* assumptions are similarly scrutinized for their ethical underpinnings. Toulmin argument, then, insists that logic alone cannot resolve complex human issues. Ethics and values play as important a role in argumentation as logical reasoning.

Let's take a closer look at the elements that comprise Toulmin argument.

Stephen Toulmin (1922–2009) is a philosopher of science with a special interest in the role that rhetoric plays in conveying ideas about ethics and morality. His context-based theory of argument provides an influential alternative to rigid, logic-driven theories.

Sijmen Hendriks Photography

The Toulmin Model of Argument

The terms we encounter in the Toulmin model immediately call attention to the complexity of the social interaction required for responsible argumentation:

- An argument begins with a *claim* to be made, which must be articulated as clearly and as accurately as possible. The claim is the thesis or premise of your argument that you want your audience to accept.

- To accomplish this goal, you must produce compelling *data*, the grounds or evidence. It is important to keep in mind that "evidence" means different things in different disciplines. In the sciences, for example, the data probably consist of results obtained from experiments, close observations, or mathematical analyses. In other contexts, the data probably consist of rules, laws, policies, highly valued social customs, or quotations from works of literature.

- Next, you need to ask of any argument whether the data used to support the claim truly are valid and are based on a sound sense of values. In other words, you must determine one or more underlying warrants, assurances that the data are based on some sensible and ethical foundation. Anyone can conjure up all sorts of data and manipulate them to give the appearance of validating a claim. As Shakespeare in *The Merchant of Venice* reminds us through the mouth of the merchant Antonio, "The Devil can cite Scripture for his purpose." For example, sometimes it is not enough to cite a law; it may be necessary to decide if the law is just or unjust.

- Just as the validity of the data is reinforced and sanctioned by one or more underlying warrants, so too must the validity of the warrants be reinforced. As Stephen Toulmin himself explains in *An Introduction to Reasoning* (1979), "Warrants are not-self-validating . . . [and] normally draw their strength and solidity from further substantial supporting considerations" (58). These further supporting considerations Toulmin calls the *backing*. To return to the example of unjust laws, the arguer would need to ask: What *assurance* can I give that the law is unjust?

- Finally, you must be prepared to bring in one or more *qualifiers* to your claim—that is, be prepared to call attention to any exceptions to the claim under certain circumstances. Consider: "The right of free speech must be protected in all situations except when it can endanger life or safety, such as yelling 'Fire!' in a crowded theater." The qualifier—the exception to the rule—prevents the claim from losing touch with complex social situations. The ability to anticipate qualifiers to one's claim is the mark of a responsible arguer. Toulmin refers to this phase of argument as the *rebuttal*. Of course, no arguer can anticipate every possible exception, and that is why audience feedback is so important in argumentation.

Now let us examine each of these elements in more detail.

The Claim

You know this feature as the thesis, premise, or central assumption. Toulmin chooses to call it the *claim* because that term suggests a thesis or assertion that is particularly *open to challenge*. The term comes from the Latin word *clamare*, meaning "to cry out," reminding us of the spontaneity with which claims are often made and hence how easily they can reach human ears and eyes without sufficient evidence to support them. The Latin root also reminds us to pay attention to how open to public scrutiny the claim is likely to be once it is presented as a speech or as a printed document in a periodical or book, on the Internet, in a court of law, or in a college paper.

For an argument to succeed, the writer first must ensure that the claim offered is worthy of deliberation. Some claims are not arguable. For example, it would be foolish to argue seriously that in general, red is a superior color to blue. The claim is too dependent on subjective taste to be arguable. As the Latin maxim goes, *De gustibus non est disputandum*—of taste there is no disputing. But let's say you are an interior decorator and you have studied the effects of color on mood. You might argue that particular colors work best in particular types of rooms within a house. Here the claim is based not on personal taste but on statistical fact: Researchers have shown that pale blue helps relax people; therefore, pale blue would be an appropriate color for bedroom walls.

There are two basic types of claims, objective and subjective. *Objective claims* assert that something *actually* exists and present evidence that is demonstrably factual—not only in the sense of scientifically factual but legally factual, as in the case of laws, regulations, and policies. Here are some examples of objective claims:

- Video games heighten a child's hand-eye coordination and visual perception, but they impede the development of language processing skills.

- It is a myth that science is based only on logical reasoning and that art is based only on imagination. Logical reasoning and imagination are equally important to science and to art.

- Those who wish to speak out against the U.S. Constitution have just as much constitutional right to communicate their views in public as those who support the Constitution.

The above claims present themselves as objective truths. But they are not *self-evident* truths; they must be supported with the appropriate evidence before readers can accept them as factual. Thus, before the first claim can be accepted as factual, the arguer must show, for example, that psychologists have compared the learning behaviors of children who play video games with those children who do not and have found enough evidence to establish a causal link between video-game playing and abstract reasoning.

Before the second claim can be accepted as factual, the arguer must provide convincing examples of the way imagination works in science and the way logical reasoning works in art. For example, the arguer might refer to autobiographical statements of scientists such as Albert Einstein or mathematicians such as Jules Henri Poincaré, who at various times obtained scientific understanding through dreams or imaginary "thought experiments."

Before the third claim can be accepted as factual, the arguer must demonstrate how the Constitution, paradoxical as it may seem, actually protects the rights of those who wish to speak out against it. This proof would entail careful analysis and interpretation of selected passages from the Constitution.

Subjective claims, on the other hand, assert that something *should* exist and present evidence derived from ethical, moral, or aesthetic convictions. Someone who argues, for example, that all college students should be required to take at least one course in literature to graduate or that animals should be treated with dignity is making a subjective claim. Although each claim is based on personal values, one cannot dismiss them as a kind of anything-goes relativism. The arguer, for example, might demonstrate that the benefits derived from studying literature improve one's ability to understand human nature, a valuable asset when one interacts with people.

The Data or Grounds

The Toulmin model demands that writers take pains to ensure that the supporting evidence fully validates the claim. The word *data* suggests "hard facts"—results from experiments or statistics from surveys, as well as historical, legal, and biographical facts. For more indirect kinds of evidence, such as testimonials or interpretations, the term *grounds* is more appropriate.

Thus, we can identify five different kinds of data to authenticate a claim: (1) *legal data* (such as laws, policies, regulations, and codes); (2) *scientific data*, such as findings obtained from mathematical calculations and laboratory experiments (keep in mind that experiments such as DNA testing and ballistics analyses, used to help solve crimes, are an inherent part of legal data and are often referred to as *forensic* data); (3) *testimonial* or *experiential* data, which is based on firsthand experience (for example, eyewitness testimony and oral histories as gathered by anthropologists); (4) *scholarly* or *documentary* data (that is, data obtained from secondary sources published in book or electronic form); and (5) *statistical data*, which may be obtained firsthand (in which case it would be akin to but not identical to scientific data unless the statistics were derived from laboratory experiments instead of, say, opinion polls).

Like claims, data or grounds must be presented as accurately and as unambiguously as possible. Someone who argues, for example, that essay exams test student comprehension of literature better than multiple-choice exams do, and who in so arguing relies on the testimonials of students, would want to make sure that those testimonials contain clear *demonstrations* of better comprehension for students taking essay exams. Of course, the criteria for "better comprehension" would need to be clarified before they could be used as valid grounds for a claim. The criteria might include richly detailed (as opposed to generalized) recollection of the content of literary works; they might also include insightful critical assessment or comparison of the thematic material of the works (as opposed to, say, superficial explanation of its strengths and weaknesses).

The Warrant and Its Backing

A warrant is the assurance that the evidence brought in to support the claim is completely reliable and that it rests on sound principles or values. Thus, just as the data legitimate the claim, a warrant, often implicit in the argument, legitimates the data. As Stephen Toulmin writes in *The Uses of Argument*, warrants "indicate the bearing of [the] conclusion of the data already produced" (98). By "bearing," Toulmin is referring to the need for readers to recognize and accept an appropriate direction in which the argument takes shape from claim to data to warrant. Warrants remind us of the humanizing dimension of argument: An argument, no matter how "heated," must always be principled rather than stem from vague or questionable motives.

Let us see how warrants operate in a given argument. Consider an essay in which a student, Melissa, argues for the abolition of letter grades in formal education. Melissa's claim is as follows:

```
Letter grades should be abolished because they result in unhealthy
competition, distract students from truly learning the subject
matter, and constitute an inadequate gauge of student performance.
```

Melissa chooses to support her claim with data that compares the performance of students in a letter-graded class with the performance of students in a Pass/No Pass class. Melissa's warrant might go something like this: "Learning for its own sake is more satisfying to students than learning to achieve predetermined standards of proficiency." As backing for this warrant, Melissa might conclude something like the following: "The more satisfying the learning experience, the more students are likely to learn." Melissa may not need to state these sentences explicitly, but the evidence she uses to support her claim should make the warrant and backing apparent.

We might diagram the relationships among Melissa's claim, data, warrant, and backing as in Figure 4.1.

Compelling warrants are just as vital to the force of an argument as are compelling data because they reinforce the trustworthiness of the data. Unsuccessful warrants often seem disconnected from, or even contradictory to, the evidence. Consider the following claim:

Students should not be required to attend class.

FIGURE 4.1

Relationships among the Claim, Data, Warrant, and Backing

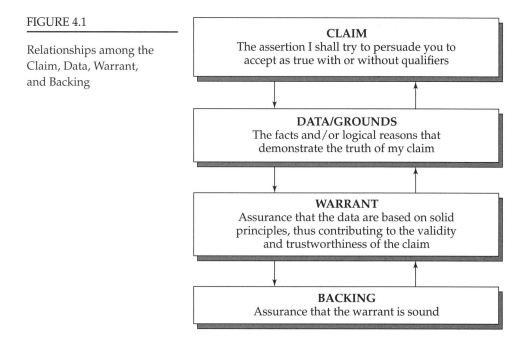

CLAIM
The assertion I shall try to persuade you to accept as true with or without qualifiers

DATA/GROUNDS
The facts and/or logical reasons that demonstrate the truth of my claim

WARRANT
Assurance that the data are based on solid principles, thus contributing to the validity and trustworthiness of the claim

BACKING
Assurance that the warrant is sound

If the evidence presented is the college's pledge to inculcate self-reliance in students, then the warrant—the conviction that self-reliance is compromised when professors require students to attend class—would seem contradictory to many readers because it is often assumed that such requirements are designed to *promote* self-reliance. Similarly, backing can be faulty. For example, in an argument claiming that every sixteen-year-old who drops out of school should be denied a driver's license, a warrant might involve the conviction that there is never any legitimate justification for dropping out of school; however, it would be difficult to find backing for this warrant that would apply in every circumstance.

There are three kinds of warrants, which roughly correspond to the three kinds of appeals in Classical argument: logical or scientific warrants, ethical or forensic-based warrants, and emotional or artistic-based warrants.

1. *Logical or scientific warrants.* These warrants reinforce the trustworthiness of logical progression of scientific reasoning. If a meteorologist predicts a smog alert on the basis of 90-degree temperatures, little or no winds, and heavy traffic, her warrant would be that such a formula for smog predication is reliable.

2. *Ethical or forensic-based warrants.* A warrant is ethical when it relates to values or codes of conduct such as honor, integrity, altruism, honesty, and compassion. If one argues that underrepresented minorities should be allowed the opportunity to attend college even if their admissions test scores are not quite as high as those of the majority of admissions candidates, and uses as evidence the success rate of those given such opportunity, the warrant is that society is ethically obligated to compensate minorities for past injustices by giving them such opportunities. Where affirmative action measures have become law, we could say that the warrant justifies enactment of that law.

3. *Emotional or artistic-based warrants.* If someone argues that profanity in films weakens instead of strengthens his enjoyment of those films and uses personal testimony as evidence, the arguer's warrant is that such negative reactions to profanity in movies is a reliable criterion for evaluating the strength or weakness of a film.

Backing may also be logical, ethical, and emotional.

Keep in mind when analyzing the arguments of others (and even your own arguments) that, as stated earlier, warrants—and, consequently, backing—often remain unstated. They may be certain fundamental principles or beliefs that the writer simply assumes his or her reader shares. In fact, such principles or beliefs may well be open to challenge, thus undermining the claim of the argument. But to make such a challenge, you first have to identify the unstated warrant. In making arguments of your own, consider the possibility that a good number of your readers may not share your warrant. If that is the case, it is best to state the warrant and backing directly, and perhaps even offer some defense for one or both.

The Qualifier

Claims are rarely absolute; that is, a claim may be valid in many circumstances, but not necessarily in all. If that is the case, an arguer would want to *qualify* the claim so that her readers would understand how she is limiting its range. For example, someone who claims that dress codes should be eliminated in the workplace might qualify that claim by excluding workplaces where uniforms are required for reasons of security (as is the case with police or military uniforms) or where certain articles of clothing are prohibited for reasons of personal safety (for example, someone cannot wear a necktie when operating heavy machinery). Someone writing about the negative influence of television on learning might qualify the claim by noting that watching television for the specific purpose of studying its negative effects could have a positive benefit on learning.

A radical form of qualification is known as the *rebuttal*. This is similar to refutation in Classical argument (see page 111), except that in the Toulmin scheme, rebuttal aims not to invalidate the claim but to show that the claim may not be valid in certain situations. Let's use the example of dress codes mentioned earlier. Instead of merely qualifying the claim that dress codes should be eliminated *except for* police uniforms, the arguer might rebut the claim entirely by agreeing that dress codes should be maintained without exception whenever there is consensus among employers and employees alike that it is necessary or desirable.

A Sample Analysis Using the Toulmin Model

Read the following argument by Virginia Woolf, noting the claim, data, warrant, and backing, as indicated by the marginal annotations.

Professions for Women | Virginia Woolf

Woolf begins by providing necessary background information for her argument.

When your secretary invited me to come here, she told me that your Society is concerned with the employment of women and she suggested that I might tell you something about my own professional experiences. It is true I am a woman; it is true I am employed; but what professional experiences have I had? It is difficult to say. My profession is literature; and in that profession there are fewer experiences for women than in any other, with the exception of the stage—fewer, I mean, that are peculiar to women. For the road was cut many years ago—by Fanny Burney, by Aphra Behn, by Harriet Martineau, by Jane Austen, by George Eliot—many famous women, and many more unknown and forgotten, have been before me, making the path smooth, and regulating my steps. Thus, when I came to write, there were very few material obstacles in my way. Writing was a reputable and harmless occupation. The family peace was not broken by the scratching of a pen. No demand was made upon the family purse. For ten and sixpence one can buy paper enough to write all the plays of Shakespeare—if one has a mind that way. Pianos and models, Paris, Vienna, and Berlin, masters and mistresses, are not needed by a writer. The cheapness of writing paper is, of course, the reason why women have succeeded as writers before they have succeeded in the other professions.

But to tell you my story—it is a simple one. You have only got to figure to yourselves a girl in a bedroom with a pen in her hand. She had only to move that pen from left to right—from ten o'clock to one. Then it occurred to her to do what is simple and cheap enough after all—to slip a few of those pages into an envelope, fix a penny stamp in the corner, and drop the envelope into the red box at the corner. It was thus that I became a journalist; and my effort was rewarded on the first day of the following month—a very glorious day it was for me—by a letter from an editor containing a cheque for one pound ten shillings and sixpence. But to show you how little I deserve to be called a professional woman, how little I know of the struggles and difficulties of such lives, I have to admit that instead of spending that sum upon bread and butter, rent, shoes and stockings, or butcher's bills, I went out and bought a cat—a beautiful cat, a Persian cat, which very soon involved me in bitter disputes with my neighbors.

What could be easier than to write articles and to buy Persian cats with the profits? But wait a moment. Articles have to be about something. Mine, I seem to remember, was about a novel by a famous man. And while I was writing this review, I discovered that if I were going to review books I should need to do battle with a certain phantom. And the phantom was a woman, and when I came to know her better I called her after the heroine of a famous poem. The Angel in the House. It was she who used to come between me and my paper when I was writing reviews. It was she who bothered me and wasted my time and so tormented me that at last I killed her. You who come of a younger and happier generation may not have heard of her—you may not know what I mean by The Angel in the House. I will describe her as shortly as

Woolf's claim emerges here through implication: Women who aspire to write must do all they can to "kill" the Angel in the House.

I can. She was intensely sympathetic. She was immensely charming. She was utterly unselfish. She excelled in the difficult arts of family life. She sacrificed herself daily.

If there was chicken, she took the leg; if there was a draught she sat in it—in short she was so constituted that she never had a mind or a wish of her own, but preferred to sympathize always with the minds and wishes of others. Above all—I need not say it—she was pure. Her purity was supposed to be her chief beauty—her blushes, her great grace. In those days—the last of Queen Victoria—every house had its Angel. And when I came to write I encountered her with the very first words. The shadow of her wings fell on my page; I heard the rustling of her skirts in the room. Directly, that is to say, I took my pen in my hand to review that novel by a famous man, she slipped behind me and whispered: "My dear, you are a young woman. You are writing about a book that has been written by a man. Be sympathetic; be tender; flatter; deceive; use all the arts and wiles of our sex. Never let anybody guess that you have a mind of your own. Above all, be pure." And she made as if to guide my pen. I now record the one act for which I take some credit to myself, though the credit rightly belongs to some excellent ancestors of mine who left me a certain sum of money—shall we say five hundred pounds a year?—so that it was not necessary for me to depend solely on charm for my living. I turned upon her and caught her by the throat. I did my best to kill her. My excuse if I were to be had up at a court of law, would be that I acted in self-defense. Had I not killed her she would have killed me. She would have plucked the heart out of my writing. For as I found directly, as I put pen to paper, you cannot review even a novel without having a mind of your own, without expressing what you think to be the truth about human relations, morality, sex. And all these questions, according to the Angel of the House cannot be dealt with freely and openly by women; they must charm, they must conciliate, they must—to put it bluntly—tell lies if they are to succeed. Thus, whenever I felt the shadow of her wing or the radiance of her halo upon my page, I took up the inkpot and flung it at her. She died hard. Her fictitious nature was of great assistance to her. It is far harder to kill a phantom than a reality. She was always creeping back when I thought I had dispatched her. Though I flatter myself that I killed her in the end, the struggle was severe; it took much time that

Woolf is more explicit about her claim here: The "Angel," if not killed, will pluck the heart out of a woman's writing.

The *data* (grounds) Woolf uses to support her claim: Women writers are forced to conciliate, tell lies.

had better have been spent upon learning Greek grammar; or in roaming the world in search of adventures. But it was a real experience; it was an experience that was bound to befall all women writers at that time. Killing the Angel in the House was part of the occupation of a woman writer.

Woolf's *warrant*, implied here, is that women writers must be free to be themselves, whatever that might be.

But to continue my story. The Angel was dead; what then remained? You may say that what remained was a simple and common object—a young woman in a bed-room with an inkpot. In other words, now that she had rid herself of falsehood, that young woman had only to be herself. Ah, but what is "herself"? I mean, what is a woman? I assure you, I do not know. I do not believe that you know. I do not believe that anybody can know until she has expressed herself in all the arts and profes-sions open to human skill. That indeed is one of the rea-sons why I have come here—out of respect for you, who are in process of showing us by your experiments what a woman is, who are in process of providing us, by your failures and successes, with that extremely important piece of information.

But to continue the story of my professional experi-ences. I made one pound ten and six by my first review; and I bought a Persian cat with the proceeds. Then I grew ambitious. A Persian cat is all very well, I said; but a Per-sian cat is not enough. I must have a motor-car. And it was thus that I became a novelist—for it is a very strange thing that people will give you a motor-car if you will tell them a story. It is a still stranger thing that there is nothing so delightful in the world as telling stories. It is far pleasanter than writing reviews of famous novels. And yet, if I am to obey your secretary and tell you my professional experiences as a novelist, I must tell you about a very strange experience that befell me as a nov-elist. And to understand it you must try first to imagine a novelist's state of mind. I hope I am not giving away professional secrets if I say that a novelist's chief desire is to be as unconscious as possible. He has to induce in himself a state of perpetual lethargy. He wants life to pro-ceed with the utmost quiet and regularity. He wants to see the same faces, to read the same books, to do the same things day after day, month after month, while he is writ-ing, so that nothing may break the illusion in which he is living—so that nothing may disturb or disquiet the mys-terious nosings about, feelings round, darts, dashes, and sudden discoveries of that very shy and illusive spirit, the imagination. I suspect that this state is the same both for men and women. Be that as it may, I want you to imagine me writing a novel in a state of trance. I want you to figure to yourselves a girl sitting with a pen in her hand, which for minutes, and indeed for hours, she never dips into the inkpot. The image that comes to my mind when I think of this girl is the image of a fisherman lying sunk in dreams on the verge of a deep lake with a rod held out over the water. She was letting her imagination sweep unchecked round every rock and cranny of the world that lies submerged in the depths of our unconscious being. Now came the experience that I believe to be far commoner with women writers than with men. The line raced through the girl's fingers. Her imagination had rushed away. It had sought the pools, the depths, the dark places where the largest fish slumber. And then there was a smash. There was an explosion. There was foam and confusion. The imagination had dashed itself against something hard. The girl was roused from her dream. She was indeed in a state of the most acute and difficult distress. To speak without figure, she had thought of something, something about the body, about the passion, which it was unfitting for her as a woman to say. Men, her reason told her, would be shocked. The consciousness of what men will say of a woman who speaks the truth about her passions had roused her from her artist's state of unconsciousness. She could write no more. The trance was over. Her imagination could work no longer. This I believe to be a very common experience with women writers—they are impeded by the extreme conventionality of the other sex. For though men sensibly allow themselves great freedom in these respects, I doubt that they realize or can control the extreme severity with which they condemn such freedom in women.

These then were two very genuine experiences of my own. These were two of the adventures of my professional life. The first—killing the Angel in the House—I think I solved. She died. But the second, telling the truth about my own experiences as a body, I do not think I solved. I doubt that any woman has solved it yet. The obstacles against her are still immensely powerful—and yet they are very difficult to define. Outwardly, what is simpler than to write books? Outwardly, what obstacles

To provide backing to her warrant, Woolf describes her own experience as a writer to demonstrate how uncompromising one must be in communicating his or her true convictions.

Woolf qualifies her claim by emphasizing the fact that the obstacles facing women have not yet been overcome.

are there for a woman rather than for a man? Inwardly, I think, the case is very different; she has still many ghosts to fight, many prejudices to overcome. Indeed it will be a long time still, I think, before a woman can sit down to write a book without finding a phantom to be slain, a rock to be dashed against. And if this is so in literature, the freest of all professions for women, how is it in the new professions which you are now for the first time entering?

Those are the questions that I should like, had I time, to ask you. And indeed, if I have laid stress upon these professional experiences of mine, it is because I believe that they are, though in different forms, yours also. Even when the path is nominally open—when there is nothing to prevent a woman from being a doctor, a lawyer, a civil servant—there are many phantoms and obstacles, as I believe, looming in her way. To discuss and define them is I think of great value and importance; for thus only can the labour be shared, the difficulties be solved. But besides this, it is necessary also to discuss the ends and the aims for which we are fighting, for which we are doing battle with these formidable obstacles. Those aims cannot be taken for granted; they must be perpetually questioned and examined. The whole position, as I see it—here in this hall surrounded by women practising for the first time in history I know not how many different professions—is one of extraordinary interest and importance. You have won rooms of your own in the house hitherto exclusively owned by men. You are able, though not without great labour and effort, to pay the rent. You are earning your five hundred pounds a year. But this freedom is only a beginning; the room is your own, but it is still bare. It has to be furnished; it has to be decorated; it has to be shared. How are you going to furnish it, how are you going to decorate it? With whom are you going to share it, and upon what terms? These, I think are questions of the utmost importance and interest. For the first time in history you are able to ask them; for the first time you are able to decide for yourselves what the answers should be. Willingly would I stay and discuss those questions and answers—but not tonight. My time is up; and I must cease. ◎/◎

The Toulmin Model in Action

In contrast to other methods of argument, the Toulmin method foregrounds the ethical or values-based underpinnings of an argument, as we can see in Woolf's "Professions for Women." Not only does Woolf explicitly describe the pressure that female writers of her day experience in order to adhere to male standards of composition and points of view, she also implies that it is unjust for such double standards to continue. As backing for this warrant Woolf draws from her own example of breaking free of the male-writer's paradigm.

Let's consider another example. Imagine that you are a member of a board of ethics whose task it is to decide who is most responsible for smoking-related illnesses: the tobacco industry or individual smokers. Your first step will be to locate the data (evidence) to support your claim. Next, you will look for ethical validation (warrant) of your data, making sure that you have sufficient backing to reinforce your warrant. In the following exercise, then student Daniel Neal has decided to argue that the burden of responsibility lies with the individual smoker.

Exercise 4.1

Read Daniel's argument and then respond to the questions at the end.

```
                        Daniel Neal


            Tobacco: Ignorance Is No Longer an Excuse

    Any individual who chooses to use tobacco today is making an
informed decision. The negative effects of tobacco are known,
admitted, and even advertised by tobacco companies. Simply put,
ignorance is no longer an excuse for smoking. And since the
government has settled with the tobacco companies, ignorance is
no longer an excuse for legal action. Because of the tobacco
settlement, individuals must now be responsible for the conse-
quences of choosing to use tobacco.
    Part of this settlement requires the tobacco companies to
begin "spending hundreds of millions of dollars on efforts to
discourage and deglamorize tobacco use" (Klein 463). Because it
will highlight the dangers of tobacco, some argue that this will
in fact encourage youth tobacco use. Richard Klein holds that
"emphasizing that tobacco is dangerous and disapproved will en-
hance the glamour, prestige, and attractiveness of cigarettes,
```

particularly among the young" (463). Klein's point is valid: Teenagers are attracted to what is dangerous and disapproved. No one
debates that youth tobacco use is undesirable and should be prevented. It is wrong, however, to blame tobacco companies for youth
tobacco use for the simple reason that they are not the ones directly selling it to minors. The tobacco companies cannot be held
accountable for the actions of independent retailers who choose to
sell tobacco to children. Instead of arguing that the settlement
will increase youth tobacco use, those who are concerned should
attack the way teens get tobacco: dishonest retailers willing to
sell tobacco products illegally to minors. The tobacco settlement
has not changed the illegality of underage tobacco use—that minors
may choose to smoke illegally is irrelevant. It is unquestionably
positive, however, that the tobacco settlement will fund education
efforts so that these minors, when adults, can make informed and
responsible decisions about tobacco use.

   Other critics of the settlement feel that the tobacco industry will receive unfair protection from further lawsuits. In her
essay ". . . Or a Payoff to Purveyors of Poison?" Elizabeth M.
Whelan writes:

> Whatever the parties' motivation, the deal that
> resulted gave the tobacco industry a major boost by
> providing limited immunity against future litigation.
> While technically allowing smokers (or their survi-
> vors) to continue to sue cigarette companies for
> damages caused by smoking, the settlement would put
> a yearly cap of $5 billion on damages, an amount that
> is a trivial cost of doing business for the indus-
> try. This cap will serve as a disincentive to future
> plaintiff's attorneys, who will incur enormous costs
> in any challenges they choose to mount against the
> wealthy tobacco companies (467).

   If the dangers of tobacco were still concealed by the tobacco
companies, Whelan's argument would be quite valid. However, that
tobacco use is harmful to one's health is plain knowledge today.

Since anyone considering tobacco use today has been fully informed of the dangers by many sources (including the tobacco industry), how can anyone but that individual be responsible for damages resulting from smoking? While Whelan holds that limited immunity for tobacco companies is a negative thing, it is in fact quite positive: By setting limits on the liability of tobacco companies, the government is forcing individuals to take responsibility for their actions. Later in her essay, Whelan continues: "This is analogous to a scenario in which a corporation admits to polluting the water supply, pays some damages, then returns immediately to dumping toxins down the well—and gets away with it" (467). In this analogy Whelan neglects to include a key participant: the individual choosing to use tobacco. Borrowing her terms, while the well may be toxic, not only is it clearly labeled so, but no one is forced to drink from it. The tobacco settlement is quite fair because it places the responsibility for tobacco use into the hands of the informed consumers who use it.

Instead of continuing to demonize the tobacco industry, we should demand that the individuals who choose to use tobacco take personal responsibility for the damages caused by it. Consider alcohol, a substance harmful both when used as intended (killing brain cells) and when abused (driving while intoxicated, alcohol poisoning, alcoholism, etc.). We have, as a society, accepted the idea of individual responsibility for the consequences of alcohol use. It is time we do the same for tobacco. An individual choosing to smoke today must realize that he or she has been amply warned. By providing the tobacco industry protection against future litigation, the tobacco settlement has justly moved the onus of responsibility from the corporation to the informed consumer.

Works Cited

Klein, Richard. "The Tobacco Deal: Prohibition II . . ." *Wall Street Journal* 26 June 1997: A-18. Print.

Whelan, Elizabeth M. ". . . Or a Payoff to Purveyors of Poison?" Wall Street Journal 26 June 1997: A-18. Print.

1. Identify Daniel's claim, data, warrant, and backing (keeping in mind that the final two may be implied).

2. How effectively does Daniel use the Toulmin method? What might he do differently?

3. Critique Daniel's method of organizing the argument. Which parts of the essay, if any, could he organize more effectively? Why?

Organizing Your Argument Using the Toulmin Model

Preparing to write an argument using the Toulmin model puts you into an intense questioning mode about the nature of your claim, the reliability of your data, and the ethical strength of your warrant and backing.

To begin, write down your claim, data, warrant, and backing. Then jot down questions about each of them. One student, organizing an argument on the hazards of secondhand cigarette smoke, prepares the following list:

My Claim

Secondhand cigarette smoke is hazardous enough to justify prohibiting smoking in all public places.

Questions About My Claim

1. Is it valid? What makes it valid?
2. Is it practical? Can it actually be acted on?
3. Are there qualifications I must make to my claim?
4. What will be some of the possible challenges to my claim?
5. Who could benefit most from accepting my claim? Benefit least or be harmed?

My Data

1. Statistical information from the American Cancer Society, the American Lung Association, and the American Medical Association
2. The most recent Surgeon General's report on secondhand smoke
3. Personal testimonials of those who became seriously ill as a result of long-term exposure to secondhand smoke

Questions About My Data

1. Do I have sufficient data to support my claim?
2. Are there other important sources of information that I have overlooked?
3. Are my data reliable (not biased or manipulated)? Timely? Accurate?
4. How can I test the data for reliability, timeliness, and accuracy?
5. Which data are the most compelling? Least compelling?

My Warrant

It is more important for people to have the freedom to breathe clean air than for smokers to have the freedom to befoul the air.

Questions About My Warrant

1. Do I really believe that "freedom" in the context of smoking has to be qualified to include freedom from encroaching on one's right to breathe smoke-free air?
2. What other warrants might underlie the one I have identified? Am I too intolerant of smokers? Am I exaggerating the seriousness of the problem?
3. Am I prepared to stand behind my warrant, regardless of how others might challenge it?

My Backing

Freedom from things that cause distress in others is more important than freedom to do things that cause distress in others.

Questions About My Backing

1. Does my backing apply in all cases? For example, does ambient smoke <u>always</u> cause distress in others?
2. What makes me so sure that "freedom from" things that might cause distress is <u>more</u> important than "freedom to do" things that might cause distress?

The student then prepares the following tentative outline based on this list:

Thesis

Because secondhand smoke is so hazardous, smoking should be banned from all public facilities.

I. Introduction: The problem of secondhand smoke

    A. First example: Woman breathes in secondhand smoke in a restaurant and has an asthma attack

    B. Second example: Child in a shopping mall, allergic to secondhand smoke, becomes seriously ill when a group of smoking teens pass by him

    C. Claim, with allusions to underlying warrants, that secondhand smoke is hazardous enough to justify banning smoking from all public places

II. Data in support of the claim

    A. Scientific data from ACS, ALA, and AMA + discussion of data

    B. Testimonial data from physicians + discussion

III. Deeper considerations (warrants and backing) behind the claim

[*Note:* This discussion would approximate refutation in the classical model but would give more emphasis to a shared value system with the audience.]

IV. Concluding remarks

◎⁄◎   Exercise 4.2

1. For each of the following claims, suggest at least one qualifier, two kinds of evidence, and one warrant for which you may also discover backing. Also suggest a counterclaim with counterdata and a counterwarrant for each.

    a. Our mayor should be removed from office because we just learned that he was once arrested for possession of marijuana.

    b. Any novel that includes the use of racial slurs should be banned from public school classrooms.

    c. Beef in restaurants should be prepared well-done regardless of customer preference because of the danger of *E. coli* infection.

2. Work up two versions of an outline for an essay on improving conditions where you live. Use the Classical model to structure the first outline and the Toulmin model to structure the second. Which of the two outlines would you use as the basis for the paper, and why?

3. Rewrite each of the following claims by using more specific terms or references. *Example:* UFO sightings are a bunch of nonsense. *Rewrite:* UFO sightings are difficult to document because trick photography is easy to accomplish.

    a. Books are an environmental problem.

    b. Cats make better pets than dogs.

    c. Students should be admitted to college on the basis of merit only.

4. Suggest one or two possible warrants for each of the following claims:

   a. All college students should be required to take at least one course in economics.

   b. More college courses should be conducted over the Internet.

   c. High school sex-education courses are inadequate.

5. Suggest at least one backing for the warrants you proposed in question 4.

◎/◎   **Exercise 4.3**

Read Thomas Jefferson's Declaration of Independence and identify its claim, data, warrant, and backing.

Declaration of Independence | Thomas Jefferson

When in the Course of human events, it becomes necessary for one people to dissolve the political bands which have connected them with another, and to assume among the Powers of the earth, the separate and equal station to which the Laws of Nature and of Nature's God entitle them, a decent respect to the opinions of mankind requires that they should declare the causes which impel them to the separation.—We hold these truths to be self-evident, that all men are created equal, that they are endowed by their Creator with certain unalienable Rights, that among these are Life, Liberty and the pursuit of Happiness.—That to secure these rights, Governments are instituted among Men, deriving their just powers from the consent of the governed.—That whenever any Form of Government becomes destructive of these ends, it is the Right of the People to alter or to abolish it, and to institute new Government, laying its foundation on such principles and organizing its powers in such form, as to them shall seem most likely to effect their Safety and Happiness. Prudence, indeed, will dictate that Governments long established should not be changed for light and transient causes; and accordingly all experience hath shewn, that mankind are more disposed to suffer, while evils are sufferable, than to right themselves by abolishing the forms to which they are accustomed. But when a long train of abuses and usurpations, pursing invariably the same Object evinces a design to reduce them under absolute Despotism, it is their right, it is their duty, to throw off such Government, and to provide new Guards for their future security.—Such has been the patient sufferance of these Colonies; and such is now the necessity which constrains them to alter their former Systems of Government. The history of the present King of Great Britain is a history of repeated injuries and usurpations, all having in direct object the establishment of an absolute Tyranny over these States. To prove this, let Facts be submitted to a candid world.—He has refused his Assent to Laws, the most wholesome and necessary for the public good.—He has forbidden his Governors to pass.

Laws of immediate and pressing importance, unless suspended in their operation till his Assent should be obtained; and when so suspended, he has utterly neglected to attend to them.—He has refused to pass other Laws for the accommodation of large districts of people, unless those people would relinquish the right of Representation in the Legislature, a right inestimable to them and formidable to tyrants only.—He has called together legislative bodies at places unusual, uncomfortable, and distant from the depository of their public Records, for the sole purpose of fatiguing them into compliance with his measures.—He has dissolved Representative Houses repeatedly, for opposing with manly firmness his invasions of the rights of the people.— He has refused for a long time, after such dissolutions, to cause others to be elected; whereby the Legislative powers, incapable of Annihilation, have returned to the People at large for their exercise; the State remaining in the mean time exposed to all the dangers of invasion from without, and convulsions within.—He has endeavoured to prevent the population of these States; for that purpose obstructing the Laws of Naturalization of Foreigners; refusing to pass others to encourage their migrations hither, and raising the conditions of new Appropriations of Lands.—He has obstructed the Administration of Justice, by refusing his Assent to Laws for establishing Judiciary powers.—He has made Judges dependent on his Will alone, for the tenure of their offices, and the amount and payment of their salaries.—He has erected a multitude of New Offices, and sent hither swarms of Officers to harass our people, and eat out their substance.—He has kept among us, in times of peace, Standing Armies without the Consent of our legislatures.— He has affected to render the Military independent of and superior to the Civil power.—He has combined with others to subject us to a jurisdiction foreign to our constitution, and unacknowledged by our laws; giving his Assent to their Acts of pretended Legislation:—For quartering large bodies of armed troops among us:—For protecting them, by a mock Trial, from punishment for any Murders which they should commit on the Inhabitants of these States:—For cutting off our Trade with all parts of the world:—For imposing Taxes on us without our Consent:—For depriving us in many cases, of the benefits of Trial by Jury:—For transporting us beyond Seas to be tried for pretended offences:—For abolishing the free System of English Laws in a neighbouring Province, establishing therein an Arbitrary government, and enlarging its Boundaries so as to render it at once an example and fit instrument for introducing the same absolute rule into these Colonies:—For taking away our Charters, abolishing our most valuable Laws, and altering fundamentally the Forms of our Governments:—For suspending our own

Legislatures, and declaring themselves invested with power to legislate for us in all cases whatsoever.—He has abdicated Government here, by declaring us out of his Protection and waging War against us.—He has plundered our seas, ravaged our Coasts, burnt our towns, and destroyed the Lives of our people.—He is at this time transporting large Armies of foreign Mercenaries to complete the works of death, desolation and tyranny, already begun with circumstances of Cruelty and perfidy scarcely paralleled in the most barbarous ages, and totally unworthy the Head of a civilized nation.—He has constrained our fellow Citizens taken Captive on the high Seas to bear Arms against their Country, to become the executioners of their friends and Brethren, or to fall themselves by their Hands.— He has excited domestic insurrections amongst us, and has endeavoured to bring on the inhabitants of our frontiers, the merciless Indian Savages, whose known rule of warfare, is an undistinguished destruction of all ages, sexes, and conditions. In every stage of these Oppressions We have Petitioned for Redress in the most humble terms: Our repeated Petitions have been answered only by repeated injury. A Prince, whose character is thus marked by every act which may define a Tyrant, is unfit to be the ruler of a free people. Nor have We been wanting in attentions to our British brethren. We have warned them from time to time of attempts by their legislature to extend an unwarrantable jurisdiction over us. We have reminded them of the circumstances of our emigration and settlement here. We have appealed to their native justice and magnanimity, and we have conjured them by the ties of our common kindred to disavow these usurpations, which, would inevitably interrupt our connections and correspondence. They too have been deaf to the voice of justice and of consanguinity. We must, therefore, acquiesce in the necessity, which denounces our Separation, and hold them, as we hold the rest of mankind, Enemies in War, in Peace Friends.—

We, therefore, the Representatives of the *United States of America*, in General Congress, Assembled, appealing to the Supreme Judge of the world for the rectitude of our intentions, do, in the Name, and by Authority of the good People of these Colonies, solemnly publish and declare, That these United Colonies are, and of Right ought to be *Free and Independent States;* that they are Absolved from all Allegiance to the British Crown, and that all political connection between them and the State of Great Britain, is and ought to be totally dissolved; and that as Free and Independent States, they have full Power to levy War, conclude Peace, contract Alliances, establish Commerce, and to do all other Acts and Things which Independent States may of right do.—And for the support of this Declaration, with a firm reliance on the protection of divine Providence, we mutually pledge to each other our Lives, our Fortunes and our sacred Honor. ◎/◎

FIGURE 4.2

Toulmin Model
Flowchart

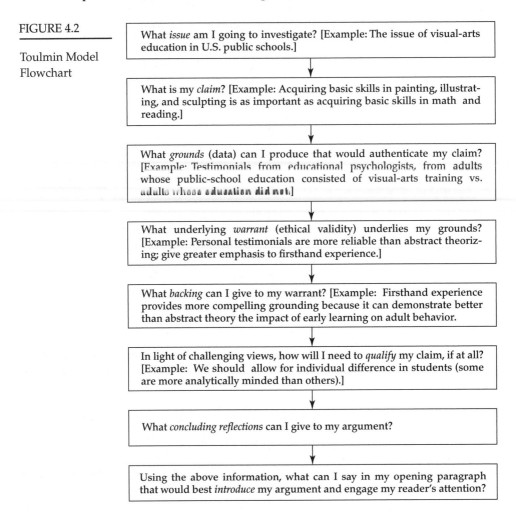

What *issue* am I going to investigate? [Example: The issue of visual-arts education in U.S. public schools.]

What is my *claim*? [Example: Acquiring basic skills in painting, illustrating, and sculpting is as important as acquiring basic skills in math and reading.]

What *grounds* (data) can I produce that would authenticate my claim? [Example: Testimonials from educational psychologists, from adults whose public-school education consisted of visual-arts training vs. adults whose education did not.]

What underlying *warrant* (ethical validity) underlies my grounds? [Example: Personal testimonials are more reliable than abstract theorizing; give greater emphasis to firsthand experience.]

What *backing* can I give to my warrant? [Example: Firsthand experience provides more compelling grounding because it can demonstrate better than abstract theory the impact of early learning on adult behavior.

In light of challenging views, how will I need to *qualify* my claim, if at all? [Example: We should allow for individual difference in students (some are more analytically minded than others).]

What *concluding reflections* can I give to my argument?

Using the above information, what can I say in my opening paragraph that would best *introduce* my argument and engage my reader's attention?

Reinforcing the Toulmin Model with Visuals

Visuals can reinforce a Toulmin-type argument in at least three ways: they can help readers visualize a claim, help readers better comprehend the data, and/or heighten awareness of the warrant. Let's consider adding illustrations to the Declaration of Independence (pages 145–147) in order to reinforce the warrant that the policies of the King of Great Britain against the American Colonists are morally wrong. What kinds of visuals would you paste into it, and where, that would reinforce the Declaration's argument? Here are two possibilities; perhaps you can think of others:

1. To illustrate "He [the King of Great Britain] has made Judges dependent on his Will alone," create a caricature of the King's soldiers muzzling the colonial judges.

2. To illustrate the King's imposition "of taxes on us without our Consent," draw the King as a burglar sneaking out the window of a colonist's home, a bag of money in tow.

◎/◎ Exercise 4.4

Suggest what kinds of visuals might be incorporated (and where) into each of the following articles:

1. "Professions for Women," pages 133–138

2. "Tobacco: Ignorance Is No Longer an Excuse," pages 139–141

3. "Academic Performance of Student Athletes," pages 326–331

Chapter Summary

The Toulmin model of argument goes beyond Classical argument in its efforts to bring values to bear on reasoning. Toulmin argument recognizes that logical reasoning, while necessary, is not enough to resolve complex social issues. For that reason, it is especially suitable in courts of law. The Toulmin argumentation method consists of presenting a carefully articulated claim (thesis to be argued). It recognizes that a claim, whether objective (based on scientific or logical issues) or subjective (based on aesthetic, ethical, or moral issues), must be grounded by data—hard facts, statistics, experimental results, valid testimony, and/or logical analysis, depending upon the nature of the claim. The claim must also be tested for possible qualifiers, exceptions to the rule; this is the rebuttal phase of an argument. Perhaps the most distinctive feature of the Toulmin method of argument is that it does not assume the data to be automatically self-justifying. Instead, the data must rest on one or more warrants, trustworthy foundations that give validity to the data. There must also be assurance—through backing—that the warrants themselves are sound.

Checklist

1. Have I stated my claim clearly and accurately enough for public scrutiny, making sure that it is arguable?

2. Have I added one or more qualifiers to my claim, that is, anticipated possible exceptions to it?

3. Have I included the right kinds of data (evidence) appropriate to my claim in order to support it convincingly?

4. Have I ensured that my data are reliable, timely, accurate, and sufficient for demonstrating the validity and truthfulness of my claim?

5. Have I included one or more warrants to validate the trustworthiness of my data?

6. Have I ensured that my warrants, in turn, are valid? In other words, do my warrants have sufficient backing?

Writing Projects

1. Prepare an argumentative essay on a topic of your own or your instructor's choosing that follows the Toulmin model. Include a preliminary synopsis of your argument, divided into five sections: (1) your claim; (2) a qualifier to your claim; (3) your data, subdivided into hard facts and reason-based evidence, both objective and subjective; (4) your warrant, which renders your data trustworthy; (5) your backing, which reinforces and legitimizes the warrant.

2. Write a Toulmin-based argument in which you defend or challenge the view that anyone elected to public office (mayor, governor, secretary of state, president of the United States, and so on) is obliged to live a morally exemplary life. Be sure to define "morally exemplary."

5 | The Rogerian Model of Argument

> The relationship which I have found helpful is character-
> ized by . . . an acceptance of [the] other person as a separate
> person with value in his own right, and by a deep
> empathic understanding which enables me to see his
> private world through his eyes.
>   —Carl Rogers

CONSIDERING THE DISCIPLINES

If you read the lyrics to Lady Gaga's "Born This Way" (available at http://www.ladygaga
.com/lyrics), you may find that the song is not quite as confrontational as the music video
may lead a viewer to believe. Or is it? It does take a clear position; but does it leave room at
the table for all to sit, regardless of gender, sexual preference, or economic status? In examining just the lyrics to Lady Gaga's song, does one detect a tolerance for "opposing" viewpoints in an effort to find common ground with those whose values differ from our own?
As this example indicates, argument is not restricted to academic texts or academic fields
or even to print texts; Rogerian argument is sometimes seen in visuals such as television
commercials and may be applicable when one is entering fields such as marketing and communication, among others. This chapter provides an example of the Rogerian approach in
the matter of civil disobedience. In Rogerian persuasion, developed by psychologist Carl
Rogers (1902–1987), the traditional paradigm of argument, with the outcome resulting in
a winner and a loser, is abandoned for a more humanist paradigm of striving for cooperative
interaction. Professionals in a given discipline inevitably bring different values, different
levels of understanding, different agendas, to bear on their views about a topic. In this chapter
the principles of Rogerian argument are explained.

In the last two chapters, we have examined the art of effective argumentation as
it has been practiced in Western culture since ancient times. Classical argument
continues to function as a versatile basis for presenting and defending a point of
view. Toulmin argument has enhanced the dynamics of Classical argument to
meet the complexities of contemporary situations, adding, as you'll recall from
Chapter 4, an ethical emphasis (by way of warrants and their backing) to the
presentation of evidence, an emphasis that is not explicitly included in Classical

argument. Toulmin argument also embraces the complexity of a claim: It must often be qualified, even refuted in certain contexts, by the arguer. This last feature might be regarded as a precursor to the method of modern argument we consider in this chapter: Rogerian argument.

Carl Rogers (1902–1987) was a psychologist of the "humanist" school, seeing cooperative interpersonal relationships as the key to a healthy society. As a therapist, Rogers urged self-realization and believed that to function fully as a person in society, one must be open to new experiences. Rigidity of thought and defensiveness breed intolerance. One way such openness is cultivated is through cooperative methods of communication.

The Rogerian Model of Argument

From Rogers's view, the Classical model of argument and even the more flexible Toulmin model tend to divide people into two camps: proponents and opponents, "good guys" versus "bad guys." The traditional language of argument, for example, is filled with militaristic metaphors: We *win* or *lose* arguments rather than resolve them. We *attack* someone's thesis rather than work to build consensus for resolving points of disagreement. We *marshal* evidence as if gathering troops. Even the seemingly neutral term *debate* is of military origin (from *battre*, "to do battle"). For Rogers, this combative approach to argument does more harm than good; it generates ill will and antagonism between discussants rather than cooperation.

Finding Common Ground

But, you ask, how can people cooperate or interact harmoniously if they hold diametrically opposed views about an issue? Rogers's answer is that you find a common ground and start from there. Returning to the rhetorical rhombus (see Figure 1.2), we see the emphasis here on *audience.* A paper in the Rogerian mode assumes that readers firmly hold differing views and therefore will resist hearing others' positions. Yet no matter how debatable or controversial a view is, one can locate views on the issue on which both can agree. It might take a while to find them, but they are there. Consider the controversy for and against capital punishment, for example:

- Both sides consider human life to be sacred and precious.

- Both sides feel that capital crimes must be deterred as effectively as possible.

- Both sides agree that someone convicted of a capital crime is a threat to society.

The virtue of finding common ground is that one can isolate and resolve the points of opposition more effectively after identifying the points of agreement because one can reduce any hostility the audience has by demonstrating a true understanding of the audience's perspective.

The Rogerian model modifies the Classical model by emphasizing common ground (points of agreement) *before* calling attention to points of disagreement.

The writer's goal is not to win or to prove wrong; it is to work together cooperatively to arrive at an agreed-on truth. From its opening sentence, a Rogerian argument communicates a desire for harmonious interaction rather than combative opposition.

I. Introduction: What is our shared problem? Let's see if we can work together to resolve it.

II. What we agree on.

III. Where we differ: misunderstandings, such as drawbacks or limited application to others' solutions, and the possible reasons behind these drawbacks or limitations.

IV. Possible drawbacks or limitations to writers' solutions, followed by greater benefits of writers' solutions.

V. How we can resolve our differences; or, an exhortation to resolving differences together.

Developing Multiple Perspectives

Rogerian persuasion requires writers to work hard at developing multiple perspectives toward issues. You must be tolerant and respectful enough of differing viewpoints to take the time to fathom the value systems that underlie them. The first step toward achieving this goal, according to Rogers, is deceptively simple: *to listen with understanding.*

Listening with understanding is a skill that takes time to develop. You may think you are listening with understanding when you permit challengers to speak their minds, but you may be only allowing them their say rather than genuinely paying close attention to what they are telling you.

Here are some suggestions for listening with understanding, in Rogers's sense of the phrase, that also can be applied to reading with understanding:

- Be as attentive as possible. Assume that the speaker's remarks have value.

- Suspend your own judgments while listening, keeping an open mind so as not to run the risk of prematurely judging the speaker's views before you have the chance to consider them carefully.

- If anything is unclear to you or you find yourself disagreeing with anything, ask questions—but only after the person has finished speaking.

- Try to see the speaker's claims in terms of his or her warrants (underlying values or ideology on which the claims are based). One better understands and appreciates a speaker's position if one is aware of these warrants.

- Think of ways in which the speaker's point of view and your own can somehow work together, despite seeming contradictory. Even if you oppose capital punishment and the speaker supports it, both of you could approach a common ground by thinking of extreme situations on either side that would discourage an inflexible stance.

Carl Rogers (1902–1987) was known for his "humanist," client-centered approach to therapy. He advocated nonthreatening methods of interpersonal communication.

Using Rogerian argument in conversation is one thing; using it in writing is another. When writing, you do not have your audience in front of you to give you immediate feedback. Instead, you have to anticipate questions and counter-responses that challengers would have for you (in other words, automatically consider the needs of your audience). By considering the audience's needs and values, and the merits of their beliefs, you will be more inclined to take a cooperative stance rather than a defensive or combative one.

Arguing cooperatively also means including in your Rogerian essay specific instances in which the differing views are logically sound. That way, you show yourself to have listened well to those perspectives. This, in turn, prepares your audience for listening more carefully and sympathetically to *your* side of things. You also demonstrate your awareness of the limitations to your proposal—no position is perfect, after all—even while you show how your position works in more varied or complex or more frequent occurrences of the common problem. You and your audience both become receptive to "give and take."

Arguing from Problem to Solution

Because the hallmark of Rogerian argument is working cooperatively with those who would otherwise be characterized as "opponents," the traditional "pro-con" combative stance, more characteristic of classical argument, is replaced by a problem-to-solution approach. Instead of asserting, in effect, "Here's why I'm right and you're wrong," the Rogerian arguer instead asserts, "Let's all of us work together in an effort to reach consensus on identifying the problem, and then determining a mutually satisfactory conclusion."

Now keep in mind that this approach will not *necessarily* vanquish opposition. The point is that the Rogerian arguer considers the issue from different perspectives, from different beliefs or value systems—but without undermining his or her own moral convictions. For example, in his famous "Letter from Birmingham Jail" (see Exercise 5.2), Martin Luther King, Jr., in his effort to establish common ground with his fellow clergymen, reminds them of what they presumably already are committed to, ensuring that human laws be morally consistent with God's laws in order for them to be considered just; and since laws that segregate people on the basis of race are inconsistent with God's unconditional love for humanity, they must be unjust. By means of such reasoning, King is not only reminding his fellow clergymen that they are on the same side, but that they can work together to solve the problem of racial injustice in America.

In brief, then, Rogerian problem-to-solution works like this:

1. The arguer first formulates the problem as a common problem and explains the problem as he or she sees it.

2. The arguer fairly considers the positions of those whose solutions differ from that of the arguer, showing how in some instances and to certain extents, those solutions may be viable, but the arguer then modifies the solution(s) to propose the solution the arguer endorses.

3. The modified problem is then discussed in terms of a mutually satisfying solution, with points of dissent isolated and examined for their flaws in reasoning, inconsistencies, omissions, and so on.

Organizing Your Argument Using the Rogerian Model

To write an argument based on the Rogerian ideals of cooperation, find common ground with your audience regardless of their views about your claim. You need to become especially sensitive to attitudes and values other than your own. You should focus on the *issue* and the best way to resolve it, not on "winning" the argument over your "opposition."

As with the Classical and Toulmin models, begin thinking about your essay with questions about your audience, the similarities between your views and your audience's (insofar as you are aware of them), and the points at which you differ most, along with possible strategies for resolving those differences. Consider these questions:

1. Can I be objective enough to represent views and evaluate evidence fairly?

2. How much sense do the points of difference make? Do they make more sense than some of my views? If so, do I have the courage to adopt them, or at least modify them to accommodate my views?

3. Am I genuinely interested in establishing a common ground with my audience? What else can I include that could better facilitate this goal?

When constructing an outline for a Rogerian argument, think in terms of thesis, support of thesis, and concluding judgments based on that support—just as you do when using the Classical and Toulmin models. But with the Rogerian model, you are more concerned with establishing common ground with readers who otherwise would reject the thesis. Here is how an argument using the Rogerian approach might take shape:

I. Introduction to the problem

   A. First scenario: A vignette that illustrates the problem, for example

   B. Second scenario: Another vignette that illustrates the problem, but one with greater complexity that some solutions would not handle well

   C. Thesis

II. Alternative views worth sharing with the target audience, and why these views are worth considering

III. Points of difference, along with reflection on how to resolve them

IV. Conclusion: The implications of finding a solution in light of the evidence presented that would benefit everyone, plus discussion of the great benefits derived from the solution that all audience members would most likely find to their liking

◎/◎ Exercise 5.1

Read the following essay in which the author uses the Rogerian method to tackle the difficult issue of sexual harassment in the early teen years. Then answer the questions that follow.

Let's Talk about Sexual Harassment in Middle School | Kimberly Shearer Palmer

Like every new employee at the *Washington Post*, I was given a "Codes of Conduct" packet—the company's policies on everything from smoking to taking medical leave.[1] It was the section on sexual harassment that startled me most. Perhaps it shouldn't have. But the

Source: Kimberly Shearer Palmer, "Let's Talk About Sexual Harassment in Middle School," *Social Education*, May–June 2003, p. M2. © National Council for the Social Studies. Reprinted by permission.

prohibition against vulgar jokes and "brushing up against another's body" brought home to me the stark contrast between the informal codes of conduct my friends and I had learned to live by in middle school and what's permissible in the working world today.

The situations are very different, of course: There aren't the same sort of power relationships in school that make harassment such a complex problem in the working world. But, looking back, I'm still left wondering why so many teenagers I knew put up with unwelcome sexual behavior. And why adults consistently turned a blind eye. Twelve years ago, when I was in middle school, overt sexual advances were everyday events and usually overlooked by teachers. Boys grabbed girls' breasts in the stairwells and cafeteria as casually as they would say "hello," and our daily routines were punctuated by unwelcome slaps on the behind.

As it turns out, my experience wasn't unusual. According to the American Association of University Women, 65 percent of girls in public school, grades eight to eleven, say they experience "touching, grabbing, and/or pinching in a sexual way."[2] My friends and I used to let boys touch, grab, and pinch us, and I don't think things have gotten all that much better. Sure, there's greater awareness: today, the districts have a sexual harassment policy that schools rely on and teachers can refer to. But the issue doesn't always reach administrators, much less the students. My recent conversations with today's teenagers suggest that it wasn't just my grade; it wasn't just my school; and it wasn't just back then. Many kids think—as my friends and I did—that the unwanted touching is just flirtation.

I have since learned to fight back when men harass me. In Paris a few years ago, when a guy grabbed my breasts, I shoved him away from me and yelled at him. After that, he left me alone. Now, when I think back to all the times in middle school when I didn't make guys leave me alone, I feel angry. So I decided to go back and find boys from my class and ask them why. I got out my old phone directory and called the same boys who would have been too cool for me to call in middle school. Most had moved, and the listed numbers were no longer valid. The ones I found shared my memories of unwanted touching in the hallways. They are, as far as I can tell,

The shared sex harassment problems children in grades 8 through 11 have faced good boyfriend material. They are by all accounts sensitive and perceptive; my younger sister knows one well, and my close friend at college dated another. I found out they were just as confused as we girls were in those adolescent years.

One old classmate remembers the casual touching. "Even good guys did that," he said. "It wasn't sexual. . . . I don't know what it was. I can't think it's a good thing." He also recalled walking girls to class because they felt threatened. We didn't speak in terms of apologies, but wonderment. It seemed so very strange that touching someone's breasts or bottom in the hallways was considered friendly behavior. Another one of my classmates told me that he remembered the same sorts of things. "Not until tenth grade would guys . . . realize it was not the best way to get a girl to like you," he said. Grabbing girls was normal behavior, we both agreed. It happened in public, in front of teachers. No one told us it was wrong. No one even seemed worried about the possibility of lawsuits, despite the 1992 Supreme Court decision that warned schools they could be held responsible for harassment.[3] Maybe the teachers looked at our sometimes giggly and embarrassed reactions and thought there wouldn't be a problem.

Basis for the
misunderstandings

One male graduate told me that boys bothered girls back then because they didn't know what else to do. "No one knows how to act [at that age]. . . . You're self-conscious, no one has self-esteem." Boys, I realized, were just as insecure as I remember feeling. We were blindly following what we assumed was routine social conduct— grabbing, pinching, being pinched. Who knew there was another way to flirt? Boys, he told me, were just trying to bridge the gap between girls and guys. "It wasn't meant to hurt," he said.

Looking back now, he knows that what some boys did probably bothered some girls. But the girls didn't show it. "They probably didn't want to seem snobby or stuck up," he remembered. As I spoke to these men, I realized how different they were from the guy who bothered me in Paris. The rules were so blurry to both girls and boys in middle school that neither gender really knew when lines were crossed. For example, when my crotch was grabbed on a school bus one afternoon, it wasn't okay with me, but I didn't even tell my parents because at some level it seemed so similar to what happened every day in school. I still feel mad, but I could hardly blame my former classmates when they were just acting out of friendship or flirtation—however misguided that was. And the more I talked with my female friends, the more I realized how often we gave the wrong signals. Some girls remembered enjoying the attention, sometimes laughing along. One recalled two boys dragging her into the boys' bathroom, as she tried to kick her way free. But she didn't remember being angry. "It was the only way to express ourselves," she now says. But something else gave her further pause. She said she thought that "teachers let it slide" like the other dumb behavior that happens among adolescents.

Fault lay with the teachers who avoided dealing with the problem.

They shouldn't have. I remember only one teacher who stood in the front of her class and yelled at the boys for grabbing girls. Finally a teacher noticed, I remember thinking. Why was she the only one? And if the teacher noticed, why didn't she inform the principal, and start a school-wide discussion? My annoyance with my former classmates redirected itself as I realized that adults who could have explained and enforced the differences between right and wrong behavior—our teachers—often did not. The fact is, no one taught us the right way to act. But as Peggy Orenstein, author of *Schoolgirls: Young Women, Self-Esteem, and the Confidence Gap*, says, "It still must stop."[4] For me, it stopped as soon as I emerged from the achingly self-conscious early teenage years. Assertiveness came from the natural confidence that comes with getting rid of braces and glasses.

And yet, would early lessons have done much good?

Shouldn't we have been helped to learn those lessons earlier? An insecure seventh-grade girl shouldn't have to deal with aggressive boys grabbing her. But I keep asking myself: What would I have wanted my parents to tell me? What could they have possibly told me? "Don't let boys touch you"? "Tell me if anyone's bothering you"? I'm sure they told me those things. I'm sure I dismissed them, way too embarrassed to talk to them about anything dealing with boy-girl relationships. How can you help a shy seventh-grade girl who doesn't even know whether to feel grateful for the attention or angry at the violation?

Admission that solutions are difficult

There are no easy solutions. Zero-tolerance policies make no sense, considering the level of confusion surrounding social behavior. Parents can try to teach their daughters to be tough; teachers can integrate into class discussions of what distinguishes flirtation from harassment. There's plenty of inspiration, in anything from the writings of Shakespeare to Maya Angelou, as Wellesley College sexual harassment scholar Nan Stein suggests in *Flirting or Hurting? A Teacher's Guide on Student-to-Student Sexual Harassment in Schools.*[5] And adults can talk to boys about limits.

Yet one thing remains clear

The fact is, my former classmates did not turn into bad men. They don't bother women at work or college. And the women I know in school have also learned where to draw the line. But we should all have learned the rules earlier, well before it comes time to sign those company policies. ◎/◎

Notes

1. This essay first appeared in the *Washington Post* on August 20, 2000. Reprinted by permission.
2. American Association of University Women, *Hostile Hallways: Bullying, Teasing, and Sexual Harassment in School* (Washington: AAUW, 2001).
3. Office of Civil Rights, "Revised Sexual Harassment Guidance" (Washington, DC: U.S. Department of Education, 2001), http://www.ed.gov/offices//OCR/shguide/index.html.
4. Peggy Orenstein, *Schoolgirls: Young Women, Self-Esteem, and the Confidence Gap* (Landover Hills: Anchor, 1995).
5. Nan Stein, *Flirting or Hurting? A Teacher's Guide on Student-to-Student Sexual Harassment in Schools* (Washington, DC: National Education Association, 1994).

1. What rhetorical devices—phrases, words, tone, details—suggest that Palmer is using the Rogerian method of argument?

2. What is most Rogerian about Palmer's approach to her topic? Least Rogerian?

3. Briefly, what is Palmer's position on the matter of sexual harassment in middle school?

4. Critics sometimes say that Rogerian argument is "wishy-washy." Is Palmer being wishy-washy about her middle school experiences with sexual harassment? Why or why not?

5. What, if anything, would you suggest to Palmer to strengthen her argument?

◎/◎ Exercise 5.2

In April 1963, Martin Luther King, Jr., was sentenced to a week in jail because of his antisegregationist campaign in Birmingham, Alabama. While in jail, Dr. King wrote the following letter defending his activities to eight members of the Birmingham clergy. As you read this masterpiece of persuasive writing, notice how King makes a concerted effort to seek common ground with his audience and to avoid the "good guys" versus "bad guys" combative stance. Look for specific points of emphasis and specific explanations that make his stance Rogerian. After reading, answer the questions that follow.

Letter from Birmingham Jail | Martin Luther King, Jr.

April 16, 1963

My Dear Fellow Clergymen:

While confined here in the Birmingham city jail, I came across your recent statement calling my present activities "unwise and untimely."[1] Seldom do I pause to answer criticism of my work and ideas. If I sought to answer all the criticisms that cross my desk, my secretaries would have little time for anything other than such correspondence in the course of the day, and I would have no time for constructive work. But since I feel that you are men of genuine good will and that your criticisms are sincerely set forth, I want to try to answer your statement in what I hope will be patient and reasonable terms.

I think I should indicate why I am here in Birmingham, since you have been influenced by the view which argues against "outsiders coming in." I have the honor of serving as president of the Southern Christian Leadership Conference, an organization operating in every southern state, with headquarters in Atlanta, Georgia. We have some eighty-five affiliated organizations across the South, and one of them is the Alabama Christian Movement for Human Rights. Frequently we share staff, educational, and financial resources with our affiliates. Several months ago the affiliate here in Birmingham asked us to be on call to engage in a nonviolent direct-action program if such were deemed necessary. We readily consented, and when the hour came we lived up to our promise. So I, along with several members of my staff, am here because I was invited here. I am here because I have organizational ties here.

But more basically, I am in Birmingham because injustice is here. Just as the prophets of the eighth century B.C. left their villages and carried their

Source: Martin Luther King Jr., "Letter from Birmingham Jail," April 16, 1963. Reprinted by arrangement with the Heirs to the Estate of Martin Luther King Jr., c/o Writers House as agent for the proprietor, New York, NY. Copyright 1963 Dr. Martin Luther King Jr., copyright renewed 1991 Coretta Scott King.

"thus saith the Lord" far beyond the boundaries of their home towns, and just as the Apostle Paul left his village of Tarsus and carried the gospel of Jesus Christ to the far corners of the Greco-Roman world, so am I compelled to carry the gospel of freedom beyond my own home town. Like Paul, I must constantly respond to the Macedonian call for aid.

Moreover, I am cognizant of the interrelatedness of all communities and states. I cannot sit idly by in Atlanta and not be concerned about what happens in Birmingham. Injustice anywhere is a threat to justice everywhere. We are caught in an inescapable network of mutuality, tied in a single garment of destiny. Whatever affects one directly, affects all indirectly. Never again can we afford to live with the narrow, provincial "outside agitator" idea. Anyone who lives inside the United States can never be considered an outsider anywhere within its bounds.

You deplore the demonstrations taking place in Birmingham. But your statement, I am sorry to say, fails to express a similar concern for the conditions that brought about the demonstrations. I am sure that none of you would want to rest content with the superficial kind of social analysis that deals merely with effects and does not grapple with underlying causes. It is unfortunate that demonstrations are taking place in Birmingham, but it is even more unfortunate that the city's white power structure left the Negro community with no alternative.

In any nonviolent campaign there are four basic steps: collection of the facts to determine whether injustices exist; negotiation; self-purification; and direct action. We have gone through all these steps in Birmingham. There can be no gainsaying the fact that racial injustice engulfs this community. Birmingham is probably the most thoroughly segregated city in the United States. Its ugly record of brutality is widely known. Negroes have experienced grossly unjust treatment in the courts. There have been more unsolved bombings of Negro homes and churches in Birmingham than in any other city in the nation. These are the hard, brutal facts of the case. On the basis of these conditions, Negro leaders sought to negotiate with the city fathers. But the latter consistently refused to engage in good-faith negotiation.

Then, last September, came the opportunity to talk with leaders of Birmingham's economic community. In the course of the negotiations, certain promises were made by the merchants—for example, to remove the stores' humiliating racial signs. On the basis of these promises, the Reverend Fred Shuttlesworth and the leaders of the Alabama Christian Movement for Human Rights agreed to a moratorium on all demonstrations. As the weeks and months went by, we realized that we were the victims of a broken promise. A few signs, briefly removed, returned; the others remained.

As in so many past experiences, our hopes had been blasted, and the shadow of deep disappointment settled upon us. We had no alternative except to prepare for direct action, whereby we would present our very bodies as a means of laying our case before the conscience of the local and the national community. Mindful of the difficulties involved, we decided to undertake a process of self-purification. We began a series of workshops on nonviolence, and we repeatedly asked ourselves: "Are you able to accept blows without retaliating?" "Are you able to endure the ordeal of jail?" We decided to schedule our direct-action program for the Easter season, realizing that except for Christmas, this is the main shopping period of the year. Knowing that a strong economic-withdrawal program would be the byproduct of direct action, we felt that this would be the best time to bring pressure to bear on the merchants for the needed change.

Then it occurred to us that Birmingham's mayoralty election was coming up in March, and we speedily decided to postpone action until after election day. When we discovered that the Commissioner of Public Safety, Eugene "Bull" Connor, had piled up enough votes to be in the run-off, we decided again to postpone action until the day after the run-off so that the demonstrations could not be used to cloud the issues. Like many others, we waited to see Mr. Connor defeated, and to this end we endured postponement after postponement. Having aided in this community need, we felt that our direct-action program could be delayed no longer.

You may well ask: "Why direct action? Why sit-ins, marches, and so   10 forth? Isn't negotiation a better path?" You are quite right in calling for negotiation. Indeed, this is the very purpose of direct action. Nonviolent direct action seeks to create such a crisis and foster such a tension that a community which has constantly refused to negotiate is forced to confront the issue. It seeks so to dramatize the issue that it can no longer be ignored. My citing the creation of tension as part of the work of the nonviolent-resister may sound rather shocking. But I must confess that I am not afraid of the word "tension." I have earnestly opposed violent tension, but there is a type of constructive, nonviolent tension which is necessary for growth. Just as Socrates felt that it was necessary to create a tension in the mind so that individuals could rise from the bondage of myths and half-truths to the unfettered realm of creative analysis and objective appraisal, so must we see the need for nonviolent gad-flies to create the kind of tension in society that will help men rise from the dark depths of prejudice and racism to the majestic heights of understanding and brotherhood.

The purpose of our direct-action program is to create a situation so crisis-packed that it will inevitably open the door to negotiation. I therefore concur with you in your call for negotiation. Too long has our beloved Southland been bogged down in a tragic effort to live in monologue rather than dialogue.

One of the basic points in your statement is that the action that I and my associates have taken in Birmingham is untimely. Some have asked: "Why didn't you give the new city administration time to act?" The only answer that I can give to this query is that the new Birmingham administration must be prodded about as much as the outgoing one, before it will act. We are sadly mistaken if we feel that the election of Albert Boutwell as mayor will bring the millennium to Birmingham. While Mr. Boutwell is a much more gentle person than Mr. Connor, they are both segregationists, dedicated to maintenance of the status quo. I have hope that Mr. Boutwell will be reasonable enough to see the futility of massive resistance to desegregation. But he will not see this without pressure from devotees of civil rights. My friends, I must say to you that we have not made a single gain in civil rights without determined legal and nonviolent pressure. Lamentably, it is an historical fact that privileged groups seldom give up their privileges voluntarily. Individuals may see the moral light and voluntarily give up their unjust posture; but as Reinhold Niebuhr[2] has reminded us, groups tend to be more immoral than individuals.

We know through painful experience that freedom is never voluntarily given by the oppressor; it must be demanded by the oppressed. Frankly, I have yet to engage in a direct-action campaign that was "well timed" in the view of those who have not suffered unduly from the disease of segregation. For years now I have heard the word "Wait!" It rings in the ear of every Negro with piercing familiarity. This "Wait" has almost always meant "Never." We must come to see, with one of our distinguished jurists, that "justice too long delayed is justice denied."[3]

We have waited for more than 340 years for our constitutional and God-given rights. The nations of Asia and Africa are moving with jetlike speed toward gaining political independence, but we still creep at horse-and-buggy pace toward gaining a cup of coffee at a lunch counter. Perhaps it is easy for those who have never felt the stinging darts of segregation to say, "Wait." But when you have seen vicious mobs lynch your mothers and fathers at will and drown your sisters and brothers at whim; when you have seen hate-filled policemen curse, kick, and even kill your black brothers and sisters; when you see the vast majority of your twenty million Negro brothers smothering in an airtight cage of poverty in the midst of an affluent society; when you suddenly find your tongue twisted and your speech stammering as you seek to explain to your six-year-old daughter why she can't go to the public amusement park that has just been advertised on television, and see tears welling up in her eyes when she is told that Funtown is closed to colored children, and see ominous clouds of inferiority beginning to form in her little mental sky, and see her beginning to distort her personality by developing an unconscious bitterness toward white people; when you have to concoct an answer for a five-year-old son who is asking: "Daddy, why do white people treat colored people so mean?"; when you take a cross-country drive and find it necessary to sleep night after night in the uncomfortable corners of your automobile because no motel will accept you; when you are humiliated day in and day out by nagging signs reading "white" and "colored"; when your first name becomes "nigger," your middle name becomes "boy" (however old you are) and your last name becomes "John," and your wife and mother are never given the respected title "Mrs."; when you are harried by day and haunted by night by the fact that you are a Negro, living constantly at tiptoe stance, never quite knowing what to expect next, and are plagued with inner fears and outer resentments; when you are forever fighting a degenerating sense of "nobodiness"—then you will understand why we find it difficult to wait. There comes a time when the cup of endurance runs over, and men are no longer willing to be plunged into the abyss of despair. I hope, sirs, you can understand our legitimate and unavoidable impatience.

You express a great deal of anxiety over our willingness to break laws.   15 This is certainly a legitimate concern. Since we so diligently urge people to obey the Supreme Court's decision of 1954 outlawing segregation in the public schools, at first glance it may seem rather paradoxical for us consciously to break laws. One may well ask: "How can you advocate breaking some laws and obeying others?" The answer lies in the fact that there are two types of laws: just and unjust. I would be the first to advocate obeying just laws. One has not only a legal but a moral responsibility to obey just laws. Conversely, one has a moral responsibility to disobey unjust laws. I would agree with St. Augustine that "an unjust law is no law at all."

Now, what is the difference between the two? How does one determine whether a law is just or unjust? A just law is a man-made code that squares with the moral law or the law of God. An unjust law is a code that is out of harmony with the moral law. To put it in the terms of St. Thomas Aquinas: An unjust law is a human law that is not rooted in eternal law and natural law. Any law that uplifts human personality is just. Any law that degrades human personality is unjust. All segregation statutes are unjust because segregation distorts the soul and damages the personality. It gives the segregator a false sense of superiority and the segregated a false sense of inferiority. Segregation, to use the terminology of the Jewish philosopher Martin Buber, substitutes an "I-it" relationship for an "I-thou" relationship and ends up relegating persons to the status of things. Hence segregation is not only politically, economically, and sociologically unsound, it is morally wrong and sinful. Paul Tillich[4] has said that sin is separation. Is not segregation an existential expression of man's tragic separation, his awful estrangement, his terrible sinfulness? Thus it is that I can urge men to obey the 1954 decision of the Supreme Court, for it is morally right; and I can urge them to disobey segregation ordinances, for they are morally wrong.

Let us consider a more concrete example of just and unjust laws. An unjust law is a code that a numerical or power majority group compels a minority group to obey but does not make binding on itself. This is *difference* made legal. By the same token, a just law is a code that a majority compels a minority to follow and that it is willing to follow itself. This is *sameness* made legal.

Let me give another explanation. A law is unjust if it is inflicted on a minority that, as a result of being denied the right to vote, had no part in enacting or devising the law. Who can say that the legislature of Alabama which set up that state's segregation laws was democratically elected? Throughout Alabama all sorts of devious methods are used to prevent Negroes from becoming registered voters, and there are some counties in which, even though Negroes constitute a majority of the population, not a single Negro is registered. Can any law enacted under such circumstances be considered democratically structured?

Sometimes a law is just on its face and unjust in its application. For instance, I have been arrested on a charge of parading without a permit. Now, there is nothing wrong in having an ordinance which requires a permit for a parade. But such an ordinance becomes unjust when it is used to maintain segregation and to deny citizens the First Amendment privilege of peaceful assembly and protest.

I hope you are able to see the distinction I am trying to point out. In no   20 sense do I advocate evading or defying the law, as would the rabid segregationist. That would lead to anarchy. One who breaks an unjust law must do so openly, lovingly, and with a willingness to accept the penalty. I submit that an individual who breaks a law that conscience tells him is unjust, and who willingly accepts the penalty of imprisonment in order to arouse the conscience of the community over its injustice, is in reality expressing the highest respect for law.

Of course, there is nothing new about this kind of civil disobedience. It was evidenced sublimely in the refusal of Shadrach, Meshach, and Abednego to obey the laws of Nebuchadnezzar, on the ground that a higher moral law was at stake. It was practiced superbly by the early Christians, who were willing to face hungry lions and the excruciating pain of chopping blocks rather than submit to certain unjust laws of the Roman Empire. To a degree, academic freedom is a reality today because Socrates practiced civil disobedience. In our own nation, the Boston Tea Party represented a massive act of civil disobedience.

We should never forget that everything Adolf Hitler did in Germany was "legal" and everything the Hungarian freedom fighters did in Hungary was "illegal." It was "illegal" to aid and comfort a Jew in Hitler's Germany. Even so, I am sure that, had I lived in Germany at the time, I would have aided and comforted my Jewish brothers. If today I lived in a Communist country where certain principles dear to the Christian faith are suppressed, I would openly advocate disobeying that country's anti-religious laws.

I must make two honest confessions to you, my Christian and Jewish brothers. First, I must confess that over the past few years I have been gravely disappointed with the white moderate. I have almost reached the regrettable conclusion that the Negro's great stumbling block in his stride toward freedom is not the White Citizen's Counciler or the Ku Klux Klanner, but the white moderate, who is more devoted to "order" than to justice; who prefers a negative peace which is the absence of tension to a positive peace which is the presence of justice; who constantly says: "I agree with you in the goal you seek, but I cannot agree with your methods of direct action"; who paternalistically believes he can set the timetable for another man's freedom; who lives by a mythical concept of time and who constantly advises the Negro to wait for a "more convenient season." Shallow understanding from people of good will is more frustrating than absolute misunderstanding from people of ill will. Lukewarm acceptance is much more bewildering than outright rejection.

I had hoped that the white moderate would understand that law and order exist for the purpose of establishing justice and that when they fail in this purpose they become the dangerously structured dams that block the flow of social progress. I had hoped that the white moderate would understand that the present tension in the South is a necessary phase of the transition from an obnoxious negative peace, in which the Negro passively accepted his unjust plight, to a substantive and positive peace, in which all men will respect the dignity and worth of human personality. Actually, we who engage in nonviolent direct action are not the creators of tension. We merely bring to the surface the hidden tension that is already alive. We bring it out in the open, where it can be seen and dealt with. Like a boil that can never be cured so long as it is covered up but must be opened with all its ugliness to the natural medicines of air and light, injustice must be exposed, with all the tension its exposure creates, to the light of human conscience and the air of national opinion before it can be cured.

In your statement you assert that our actions, even though peaceful, must be condemned because they precipitate violence. But is this a logical assertion? Isn't this like condemning a robbed man because his possession of money precipitated the evil act of robbery? Isn't this like condemning Socrates because his unswerving commitment to truth and his philosophical inquiries precipitated the act by the misguided populace in which they made him drink hemlock? Isn't this like condemning Jesus because his unique God-consciousness and never-ceasing devotion to God's will precipitated the evil act of crucifixion? We must come to see that, as the federal courts have consistently affirmed, it is wrong to urge an individual to cease his efforts to gain his basic constitutional rights because the quest may precipitate violence. Society must protect the robbed and punish the robber.

I had also hoped that the white moderate would reject the myth concerning time in relation to the struggle for freedom. I have just received a letter from a white brother in Texas. He writes: "All Christians know that the colored people will receive equal rights eventually, but it is possible that you are in too great a religious hurry. It has taken Christianity almost two thousand years to accomplish what it has. The teachings of Christ take time to come to earth." Such an attitude stems from a tragic misconception of time, from the strangely irrational notion that there is something in the very flow of time that will inevitably cure all ills. Actually, time itself is neutral; it can be used either

25

destructively or constructively. More and more I feel that the people of ill will have used time much more effectively than have the people of good will. We will have to repent in this generation not merely for the hateful words and actions of the bad people but for the appalling silence of the good people. Human progress never rolls in on wheels of inevitability; it comes through the tireless efforts of men willing to be co-workers with God, and without this hard work, time itself becomes an ally of the forces of social stagnation. We must use time creatively, in the knowledge that the time is always ripe to do right. Now is the time to make real the promise of democracy and transform our pending national elegy into a creative psalm of brotherhood. Now is the time to lift our national policy from the quicksand of racial injustice to the solid rock of human dignity.

You speak of our activity in Birmingham as extreme. At first I was rather disappointed that fellow clergymen would see my nonviolent efforts as those of an extremist. I began thinking about the fact that I stand in the middle of two opposing forces in the Negro community. One is a force of complacency, made up in part of Negroes who, as a result of long years of oppression, are so drained of self-respect and a sense of "somebodiness" that they have adjusted to segregation; and in part of a few middle-class Negroes who, because of a degree of academic and economic security and because in some ways they profit by segregation, have become insensitive to the problems of the masses. The other force is one of bitterness and hatred, and it comes perilously close to advocating violence. It is expressed in the various black nationalist groups that are springing up across the nation, the largest and best-known being Elijah Muhammad's Muslim movement. Nourished by the Negro's frustration over the continued existence of racial discrimination, this movement is made up of people who have lost faith in America, who have absolutely repudiated Christianity, and who have concluded that the white man is an incorrigible "devil."

I have tried to stand between these two forces, saying that we need emulate neither the "do-nothingism" of the complacent nor the hatred and despair of the black nationalist. For there is the more excellent way of love and nonviolent protest. I am grateful to God that, through the influence of the Negro church, the way of nonviolence became an integral part of our struggle.

If this philosophy had not emerged, by now many streets of the South would, I am convinced, be flowing with blood. And I am further convinced that if our white brothers dismiss as "rabble-rousers" and "outside agitators" those of us who employ nonviolent direct action, and if they refuse to support our nonviolent efforts, millions of Negroes will, out of frustration and despair, seek solace and security in black-nationalist ideologies—a development that would inevitably lead to a frightening racial nightmare.

Oppressed people cannot remain oppressed forever. The yearning for freedom eventually manifests itself, and that is what has happened to the   30

American Negro. Something within has reminded him of his birthright of freedom, and something without has reminded him that it can be gained. Consciously or unconsciously, he has been caught up by the *Zeitgeist*,[5] and with his black brothers of Africa and his brown and yellow brothers of Asia, South America, and the Caribbean, the United States Negro is moving with a sense of great urgency toward the promised land of racial justice. If one recognizes this vital urge that has engulfed the Negro community, one should readily understand why public demonstrations are taking place. The Negro has many pent-up resentments and latent frustrations, and he must release them. So let him march; let him make prayer pilgrimages to the city hall; let him go on freedom rides—and try to understand why he must do so. If his repressed emotions are not released in nonviolent ways, they will seek expression through violence; this is not a threat but a fact of history. So I have not said to my people: "Get rid of your discontent." Rather, I have tried to say that this normal and healthy discontent can be channeled into the creative outlet of nonviolent direct action. And now this approach is being termed extremist.

But though I was initially disappointed at being categorized as an extremist, as I continued to think about the matter I gradually gained a measure of satisfaction from the label. Was not Jesus an extremist for love: "Love your enemies, bless them that curse you, do good to them that hate you, and pray for them which despitefully use you, and persecute you." Was not Amos an extremist for justice: "Let justice roll down like waters and righteousness like an ever-flowing stream." Was not Paul an extremist for the Christian gospel: "I bear in my body the marks of the Lord Jesus." Was not Martin Luther an extremist: "Here I stand; I cannot do otherwise, so help me God." And John Bunyan: "I will stay in jail to the end of my days before I make a butchery of my conscience." And Abraham Lincoln: "This nation cannot survive half slave and half free." And Thomas Jefferson: "We hold these truths to be self-evident, that all men are created equal. . . ." So the question is not whether we will be extremists, but what kind of extremists we will be. Will we be extremists for hate or for love? Will we be extremists for the preservation of injustice or for the extension of justice? In that dramatic scene on Calvary's hill three men were crucified. We must never forget that all three were crucified for the same crime—the crime of extremism. Two were extremists for immorality, and thus fell below their environment. The other, Jesus Christ, was an extremist for love, truth, and goodness, and thereby rose above his environment. Perhaps the South, the nation, and the world are in dire need of creative extremists.

I had hoped that the white moderate would see this need. Perhaps I was too optimistic; perhaps I expected too much. I suppose I should have realized that few members of the oppressor race can understand the deep groans and passionate yearnings of the oppressed race, and still fewer have the vision to see that injustice must be rooted out by strong, persistent, and determined action. I am thankful, however, that some of our white brothers in the South have grasped the meaning of this social revolution and committed themselves to it. They are still all too few in quantity, but they are big in quality. Some—such as Ralph McGill, Lillian Smith, Harry Golden, James McBride Dabbs, Ann Braden, and Sarah Patton Boyle—have written about our struggle in eloquent and prophetic terms. Others have marched with us down nameless streets of the South. They have languished in filthy, roach-infested jails, suffering the abuse and brutality of policemen who view them as "dirty nigger-lovers." Unlike so many of their moderate brothers and sisters, they have recognized the urgency of the moment and sensed the need for powerful "action" antidotes to combat the disease of segregation.

Let me take note of my other major disappointment. I have been so greatly disappointed with the white church and its leadership. Of course, there are some notable exceptions. I am not unmindful of the fact that each of you has taken some significant stands on this issue. I commend you, Reverend Stallings, for your Christian stand on this past Sunday, in welcoming Negroes to your worship service on a nonsegregated basis. I commend the Catholic leaders of this state for integrating Spring Hill College several years ago.

But despite these notable exceptions, I must honestly reiterate that I have been disappointed with the church. I do not say this as one of those negative critics who can always find something wrong with the church. I say this as a minister of the gospel, who loves the church; who was nurtured in its bosom; who has been sustained by its spiritual blessings and who will remain true to it as long as the cord of life shall lengthen.

When I was suddenly catapulted into the leadership of the bus protest   35 in Montgomery, Alabama, a few years ago, I felt we would be supported by the white church. I felt that the white ministers, priests, and rabbis of the South would be among our strongest allies. Instead, some have been outright opponents, refusing to understand the freedom movement and misrepresenting its leaders; all too many others have been more cautious than courageous and have remained silent behind the anesthetizing security of stained-glass windows.

In spite of my shattered dreams, I came to Birmingham with the hope that the white religious leadership of this community would see the justice of our cause and, with deep moral concern, would serve as the channel through which our just grievances could reach the power structure. I had hoped that each of you would understand. But again I have been disappointed.

I have heard numerous southern religious leaders admonish their worshipers to comply with a desegregation decision because it is the law, but I have longed to hear white ministers declare: "Follow this decree because integration is morally right and because the Negro is your brother." In the midst of blatant injustices inflicted upon the Negro, I have watched white churchmen stand on the sideline and mouth pious irrelevancies and sanctimonious trivialities. In the midst of a mighty struggle to rid our nation of racial and economic injustice, I have heard many ministers say: "Those are social issues, with which the gospel has no real concern." And I have watched many churches commit themselves to a completely otherworldly religion which makes a strange, unbiblical distinction between body and soul, between the sacred and the secular.

I have traveled the length and breadth of Alabama, Mississippi, and all the other southern states. On sweltering summer days and crisp autumn mornings I have looked at the South's beautiful churches with their lofty spires pointing heavenward. I have beheld the impressive outlines of her massive religious-education buildings. Over and over I have found myself asking: "What kind of people worship here? Who is their God? Where were their voices when the lips of Governor Barnett dripped with words of interposition and nullification? Where were they when Governor Wallace gave a clarion call for defiance and hatred? Where were their voices of support when bruised and weary Negro men and women decided to rise from the dark dungeons of complacency to the bright hills of creative protest?"

Yes, these questions are still in my mind. In deep disappointment I have wept over the laxity of the church. But be assured that my tears have been tears of love. There can be no deep disappointment where there is not deep love. Yes, I love the church. How could I do otherwise? I am in the rather unique position of being the son, the grandson, and the great-grandson of preachers. Yes, I see the church as the body of Christ. But, Oh! How we have blemished and scarred that body through social neglect and through fear of being nonconformists.

There was a time when the church was very powerful—in the time when the early Christians rejoiced at being deemed worthy to suffer for what they believed. In those days the church was not merely a thermometer that recorded the ideas and principles of popular opinion; it was a thermostat that transformed the mores of society. Whenever the early Christians entered a town, the people in power became disturbed and immediately sought to convict the Christians for being "disturbers of the peace" and "outside agitators." But the Christians pressed on, in the conviction that they were "a colony of heaven," called to obey God rather than man. Small in number, they were big in commitment. They were too God-intoxicated to be "astronomically intimidated." By their effort and example they brought an end to such ancient evils as infanticide and gladiatorial contests. 40

Things are different now. So often the contemporary church is a weak, ineffectual voice with an uncertain sound. So often it is an archdefender of the status quo. Far from being disturbed by the presence of the church, the power structure of the average community is consoled by the church's silent—and often even vocal—sanction of things as they are.

But the judgment of God is upon the church as never before. If today's church does not recapture the sacrificial spirit of the early church, it will lose its authenticity, forfeit the loyalty of millions, and be dismissed as an irrelevant social club with no meaning for the twentieth century. Every day I meet young people whose disappointment with the church has turned into outright disgust.

Perhaps I have once again been too optimistic. Is organized religion too inextricably bound to the status quo to save our nation and the world? Perhaps I must turn my faith to the inner spiritual church, the church within the church, as the true *ekklesia* and the hope of the world. But again I am thankful to God that some noble souls from the ranks of organized religion have broken loose from the paralyzing chains of conformity and joined us as active partners in the struggle for freedom. They have left their secure congregations and walked the streets of Albany, Georgia, with us. They have gone down the highways of the South on tortuous rides for freedom. Yes, they have gone to jail with us. Some have been dismissed from their churches, have lost the support of their bishops and fellow ministers. But they have acted in the faith that right defeated is stronger than evil triumphant. Their witness has been the spiritual salt that has preserved the true meaning of the gospel in these troubled times. They have carved a tunnel of hope through the dark mountain of disappointment.

I hope the church as a whole will meet the challenge of this decisive hour. But even if the church does not come to the aid of justice, I have no despair about the future. I have no fear about the outcome of our struggle in Birmingham, even if our motives are at present misunderstood. We will reach the goal of freedom in Birmingham and all over the nation, because the goal of America is freedom. Abused and scorned though we may be, our destiny is tied up with America's destiny. Before the pilgrims landed at Plymouth, we were here. Before the pen of Jefferson etched the majestic words of the Declaration of Independence across the pages of history, we were here. For more than two centuries our forebears labored in this country without wages; they made cotton king; they built the homes of their masters while suffering gross injustice and shameful humiliation—and yet out of a bottomless vitality they continued to thrive and develop. If the inexpressible cruelties of slavery could not stop us, the opposition we now face will surely fail. We will win our freedom because the sacred heritage of our nation and the eternal will of God are embodied in our echoing demands.

Before closing I feel impelled to mention one other point in your statement that has troubled me profoundly. You warmly commended the Birmingham police force for keeping "order" and "preventing violence." I doubt that you would have so warmly commended the police force if you had seen its dogs sinking their teeth into unarmed, nonviolent Negroes. I doubt that you would so quickly commend the policemen if you were to observe their ugly and inhumane treatment of Negroes here in the city jail; if you were to watch them push and curse old Negro women and young Negro girls; if you were to see them slap and kick old Negro men and young boys; if you were to

45

observe them, as they did on two occasions, refuse to give us food because we wanted to sing our grace together. I cannot join you in your praise of the Birmingham police department.

It is true that the police have exercised a degree of discipline in handling the demonstrators. In this sense they have conducted themselves rather "nonviolently" in public. But for what purpose? To preserve the evil system of segregation. Over the past few years I have consistently preached that nonviolence demands that the means we use must be as pure as the ends we seek. I have tried to make clear that it is wrong to use immoral means to attain moral ends. But now I must affirm that it is just as wrong, or perhaps even more so, to use moral means to preserve immoral ends. Perhaps Mr. Connor and his policemen have been rather nonviolent in public, as was Chief Pritchett in Albany, Georgia, but they used the moral means of nonviolence to maintain the immoral end of racial injustice. As T. S. Eliot has said: "The last temptation is the greatest treason: To do the right deed for the wrong reason."

I wish you had commended the Negro sit-inners and demonstrators of Birmingham for their sublime courage, their willingness to suffer, and their amazing discipline in the midst of great provocation. One day the South will recognize its real heroes. They will be the James Merediths, with the noble sense of purpose that enables them to face jeering and hostile mobs, and with the agonizing loneliness that characterizes the life of the pioneer. They will be old, oppressed, battered Negro women, symbolized in a seventy-two-year-old woman in Montgomery, Alabama, who rose up with a sense of dignity and with her people decided not to ride segregated buses, and who responded with ungrammatical profundity to one who inquired about her weariness: "My feets is tired, but my soul is at rest." They will be the young high school and college students, the young ministers of the gospel and a host of their elders, courageously and nonviolently sitting in at lunch counters and willingly going to jail for conscience' sake. One day the South will know that when these disinherited children of God sat down at lunch counters, they were in reality standing up for what is best in the American dream and for the most sacred values in our Judaeo-Christian heritage, thereby bringing our nation back to those great wells of democracy which were dug deep by the founding fathers in their formulation of the Constitution and the Declaration of Independence.

Never before have I written so long a letter. I'm afraid it is much too long to take your precious time. I can assure you that it would have been much shorter if I had been writing from a comfortable desk, but what else can one do when he is alone in a narrow jail cell, other than write long letters, think long thoughts, and pray long prayers?

If I have said anything in this letter that overstates the truth and indicates an unreasonable impatience, I beg you to forgive me. If I have said anything that understates the truth and indicates my having a patience that allows me to settle for anything less than brotherhood, I beg God to forgive me.

I hope this letter finds you strong in the faith. I also hope that circum-   50
stances will soon make it possible for me to meet each of you, not as an
integrationist or a civil-rights leader but as a fellow clergyman and a Christian brother. Let us all hope that the dark clouds of racial prejudice will soon
pass away and the deep fog of misunderstanding will be lifted from our fear-
drenched communities, and in some not too distant tomorrow the radiant
stars of love and brotherhood will shine over our great nation with all their
scintillating beauty.

—YOURS FOR THE CAUSE OF PEACE AND BROTHERHOOD,
MARTIN LUTHER KING, JR. ◎/◎

Notes

1. This response to a published statement by eight fellow clergymen from Alabama
   (Bishop C. C. J. Carpenter, Bishop Joseph A. Durick, Rabbi Milton L. Grafman, Bishop
   Paul Hardin, Bishop Nolan B. Harmon, the Reverend George M. Murray, the Reverend
   Edward V. Ramage, and the Reverend Earl Stallings) was composed under somewhat
   constricting circumstances. Begun on the margins of the newspaper in which the
   statement appeared while I was in jail, the letter was continued on scraps of writing
   paper supplied by a friendly Negro trusty, and concluded on a pad my attorneys
   were eventually permitted to leave me. Although the text remains in substance un-
   altered, I have indulged in the author's prerogative of polishing it for publication.
   [King's note.]
2. **Reinhold Niebuhr** Niebuhr (1892–1971) was a minister, political activist, author, and
   professor of applied Christianity at Union Theological Seminary. [All notes are the
   editors' unless otherwise specified.]
3. **justice . . . denied** A quotation attributed to William E. Gladstone (1809–1898), British
   statesman and prime minister.
4. **Paul Tillich** Tillich (1886–1965), born in Germany, taught theology at several German
   universities, but in 1933 he was dismissed from his post at the University of Frankfurt
   because of his opposition to the Nazi regime. At the invitation of Reinhold Niebuhr,
   he came to the United States and taught at Union Theological Seminary.
5. *Zeitgeist* German for "spirit of the age."

1. King chose to present his views in the form of a letter instead of, say, a mani-
   festo. How might King's choice be explained from a Rogerian perspective?

2. Where do you see King making an effort to establish common ground with
   his audience? Explain whether you think he succeeded in doing so.

3. Do any moments in King's letter seem un-Rogerian? How so? What
   positive or negative effect might they have on his intended readers?

4. Does King use any of the three Aristotelian appeals of ethos, pathos, or
   logos described in Chapter 1? If so, which one(s)? Where do they appear?
   Why do you suppose King uses them?

5. Where does King most clearly reveal a special effort to reach his audience of
   fellow clergy?

6. Outline the key points in King's essay. Is there anything Rogerian about the way King sequences and emphasizes some of these points?

7. Should King have taken a more aggressive approach in his *Letter* (i.e., used a Classical argument strategy)? Why or why not?

FIGURE 5.1

Rogerian Model Flowchart

What issue am I going to investigate? [Example: The issue of visual arts education in U.S. public schools.]

What is my thesis? [Example: Acquiring basic skills in painting, illustrating, and sculpting is as important as acquiring basic skills in math and reading.]

What *common ground* exists between my views and those whose views differ from mine? [Example: We both agree that students must master those skills that will ensure success in practical "real-world" contexts; we both agree that analytical thinking and creative thinking are essential.]

What are the *challenging views* on the matter that I need to discuss? [Example: Mastery of math and reading skills must take priority over mastery of artistic skills.]

How can I most judiciously highlight the limitation of the *challenging views* and suggest a mutually agreeable way of overcoming those limitations? [Example: Giving priority to math and reading skills over artistic skills privileges analysis over creativity; yet we both agree that analysis and creativity are equally important; therefore we both agree that ways should be found to integrate math and reading skills with artistic skills in lesson plans.]

Based on shared views about my thesis, what can I add in the way of *evidence* that would be compatible with challenging views? [Example: If challengers say that math and reading skills must take priority, I can suggest that math and reading skills can be *integrated* with artistic design skills.]

What are my *concluding reflections* in light of the above?

Using the above information, what can I say in my opening paragraph that would best *introduce* my argument and engage my reader's attention?

Reinforcing a Rogerian Argument with Visuals

Visual aids most likely to work in a Rogerian argument would illustrate co-operation and interaction among people: photographs of individuals engaged in discussion, of planning sessions, of teamwork. An illustrated "Letter from Birmingham Jail" (pages 161–174), for example, could include, along with those well-known images of Martin Luther King leading a peaceful civil rights demonstration, a photograph of citizens removing a racial discrimination sign (e.g., "Whites Only") from a restaurant window. What additional illustrations can you suggest that would capture the spirit of Dr. King's message?

Chapter Summary

A successful argument structured along Rogerian principles, like the Classical and Toulmin models, includes thorough, accurate, and relevant evidence in support of its claim; unlike these models, however, the aim of Rogerian persuasion is not to "win" the argument but to find common ground and to build consensus on an issue troubling both the writer and the audience. Instead of being considered "opponents," those with differing views are encouraged to engage in cooperative dialogue to solve a common problem; to succeed in establishing a Rogerian approach, arguers need to listen with care and open-mindedness to divergent points of view. When considering taking a Rogerian approach to your argument, remember to ask yourself three questions: Can I represent challenging views and evaluate the evidence fairly and objectively? Do any of the challenging views make sense to some degree, and, if so, can I find a way to incorporate them into my own views? Am I sincere in my desire to establish common ground with those who take issue with me?

Summary and Comparison of the Classical, Toulmin, and Rogerian Models

Classical Model

- Based on philosophical ideals of sound thinking, incorporating the Aristotelian appeals of ethos (ethical principles, recognized authority, and shared values), pathos (stirring of emotions), and logos (dialectical reasoning)

- Follows a predetermined arrangement of elements: An *introduction* that states the problem and the thesis, presentation of the *evidence*, *refutation* of challenging views, and a *conclusion*

Toulmin Model

- Based on the pragmatics of the judicial system rather than the ideals of philosophical thinking

- Approaches an argument in terms of its *claims* (which are presented more as hypotheses being opened to challenge than as truths to be proven), its *data*, and its underlying *warrants*, and *backing* justifying those warrants, that make the data trustworthy

- Recognizes the "real-world" complexities of an argument; gives special emphasis to refutation

Rogerian Model

- Based on humanistic values that take into account the importance of social cooperation in argument (that is, finding common ground is valued over "beating the opposition")

- Emphasizes points of agreement over points of disagreement, and treats the issue as a common problem for both the writer and the audience

- Urges arguers to cultivate multiple perspectives toward issues

Checklist

1. Do I find common ground with those whose views differ from my own?

2. Do I carefully consider the weaknesses or limitations of my point of view, as well as those of others'? Do I share these with my readers?

3. Is my tone cooperative rather than confrontational?

4. Do I encourage multiple perspectives rather than a singular one toward the issue?

5. Do I treat views with which I disagree respectfully? Do I give more emphasis to the points of agreement than the points of disagreement?

Writing Projects

1. Write an argumentative essay, following the Rogerian model, in which you defend or challenge one of the following issues:

   a. Books, especially textbooks, should be published online.

  b. Because the Second Amendment to the U.S. Constitution gives citizens the right to bear arms, students over the age of eighteen cannot be prohibited from bringing firearms onto campus if they feel the need for self-protection.

  c. Libraries should become media centers, using more of their budgets for electronic resources than for print resources.

2. Write an essay in which you use the Rogerian model to argue for one feasible way of improving living conditions with one or more roommates.

3. Write a comparative evaluation of the Classical, Toulmin, and Rogerian models of argument.

4. Read the following essay, "Who Owns Our Children?", by student Daniela Gibson. Then critique it in terms of her use of Rogerian persuasion.

Daniela Gibson

Who Owns Our Children?

Every morning when I go to the bus stop, I pass by a poster with a smiling mother and toddler. On the poster, it says, "You are your child's first teacher." Unfortunately, today, many parents feel that this caring and loving relationship with their children is threatened by a dark force—child violence. The reality of this threat is manifested in tragic events such as the shooting at Columbine, where two high school students killed twelve students and a teacher, leaving several wounded. In the face of such tragedies, it is not surprising that parents are desperately seeking a cause. Recently, many have turned to the media and argued that violence on TV is responsible for violence among children. Many parents now feel that only TV censorship by the government can bring child violence to a halt.

These parents, together with several journalists, sociologists, and psychologists, see a parallel between TV violence and child violence. In support of their claim, they cite people like David Walsh, director of the National Institute of Media and the Family, who notes that "it is estimated the average American kid has seen 200,000 acts of violence on television by the time he or she graduates from high school" (Hunt). They further refer to Professor Brandon Centerwall, whose studies suggest that "when English-language TV came to South Africa in 1975, having previously been banned by the Afrikaans-speaking government . . . there was a spectacular increase in violent crime, most especially among the young" (Kristol). Another argument against TV is that its violence desensitizes both adults and children from the violence in the real world "to the point where nothing is revolting. Where nothing makes us blush" (Jacoby). Arguments like these have let people conclude that "the government . . . will have to step in to help the parents"—a call, of course, for censorship (Kristol).

These reactions are understandable and reflect the fears and concerns of the parents. I think that everybody will agree that violence is bad, that TV can promote violence among young children, and that this is especially the case when TV replaces a parent or other caretaker. It clearly is in the interest of our children and our society that children do not have unlimited access to television. The question is, however, who should be in charge of regulating TV for our children. The government or the parents? I strongly believe that the latter should be in charge. I believe that child violence can only be reduced if parents stop holding the TV media responsible for the violence and instead acknowledge and act upon their responsibilities as parents.

To blame the media for child violence and call for censorship of television is a mistake, for the causal link between child violence and TV has not been sufficiently established and censorship is not only impractical but also dangerous. First, if we see television as the main cause for child violence, we mistake a correlation for a cause. As one author explains: "epidemiological research . . . consists of observing groups of people and then showing statistical associations between their life-styles or behavior and what happens to them later. Scientists know, as the public often does not, that such [. . .] research tells us nothing about cause and effect" (Glasser). The same author continues, "many people will falsely conclude after reading such statistical associations" that "'[t]elevision is the cause' [of violence]." To illustrate the problems with this epidemiological research,

let us look at the argument that TV brought violence to South
Africa. This claim is based on a correlation of the introduction
of English-language TV and an increase in "violent crime, most
especially among the young." To say, however, that TV is the
cause of the crime is to exclude all kinds of other factors. For
example, we know that in the particular case in South Africa,
English-language TV had previously "been banned by the Afrikaans-
speaking government." This information suggests tension between
the native population and a pro-English movement. Now, I am not
saying that I can prove this tension or that it is the real cause
for the increase in violence. What I am saying is that we cannot
conclude a cause if we only have a simple correlation. To say
that English-language TV is the cause for growing violence is to
say that "owning more than one television set caused heart disease"
just because an "epidemiologic research showed a statistical
association between heart disease and the number of television
sets a person owned" (in fact, "[c]linical trials demonstrated
that cholesterol, but not the number of television sets one
owned, was causally related") (Glasser).

Furthermore, not only are the grounds for TV censorship shaky,
but such censorship would also be impractical and potentially
dangerous. The following quote points at the impracticality of
censorship: "claiming we have to reprogram the media watched by
99.99 percent of us to influence the behavior of 0.01 percent is
to be rendered helpless by a much smaller problem" (Jenkins).
Although I am not sure about the accuracy of these numbers, I do
think that the statement demonstrates well the unwillingness of
many people to give up their freedom of watching whatever they
want on TV in favor of child sensitive censorship. Furthermore,
to trust the government with the regulation of TV programs is
also dangerous, for it would be unclear by which and whose standards this censorship would be carried out. The difficulty of
finding a standard that corresponds to the values of all parents
is demonstrated by the claim of an author who argues that most
TV shows are in fact portraying the right values. In support of
his claim, he refers to the TV show *Friends* and asks, "Is there

a more wholesome group of kids than the cute boys and girls on *Friends*. They are all white and hetero" (Hirschorn). Now, I know several parents who would strongly object to "all white and hetero" as the right message. On the other hand, I also know parents who would endorse such a message. Not only does this disagreement show the difficulty of having someone else than the parents, namely the government, define the "right" values for children, but it also points to the danger of children being indoctrinated with values that conflict with those of their parents.

Being aware of the shortcomings of TV censorship, it is important now to look at the benefits of responsible parenting with respect to TV and violence. I believe that parent regulation of TV shows, a dialogue between parent and child about TV shows, and the offering of alternatives to TV can not only reduce child violence but also increase the happiness of child and parent.

First, responsible parents should regulate the TV exposure of their children. This allows parents not only to reduce the violence their children are exposed to while watching TV but also to monitor the time their children spend in front of the TV. For reasons that I will address under point three, I believe that it is important for the mental and physical health of the child that the time spent in front of a TV is limited. The danger with government regulation is that it might give parents a false sense of security. They think because violence has been censored, TV can no longer harm their children. They will feel comfortable about their children watching TV. Suddenly, the TV has become a convenient babysitter.

But responsible parents know not only what and when their children watch TV but also how they respond to what they see. This brings me to my second attribute of responsible parents: Responsible parents also use TV shows as an opportunity for dialogue with their children. In the case where children actually do watch violence, parents could ask, "Can you imagine how much this must hurt?" to give children a sense of the pain that accompanies violence. And of course, parents should also disagree with the violence shown and tell the child, "I really disagree with the way the character treated his friend. I think it would have been much better if he had talked to him instead of beating him." The point is that watching TV together with your child is more than just a means to shield your child from an overdose of TV violence. It can also be a great opportunity to encourage conversations that foster critical thinking skills and verbal skills and allow parents to understand their children better.

And third, responsible parents should also offer their children alternatives to TV. If a child spends most of his or her time in front of a TV, even if the violence is minimal, the child's physical and mental well-being is threatened. The hour-long sitting prohibits the child from getting enough exercise. Furthermore, the lonely hours in front of the TV would cause the child to become alienated from others and to be less and less able to distinguish reality from the world on TV. On the other hand, spending time with the child on other activities can be very rewarding both for the child and the parent. An example is the weekend my husband and I spent with our five-year-old nephew, Mason. He arrived with a video that he was determined to watch. However, when we suggested going to the park, the video was soon forgotten. Moreover, walking all over the park and visiting the planetarium, aquarium, and playground was time well spent: Mason felt proud that he could keep up with us grownups without being carried on my husband's shoulders; he got plenty of exercise, not only from the walking but also from the playground; he became completely fascinated with the planetarium; he got the sense that he was important and loved; and he just had a real fun time. At the same time, because this day was full of interaction and talking with Mason, my husband and I learned so much more about our nephew than we would have ever done if we had watched TV. (Also all these activities caused Mason to fall asleep after dinner, so that my husband and I had a calm and restful evening—something that TV would have never accomplished.)

Censorship might shield children from TV violence. But responsible parenting can do the same. And while TV censorship is problematic its causal grounds are shaky, its practicality and standards are doubtful—responsible parenting is so much more rewarding. When parents not only monitor the shows their children watch and the hours their children spend in front of a TV, but also encourage dialogue about the shows and offer alternative activities to TV, the children will learn to think critically, feel loved, have ample opportunities to release extra energies, and be much happier. And having happier children appears to be the best prevention of violence. In the end, I still believe in the truth of the poster, that "you are your child's first teacher."

Works Cited

Glasser, Ira. "TV Causes Violence? Try Again." *New York Times* 15 June 1994: A19. Print.

Hirschorn, Michael. "The Myth of Television Depravity." *New York Times* 4 Sept. 1995: A21. Print.

Hunt, Albert R. "Teen Violence Spawned by Guns and Cultural Rot." *Wall Street Journal* 11 June 1998: 12. Print.

Jacoby, Jeff. "A Desensitized Society Drenched in Sleaze." *Boston Globe* 8 June 1995: 16. Print.

Jenkins, Holman W. "Violence Never Solved Anything but It's Entertaining." *Wall Street Journal* 28 Oct. 1998: 14. Print.

Kristol, Irving. "Sex, Violence, and Videotape." *Wall Street Journal* 31 May 1998: 28. Print.

6 | Reasoning: Methods and Fallacies

Come now, and let us reason together.
—Isaiah 1:18

As we have seen in the preceding chapters, argumentative writing involves the use of many skills: making rhetorical choices regarding audience, purpose, expectations, and the nature of the subject matter; outlining and drafting arguments; and deciding to use Classical, Toulmin, or Rogerian methods of argument. This chapter looks closely at another fundamental skill for writers of arguments—reasoning. By taking care to improve your ability to think critically and logically, you will be less likely to slip into errors of reasoning when supporting a claim.

Argumentative Reasoning

All arguments are imperfect to some degree. Unlike the tight logic of mathematics, in which a problem is solved methodically and objectively and turns out either correct or incorrect, most genuine arguments are based on complex human situations—complex because they have unpredictable elements. It is one thing to prove that force is equal to the product of mass times acceleration ($F = ma$) or that Socrates is mortal (given the fact that all humans are mortal); it is quite another matter to prove that reading to children, say, dramatically increases their chances of college success. To argue that claim convincingly, you would first need to be aware of variables such as the availability of controlled studies on this topic, the characteristics of the students used in the studies, the types of readings the children had been exposed to, the frequency of being read to, and so on. Because of such complex variables, no argument can be 100 percent beyond dispute.

Thus, opportunities to make an argument stronger than it is always exist. Good arguers, however, strive to create not the perfect argument but the most efficient one—the one that will ethically and logically persuade the readers. An argument, then, is most successful when its weaknesses are minimized as much as possible. As a writer of arguments, you should familiarize yourself with the most common argumentative errors, which are known as *fallacies.* Learning to recognize fallacies does not guarantee that you will always avoid them, but it does increase the likelihood that you'll recognize them. You can use the information about fallacies to read others' arguments, resources, and your own drafts so that your ability to recognize fallacies will eventually improve your ability to construct sound and convincing arguments.

The Nature of Fallacies

Arguers rarely use fallacies deliberately. Inadvertent lapses in judgment, fallacies usually arise from lack of experience with the subject matter, lack of familiarity with other points of view, and undeveloped methods of argumentative reasoning. Let us examine each of these problems.

- **Lack of experience with the subject matter.** The more informed you are, the more material you have to defend your views. Most arguments fail to convince because they do not draw sufficiently from experience (personal experience as well as experience acquired from intensive research). You may feel passionately about the need to save the rain forests, but unless you thoroughly understand the nature of rain forests, the reasons they are so precious, and the ways in which they are so threatened, your argument will lack substance. You would have no choice but to rely on broad generalities, such as "Rain forests are filled with important species." Unless you can name and describe such species and describe their importance, readers are unlikely to be convinced that the assertion was valid.

- **Lack of familiarity with other points of view.** In addition to acquiring a knowledge base about the topic, you also need to be familiar with the range of representative views on that topic. Before you can defend your views on an issue, you need to understand challenging arguments, find reasons why those arguments are not as effective as yours, and be open to the possibility of adjusting your position if another is actually more reasonable.

- **Underdeveloped methods of argumentative reasoning.** You not only need to be knowledgeable about issues and familiar with the spectrum of views on those issues, but you also need to know how arguments progress logically from one point to the next. In addition to the methods of presenting an argument (the Classical, Toulmin, and Rogerian methods discussed in Chapters 3 through 5), there are particular *reasoning strategies* or patterns of thinking that enable you to frame an assertion logically.

Strategies of Reasoning

The reasoning strategies most relevant to argumentative writing are as follows:

- **Deduction:** Drawing conclusions from assertions that you know to be true (insofar as you can determine); reasoning from the general to the specific

- **Induction:** Arriving at a conclusion that is based on what you judge to be sufficient (not necessarily conclusive) available evidence; reasoning from the specific to the general

- **Categorization:** Placing an idea or issue in a larger context using the strategies of definition, classification, and division

- **Analogy:** Attempting to enhance the validity of a claim by finding a similar situation in a different context

- **Authorization:** Establishing the validity of a claim by invoking authority, either in the form of personal testimonial from an expert or of preestablished policy or law

- **Plea:** Using emotionally charged expressions of feeling to aid in defending an assertion

The sections that follow look more closely at the ways in which each of these reasoning strategies operates.

Deduction

When you reason deductively, you break down an assertion into formal statements that are logically connected. A *syllogism* is one formula used in deductive reasoning, consisting of a *major premise*, a *minor premise*, and a *conclusion*.

Major premise: All cats meow.

Minor premise: Cordelia is a cat.

Conclusion: Therefore, Cordelia meows.

As this simple example reveals, to reason deductively means to accept the major premise without question. To call the major premise into question ("Is it true that all cats meow?") is to move from deduction to induction, whereby one looks at the evidence leading up to the hypothesis to determine its truthfulness.

In commonplace arguments, an assumption often goes unstated because it is taken for granted that the audience already shares it. From the perspective of formal logic, this is considered an incomplete syllogism; but from the perspective of argumentative discourse, it is considered sufficient and is referred to as an *enthymeme*. Thus, the statement "Cordelia meows because she is a cat" is an enthymeme because the writer takes for granted that the audience accepts the unstated assumption that all cats meow.

Deductive reasoning can be especially powerful when one is refuting a claim. (If you need to refresh your memory about the process of refutation, review the discussion of Classical argument in Chapter 3.) For example, if a friend claims that to accept a government-run program is to reject a free-market economy, you could refute the claim by asserting that a government program and a free-market economy are not as mutually exclusive as the friend's claim implies. Such dichotomous ("either-or") thinking is a commonly occurring example of flawed deductive reasoning. By calling attention to the many-sided complexity of a problem, you raise the consciousness of your audience; you in effect *teach* your readers to recognize the "gray areas" that aren't as conspicuous as the "black-and-white areas" but that usually bring the truth much closer.

To refute a claim, you may need to do a deductive analysis of the author's reasoning strategies. Here is a five-step method for such analysis:

1. Identify contradictions.

2. Identify inconsistencies.

3. Identify omissions or oversights.

4. Reduce an unsound claim to its logical absurdity (*reductio ad absurdum*) so as to expose the flawed reasoning more conspicuously.

5. Identify oversimplifications.

Identify Contradictions   Someone asserts that making handgun sales illegal would increase crime because more guns would be obtained illegally. You could reveal a contradiction by showing (using statistics from a reputable survey) how that claim contradicts reality: that crime actually has decreased by a certain percentage in one or more places where such a law had been enacted. Similarly, if a writer asserts that playing video games excessively damages one's ability to think effectively and then proceeds to describe her own experiences with video games in an effective manner, you could point out the contradiction between the author's writing effectively and the alleged damage to her thinking skills from years of playing video games.

Identify Inconsistencies   If you claim that people should give up eating meat but then proceed to eat a bowl of chicken soup, reasoning that such a small quantity of chicken is negligible or that even vegetarians need a "meat break" now and then, you are being logically inconsistent. Or consider this somewhat more complex example: Arlene is against abortion because she equates abortion with murder. However, Arlene agrees that in cases of rape, incest, or grave danger to the mother's life, abortion is permissible. Arlene is being logically inconsistent because her exceptions seem irrelevant to her own definition of abortion as fetal murder.

Identify Omissions or Oversights   A friend advises you not to take a course from Professor Krupp because Krupp gives difficult exams, grades rigorously, and assigns a heavy reading load. At first, you think that these are pretty good reasons for not enrolling in Professor Krupp's course. But then you wonder whether any positive things about this professor might balance out the bad, so you ask: "Did you learn a lot in her course?" Your friend replies, "Oh, yes—more than in any other course I've taken." You have just identified a deliberate omission or an accidental oversight in your friend's assessment of Professor Krupp.

Reduce an Unsound Claim to Its Logical Absurdity   Someone argues against a company's policy that employees wear shirts and ties or dresses and skirts by claiming that employees can think well even when dressed casually in jeans and T-shirts. You could refute that claim by taking it to the logical extreme. Why wouldn't the first person show up in pajamas or a swimsuit for work, then? The point of the dress code is not to affect one's ability to think but to present a certain image of the company.

Identify Oversimplifications   Recall the earlier example of the friend who argues that a government-run program is never compatible with a free-market economy. This kind of dichotomous thinking oversimplifies the reality of a free-market society such as that of the United States, where government programs such as Social Security and NASA are quite compatible with a market economy. Oversimplification results from an insufficiently investigated or thought-out premise on which the argument rests.

◎/◎   Exercise 6.1

1. Examine the following four arguments and describe the method or methods of deductive reasoning that each author is using or representing.

   a. Watching the Republican Party try to come to terms with several million gay voters reminds me a little of my uncle. He's the only family member I'm estranged from, because he regards my sexual orientation as a deliberate rebuke to God. When he heard I had contracted HIV, he told me in a letter, in so many words, that I deserved it and that only the Holy Spirit could cure me. He's also, I might add, a good person: kind, loving, and decent, if not the brightest bulb on the Christmas tree.

The human question is: How do I get along with him? My human answer: I don't. After his letter about my illness, in which he couldn't even bring himself to ask how I was, I cut him off. In most families with gay members there's something of this sort going on. So I completely understand the impulse to ostracize someone who has decided that a religious fiat, which by definition cannot be challenged, requires him to reject and hurt a loved one.

In a family, we can get away with such anger and hurt. But in politics such emotionally satisfying options come at a price: impasse, conflict, and little progress. That's why the knee-jerk attempt to turn George W. Bush into a homophobe is, in my view, misguided. It's misguided, first of all, because it's clear he isn't one. And it's misguided also because it will create an atmosphere that, while making a few gays feel better, makes many more worse off. We need to change a paradigm in which one side sees only bigots and the other side sees only perverts. This election presents us with a chance.

How? The first step is to resist at every opportunity the notion that homosexuals are defined by victimhood. If you look at the agenda of, say, the leading gay lobby, the Human Rights Campaign, you'll see what I mean. Its priorities are laws that protect gays from hate crimes and employment discrimination. Both proposals rely for their effectiveness on the notion that gay men and women be seen as the objects of physical violence and routine oppression in the workplace. But the number of hate crimes perpetrated against gay people is relatively puny, and such crimes are already covered under existing criminal law. And it's ludicrous to look at the gay population and see millions of people who have a hard time finding or keeping a job. In those states where anti-discrimination laws for gays are in effect, the number of lawsuits filed is negligible. But the real harm of these campaigns isn't just that they add new, largely pointless laws; it's that they portray homosexuals as down-trodden and weak.

To put it bluntly, we're not. We have survived a health crisis that would have destroyed—and is destroying—other populations, due in no small part to our tenacity, compassion, and organization. We are represented in almost every major cultural, political, and social organization, often leading them. Gay strength can be seen everywhere—from courageous high school kids organizing support groups to a young lesbian serving as an indispensable aide to Dick Cheney's vice presidential campaign. The media is saturated with gay talent, images, and skill. An honest gay agenda should capitalize on this truth, not flee from it. —Andrew Sullivan

b. If the Darwinian [evolutionary] process really took place, remains of plants and animals [that is, the fossil record] should show a gradual and continual change from one type of animal or plant into another. One of the things that worried Darwin in his day, as well as [what worries] modern evolutionists, was that the fossil record did not supply these intermediate life forms. —Donald E. Chittick

c. Until the census is focused on individuals, not households, the situation of women and children may continue to be distorted—just as it might be if there were only one vote per household. There is such a wide range of constituencies with an interest in Census Bureau policies that journalists have coined the phrase "census politics." But social justice movements haven't yet focused on the fact that census categories also determine what is counted as work, and who is defined as a worker. . . . —Gloria Steinem

d. Aristotle felt that the mortal horse of Appearance which ate grass and took people places and gave birth to little horses deserved far more attention than Plato was giving it. He said that the horse is not mere Appearance. The Appearances cling to something which is independent of them and which, like Ideas, is unchanging. The "something" that Appearances cling to he named "substance." And at that moment . . . our modern scientific understanding of reality was born. —Robert Pirsig

2. Bring in a short article such as a newspaper editorial and discuss it in terms of its use of deductive reasoning. Point out any flaws you see in the deductive reasoning.

Induction

You engage in inductive reasoning when you strive to make sense of things you experience. Unlike deductive reasoning, you do not begin with a premise assumed to be true and then determine a logical foundation for supporting it. Instead, you build a hypothesis out of your observations of phenomena. To return to our simple example of whether all cats meow, the inductive writer would examine the evidence—Cat A, Cat B, Cat C, and so on—until observing enough cats to warrant the conclusion, "Yes, all cats meow," or to reject it ("No, not all cats meow; Siberian tigers are cats, and they growl"), or to qualify it ("Yes, all cats meow, provided they're members of the subgenus *Felix domesticus*").

Because in inductive reasoning the strength of the conclusion rests entirely on the sufficiency of the evidence observed, you must use an adequate number of reliable samples.

Number of Samples   How many samples must be observed before it is reasonable to make the "inductive leap"? Technically, of course, no conclusion arrived at inductively is absolutely indisputable. For that to be the case in our cat argument, for example, you would have to observe every domestic cat on earth! At some point, every inductive reasoner must say, "I have observed enough to draw a reliable conclusion." This decision can be tricky and, indeed, is a major point of disputation in science—which relies preeminently on the inductive method (better known as the *scientific method*) for testing the validity of hypotheses.

Reliability of Samples   If the purpose of your paper is to argue whether a clear correlation exists between alcohol consumption and health problems, you may decide first to conduct a campus survey to see whether health problems are more frequent among drinking students than among nondrinking ones. In addition to interviewing an adequate number of students from each group (a 20 to 25 percent response rate to your survey from the total student population would be considered substantial), you will want the sample to be reliable in other ways. For example, it should be representative of different groups within the student body. Having only women, only men, only athletes, or only Mormons included would make your sample survey on college drinking unreliable.

◎/◎ Exercise 6.2

Describe the sequence of likely steps in inductive reasoning one might take for each of the following tasks:

1. Buying a new or a used car

2. Choosing a birthday gift for a friend or parent

3. Determining the chemical composition of an unknown gas

Categorization

Without systems of classification and division, we would be unable to make much sense out of reality. Perhaps the best illustration of this is the Linnaean system of taxonomy. With its binomial schema (genus name + species name, as in *Felix domesticus* or *Homo sapiens*), all life on earth has been classified. Think for a moment about how valuable such a schema is for understanding the relationship of life forms to each other.

People categorize foods into groups such as *savory* or *sweet*, or *main course* or *dessert*, to determine what they'll serve for dinner—a useful strategy for knowing what to buy for a dinner party. People break the large category of sports into basketball, baseball, and so on, and then divide those subgroups further into professional and amateur leagues. College football teams would fall into amateur leagues, which then play on their NCAA division level—IA, IAA, IIA, and so on. Imagine the injuries without such classification—an NFL football team playing a IIIA college team! Categorization in sports helps ensure a level playing field.

Categorization is just as important outside of science; for example, we can plan our day better by grouping our activities into "chores," "business transactions," "recreation," and so on. However, problems often arise. When people try to categorize human beings neatly according to ethnicity or cultural differences, the danger of stereotyping arises. Superficial differences such as skin color or manner of dress or speech are given more significance than they deserve. Racism, homophobia, and gender-based discrimination are often the ugly results. Categorizing works best when it serves as an initial gauge for differentiating A from B or A and B from C, and so forth. For example, if you were examining the study habits of college students, you might group your sample students by gender or age or major, just in case a correlation between the category selected and the kind of study habits would show up.

Another facet of categorization is definition, which is necessary for "fine-tuning" the distinctions between one thing and another within the same category. The very word *define* means "to determine or fix the boundaries or extent of" (*Random House Webster's College Dictionary*). Formal definitions use categorizing techniques themselves. In the definition of the word *chaplet*, for example—"a wreath or garland for the head" (*Random House Webster's College Dictionary*)—the first half of the definition ("a wreath or garland") establishes the broad category, or genus, and the second half ("for the head") pinpoints its distinguishing (specific) characteristics.

◎/◎ Exercise 6.3

1. Study the definitions of the following words in two unabridged dictionaries (e.g., *The Oxford English Dictionary* and *Webster's Unabridged Dictionary*). Report the differences in the way each dictionary presents the broad category (genus) and the distinguishing (specific) characteristics:

   a. volcano

   b. emphysema

   c. magician

   d. cathedral

2. Write a brief explanation of the way knowledge is categorized in your major field of study (or in a subject you are currently studying).

Analogy

To make an analogy is to draw a correspondence between two things that are superficially different but not essentially different. Analogies are used to enhance comprehension. If you are trying to help readers understand the nature of a radio wave, for example, you might use the more familiar analogy of a water wave. A river and an artery are not superficially alike, but they behave in similar enough ways for one to say that water flows in a river the way blood flows in an artery. A more readily perceived phenomenon like a flowing river is easier to understand than the flow of blood through an artery. The author's goal is to enable ease of understanding over precision of explanation.

However, to say that people are like ants because they swarm in large numbers to sporting events is to generate a distorted (and demeaning) image of fans' behavior. Using analogy in argumentative writing is a give-and-take situation: You give your readers greater comprehension of the idea, but you take away precision. The rule of thumb, then, is to use analogies carefully.

◎/◎ Exercise 6.4

Create an analogy to help explain each of the following concepts:

1. Doppler effect
2. Cardiac function
3. Eye function
4. Heaven

Authorization

Writers sometimes need to support an assertion by including the testimony of an expert in the field in question. If you are arguing about the dangers of ultraviolet radiation and urging people to consider sunbathing a risky activity due to the alleged link between ultraviolet radiation and skin cancer, you are likely to present empirical evidence from, say, several medical studies. You could also add drama to your claim by quoting a startling statement made by a leading skin cancer expert. In such a situation, you are resorting to the ethos, or the reliable character, of the expert.

Sometimes, finding the appropriate authority to obtain testimony in support of a claim can be tricky, depending on the claim. If you wish to argue that using genetic material from human embryos is unethical, should you include testimony from geneticists or religious leaders, or other kinds of experts? It might be easy to find experts who will agree with you—but are they the right experts?

◎/◎   **Exercise 6.5**

Suggest appropriate credentials for one or more authority figures brought in to offer testimony for each of the following topics:

1. Depletion of South American rain forests

2. The need for greater tsunami preparedness in certain regions of the world

3. A new dieting program

4. Cultivating the habit of reading in children

Plea

Emotional response is often highly persuasive. In formal argument, therefore, you may try to persuade your audience to accept your views by way of sympathy or compassion as well as by way of logical reasoning. Thus, if your goal is fundraising for the homeless, you might tell stories about the way homeless people suffer when they have to go without eating for two or three days, or shiver during cold winter nights on a park bench. If you wish to emphasize the importance of reading aloud to children, you might create a little scenario in which you dramatize the way in which listening to stories delights and heightens the intellectual curiosity of young children who are absorbed in what their parents are reading to them.

The plea strategy uses the Aristotelian appeals to emotion or to ethics. Appealing to the audience's compassion, ethical responsibility, need for security, comfort, and so on reinforces rather than counteracts the logical and analytical; for that reason, such appeals are an important rhetorical tool in the art of persuasion.

◎/◎   **Exercise 6.6**

Suggest possible uses of the plea strategy for each of the following topics:

1. An article on improving airport security

2. An article on preserving the individual's right to privacy

3. An article on teaching children to swim before age five

4. An article on reducing the risk of drowning accidents among children

Errors in Reasoning: A Taxonomy

Now that we have examined the methods of reasoning, it is time to look closely at the pitfalls that can occur. To some degree, errors in reasoning are almost unavoidable because reasoning is a complex mental act that requires a concerted effort to perfect. Nonetheless, the more alert you become to the way in which a given line of reasoning violates a principle of logic, of ethics, or of emotional integrity, the less likely it is that your arguments will be criticized for their fallacies.

Let us begin by becoming familiar with the common fallacies; we then examine each of them in more detail and look at the ways they subtly creep into an argument. We also examine these fallacies to identify faulty logic in the sources we may consult for our topics. Seeing faulty logic in supposedly informed sources helps us to decide not to use such sources ourselves and to know what we can rebut in arguments that challenge our own.

Errors of Deduction

In this group of fallacies, the line of reasoning that stems from statements assumed to be true is flawed, or the statements themselves may be flawed. Many errors in deductive reasoning occur because the author fails to connect premises to conclusions logically. Some common types of deductive fallacies follow.

Fourth Term   Careless arguers sometimes substitute one term for another, assuming the terms mean or suggest the same things, when in fact the terms have different meanings. The way to demonstrate the illogic of such a substitution is to think about the terms in a formal syllogism (the pattern of formal deductive reasoning discussed on pages 186–187): major, minor, and middle, as follows:

	[Maj] [Maj]
Major premise:	All **dogs** are **mammals.**
	[Minor] [Maj]
Minor premise:	**Rascal** is a **dog.**
	[Minor] [Maj]
Conclusion:	Therefore, **Rascal** is a **mammal.**

In any valid syllogism, the major term is the subject that must be equated with both a generic classification (middle term) and an individual one (minor term). In the above example, the major term *dog* is equated with the middle term *mammal* (dog 5 mammal) and the minor term Rascal (dog = Rascal).

Now consider this syllogism:

All prerequisites for the major in chemistry are difficult.

Chem. 50 is highly recommended for the major in chemistry.

Therefore, Chem. 50 is difficult.

Instead of seeing the major term *prerequisites* appear in the minor premise, a substitute fourth term—*highly recommended*—appears, thus rendering the syllogism invalid (even though the conclusion may be true).

Non Sequitur   In a non sequitur ("It does not follow"), an assertion cannot be tied logically to the premise it attempts to demonstrate. Consider the premise, "Nellie is obsessed with basketball." The reason presented is "because she attends a basketball game every week." The fact that one attends a basketball game every week—or every day—does not in itself demonstrate an obsession. Nellie could be an employee at the arena, or her brother could be one of the players, or she could be a sportswriter, or she could be conducting research on the game of basketball, or she could simply love the game in a positive sense. *Obsession* implies that something in one's behavior is beyond control; if that is the case, then your statements should reflect it: "Nellie is obsessed with basketball because, despite being threatened with losing her job if she doesn't go to work rather than the basketball games, she attends them anyway."

Ad Hominem   An ad hominem ("against the individual person") is a form of non sequitur in which the arguer argues against an individual's qualifications by attacking his or her personal life or trying to create a negative link between life and work. "Sherwood would not make a good mayor because he spends too much of his free time reading murder mysteries." The reverse situation—pro *hominem*—is equally fallacious, even though it would seldom be reported: "Sherwood would make a terrific mayor because he spends a lot of his time reading the Bible."

Denying the Antecedent/Affirming the Consequent   This fallacy occurs in hypothetical ("if–then") assertions. The first part of the assertion (the "if" clause) is called the *antecedent*; the second part (the "then" clause) is called the *consequent*. In a valid hypothetical assertion, the antecedent may be affirmed or the consequent denied—but not vice versa. Thus, in the hypothetical assertion,

If it snows today, then classes will be canceled.

the antecedent may correctly be affirmed (*It is snowing today*; therefore, classes are canceled), or the consequent correctly denied (*Classes were not canceled today*; therefore, it must not be snowing). But asserting the opposite in each case would be fallacious, as follows:

Antecedent denied: "*It is not snowing today*; therefore, classes are not canceled." (Classes could still be canceled even if it weren't snowing—for example, teachers may have gone on strike.)

Consequent affirmed: "*Classes have been canceled today*; therefore, it is snowing." (Again, classes could have been canceled for reasons other than snowfall.)

Errors of Induction

In this group of fallacies, the process of drawing conclusions or arriving at reliable generalizations based on observed particulars is faulty.

Unsupported Generalization   Generalizing is an important tool for critical thinkers, but a good generalization is derived from evidence. When the *evidence* is lacking, we say that the generalization is unsupported. *Evidence* in this context refers not only to statistics such as trends, tallies, or percentages but also to cases in point. For example, if you read somewhere that more physicians are being sued for malpractice in the current year than in the year preceding, you would be making an unsupported generalization if you neglected to provide statistical support for your assertion. It would also be a good idea to refer to individual cases that *demonstrated* incompetence. Why? Perhaps the increase in malpractice suits was based on other factors, such as more aggressive efforts to sue for malpractice; or perhaps the criteria defining *malpractice* had changed from one year to the next. As a critical thinker, you always need to be aware of alternative possibilities and explanations.

Another example of an unsupported generalization might be termed an assumption of hidden motive (or hidden agenda), or simply the *motive fallacy*, as the British philosopher Jamie Whyte terms it in his witty and incisive exposé of muddled thinking, *Crimes against Logic* (2004). If you're a manager and one of your employees praises you for landing an important contract, you will fall prey to the motive fallacy if you assume that the employee's motive for praise was, say, to reinforce his or her job security rather than simply wanting to praise you for your achievement. Whyte uses a courtroom example of the motive fallacy. A juror might secretly assume that a defense attorney is "motivated" to defend her client's innocence only because she is being paid to do so; but that juror obviously must consider only the evidence, not any hidden motives. "If we followed the method of the motive fallacy in civil trials," Whyte quips, "they would be rather simple. Decide against the side of the lawyer who was paid more. She has the greater corrupting motive" (12).

Hasty Generalization   A hasty generalization occurs when one leaps to a *premature conclusion*—not because the arguer provided faulty evidence or no evidence at all but because the evidence provided was insufficient to convincingly support the claim being made. Writers of argument can fall prey to hasty generalization when they do not check out enough cases before reaching their conclusion. If you claim, for example, that burglary has increased in your neighborhood and use as your only evidence the fact that two houses on your block have been burglarized, you would be guilty of a hasty generalization—*unless* you could also demonstrate that this number is greater for the same time frame of a year ago. Always make sure your evidence is thorough.

Red Herring   In British fox hunting, red herrings (very odorous) are sometimes dragged across a trail to throw the dogs off scent. This practice serves as a metaphor for raising an issue that has little or nothing to do with what is being argued in order to force the argument in a new direction. For example, say that after listening to a voter's concern that the community's high school needs to receive major funds to upgrade its facilities, a candidate responds, "I understand your concern and have asked the school board to review its policies." The candidate has thrown the voter a red herring by changing the subject from inadequate facilities to the school board's educational policies.

Poisoning the Well   Like the red herring, this fallacy aims to interfere with normal argumentative progression. But whereas the red herring aims to derail an argument in progress, poisoning the well aims to corrupt the argument before it even begins—usually by passing judgment on the quality of the argument before listeners have a chance to evaluate it. If you ask your friends to listen to a debate on whether the public library should be funded for building a videotape collection but then say that one of the debaters will be presenting an argument that has already been successfully repudiated, you would be guilty of poisoning the well with your own evaluation before giving your friends the opportunity to judge for themselves.

Misreading the Evidence   One of the biggest challenges in coming up with good evidence to support a claim is interpreting it properly. Findings based on polls, for example, can qualify as valid evidence, but such findings can easily be misinterpreted. For example, if a poll reveals that the majority of people polled felt that a human mission to Mars is too expensive and should not be federally funded, you would be misreading the evidence if you interpreted that statistic as an indication that most *Americans* felt that a human mission to Mars should not be federally funded, or that most people polled felt that human exploration of space was a waste of resources, or that most people polled felt that the cost of a human expedition to Mars was much higher than the U.S. government could afford. Notice that the majority is of a subset of the population at large, so you can claim only that the majority of those polled felt a certain way.

Slighting the Opposition   It can sometimes be tempting, in an argument, to downplay points of view with which we disagree, or to conveniently omit information that would make those views more persuasive and our own views less persuasive. By doing so, you commit the fallacy of slighting the opposition. Let's say you're arguing that cell phone use should not be permitted in flight, on the grounds that cell phone conversations would annoy many of the nearby passengers and that it could pose a security problem. You're aware of the counterarguments that a sizeable percentage of passengers would find cell phone conversations a more pleasant way to pass the time, would permit transacting important business, that new technology has rendered cell phone operation during flight perfectly safe, and that passengers not wanting to be seated near anyone with a cell phone would be accommodated—however, because you fear that mentioning the last counterargument would seriously undermine your own stance, you don't bother to mention it.

Post Hoc Ergo Propter Hoc   The phrase (sometimes simply post hoc) means "after the fact, therefore because of the fact." An effect (say, tripping and falling) is attributed to a cause (say, the sudden appearance of a black cat) only because of proximity, not because of any logical connection. The post hoc fallacy forms the basis for superstitious thinking and preempts any effort to determine a logical cause (for example, the ground was slippery or the person who fell was not paying any attention to the ground).

Begging the Question   This is an error of both deductive and inductive reasoning. As a deductive fallacy, question-begging takes the form of circular reasoning in which a conclusion is nothing more than a reworded premise, as in this example:

> A required course is one that is essential for a well-rounded education.
>
> Composition is essential for a well-rounded education.
>
> Therefore, composition is a required course.

The reasoning looks sound at first glance, but nothing has been "reasoned" at all. "Required course" is just another way of saying "necessary for a well-rounded education" in the context of the above syllogism. The question that remains—that is "begged"—is "What is meant by 'necessary for a well-rounded education'"?

Question-begging can also present itself as an error in inductive reasoning. Essentially, it voices a conclusion that requires inductive testing as if the testing had already been conducted, as in the assertion, "Impractical courses like Ancient History will no longer be required for graduation." Instead of applying a test of impracticality (whatever such a test would be like) to the course in question, the speaker assumes by her phrasing that such a test would be unnecessary.

Slippery Slope   This is an example of induction run rampant. Here, a person forecasts a series of events (usually disastrous) that will befall one if the first stated step is taken. Thus, the person who asserts the following is committing a slippery slope fallacy:

> If medical researchers continue to increase human longevity, then the population will soar out of control, mass famine will occur, the global economy will collapse, and the very survival of the species will be threatened.

Factors capable of compensating for the consequences of population increase have not been considered.

Errors of Categorization

In this group of fallacies, arguers tend to see things in terms of black and white instead of color gradations, so to speak—or they confuse one group of objects or ideas with another.

False Dichotomy (Either/Or)   This error of reasoning assumes there are only two options to resolving a given situation, when in fact there may be many. Assertions such as, "If you're not part of the solution, you're part of the problem," "America: love it or leave it," or "If you love nature, then you cannot possibly support industrial development" are examples of dichotomous thinking. To address the last example mentioned, for instance, factors that complicate the industry/nature dichotomy include the fact that recycling, land-reclaiming, and alternative energy use (wind, solar, geothermal, biomass) are industries.

Apples and Oranges   We often hear people comparing two things that are not comparable (because they are not part of the same category). A statement like "The physics lecture was not as good as the dinner we had at Antoine's last night" does not convey much meaning. Likewise, it is illogical to claim that Placido Domingo is a better singer than Johnny Cash, because opera and country-western are two different kinds of music, with fundamentally different criteria for excellence.

Errors of Analogy

Errors in analogies occur when the analogy distorts, misrepresents, or oversimplifies the reality.

False or Invalid Analogy   An analogy is considered false when it distorts what is essentially true about what is being analogized. If a student dislikes an instructor's strict, regimented classroom tactics and says that the classroom is like Hitler's Third Reich, the student is using a false analogy. Yes, it is true that Hitler used strict military tactics; but that fact alone cannot serve to parallel the situation in a classroom—unless the professor hired secret police agents (Gestapo), put dissenters into horrific concentration camps, and instituted mass extermination plans. Parallel activities of students and professionals often breed false analogies: "It isn't fair that I can't write on anything I want, any way I want. Nobody tells Amy Tan or Stephen King how or what to write!"

Faulty Analogy   Sometimes, the analogy we use to parallel an idea or object is something of a half-truth instead of a complete falsehood; that is, it might work in one context, but not in others. To compare human courtship rituals to those of peacocks, for example, might amusingly highlight the similarities, but the differences are too major to take the analogy seriously.

Tu Quoque   (pronounced *too qwo-kway*, Latin for "you also") You'd think that the likelihood of committing this fallacy would have vanished shortly after one's tenth birthday, but for some reason it lingers into adulthood. This is the error of analogy whereby Teddy says to Betty, "Don't you dare accuse *me* of cheating on the exam; I saw you cheating also."

Errors of Authorization

In this group of fallacies, authority figures or their testimonials are used vaguely or erroneously.

Vague Authority   In the sentence, "Science tells us that a catastrophic earthquake will strike Southern California within the next ten years," we would do well to question the term *science*. (In a similar vein, recall the commercial that begins, "Four out of five doctors recommend. . . .") We have no idea who or even what authority *science* is referring to, since *science* refers to a vast body of disciplines, not any particular authority. To remove the vagueness, the author would have to say something to this effect: "Seismologists at Cal Tech [or, better yet, Dr. So-and-So, a seismologist at Cal Tech] predicts that a catastrophic earthquake will strike Southern California within the next ten years."

Suspect Authority   Sometimes, it is not easy to tell whether an authority is reliable. Using the above example, if the credentials of the scientist predicting the earthquake are not disclosed—or if her field of expertise is a discipline other than seismology—we have a right to suspect her authority.

The suspect authority fallacy is encountered most frequently in advertisements. When a film star tells us that a certain brand of shampoo gives a "deep-bodied" luster to hair, we wonder what the basis for authority possibly could be, even assuming that everyone agrees on how a "deep-bodied" luster looks.

Keep in mind, of course, that such a commercial is not an example of false advertising. The commercial never states that the film star has the proper credentials to evaluate a product's quality, only that the product is the star's personal choice. The audience is left to make any further inferences, such as, "Gosh, if Wilma Superstar uses that shampoo, then it *must* be terrific."

Errors of Pleading

These fallacies stem from erroneous or improper use of the Aristotelian appeals discussed in Chapter 1.

Appeal to Fear   Anyone who has heard commercials for security alarm systems or auto-theft prevention devices is quite familiar with this appeal. The advertiser typically presents scenarios of coming home to find the place ransacked. "Better to be safe than sorry" is the common phrase brandished here. Keep in mind that this appeal becomes an error in pleading when it is excessive or when the scenarios presented are so extreme as to distort reality. If the advertiser for security alarms paints a lurid picture of you and your family being tortured or murdered by burglars, for example, such an appeal to fear likely would be excessive and thus erroneous.

Appeal to the Bandwagon   Appeal to the bandwagon is the fallacy behind peer pressure. "Hey, everyone else is going to the beach today; don't be a nerd and stay cooped up in the library on such a gorgeous day!" Being able to say no, to maintain your own integrity, and to do what is most responsible and best for you in the long term are hard when you are the only one following that path.

If you discover that everyone is suddenly buying or selling shares of stock that you own, the temptation is great to do likewise. It sometimes takes courage to say, "I'm going to think this out on my own and not follow the crowd."

Of course, an appeal to the bandwagon sometimes makes sense, as in the case of sound medical or health-care advice: "Millions of people get their teeth cleaned regularly (because they are far less likely to suffer from gum disease if they do so), so you should get your teeth cleaned too."

Appeal to Ignorance   The basis of the appeal here is that we can decide based on what is *not* known. For example, "We have every reason to believe that Martians exist because we have no way of knowing that they *don't exist*." The problem with this kind of reasoning, of course, is that there is no way to prove or disprove the claim.

One often encounters appeals to ignorance in informal scientific speculation. Have you ever gotten into a conversation about the likelihood of intelligent life on other worlds? You might commonly hear a line of reasoning that goes something like this:

> True, we haven't the slightest blip of evidence that intelligent beings exist beyond earth; but the universe is so vast and our understanding of what the universe could contain is so meager that there must be intelligent life out there somewhere!

Although one might argue that the probability of intelligent life increases in proportion to the size of the field, that probability does not necessarily approach inevitability unless compelling evidence is uncovered (indirect evidence of intelligent habitation, such as industrial pollutants in the atmosphere of a distant planet, for example).

◎/◎   Exercise 6.7

1. What is the connection between a method of reasoning and an error in reasoning?

2. State the principal difference between inductive and deductive reasoning.

3. For each of the following passages,

   - give the method of reasoning it belongs to;

   - indicate whether it is an appropriate or erroneous use of that method; and

   - if the latter, identify the error and suggest a way to resolve it.

   Note: There may be more than one error in a given passage or no errors at all.

a. Cats are just like people: They're intensely curious, and they get into trouble as a result of their curiosity.

b. The idiots who gave my car a tune-up forgot to clean the fuel injection system.

c. God is beyond logical understanding; therefore, one should never question the truth of God's existence.

d. All honors students are high achievers. José is a straight-A student. Therefore, José is a high achiever.

e. Jane: What do you think of my new boyfriend?

   Ann: I think he's a jerk.

   Jane: You just say that because you want him for yourself!

f. After interviewing a dozen students about their reading habits, I am convinced that students these days do not like to read poetry.

g. All of my friends who want to attend law school have signed up for the Advanced Argumentation course. Since you plan on going to law school, you should take this course too.

h. It's a good idea to wash fresh fruit before eating it; the last time I forgot to wash the strawberries I ate, I came down with food poisoning.

i. Music appreciation classes seem like a waste of time. I know what I like to listen to, and no music expert is going to change my mind about it.

j. Chicken is much tastier than oatmeal.

k. Libraries are clearly becoming obsolete because the Internet is growing so rapidly.

l. To answer your question about whether taxes should be raised, let me first call your attention to the fact that the unemployment rate in this state is lower than it has ever been.

m. Sound waves, just like light waves, can be low-frequency or high-frequency.

n. If children love to read, they will do well in school. Erika does well in school. Therefore, Erika loves to read.

o. Why should I vote? You haven't voted in years.

4. For each of the above passages, suggest ways in which the error, if one exists, may be corrected.

◎/◎   **Exercise 6.8**

Read "Love Is a Fallacy" by Max Shulman, a mid-twentieth-century humorist. In
it he attempts to demonstrate logical fallacies in action. Then answer the questions that follow.

Love Is a Fallacy | Max Shulman

Cool was I and logical. Keen, calculating, perspicacious, acute and astute—
I was all of these. My brain was as powerful as a dynamo, as precise as
a chemist's scales, as penetrating as a scalpel. And—think of it!—I was only
eighteen.

It is not often that one so young has such a giant intellect. Take, for example,
Petey Burch, my roommate at the University of Minnesota. Same age, same
background, but dumb as an ox. A nice enough fellow, you understand, but
nothing upstairs. Emotional type, unstable. Impressionable. Worst of all, a
faddist. Fads, I submit, are the very negation of reason. To be swept up in
every new craze that comes along, to surrender yourself to idiocy just because
everybody else is doing it—this, to me, is the acme of mindlessness. Not,
however, to Petey.

One afternoon I found Petey lying on his bed with an expression of such
distress on his face that I immediately diagnosed appendicitis. "Don't move,"
I said. "Don't take a laxative. I'll get a doctor."

"Raccoon," he mumbled thickly.

"Raccoon?" I said, pausing in my flight.   5

"I want a raccoon coat," he wailed.

I perceived that his trouble was not physical, but mental. "Why do you
want a raccoon coat?"

"I should have known it," he cried, pounding his temples. "I should have
known they'd come back when the Charleston came back. Like a fool I spent
all my money for textbooks, and now I can't get a raccoon coat."

"Can you mean," I said incredulously, "that people are actually wearing
raccoon coats again?"

"All the Big Men on Campus are wearing them. Where've you been?"   10

"In the library," I said, naming a place not frequented by Big Men on
Campus.

He leaped from the bed and paced the room. "I've got to have a raccoon
coat," he said passionately. "I've got to!"

"Petey, why? Look at it rationally. Raccoon coats are unsanitary. They
shed. They smell bad. They weigh too much. They're unsightly. They—"

"You don't understand," he interrupted impatiently. "It's the thing to do. Don't you want to be in the swim?"

"No," I said truthfully.   15

"Well, I do," he declared. "I'd give anything for a raccoon coat. Anything!"

My brain, that precision instrument, slipped into high gear. "Anything?" I asked, looking at him narrowly.

"Anything," he affirmed in ringing tones.

I stroked my chin thoughtfully. It so happened that I knew where to get my hands on a raccoon coat. My father had had one in his undergraduate days; it lay now in a trunk in the attic back home. It also happened that Petey had something I wanted. He didn't *have* it exactly, but at least he had first rights on it. I refer to his girl, Polly Espy.

I had long coveted Polly Espy. Let me emphasize that my desire for this   20
young woman was not emotional in nature. She was, to be sure, a girl who excited the emotions, but I was not one to let my heart rule my head. I wanted Polly for a shrewdly calculated, entirely cerebral reason.

I was a freshman in law school. In a few years I would be out in practice. I was well aware of the importance of the right kind of wife in furthering a lawyer's career. The successful lawyers I had observed were, almost without exception, married to beautiful, gracious, intelligent women. With one omission, Polly fitted these specifications perfectly.

Beautiful she was. She was not yet of pin-up proportions, but I felt sure that time would supply the lack. She already had the makings.

Gracious she was. By gracious I mean full of graces. She had an erectness of carriage, an ease of bearing, a poise that clearly indicated the best of breeding. At table her manners were exquisite. I had seen her at the Kozy Kampus Korner eating the specialty of the house—a sandwich that contained scraps of pot roast, gravy, chopped nuts, and a dipper of sauerkraut—without even getting her fingers moist.

Intelligent she was not. In fact, she veered in the opposite direction. But I believed that under my guidance she would smarten up. At any rate, it was worth a try. It is, after all, easier to make a beautiful dumb girl smart than to make an ugly smart girl beautiful.

"Petey," I said, "are you in love with Polly Espy?"   25

"I think she's a keen kid," he replied, "but I don't know if you'd call it love. Why?"

"Do you," I asked, "have any kind of formal arrangement with her? I mean are you going steady or anything like that?"

"No. We see each other quite a bit, but we both have other dates. Why?"

"Is there," I asked, "any other man for whom she has a particular fondness?"

"Not that I know of. Why?"   30

I nodded with satisfaction. "In other words, if you were out of the picture, the field would be open. Is that right?"

"I guess so. What are you getting at?"

"Nothing, nothing," I said innocently, and took my suitcase out of the closet.

"Where are you going?" asked Petey.

"Home for the weekend." I threw a few things into the bag.   35

"Listen," he said, clutching my arm eagerly, "while you're home, you couldn't get some money from your old man, could you, and lend it to me so I can buy a raccoon coat?"

"I may do better than that," I said with a mysterious wink and closed my bag and left.

"Look," I said to Petey when I got back Monday morning. I threw open the suitcase and revealed the huge, hairy, gamy object that my father had worn in his Stutz Bearcat in 1925.

"Holy Toledo!" said Petey reverently. He plunged his hands into the raccoon coat and then his face. "Holy Toledo!" he repeated fifteen or twenty times.

"Would you like it?" I asked.   40

"Oh yes!" he cried, clutching the greasy pelt to him. Then a canny look came into his eyes. "What do you want for it?"

"Your girl," I said, mincing no words.

"Polly?" he said in a horrified whisper. "You want Polly?"

"That's right."

He flung the coat from him. "Never," he said stoutly.   45

I shrugged. "Okay. If you don't want to be in the swim. I guess it's your business."

I sat down in a chair and pretended to read a book, but out of the corner of my eye I kept watching Petey. He was a torn man. First he looked at the coat with the expression of a waif at a bakery window. Then he turned away and set his jaw resolutely. Then he looked back at the coat, with even more longing in his face. Then he turned away, but with not so much resolution this time. Back and forth his head swiveled, desire waxing, resolution waning. Finally he didn't turn away at all; he just stood and stared with mad lust at the coat.

"It isn't as though I was in love with Polly," he said thickly. "Or going steady or anything like that."

"That's right," I murmured.

"What's Polly to me, or me to Polly?"   50

"Not a thing," said I.

"It's just been a casual kick—just a few laughs, that's all."

"Try on the coat," said I.

He complied. The coat bunched high over his ears and dropped all the way down to his shoe tops. He looked like a mound of dead raccoons. "Fits fine," he said happily.

I rose from my chair. "Is it a deal?" I asked, extending my hand.   55

He swallowed. "It's a deal," he said and shook my hand.

I had my first date with Polly the following evening. This was in the nature of a survey; I wanted to find out just how much work I had to do to get her mind up to the standard I required. I took her first to dinner. "Gee, that was a delish dinner," she said as we left the restaurant. Then I took her to a movie. "Gee, that was a marvy movie," she said as we left the theater. And then I took her home. "Gee, I had a sensaysh time," she said as she bade me good night.

I went back to my room with a heavy heart. I had gravely underestimated the size of my task. This girl's lack of information was terrifying. Nor would it be enough merely to supply her with information. First she had to be taught to *think*. This loomed as a project of no small dimensions, and at first I was tempted to give her back to Petey. But then I got to thinking about her abundant physical charms and about the way she entered the room and the way she handled a knife and fork, and I decided to make an effort.

I went about it, as in all things, systematically. I gave her a course in logic. It happened that I, as a law student, was taking a course in logic myself, so I had all the facts at my finger tips. "Polly," I said to her when I picked her up on our next date, "tonight we are going over to the Knoll and talk."

"Oo, terrif," she replied. One thing I will say for this girl: you would go   60
far to find another so agreeable.

We went to the Knoll, the campus trysting place, and we sat down under an old oak, and she looked at me expectantly. "What are we going to talk about?" she asked.

"Logic."

She thought this over for a minute and decided she liked it. "Magnif," she said.

"Logic," I said, clearing my throat, "is the science of thinking. Before we can think correctly, we must first learn to recognize the common fallacies of logic. These we will take up tonight."

"Wow-dow!" she cried, clapping her hands delightedly.   65

I winced, but went bravely on. "First let us examine the fallacy called Dicto Simpliciter."

"By all means," she urged, batting her lashes eagerly.

"Dicto Simpliciter means an argument based on an unqualified generalization. For example: Exercise is good. Therefore everybody should exercise."

"I agree," said Polly earnestly. "I mean exercise is wonderful. I mean it builds the body and everything."

"Polly," I said gently, "the argument is a fallacy. *Exercise is good* is an un-   70
qualified generalization. For instance, if you have heart disease, exercise is bad, not good. Many people are ordered by their doctors *not* to exercise. You must *qualify* the generalization. You must say exercise is *usually* good, or exercise is good *for most people*. Otherwise you have committed a Dicto Simpliciter. Do you see?"

"No," she confessed. "But this is marvy. Do more! Do more!"

"It will be better if you stop tugging at my sleeve," I told her, and when she desisted, I continued. "Next we take up a fallacy called Hasty Generalization. Listen carefully: You can't speak French. I can't speak French. Petey Burch can't speak French. I must therefore conclude that nobody at the University of Minnesota can speak French."

"Really?" said Polly, amazed. *"Nobody?"*

I hid my exasperation. "Polly, it's a fallacy. The generalization is reached too hastily. There are too few instances to support such a conclusion."

"Know any more fallacies?" she asked breathlessly. "This is more fun than   75
dancing even."

I fought off a wave of despair. I was getting nowhere with this girl, absolutely nowhere. Still, I am nothing if not persistent. I continued. "Next comes Post Hoc. Listen to this: Let's not take Bill on our picnic. Every time we take him out with us, it rains."

"I know somebody just like that," she exclaimed. "A girl back home—Eula Becker, her name is. It never fails. Every single time we take her on a picnic—"

"Polly," I said sharply, "it's a fallacy. Eula Becker doesn't *cause* the rain. She has no connection with the rain. You are guilty of Post Hoc if you blame Eula Becker."

"I'll never do it again," she promised contritely. "Are you mad at me?"

I sighed deeply. "No, Polly, I'm not mad."   80

"Then tell me some more fallacies."

"All right. Let's try Contradictory Premises."

"Yes, let's," she chirped, blinking her eyes happily.

I frowned, but plunged ahead. "Here's an example of Contradictory Premises: If God can do anything, can He make a stone so heavy that He won't be able to lift it?"

"Of course," she replied promptly.   85

"But if He can do anything, He can lift the stone," I pointed out.

"Yeah," she said thoughtfully. "Well, then I guess He can't make the stone."

"But He can do anything," I reminded her.

She scratched her pretty, empty head. "I'm all confused," she admitted.

"Of course you are. Because when the premises of an argument contradict   90
each other, there can be no argument. If there is an irresistible force, there can be no immovable object. If there is an immovable object, there can be no irresistible force. Get it?"

"Tell me some more of this keen stuff," she said eagerly.

I consulted my watch. "I think we'd better call it a night. I'll take you home now, and you go over all the things you've learned. We'll have another session tomorrow night."

I deposited her at the girl's dormitory, where she assured me that she had had a perfectly terrif evening, and I went glumly home to my room. Petey lay snoring in his bed, the raccoon coat huddled like a great hairy beast at his feet. For a moment I considered waking him and telling him that he could have his girl back. It seemed clear that my project was doomed to failure. The girl simply had a logic-proof head.

But then I reconsidered, I had wasted one evening; I might as well waste another. Who knew? Maybe somewhere in the extinct crater of her mind, a few embers still smoldered. Maybe somehow I could fan them into flame. Admittedly it was not a prospect fraught with hope, but I decided to give it one more try.

Seated under the oak the next evening I said, "Our first fallacy tonight is 95 called Ad Misericordiam."

She quivered with delight.

"Listen closely," I said. "A man applies for a job. When the boss asks him what his qualifications are, he replies that he has a wife and six children at home, the wife is a helpless cripple, the children have nothing to eat, no clothes to wear, no shoes on their feet, there are no beds in the house, no coal in the cellar, and winter is coming."

A tear rolled down each of Polly's pink cheeks. "Oh, this is awful, awful," she sobbed.

"Yes, it's awful," I agreed, "but it's no argument. The man never answered the boss's question about his qualifications. Instead he appealed to the boss's sympathy. He committed the fallacy of Ad Misericordiam. Do you understand?"

"Have you got a handkerchief?" she blubbered. 100

I handed her a handkerchief and tried to keep from screaming while she wiped her eyes. "Next," I said in a carefully controlled tone, "we will discuss False Analogy. Here is an example: Students should be allowed to look at their textbooks during examinations. After all, surgeons have X-rays to guide them during an operation, lawyers have briefs to guide them during a trial, carpenters have blueprints to guide them when they are building a house. Why, then, shouldn't students be allowed to look at their textbooks during an examination?"

"There now," she said enthusiastically, "is the most marvy idea I've heard in years."

"Polly," I said testily, "the argument is all wrong. Doctors, lawyers, and carpenters aren't taking a test to see how much they have learned, but students are. The situations are altogether different, and you can't make an analogy between them."

"I still think it's a good idea," said Polly.

"Nuts," I muttered. Doggedly I pressed on. "Next we'll try Hypothesis 105 Contrary to Fact."

"Sounds yummy," was Polly's reaction.

"Listen: If Madame Curie had not happened to leave a photographic plate in a drawer with a chunk of pitchblende, the world today would not know about radium."

"True, true," said Polly, nodding her head. "Did you see the movie? Oh, it just knocked me out. That Walter Pidgeon is so dreamy. I mean he fractures me."

"If you can forget Mr. Pidgeon for a moment," I said coldly, "I would like to point out that the statement is a fallacy. Maybe Madame Curie would have discovered radium at some later date. Maybe somebody else would have discovered it. Maybe any number of things would have happened. You can't start with a hypothesis that is not true and then draw any supportable conclusions from it."

"They ought to put Walter Pidgeon in more pictures," said Polly. "I hardly ever see him any more." 110

One more chance, I decided. But just one more. There is a limit to what flesh and blood can bear. "The next fallacy is called Poisoning the Well."

"How cute!" she gurgled.

"Two men are having a debate. The first one gets up and says, 'My opponent is a notorious liar. You can't believe a word that he is going to say.' Now, Polly, think. Think hard. What's wrong?"

I watched her closely as she knit her creamy brow in concentration. Suddenly a glimmer of intelligence—the first I had seen—came into her eyes. "It's not fair," she said with indignation. "It's not a bit fair. What chance has the second man got if the first man calls him a liar before he even begins talking?"

"Right!" I cried exultantly. "One hundred percent right. It's not fair. The 115 first man has *poisoned the well* before anybody could drink from it. He has hamstrung his opponent before he could even start. . . . Polly, I'm proud of you."

"Pshaw," she murmured, blushing with pleasure.

"You see, my dear, these things aren't so hard. All you have to do is concentrate. Think—examine—evaluate. Come now, let's review everything we have learned."

"Fire away," she said with an airy wave of her hand.

Heartened by the knowledge that Polly was not altogether a cretin, I began a long, patient review of all I had told her. Over and over and over again I cited instances, pointed out flaws, kept hammering away without let up. It was like digging a tunnel. At first everything was work, sweat, and darkness. I had no idea when I would reach the light, or even *if* I would. But I persisted. I pounded and clawed and scraped, and finally I was rewarded. I saw a chink of light. And then the chink got bigger and the sun came pouring in and all was bright.

Five grueling nights this took, but it was worth it. I had made a logician 120 out of Polly; I had taught her to think. My job was done. She was worthy of me at last. She was a fit wife for me, a proper hostess for my many mansions, a suitable mother for my well-heeled children. It must not be thought that I was without love for this girl. Quite the contrary. Just as Pygmalion loved the perfect woman he had fashioned, so I loved mine. I determined to acquaint her with my feelings at our very next meeting. The time had come to change our relationship from academic to romantic.

"Polly," I said when next we sat beneath our oak, "tonight we will not discuss fallacies."

"Aw, gee," she said, disappointed.

"My dear," I said, favoring her with a smile, "we have now spent five evenings together. We have gotten along splendidly. It is clear that we are well matched."

"Hasty Generalization," said Polly brightly.

"I beg your pardon," said I.   125

"Hasty Generalization," she repeated. "How can you say that we are well matched on the basis of only five dates?"

I chuckled with amusement. The dear child had learned her lessons well.

"My dear," I said, patting her hand in a tolerant manner, "five dates is plenty. After all, you don't have to eat a whole cake to know that it's good."

"False Analogy," said Polly promptly. "I'm not a cake. I'm a girl."

I chuckled with somewhat less amusement. The dear child had learned   130
her lessons perhaps too well. I decided to change tactics. Obviously the best approach was a simple, strong, direct declaration of love. I paused for a moment while my massive brain chose the proper words. Then I began:

"Polly, I love you. You are the whole world to me, and the moon and the stars and the constellations of outer space. Please, my darling, say that you will go steady with me, for if you will not, life will be meaningless. I will languish. I will refuse my meals. I will wander the face of the earth, a shambling, hollow-eyed hulk."

There, I thought, folding my arms, that ought to do it.

"Ad Misericordiam," said Polly.

I ground my teeth. I was not Pygmalion; I was Frankenstein, and my monster had me by the throat. Frantically I fought back the tide of panic surging through me. At all costs I had to keep cool.

"Well, Polly," I said, forcing a smile, "you certainly have learned your   135
fallacies."

"You're darn right," she said with a vigorous nod.

"And who taught them to you, Polly?"

"You did."

"That's right. So you do owe me something, don't you, my dear? If I hadn't come along you never would have learned about fallacies."

"Hypothesis Contrary to Fact," she said instantly.   140

I dashed perspiration from my brow. "Polly," I croaked, "you mustn't take all these things so literally. I mean this is just classroom stuff. You know that the things you learn in school don't have anything to do with life."

"Dicto Simpliciter," she said, wagging her finger at me playfully.

That did it. I leaped to my feet, bellowing like a bull. "Will you or will you not go steady with me?"

"I will not," she replied.

"Why not?" I demanded.   145

"Because this afternoon I promised Petey Burch that I would go steady with him."

I reeled back, overcome with the infamy of it. After he promised, after he made a deal, after he shook my hand! "The rat!" I shrieked, kicking up great chunks of turf. "You can't go with him, Polly. He's a liar. He's a cheat. He's a rat."

"Poisoning the Well," said Polly, "and stop shouting. I think shouting must be a fallacy too."

With an immense effort of will, I modulated my voice. "All right, I said. "You're a logician. Let's look at this thing logically. How could you choose Petey Burch over me? Look at me—a brilliant student, a tremendous intellectual, a man with an assured future. Look at Petey—a knothead, a jitterbug, a guy who'll never know where his next meal is coming from. Can you give me one logical reason why you should go steady with Petey Burch?"

"I certainly can," declared Polly. "He's got a raccoon coat." ◎/◎   150

1. Shulman ironically relies on fallacies of his own (such as gender stereotyping) as a way of generating humor. Suggest ways in which the piece could be revised without having to rely on such fallacies.

2. How reliable is this piece as a gauge of problematic reasoning among college students? Although its humor is somewhat dated, does it possess enough of an underlying seriousness to warrant further analysis of the reasoning skills of today's college students?

Chapter Summary

Argumentative writing requires careful reasoning, the ability to think critically and logically about the issues you are investigating and to recognize errors in logic. Such errors—known as *fallacies* (for example, false analogy and ad hominem)—often arise when writers are not sufficiently knowledgeable about their subject or have not thought sufficiently about possible counterarguments to their thesis. The principal strategies that constitute good reasoning in argument are deduction, induction, categorization, analogy, authorization, and plea. Deduction involves identifying contradictions, inconsistencies, omissions, and oversimplifications, as well as reducing unsound claims to their logical absurdity. Induction involves determining a sufficient quantity for the sample as well as determining the reliability of that sample. Categorization involves classifying items according to similar characteristics. Analogy is used to help readers understand a concept by comparing it to one that is simpler and more familiar. Authorization refers to the use of testimony by experts as a supplement to empirical evidence to support claims. Plea refers to use of emotional appeals to motivate readers to take action. When learning to recognize errors in reasoning, don't worry excessively about using fallacies inadvertently; the goal is to become sufficiently familiar with them to reduce the likelihood of their occurring.

Checklist

1. Is the line of reasoning used in my argument logical and coherent?
2. Do I cover all facets of my argument?
3. Do I anticipate counterarguments?
4. Do I commit any errors in reasoning?
   a. Fallacies of deduction such as fourth term, non sequitur, and ad hominem?
   b. Fallacies of induction such as unsupported generalization, red herring, poisoning the well, and begging the question?
   c. Fallacies of categorization such as false dichotomy and mixing apples with oranges?
   d. Fallacies of analogy such as false analogy and faulty analogy?
   e. Fallacies of authorization such as vague authority and suspect authority?
   f. Fallacies of pleading such as appeal to fear, appeal to the bandwagon, and appeal to ignorance?

Writing Projects

1. Read several newspaper or magazine editorial or opinion pieces on a given topic; then, write a comparative evaluation of each piece based on the presence and frequency of deductive and inductive errors in reasoning you detect in them.

2. Write an essay on the importance of good reasoning in establishing healthy human relationships, such as romantic or business relationships, friendships, parent–sibling relationships, and so on. Focus on specific kinds of errors in reasoning that occur, using actual or representative examples.

3. Initiate an informal argument on one of the current debates on your campus with two or more of your classmates in a small group, and while you are arguing, jot down any fallacies you detect. (To be fair to your classmates, ask them to jot down any fallacies they catch *you* falling prey to.) Afterward, write up the argument, supporting the claim you feel most committed to. Do all you can to rid the argument of the detected fallacies.

7 | Argument across the Disciplines

We see comparatively
—Emily Dickinson

CONSIDERING THE DISCIPLINES

Have you ever tried unsuccessfully to argue a point about the virtue of passion in a film you've just seen, using your notions of virtue over reason learned in your philosophy class? Quite likely, you were using a method of argument appropriate for philosophy, but not for film criticism. During your first year in college you quickly discovered that scholars in different disciplines communicate their ideas differently. A physics professor regards evidence differently from, a literature professor. Part of what it takes to succeed in college involves understanding these differences. In this chapter you will learn strategies of argument associated with several academic disciplines: the arts (fine art and literature), the social sciences, the natural sciences, and the professional disciplines of business,engineering, and law.

Argument is the engine that drives intellectual inquiry in all disciplines. New discoveries or new insights resulting from original research require explanation and interpretation, and there is always more than one way to explain or interpret new information. Two researchers of equal competence can examine the same body of facts and reach very different conclusions because experts interpret findings differently. Although they describe their methodology, report their evidence, and document their sources accurately (so that other researchers may independently determine the validity of their conclusions), they may assign greater importance to some facts more than others, or apply different value-based criteria to their findings.

How Argumentation Differs from Discipline to Discipline

Argumentative discourse is essential to the advancement of knowledge, regardless of the field of inquiry. However, every field of inquiry has developed its own manner of argument and even its own set of criteria for what qualifies as evidence. These differences can be confusing at first to students, who soon discover that evidence in literary criticism means something quite different from evidence in physics or history or economics. By comparing the different ways physicists, economists, art historians, sociologists, engineers, or literary critics argue their respective ideas, you will gain a deeper understanding of how these academic disciplines operate. The aim of this chapter is to help you become familiar with these discipline-specific methods of argument and criteria for evidence.

Strategies of Argument in the Arts

A common initial reaction students may have with regard to arguing about works of art is that art is so subjective any point of view ought to be just as valid as another. Thus, one's claim that a Jackson Pollack "splatter" canvas could just as easily have been created by a child throwing a temper tantrum with paint might be considered just as legitimate as the claim that Pollack's canvases are brilliant developments in abstract expressionism. Or that a free-verse poem by Ezra Pound is utterly lacking in technique or emotional impact.

First of all, any claim is *potentially* legitimate; but, as is true of claims in any discipline, in order for there to be true, full argument, appropriate evidence must be brought in to support the claim. Keep in mind that evidence in the arts does not mean quite the same thing as evidence in other disciplines. Appropriate evidence in the context of visual arts, for example, would include expert opinion by critics, historians, philosophers (aestheticians), and museum curators, all of whom ought to be specialists in the period and genre(s) in which the artist is working. For works of literature, appropriate evidence would include expert opinion by literary scholars with a specialty in Elizabethan drama, nineteenth-century American poetry, and so on.

Secondly, a work of art or literature should be placed in the context of a particular artistic or literary movement or its historical, social, and political milieu. However, such contextualizing is necessary only if the critical approach of the arguer is historical, social, or political. A work of art or literature can be the source of its own internal evidence—that is, the critic identifies and evaluates the artist's or writer's techniques, attempting to show how the aim of the work in question is successfully rendered by the effective use of those techniques.

Arguing Critically about a Painting

As anyone who has studied art history knows, the history of painting (and other arts such as theatre and music) has major movements and revolutions that often parallel history in general. When discussing a painting, you generally should, regardless of the critical stance you wish to take, situate the work in its historical context and then in the context of the artistic movement in which the artist seems to be working, extending, satirizing, or otherwise rebelling against. Once this contextualizing information has been conveyed, you might compare or contrast the painting (a) to paintings by other artists within the movement and

(b) to other paintings by the same artist, perhaps to show a continuity of purpose from one work to the next. Finally, readers will want to know your impressions of the painting—what you like or dislike about the artist's treatment of the subject, the techniques used (palette and brush work, lighting, mood), and so on. A good critic will also call attention to other critics' assessments of the work, and the reasons why those assessments are faulty or limited.

Example of a Short Argument about a Painting

One of the most famous—and most parodied—modern American paintings is *American Gothic* (1930) by Grant Wood, an Iowa artist, influenced by Gothic and Renaissance painting, who captured rural motifs in his charming canvases.

In the following commentary, note how art critic Jonathan Jones first places the painting in its historical and regional context, and then comments on the painting's ambiguous aspects.

American Gothic,
Grant Wood (1930)

Jonathan Jones

American Gothic, 1930 (oil on board), Wood, Grant (1892–1942)/The Art Institute of Chicago, IL, USA/© DACS/The Bridgeman Art Library International

The Guardian, Saturday 18 May 2002

Artist: Grant Wood (1892–1941) was not all he seemed. In the 1930s he became famous in the US as one of the leading figures in the Regionalist movement, an anti-modern, anti-European campaign for a purely and folklorically American art. Regionalist painters rejected the big cosmopolitan cities and depicted, in quite homely ways, rural America. This was the one American art movement that

came from, and identified with, the midwestern heartland, rather
than the east coast or California.

Wood hailed from and lived in small-town Iowa, and painted ar-
chaic visions of an America of little hamlets nestling in rounded
hills under the beacon of a white-painted church. Yet unlike
Thomas Hart Benton, the self-promoting leader of the movement,
Wood was a quiet, elusive figure with a fondness for European art.
In the 1920s he made four trips to Europe. His style was formed
by the art he saw there, most of all northern renaissance artists
such as Van Eyck, but also the 1920s German neue sachlichkeit
(new objectivity) movement.

Wood's often dreamlike paintings recall the stories of Washington Irving, imagining a small-town world that is comforting
and enclosed yet could easily be the stage for spooky nocturnal
mayhem. His painting The Midnight Ride of Paul Revere (1931), in
the Metropolitan Museum of Art, New York, despite its nationalist
theme, is an eerie vision of a lonely rider hurtling through an
ivory-coloured slumbering town by moonlight.

Subject: The models, dressed in clothes dating from the 1890s,
are Wood's sister, Nan, and their dentist, BH McKeeby of Cedar
Rapids. They pose in front of an 1880s wood-frame house—which
still exists as a tourist attraction in the Iowa town of Eldon—
built in the American Gothic or Carpenter's Gothic style.

Distinguishing features: They are keeping us out of their
world rather than showing it off. The close-packed bodies of the
19th-century farmer and his spinster daughter played by Nan and
McKeeby form a wall between us and the white wooden house. The
house itself is a second closing of space, its front wall im-
penetrably neat, with blinds pulled down over the windows. Only
behind that do we glimpse the blue sky and round puffy trees of
pastoral joy.

The farmer is at once genteelly studious, like a clerk, and
aggressive, as if he has a serious temper. He looks at us in a
no-nonsense way, and that pitchfork he holds is extremely phallic
and sharp: it could do you a nasty injury. Her gaze is anxiously
sidelong. She might be watching some boys, wondering if they are

about to steal apples, or seeing a man she had feelings for ride past with his new city wife. She wears an ornate brooch that suggests another, distant world of passion and desire, at odds with her neat white collar and tightly tied hair. Behind her ear hangs a wisp of loose, curling golden hair that suggests suppressed sensuality.

People have argued about where this painting stands on midwestern, American heartland values ever since it was first exhibited. Wood denied that it was satirical. He proclaimed his sincere belief in the values of hearth and home. And yet it is impossible to deny the strangeness of this American masterpiece, in which nothing is quite as stable as a first glance might suggest.

It is fictive in multiple ways. It is a 19th-century picture painted in the 20th century. It is an apparently naive painting by a sophisticated artist. Even the title is ambiguous. American Gothic refers to the architecture of the house, but also unavoidably has associations with Edgar Allan Poe and big-city prejudices about in-marrying, psychopathic country folk.

The weirdest ambiguities surround the house. That pointed medieval-style window suggests to some viewers a church; indeed, were it not for the potted plants on the porch and the decorative blind, we might mistake it for a house of the Lord. But in a private house, it has other implications. Given the plain self-presentation of these people, the medieval window between their heads is incongruously flamboyant, a bit of fantasy that sits oddly with the whitewashed clapboard and the sombre dress. One feels this strange architecture might have inspired the painting—as if, seeing the house, Wood had wondered about its original inhabitants. There is something odd about that window and the concealed upstairs room behind it. Anything could go on up there.

Inspirations and influences: Jan van Eyck's Arnolfini Portrait (1434) is a model for this painting, as a double domestic portrait and as a mystery.

Where is it? The Art Institute of Chicago.

Source: American Gothic, Grant Wood (1930) By Jonathan Jones The Guardian, Saturday 18 May 2002. Copyright Guardian News & Media Ltd 2002.

Notice how Jones begins his critique by providing background information about Wood and his work, in relation to other regionalist painters, before presenting his personal responses to the painting. If Jones were aiming for a scholarly audience instead of a lay audience with an interest in the arts, he probably would have compared his own reactions to the painting with those of other art critics.

◎∕◎ Exercise 7.1

1. After carefully studying Grant Wood's *American Gothic,* write your own critique of the painting. What do the two figures represent to you? Why does Wood title his painting *American Gothic?* Consider as many elements of the painting as you can before working out your own response to it. What, for example, does the pitchfork represent? What do you make of the woman's expression? The man's?

2. Critique Jonathan Jones's interpretation of the painting. Which assertions to you agree with or disagree with, and why?

Arguing Critically about a Poem

People tend to react to poems with delight or confusion or both. Much modern poetry—poems written during the twentieth and twenty-first centuries—confuses general readers and creates an aversion to poetry that stays with them a long time. But modern poetry shares many characteristics with poetry from previous ages, and uses poetic techniques that were developed centuries ago—techniques like irony, symbolism, figurative language, and wordplay.

Key Elements in a Critical Discussion of a Poem

As is true of writing about any work of art, it makes sense first to situate the poem in its historical and cultural context. For a critical discussion that aims solely to illuminate what the poem is "about"—its theme and the techniques the poet uses to convey the theme (known as *formalist criticism*)—historical or cultural information is usually omitted or presented as part of the introduction. For biographical, gender/feminist, or cultural critics, the larger context is the whole point. We cannot fully understand a poem, these critics argue, unless we know as much as we can about the poet's life and times.

Example of a Short Argument about a Poem

Study the following student critique of Shelley's famous poem "Ozymandias." First, read the poem and form your own response to it; next, read the critique, paying attention to the way Joseph Forte structures his argument in terms of introductory remarks, presentation of thesis, defense of thesis, and conclusion; finally, reread the critique to determine the effectiveness of Forte's argument and the ways it might be strengthened.

Joseph Forte

3-19-10

Introduction to Poetry

Percy Bysshe Shelley (1792-1822)

Ozymandias (1818)

Percy Bysshe Shelley

I met a traveller from an antique land
Who said: Two vast and trunkless legs of stone
Stand in the desert. Near them, on the sand,
Half sunk, a shattered visage lies, whose frown
And wrinkled lip, and sneer of cold command
Tell that its sculptor well those passions read
Which yet survive, stamped on these lifeless things,
The hand that mocked them and the heart that fed.
And on the pedestal these words appear:
"My name is Ozymandias, king of kings:
Look on my works, ye Mighty, and despair!"
Nothing beside remains. Round the decay
Of that colossal wreck, boundless and bare
The lone and level sands stretch far away.

Recession-Era Reflections on Percy Shelley's *Ozymandias*

Imagine the sense of wonder that must have overcome Giovanni
Belzoni, a nineteenth-century Italian explorer, when he discovered

the massive statue of Ramses II (whose Greek name was "Ozymandias")
dwelling inside the even larger Ramesseum temple. To Belzoni, the
huge visage of Ramses must have represented the vast, age-old power
and majesty of the early Egyptians. During Belzoni's life, the
ancient Egyptians would have seemed mysterious and powerful indeed.
In part, this was due to the European public's fad-like obsession
with the Egyptians at this time (Napoleon himself made an unsuccessful bid for the statue of Ramses). We would be naive, though,
if we did not acknowledge that the crumbling ruins of the vast
empires of old still captivate us today.

British poet Percy Shelley must have been similarly captivated
when he wrote *Ozymandias*. After viewing the statue at London's
British Museum, Shelley and his friend Horace Smith entered into
a friendly competition to see who could write the better poem
about Ramses. Shelley's poem went on to achieve world renown, and
for good reason. The poem's central theme of all peoples' inevitable decline has captivated generations just as the real statue
of Ozymandias has. *Ozymandias's* message of human impermanence is
all the more foreboding today, as America faces a century that
may see its loss of international dominance. An examination of
the poem's place in the Romantic movement as well as its place in
Shelley's own body of work can give context that supports the
poem's increasing relevance in the present.

To understand this context, we must begin with a broad understanding of what makes *Ozymandias* an essential Romantic poem. With
broad strokes, we can paint Romanticism as a reaction to the norms
of the Age of Enlightenment, particularly the idea that the natural
world and the cosmic order could be completely explained by reason.
Romanticists instead emphasized the role of intuition and emotion
in experience, as well as the power of imagination. Furthermore,
Romanticists found beauty and mystery in nature as well as the
achievements of exotic, ancient peoples. These fundamental qualities of Romanticism can be easily observed in *Ozymandias*.

For example, the tragedy of Ozymandias' ruin showcases Romantic Poetry's strength in inspiring emotion in the reader. Shelley
gives the poem an emotional core by calling attention to certain
details of the desert scene. By describing Ozymandias' "frown and

wrinkled lip, and sneer of cold command," he gives an inanimate object (the statue) the personal, emotional qualities of a human being. These very passions form the basis for the inscription of the statue, which is the poem's focal point. By personifying the object of ruin with the "spirit" of an ancient, mysterious despot, *Ozymandias* is able to make a powerful emotional plea in a manner very consistent with Romantic norms. The other imagery in the poem is also written to inspire great emotion. Shelley's descriptions of the desert surrounding the ruined stature are restrained in their content, yet still manage to evoke powerful feelings of wonder in the reader, perhaps because of their near-monolithic simplicity.

Shelley employs his mastery of diction to elicit more gut-level reactions. The traveler is from an "antique" land, not a merely "ancient" land. The sands are "lone" and level, not "desolate" and level. These word choices further pull at the reader's heartstrings, evoking the feelings of nostalgia and solitude, respectively. By imbuing every line of the poem with emotional power, Shelley enhances the personal relevance of the poem to the reader by appealing directly to his or her emotions. All this passionate use of emotion places *Ozymandias* well within the conventions of Romantic Poetry.

Yet, *Ozymandias* also delicately defies one of the Romantic Movement's ideals by implicitly disagreeing with the movement's love of nationalism. Nationalism became important to Romanticism through the movement's love for national folklore and local traditions as well as the teachings of intellectuals such as Rousseau. Eventually, Romanticism and Nationalism became intimately intertwined. For example, Delacroix's *Liberty Leading the People,* one of the most widely-known Romantic paintings, explicitly supports nationalism. *Ozymandias* seems to defy this Romantic tradition. The poem's central theme of human impermanence applies to the ousting of centuries-old monarchies by new national governments, but also applies to the upstarts doing the ousting.

Just as the aristocracy had grown bloated, corrupt, and unpopular, so are all forms of government subject to eventual decay and decline. The new national governments being formed on the ashes of the monarchies would, in time, be responsible for many of the injustices and cruelties the monarchies were accused of in the first place. Many of the 20th century's acts of evil have, in fact, been the doing of democratic nations (the Holocaust, for one, was perpetrated by an elected government.) Even today, wage slavery, wars of aggression, and corruption still exist. The seeds of democracy that were sewn in Shelley's time have borne fruit that is not unmarred by the wrongs of past governments. Even the loftiest ideals eventually give way to harsh realities. The nationalist movements of Shelley's time appear overconfident (even naïve) when viewed through the cynical lens of *Ozymandias.*

Ironically, *The Masque of Anarchy,* another famous work written by Shelley, appears (at first) to wholeheartedly endorse the nationalist rebellions of the time. *Masque* (attached) does not actually support nationalism, however. In fact, upon closer examination, the poem reveals itself as anti-violence and anti-rebellion. This affirms Shelley's defiance of the mainstream Romantic acceptance of nationalist revolutions.

> **The Masque of Anarchy** – Percy Bysshe Shelley, 1819
> Stand ye calm and resolute,
> Like a forest close and mute,
> With folded arms and looks which are
> Weapons of unvanquished war.
> And if then the tyrants dare,
> Let them ride among you there,
> Slash, and stab, and maim and hew,
> What they like, that let them do.
> With folded arms and steady eyes,
> And little fear, and less surprise
> Look upon them as they slay
> Till their rage has died away
> Then they will return with shame
> To the place from which they came,
> And the blood thus shed will speak
> In hot blushes on their cheek.
> Rise like Lions after slumber

> In unvanquishable number,
> Shake your chains to earth like dew
> Which in sleep had fallen on you—
> Ye are many — they are few.

Perhaps *Masque* could be understood to support the Nationalist revolutions of Shelley's era if only history had proceeded differently. If Europe's monarchies had been toppled peacefully with a minimum of bloodshed, then *Masque*, which supports peaceful protest, would be in concord with the actions of the era's rebels. Unfortunately, history did not unfold in this fashion. For example, the French Revolution resulted in extensive death and destruction. Hugh Gough writes in his 1998 book *The Terror in the French Revolution* that up to 40,000 French citizens were executed during the reign of terror that occurred once the forces of the Revolution had seized power.

The cruel fact that much of the French Revolution's violence was directed at the average French citizenry surely did not escape Shelley. The systemic violence against France's own populace resembled the tyranny of the very monarchs they had overthrown. The Revolution had suffered a symbolic decline similar to Ozymandias's literal one; its original ideals of fraternity and equality had almost completely decayed. *Masque,* then, can stand beside *Ozymandias* as a critique of nationalist movements. The poem offers an alternative solution to the problems caused by Europe's monarchies. By advocating pacifism and non-violent protest, *Masque* attempts to protect would-be rebels from falling for the same traps that perverted the spirit of the French Revolution.

Examining *Ozymandias*'s historical context and its relation to Shelley's other work leads us to the conclusion that even our current society, founded on principles of liberty and justice, is no more permanent than the tyranny it replaced. *Ozymandias* may seem like a rather obvious choice for an essay given our society's current trajectory: The *Wall Street Journal's* MarketWatch predicts China's GDP will overtake the USA's by the early 2020s. Now, Shelley's words seem more ominous than ever. The institutions we build for ourselves, the nations we form for protection, and the societies we create to give our lives' purpose, relate in their imperfection and impermanence. Nevertheless, this fact should not inspire feelings of hopelessness in us. On the contrary, it should inspire us to action. By realizing the limited nature of our influence, we should aim to make prudent, intelligent decisions. If we are all eventually destined to become Ozymandias, alone and forgotten, buried in the sands of time, then the least we can do is leave behind evidence of the good judgment that made us great in the first place, not the hubris that hastened our fall.

Exercise 7.2

1. What are the main assertions Forte makes about "Ozymandias"? How convincingly does he support these assertions? Are there any aspects of the poem that Forte overlooks? If so, what are they?

2. Write a textual explication of "Ozymandias," limiting your commentary to the text of the poem. For example, you might focus your attention on Shelley's use of symbolism and the way it helps convey the theme.

3. Compare "Ozymandias" to "The Masque of Anarchy," focusing on the similarities and differences of theme and technique used to convey the theme.

Strategies of Argument in the Natural Sciences

It is sometimes assumed that scientific discourse is purely objective, that phenomena are examined, measured, and reported, without recourse to critical inquiry or debate. While it is true that many *basics* of science can be demonstrated through indisputable experiment—such as dropping two balls of unequal weight to show that all objects fall at the same rate of thirty-two feet per second, or creating table salt (sodium chloride) by mixing together two poisonous substances, sodium and hydrochloric acid—more complex scientific matters, such as whether salt in certain quantities can be beneficial or harmful to human health, are open to disputation. Indeed, scientists *welcome* disputation. In the 1996 film *Contact* (based on the novel by the late Carl Sagan), astronomer Eleanor Arroway (played by Jodie Foster) shouts to her colleagues, "Make me a liar," after detecting what she thinks is an artificial signal from interstellar space. In other words, she is asking her fellow astronomers to try and *disprove* her assumption, to think of every possible alternative explanation for the signal—a communication satellite? a secret military code? a technical glitch? Only by doing everything to disprove the assumption can one reach a reliable explanation for the phenomenon.

Arguing Critically about an Issue in Space Exploration

One of the most frequent questions posed by the general public regarding space exploration is this: Why spend billions of dollars exploring other worlds, sending astronauts to the International Space Station, launching telescopes into orbit, and so on, when those funds could be used to improve the quality of life on Earth? Think of what a billion dollars could do to alleviate homelessness! Think of how much food a billion dollars could purchase for starving people in Darfur! The question is entirely legitimate. Few would disagree that more could be done to combat human suffering—if not globally, at least in our own country. And yet . . . must one endeavor exclude the other? Why can't we work harder to eliminate poverty *and* explore space? The underlying concern, of course, has to do with necessity. Why is it necessary to explore space? What benefits, if any, are derived from such an expensive and dangerous pursuit? Those are the questions that need to be carefully addressed. Although the space age is more than fifty-five years old (it officially began on October 4, 1957, when the Soviet Union launched Sputnik I, the first artificial satellite), people still tend to associate space exploration with science fiction-like fancifulness—nice for escapist entertainment but hardly relevant to solving the practical problems of the world.

A little reflection will help us realize that space exploration *has* led to solving practical problems of the world. Let's start with global communications: without having learned to launch satellites into orbit, cellular phone and GPS technology would not exist, nor would it be possible to receive live television broadcasts from the other side of the world. A quick visit to NASA's website (www.nasa.gov) reminds us of many additional practical advances produced directly or indirectly through space exploration:

- monitoring of climate change—studying carbon emissions, aerosols, and other greenhouse gases; polar ice-cap shrinkage; rising sea levels
- tracking of weather systems such as hurricanes
- changes in Earth's ozone layer; amount of solar radiation reaching the surface
- monitoring volcanoes
- imaging of natural and industrial disasters such as the Gulf oil spill

Granted, you may be thinking, there are some practical applications to space research—but there are also impractical ones. Some might argue that exploring space in order to pave the way toward colonizing the moon and Mars is an example of an impractical application. But it may be difficult to draw the line between practical and impractical. Much depends on one's values and sense of priorities. It also depends on how skillfully one can persuade others of those values and priorities.

Key Elements in a Critical Discussion of a Space Exploration Issue

As with other issues of a scientific nature, issues in space exploration will be familiar to the general reader only in the most general way. They may know, for example, that NASA has been developing plans for a human expedition to Mars, perhaps by 2035, but they may not be familiar with the reasons for or against such a mission, other than the most superficial pro/con reasons (e.g., pro: exploring the unknown is part of what it means to be human; con: such an expedition would be far too expensive to fund in light of other economic needs). Thus, when dealing with a space exploration issue, the arguer must provide more substantive analysis. This requires not only in-depth research, but presentation of the information yielded by the research—often technical in nature—in a manner that nonspecialists can understand.

Example of a Short Argument on a Space Exploration Issue

Many people favor robotic exploration of space because it is far less expensive than human exploration and does not pose a threat to humans. Others argue that human exploration is necessary—no robot can explore as thoroughly as a trained human scientist. Moreover, exploration is an essential human trait, a fundamental part of what it means to be human.

But how far are you willing to carry that rationale? You might agree that the human exploration of Mars, setting aside the enormous expense, would be a great adventure for humankind. But what about colonizing Mars? Read Robert Zubrin's case for Martian colonization and decide for yourself. Robert Zubrin is the former Chair of the National Space Society, president of the Mars Society, and author of *The Case for Mars: The Plan to Settle the Red Planet and Why We Must.*

THE CASE FOR COLONIZING MARS

Robert Zubrin

From Ad Astra July/August 1996

MARS IS THE NEW WORLD

Among extraterrestrial bodies in our solar system, Mars is singular in that it possesses all the raw materials required to support not only life, but a new branch of human civilization. This uniqueness is illustrated most clearly if we contrast Mars

Source: Ad Astra, July/August 1996. Used with permission.

with the Earth's Moon, the most frequently cited alternative
location for extraterrestrial human colonization.

In contrast to the Moon, Mars is rich in carbon, nitrogen,
hydrogen and oxygen, all in biologically readily accessible forms
such as carbon dioxide gas, nitrogen gas, and water ice and permafrost. Carbon, nitrogen, and hydrogen are only present on the
Moon in parts per million quantities, much like gold in seawater.
Oxygen is abundant on the Moon, but only in tightly bound oxides
such as silicon dioxide (SiO_2), ferrous oxide (Fe_2O_3), magnesium
oxide (MgO), and aluminum oxide (Al_2O_3), which require very high
energy processes to reduce. Current knowledge indicates that if
Mars were smooth and all its ice and permafrost melted into liquid water, the entire planet would be covered with an ocean over
100 meters deep. This contrasts strongly with the Moon, which is
so dry that if concrete were found there, Lunar colonists would
mine it to get the water out. Thus, if plants could be grown in
greenhouses on the Moon (an unlikely proposition, as we've seen)
most of their biomass material would have to be imported.

The Moon is also deficient in about half the metals of interest to industrial society (copper, for example), as well as many
other elements of interest such as sulfur and phosphorus. Mars
has every required element in abundance. Moreover, on Mars, as on
Earth, hydrologic and volcanic processes have occurred that are
likely to have consolidated various elements into local concentrations of high-grade mineral ore. Indeed, the geologic history
of Mars has been compared to that of Africa, with very optimistic inferences as to its mineral wealth implied as a corollary.
In contrast, the Moon has had virtually no history of water or
volcanic action, with the result that it is basically composed of
trash rocks with very little differentiation into ores that represent useful concentrations of anything interesting.

You can generate power on either the Moon or Mars with solar
panels, and here the advantages of the Moon's clearer skies and
closer proximity to the Sun than Mars roughly balances the disadvantage of large energy storage requirements created by the Moon's
28-day light-dark cycle. But if you wish to manufacture solar panels, so as to create a self-expanding power base, Mars holds an

enormous advantage, as only Mars possesses the large supplies of carbon and hydrogen needed to produce the pure silicon required for producing photovoltaic panels and other electronics. In addition, Mars has the potential for wind-generated power while the Moon clearly does not. But both solar and wind offer relatively modest power potential — tens or at most hundreds of kilowatts here or there. To create a vibrant civilization you need a richer power base, and this Mars has both in the short and medium term in the form of its geothermal power resources, which offer potential for large numbers of locally created electricity generating stations in the 10 MW (10,000 kilowatt) class. In the long-term, Mars will enjoy a power-rich economy based upon exploitation of its large domestic resources of deuterium fuel for fusion reactors. Deuterium is five times more common on Mars than it is on Earth, and tens of thousands of times more common on Mars than on the Moon.

But the biggest problem with the Moon, as with all other airless planetary bodies and proposed artificial free-space colonies, is that sunlight is not available in a form useful for growing crops. A single acre of plants on Earth requires four megawatts of sunlight power, a square kilometer needs 1,000 MW. The entire world put together does not produce enough electrical power to illuminate the farms of the state of Rhode Island, that agricultural giant. Growing crops with electrically generated light is just economically hopeless. But you can't use natural sunlight on the Moon or any other airless body in space unless you put walls on the greenhouse thick enough to shield out solar flares, a requirement that enormously increases the expense of creating cropland. Even if you did that, it wouldn't do you any good on the Moon, because plants won't grow in a light/dark cycle lasting 28 days.

But on Mars there is an atmosphere thick enough to protect crops grown on the surface from solar flare. Therefore, thin-walled inflatable plastic greenhouses protected by unpressurized UV-resistant hard-plastic shield domes can be used to rapidly create cropland on the surface. Even without the problems of solar flares and month-long diurnal cycle, such simple greenhouses would be impractical on the Moon as they would create unbearably high temperatures. On Mars, in contrast, the strong greenhouse effect created by such domes would be precisely what is necessary to produce a temperate climate inside. Such domes up to 50 meters in diameter are light enough to be transported from Earth initially, and later on they can be manufactured on Mars out of indigenous materials. Because all the resources to make plastics exist on Mars, networks of such 50- to 100-meter domes could be rapidly manufactured and deployed, opening up large areas of the surface to both shirtsleeve human habitation and agriculture. That's just the beginning, because it will eventually be possible for humans to substantially thicken Mars' atmosphere by forcing the regolith to outgas its contents through a deliberate program of artificially induced global warming. Once that has been accomplished, the habitation domes could be virtually any size, as they would not have to sustain a pressure differential between their interior and exterior. In fact, once that has been done, it will be possible to raise specially bred crops outside the domes.

The point to be made is that unlike colonists on any known extraterrestrial body, Martian colonists will be able to live on the surface, not in tunnels, and move about freely and grow crops in the light of day. Mars is a place where humans can live and multiply to large numbers, supporting themselves with products of every description made out of indigenous materials. Mars is thus a place where an actual civilization, not just a mining or scientific outpost, can be developed. And significantly for interplanetary commerce, Mars and Earth are the only two locations in the solar system where humans will be able to grow crops for export.

INTERPLANETARY COMMERCE

Mars is the best target for colonization in the solar system because it has by far the greatest potential for self-sufficiency. Nevertheless, even with optimistic extrapolation of robotic manufacturing techniques, Mars will not have the division of labor required to make it fully self-sufficient until its population numbers in the millions. Thus, for decades and perhaps longer, it will be necessary, and forever desirable, for Mars to be able to import specialized manufactured goods from Earth. These goods can be fairly limited in mass, as only small portions (by weight) of even very high-tech goods are actually complex. Nevertheless, these smaller sophisticated items will have to be paid for, and the high costs of Earth-launch and interplanetary transport will greatly increase their price. What can Mars possibly export back to Earth in return?

It is this question that has caused many to incorrectly deem Mars colonization intractable, or at least inferior in prospect to the Moon. For example, much has been made of the fact that the Moon has indigenous supplies of helium-3, an isotope not found on Earth and which could be of considerable value as a fuel for second generation thermonuclear fusion reactors. Mars has no known helium-3 resources. On the other hand, because of its complex geologic history, Mars may have concentrated mineral ores, with much greater concentrations of precious metal ores readily available than is currently the case on Earth — because the terrestrial ores have been heavily scavenged by humans for the past 5,000 years. If concentrated supplies of metals of equal or greater value than silver (such as germanium, hafnium, lanthanum, cerium, rhenium, samarium, gallium, gadolinium, gold, palladium, iridium, rubidium, platinum, rhodium, europium, and a host of others) were available on Mars, they could potentially be transported back to Earth for a substantial profit. Reusable Mars-surface based single-stage-to-orbit vehicles would haul cargoes to Mars orbit for transportation to Earth via either cheap expendable chemical stages manufactured on Mars or reusable cycling solar or magnetic sail-powered interplanetary spacecraft. The existence of such Martian precious metal ores, however, is still hypothetical.

But there is one commercial resource that is known to exist ubiquitously on Mars in large amount — deuterium. Deuterium, the heavy isotope of hydrogen, occurs as 166 out of every million hydrogen atoms on Earth, but comprises 833 out of every million hydrogen atoms on Mars. Deuterium is the key fuel not only for both first and second generation fusion reactors, but it is also an essential material needed by the nuclear power industry today. Even with cheap power, deuterium is very expensive; its current market value on Earth is about $10,000 per kilogram, roughly fifty

times as valuable as silver or 70% as valuable as gold. This is
in today's pre-fusion economy. Once fusion reactors go into
widespread use deuterium prices will increase. All the in-situ
chemical processes required to produce the fuel, oxygen, and plastics necessary to run a Mars settlement require water electrolysis
as an intermediate step. As a by product of these operations,
millions, perhaps billions, of dollars worth of deuterium will
be produced.

Ideas may be another possible export for Martian colonists.
Just as the labor shortage prevalent in colonial and nineteenth
century America drove the creation of "Yankee ingenuity's" flood
of inventions, so the conditions of extreme labor shortage combined with a technological culture that shuns impractical legislative constraints against innovation will tend to drive Martian
ingenuity to produce wave after wave of invention in energy production, automation and robotics, biotechnology, and other areas.
These inventions, licensed on Earth, could finance Mars even as
they revolutionize and advance terrestrial living standards as
forcefully as nineteenth century American invention changed
Europe and ultimately the rest of the world as well.

Inventions produced as a matter of necessity by a practical intellectual culture stressed by frontier conditions can make
Mars rich, but invention and direct export to Earth are not the
only ways that Martians will be able to make a fortune. The other
route is via trade to the asteroid belt, the band of small,
mineral-rich bodies lying between the orbits of Mars and Jupiter.
There are about 5,000 asteroids known today, of which about 98%
are in the "Main Belt" lying between Mars and Jupiter, with an
average distance from the Sun of about 2.7 astronomical units,
or AU. (The Earth is 1.0 AU from the Sun.) Of the remaining two
percent known as the near-Earth asteroids, about 90% orbit closer
to Mars than to the Earth. Collectively, these asteroids represent
an enormous stockpile of mineral wealth in the form of platinum
group and other valuable metals.

Miners operating among the asteroids will be unable to produce
their necessary supplies locally. There will thus be a need to
export food and other necessary goods from either Earth or Mars

to the Main Belt. Mars has an overwhelming positional advantage as a location from which to conduct such trade.

HISTORICAL ANALOGIES

The primary analogy I wish to draw is that Mars is to the new age of exploration as North America was to the last. The Earth's Moon, close to the metropolitan planet but impoverished in resources, compares to Greenland. Other destinations, such as the Main Belt asteroids, may be rich in potential future exports to Earth but lack the preconditions for the creation of a fully developed indigenous society; these compare to the West Indies. Only Mars has the full set of resources required to develop a native civilization, and only Mars is a viable target for true colonization. Like America in its relationship to Britain and the West Indies, Mars has a positional advantage that will allow it to participate in a useful way to support extractive activities on behalf of Earth in the asteroid belt and elsewhere.

But despite the shortsighted calculations of eighteenth-century European statesmen and financiers, the true value of America never was as a logistical support base for West Indies sugar and spice trade, inland fur trade, or as a potential market for manufactured goods. The true value of America was as the future home for a new branch of human civilization, one that as a combined result of its humanistic antecedents and its frontier conditions was able to develop into the most powerful engine for human progress and economic growth the world had ever seen. The wealth of America was in fact that she could support people, and that the right kind of people chose to go to her. People create wealth. People are wealth and power. Every feature of Frontier American life that acted to create a practical can-do culture of innovating people will apply to Mars a hundred-fold.

Mars is a harsher place than any on Earth. But provided one can survive the regimen, it is the toughest schools that are the best. The Martians shall do well.

Robert Zubrin is former Chairman of the National Space Society, President of the Mars Society, and author of The Case For Mars: The Plan to Settle the Red Planet and Why We Must.

Exercise 7.3

1. How convincingly does Zubrin support his thesis for colonizing Mars? Consider his use of evidence, outside sources, or expert opinion.

2. Zubrin uses the exploration of North America as an analogy for Mars exploration. How useful is this analogy?

3. Prepare a counterargument to Zubrin's thesis.

4. Comment on the language of Zubrin's commentary: Is it too technical for an audience of nonspecialists? Not technical enough?

5. Suggest particular kinds of visual aids that could enhance Zubrin's article. Be prepared to explain how a particular photograph, chart, or diagram would provide additional clarity to the part of the argument.

Arguing Critically about a Topic in Health/Nutrition

The most heated controversies of modern science are from biology, medicine, and health/nutrition. What are the best strategies for conquering antibiotic-resistant bacteria? Are foodstuffs like table salt, coffee, or diet soda more harmful than beneficial? What is the best strategy for tackling child obesity? Newspapers and magazines routinely report the results of new studies—but these results are often tentative, or rendered faulty or even invalid by subsequent studies. What we assume to be "the truth" in biological sciences is usually a matter of current consensus among specialists. New findings, or new interpretations of those findings, routinely modify what is true and what is not.

Key Elements in a Critical Discussion of an Issue in Health/Nutrition

Not surprisingly, issues relating to medicine and health are of great concern to the general public, as these issues concern the well-being of everyone. If you are going to write an article in this field, you must first understand your topic thoroughly enough to be able to communicate its more technical aspects in a non-technical manner—or at least to define technical terms and concepts in a way that most readers can understand. The next order of business is to represent challenging views as fully and objectively as possible, and to explain why these views or interpretations are outdated, flawed, or otherwise in error. CAUTION: Unless you have already acquired expertise in the field, you will need to rely on the findings and opinions of experts.

Analysis of a Short Argument in Health/Nutrition

Study the following article from the *U.C. Berkeley Wellness Letter* on the comparative benefits of raw versus cooked food.

THE RAW VS. THE COOKED

Featured Article
April 2010

The belief in the benefits of raw foods—sometimes called "living foods"—is nothing new. Sylvester Graham, for whom the cracker is named, promoted raw foods 150 years ago, just as some chefs, cookbooks, celebrities, and websites promote them today. Among other claims, raw food diets are said to eliminate headaches and allergies, improve memory and immunity, ease arthritis, and reverse diabetes. Proponents say that cooking destroys nutrients, enzymes, and the "life force" of the food itself.

The basics. A raw food diet is based mostly or exclusively on uncooked and unprocessed plant foods (often organic), including fruits, vegetables, nuts, seeds, and sprouted grains. Most followers are strict vegetarians, though some eat unpasteurized dairy foods and sometimes even raw eggs, meat, and fish. Foods are prepared using blenders, processors, and dehydrators, and can be served either cold or warm, but not hot enough to cook them. Truly dedicated raw foodists shun refined sugar, vinegar, coffee, tea, soy products, most vegetable oils, dried herbs, and alcohol.

The benefits. Raw food diets encourage people to eat lots of fresh produce and other nutritious foods that are low in saturated fat, cholesterol, and sodium, and high in fiber. Few studies have compared the health effects of a raw food diet versus other eating patterns, but vegetarians, in general, tend to have a lower risk of heart disease and are less likely to be overweight. And in a study from Roswell Park Cancer Institute in Buffalo, people who ate the most raw (as compared to cooked) cruciferous vegetables had a reduced risk of bladder cancer, possibly because the raw vegetables retain more cancer-protective isothiocyanates. Cooking, after all, does reduce some phytochemicals, including isothiocyanates, as well as many vitamins.

The drawbacks. Some nutrients and potentially beneficial plant compounds are *less* available to the body in the raw state. Heat is needed to break down a plant's cell walls and release the compounds. Cooking a carrot releases extra beta carotene, while cooking tomatoes releases more lycopene.

Of more concern, some uncooked and unpasteurized foods pose
a risk of food poisoning, which is especially dangerous for
pregnant women, young children, the elderly, people with compromised immunity, and those with chronic medical conditions, such
as liver or kidney disease. Raw sprouts, raw oysters, and raw
(unpasteurized) milk products have been the cause of many out-
breaks of foodborne illness in recent years. Heat kills patho-
gens. Depending on how strict the diet is, people on raw food
diets may also need to take supplements to make up for potential shortfalls in calcium, iron, zinc, vitamin B12, and other
nutrients.

What about the enzyme argument? Raw foodists claim that the
enzymes in raw foods (destroyed by cooking) aid digestion, prevent "toxicity" in the body, and have other curative effects. But
these enzymes are there for the plants, not us. Moreover, they
are largely inactivated by the highly acidic environment of the
stomach and thus cannot aid digestion farther down in the intestines or have other benefits. And there's no evidence that the
enzymes can become reactivated in the intestines, as some raw
foodists say. In any case, even if some enzymes do survive, the
body usually makes all the enzymes it needs to digest and absorb
food. The claim by some raw foodists that our bodies have a limited lifetime supply of enzymes makes no sense, either, and is
simply not true.

Cooking, the mother of inventions. The invention of cooking
was a crucial factor in the evolution of humans. Cooking, which
distinguishes us from other species, makes high-protein foods
softer and easier to digest, and this enabled our early ancestors
to devote more energy to other activities besides hunting, gathering, and chewing raw foods all day. Besides killing bacteria
and releasing healthful compounds from cell walls, cooking also
allows us to more easily consume pasta, rice, wheat, corn, and
potatoes. It's true that cooking at high temperature (as in grill-
ing meat or frying potatoes) creates potential cancer-causing
substances, but most things in life carry some risk, along with
benefit. If you eat a varied diet and refrain from eating a

lot of charred food, this is not a problem. To retain the most nutrients, though, cook your vegetables for as short a time as possible.

A MATTER OF BALANCE

Raw fruits, vegetables, nuts, and seeds are certainly good for you. But you don't need to—and should not—restrict yourself to raw foods only. There's no conclusive evidence that a pure raw food diet will prevent or cure any condition or disease. Plus, it's an extreme diet that's hard to maintain over the long run, deprives you of some of the tastiest and most nutritious foods, makes dining out difficult, and can be deficient in some nutrients.

U.C. Berkeley Wellness Letter, April 2010

Source: The University of California at Berkeley Wellness Letter April © 2010. www .wellnessletter.com.

Exercise 7.4

1. Critique the writer's argumentative strategy in this article, using the Rhetorical Rhombus (described in Chapter 1) as a basis for your commentary. How well is the evidence for both sides of the argument presented? How convincingly are the more debatable issues (like the alleged increased cancer risk with grilled foods) resolved?

2. Discuss the level of diction used this article. Is it too technical? Not sufficiently technical?

3. Comment on the style and formatting of the article. How helpful are the subheadings? How would you characterize the level of usage and its effectiveness?

Strategies of Argument in the Social Sciences

The social sciences, like the natural sciences, investigate phenomena as analytically and objectively as possible. Unlike the natural sciences, of course, phenomena in the social sciences (anthropology, history, international relations, law, political science, sociology) are generally too complex to reduce to axioms or laws. That's because human behavior, whether manifested individually or in groups—from families and organizations to entire cultures—is more complex. Quite commonly, the testimony of experts (cultural anthropologists, psychologists, or linguists, for example) will serve as reliable evidence to support assumptions.

Arguing Critically about an Issue in Politics or International Relations

The first challenge in writing arguments about an issue in international relations is to recognize the interdisciplinary complexity involved. Interacting with another culture—whether to establish business and trade agreements, establish alliances or cultural exchanges, or provide aid—requires a solid understanding of the history and customs of that culture, together with the politics and economics. The next challenge is to explore any controversies generated by the issue at hand and decide how or whether those controversies are going to affect American interaction. If a certain country's freedom of speech is being curtailed, should we intervene? What if such intervention threatens American trade relations with the country?

Key Elements in an Argument on International Relations

A strong argument on an issue in international relations begins by introducing the problem at hand in a larger sociopolitical context—that is, it will place the particular problem, such as the need for improved school facilities, in the context of that country's existing political and economic situation. It will look at competing scenarios, each offering different types of improvement at different timelines, and decide which scenario is the most sensible, given the degree of necessity. It might be necessary to append a breakdown of costs (for lighting fixtures, desks, blackboards, computers, textbooks, and so on).

Example of a Short Argument on International Relations

In the following essay, college senior Lauren Silk examines the problems underlying the failure of existing foreign-aid programs to African nations and offers a possible way of making these programs more successful.

Lauren Silk

Poli Sci 128: U.S. Foreign Policy

30 April 2009

Professor Senzai

Aid to Africa: Proposed Solutions

While U.S. aid to Africa has increased by more than 60% over the past eight years, little has been done to eradicate the widespread poverty, disease, and famine plaguing the continent. Rather than helping to rebuild African nations, the presence of increasing aid has slowed growth and development, leaving over half of its population still living on under a dollar a day (Moyo). While aid levels have since doubled from $12.7 billion in 1999, African per capita incomes have yet to budge and 400 million sub-Saharan Africans are expected to live under the poverty line in 2015 (Smart Aid for Africa). In 2001, roughly 46% of sub-Saharan Africans were living in extreme poverty—a figure which has since increased to 50% (A Dollar a Day). These statistics lead one to assume that Africa receives very little aid—but for the past fifty years, the U.S. has funneled over $500 billion to Africa with little progress to show for its efforts to eradicate poverty (Lerrick). While the continent's failure to progress is partly due to crippling debt repayments that continue to bankrupt African governments, much more is due to mismanagement of aid by government officials. Rather than improving the quality of life for its people, most of the aid Africa receives has gone to supporting and sustaining corrupt governments that embezzle state funds and exploit their people for personal gain. As poverty continues to grow and we prepare for an even larger and costlier aid package to Africa in an already disastrous economic climate, policymakers must address the shortcomings of our aid policy so that we can find a solution that will effectively and permanently lift its people out of poverty.

As seen by our past commitments to the tune of billions of dollars, solving Africa's problems is of great interest to the U.S. According to the Wilson Center, six million Africans die a

year from preventable causes, 26 million are infected with HIV/
AIDS and 350 million are living on less than a dollar a day
(Hamilton). While ensuring aid to Africa is largely a humanitarian
interest, it is also one of national security. Great political
and economic instability has transformed many African nations into
breeding grounds for criminal operations that threaten American
lives. Growing populations of restless and unemployed young men
with access to cheap guns has led to the growth of terrorism and
piracy. But as our deficit grows into the trillions, and the billions we have already committed have done little to help alleviate
Africa's problems, one sees the necessity of seriously reforming
our aid packages so that they effectively combat these threats and
improve economic opportunities for the African people.

As stated earlier, Africa's failure to progress is largely due
to the crippling effects that debt repayments have on their economies. As a solution, many have called for cancelling these debts
in order to provide these countries with a clean slate. While
African countries won't owe anything on previous aid, they will
continue to receive money in enormous amounts that they can't pay
back, thus sustaining the vicious cycle of debt. If funneling
billions of dollars into corrupt governments and bloated bureaucracies didn't work the first time, how can we think it will work
again?

Some argue that aid has been largely ineffective in Africa because *not enough* of it has been given to adequately address their
needs. Some even argue that in order to sufficiently develop these
countries, current aid (already over $4 billion a year) needs to
be increased by several billion dollars (Fletcher). But the current economic climate makes this request difficult to meet for
both the U.S. and its allies. France, for example, has already
been forced to cut aid by several billion dollars. And while
countries like the UK are sustaining promised levels of aid, the
decreased value in their currency makes this money worth much
less than before (Kharas). According to the Brookings Institute,
"the currency movement alone will wipe out $5 billion in aid in
2009" (Kharas). While a moral imperative to help these nations

still exists, our ever-increasing deficit has made it so that we can't afford to increase, much less sustain, current levels.

However, some argue that it isn't our level of committed aid that's the problem; it's the fractional amount of appropriated aid that actually gets out of Washington and into Africa. Much of our committed aid has already been budgeted and accounted for, but its disbursement has been tied up in bureaucratic red tape (Kharas). In order to release this money, funds would need to be moved from "consultant contracts and slow moving projects" directly to the governments themselves (Kharas). While this would certainly speed the process of getting money out o the "bureaucratic pipeline" and into the countries themselves, history has shown that funneling free money to corrupt and bloated governments not only fuels the vicious cycle of inefficient aid but fails to guarantee that the money will even get to the populations who need it.

In light of the failure of U.S. aid to adequately assist African development, some critics have called for eliminating and replacing all aid to Africa with trade and investments (Moyo). While trade and investments need to be ultimately part of the solution, the sudden removal of all assistance from these countries would be disastrous, and only exacerbate these countries' poverty levels. Just like the issues these countries face, the aid process is very complex and thus requires a complex solution (Joseph). No simple solution such as increasing aid or eliminating it altogether will sufficiently help solve Africa's problems. Therefore, I recommend a compromise between aid and investment. In our quest for "smarter aid," our aid must be able to balance both humanitarian needs and support the creation and flourishing of businesses and civil society (Smart Aid for Africa).

First, because much aid is embezzled by corrupt government officials and bloated bureaucracies, policymakers must commit to restoring transparency and accountability in African governments in order to facilitate movement of aid directly to the people. This effort can be done through creating incentives for African states to rebuild their governments and civil societies (Joseph). As advocated by the Millennium Challenge Corporation, these efforts require that aid be tied to the success and accountability of the government. Therefore, governments which "conduct honest elections, use available resources to improve the welfare of their people, and pursue sound economic policies" should be rewarded with greater levels of support (Smart Aid for Africa). This support should come in the form of investing in infrastructure, education, and healthcare development. For low-performing states, U.S. policymakers must consult with both their governments and the international community to determine the best way to balance support between he "state and civil society" as a prerequisite to aid (Smart Aid for Africa).

After working to build accountable and transparent African governments, the U.S. must restructure aid to best invigorate businesses and civil society, both of which encourage healthy democracy. This can be achieved through investment in microloans, which would loan anywhere from about $2 to $1,500 to Africans looking to start their own businesses (Mercy Corps). Influx of microloans would fuel the African economy by invigorating the private sector and providing Africans with jobs and the opportunity to become self-sufficient. Microloans provided by American banks and businesses have already proven successful in many African countries. Not only have millions of Africans been able to pull themselves out of poverty by their own innovation, but microloan providers see a 97% return on their investments—a much more promising statistic than that of current debt repayments (Mercy Corps). In addition, microlending would help phase out Western aid to Africa, helping it become more self-sufficient by growing its economy from the ground up. In doing this, we would not only succeed in our goal of reducing poverty, but would also help Africa reach its potential and alleviate economic pressure on the U.S. government.

In conclusion, reforming U.S. aid to Africa requires a two-step process. First, policymakers must work to promote the same accountability and transparency pursued in our own government in African governments. Through providing incentives and denying aid to those who don't meet requirements for accountability and transparency, we can ensure that money designed to help the African people does just that. Secondly, we must invest in the African economy. By investing in African innovation and potential, we will help them and their countries fulfill their goal of becoming self-sufficient. Ultimately these are the best means of achieving the stability we have been trying to secure for the past 60 years. By reforming African nations at the political level and investing in their people and economies, we will not only greatly reduce impending threats to our national security, but will succeed in our goal of restoring basic human rights to the African people.

Works Cited

"A Dollar a Day: Poverty Overview: Poverty around the World." 2006. *ThinkQuest*. 28 April 2009, <http://library.thinkquest .org/05aug/00282/over_world.htm#africa>.

Fletcher, Michael. "Bush Has Quietly Tripled Aid to Africa." *The Washington Post* 31 December 2006. 28 April 2009, <http:// www.washingtonpost.com/wp-dyn/content/article/2006/12/30/ AR2006123000941.html>.

Hamilton, Lee. "Helping a Troubled Continent." *Selected Commentaries*. 5 July 2005. Woodrow Wilson International Center for Scholars. 28 April 2009, <http://www.wilsoncenter.org/ index.cfm?fuseaction=director.thing&typeid=A687F6E6-1125-AADA-EA0F1BD2F5FD8AEC&itemid=B0472774-1125-AADA-EABFAD9CCD5DBE6A>.

Joseph, Richard. Interview with Jerome McDonnell. 7 April 2009. Chicago Public Radio's Worldview. 28 April 2009. The Brookings Institution. <http://www.brookings.edu/interviews/2009/0407_ africa_aid_joseph.aspx>.

Kharas, Homi. "The Financial Crisis, a Development Emergency, and the Need for Aid." The Wolfensohn Center for Development, The Brookings Institution. 11 February 2009, 27 April 2009, <http://www.brookings.edu/opinions/2009/0211_financial_crisis_ kharas.aspx>.

Lerrick, Adam. "Aid to Africa at Risk: Covering up Corruption." *International Economics Report*. December 2005. Gailliot Center for Public Policy. Carnegie Mellon University. 26 April 2009, <http://www.house.gov/jec/publications/109/12-09-05galliotcorruption.pdf>.

"Microlending Explained." *Global Envision.* 12 May 2006. Mercy Corps. 28 April 2009, <http://www.globalenvision.org/library/4/1073/>.

Moyo, Dambisa. "Why Foreign Aid is Hurting Africa." *The Wall Street Journal* 21 March 2009. 28 April 2009, <http://online.wsj.com/article/SB123758895999200083.html>.

"Smart Aid for Africa." Notes from "Aid, Governance and Development in Africa" Conference. May 12-14 2005, Northwestern University. 26 April 2009, <http://www.northwestern.edu/africanstudies/Pdfs/Smart%20Aid%20for%20Africa%20%20Northwestern%20conference%20statement.pdf>.

◎/◎ Exercise 7.5

1. How effectively does Lauren Silk introduce her thesis? If you were writing on the topic of changing the way the United States gives aid to Africa, how would you introduce your thesis? Explain your strategy.

2. Critique Silk's strategies of argumentation, making use of the Rhetorical Rhombus described in Chapter 1.

3. Compare Silk's manner of integrating her outside sources with that of the *Wellness Letter* author of "The Raw versus the Cooked" above. Suggest an underlying rationale for each method of source use.

4. Even if you agree with Silk's recommendations, suggest alternative recommendations, along with clear rationales for their implementation.

Arguing Critically about an Issue in Bioethics

As we have noted, when arguing issues in the natural sciences, such as biology, one extrapolates strictly from the phenomena under scrutiny. For example, if you're investigating how a particular species of monkey evolved in a particular part of the world, you will not be arguing whether evolutionary theory itself violates religious doctrines—that line of inquiry would take you out of biology and into theology. Similarly, an inquiry into the social or ethical implications of genetic engineering is not a topic in biology (although it must draw information from that scientific discipline), but rather in sociology.

Key Elements in a Discussion of an Issue in Bioethics

Any argument involving ethics necessarily involves commentary about people's values in relation to the more objective subject matter, be it law, biology, medicine, or business. A value system can be intrinsic or extrinsic, secular or religious, behavioral or pragmatic. An argument in bioethics introduces the elements of the ethical dilemma as objectively and accurately as possible, being careful not to inject subtle biases prematurely. For example, if one wishes to argue that stem cell extraction from human embryos is a violation of human rights, one must first objectively represent the other side: that such stem cell use will possibly lead to the saving of lives by curing or preventing crippling genetic diseases.

Example of a Short Argument on an Issue in Bioethics

Study the following argument on genetic manipulation by the bioethicist Margaret McLean, Ph.D., director of Biotechnology and Health Care Ethics at the Markkula Center for Applied Ethics, Santa Clara University.

WHEN WHAT WE KNOW OUTSTRIPS WHAT WE CAN DO

By Margaret R. McLean

Our genes contain information that scientists hope will help in the treatment of many diseases. Huntington's disease provides a window on the choices we face as medicine increases our ability to intervene in human genetics.

"*Stop pacing, Mom. It'll be all right.*" Meghan and her mother, Anne, fidget nervously in the waiting area of the genetic testing center.

"*I need to have this test, Mom,*" Meghan continues. "*I want to know if I'm going to wind up like Uncle Harry. I want to know*

Margaret R. McLean is the director of Biotechnology and Health Care Ethics at the Markkula Center for Applied Ethics.

the chances that my children will inherit Huntington's disease."
Meghan and her husband, Rick, want to start a family-a family
untouched by Huntington's bizarre dances, frightening mood
swings, and untimely death. "I'd rather not have children if it
means sentencing them to a death like that," Meghan says.

Anne halts and faces her daughter. "I wish it wasn't this way,
Meghan." Anne's family has been haunted by Huntington's since
anyone can remember; those who get it always die from it. Her
brother Harry was just fine until his mid- 40s—then came the
depression, the twitching arms.

"I would do anything to spare you," Anne says. "But, Meghan,
please understand that I don't want to be tested. 'So far, so
good' is my philosophy. I'm only 42. I want to live my life and
make my decisions without a Huntington's diagnosis hanging over
my head."

"But Mom, you're not the one being tested; I am."

Falling into the chair next to her daughter, Anne pleads,
"Don't you see? If your test is positive, it means I've got the
gene, too. And I don't want to know. I have a right not to know,
don't I?"

Anne and Meghan face a tentative future. Members of families
with a history of Huntington's disease have long known that this
neurological disorder-with its loss of motor control, personality changes, depression, dementia, and death-might eventually be
their fate.

Huntington's is a genetic disease, one that can be passed
down from parents to children. The gene for Huntington's is
dominant, which means that a single copy of the gene from
either parent triggers the disease. Children of people afflicted
with Huntington's disease have a 50/50 chance of also having the
disease.

Until recently, these people had no way of knowing whether
they were in the unlucky 50 percent until symptoms actually appeared, usually between the ages of 30 and 50. Then, in 1993,
scientists identified the gene responsible for the disorder and
made possible the test Meghan wants to take.

If Meghan is tested and found to carry the gene for Huntington's disease, her mother must also have the gene. Meghan, then,
will know what Anne does not want to know. What should Meghan do?

The Human Genome Project

Meghan's problem foreshadows the dilemmas many people will
face as scientists learn more about genetics. In 1990, an
international effort was launched to decode the language of
our genes—the Human Genome Project (HGP). The United States
is investing $3 billion over 15 years in this endeavor to map
the complete set of genes for humans-the human genome. The
project will make it easier for researchers who want to identify
the genetic components both of disease and of physical and
intellectual traits.

Thus far, the most obvious result of the HGP is the rapid proliferation of genetic information. As the new information pours
in, the traditional questions haunt us: What should we do with
this information? What does this particular genetic alteration
mean personally, medically, and socially? If we can, should we
intervene to correct or enhance an individual's genome? And when
we cannot intervene, how do we handle diagnostic information in
the absence of a cure?

Genetic screening can provide new information, not only for
potential Huntington's victims but also for sufferers of the more
than 4,000 other diseases of genetic origin. Additional ailments
are rooted in the interaction of genes with the environment. All
told, genetic disorders are the fourth leading cause of death in
the United States.

Discovering the location of a disease-causing gene on a chro-
mosome permits diagnosis before the onset of symptoms. It also
allows testing of entire populations to identify carriers as well
as those who are affected.

The long-term hope is for a precise molecular correction of
the defect so that genetic disease becomes as curable as infec-
tious disease. Such therapy might also prevent genetic patholo-
gies from moving from one generation to the next.

The Rift Between Diagnosis and Cure

Yet despite the progress of the HGP—and, indeed, primarily because of it—disease prediction continues to outpace medicine's ability to treat or cure. The test for Huntington's disease can confirm a mutation in the Huntington's gene, but it offers no treatment for the devastating symptoms. The result is a therapeutic rift between what we know and what we can do.

Meghan and Anne fearfully straddle this crevasse, hoping against hope that it will narrow. However, it seems likely that as information flows from the HGP, this therapeutic rift will continue to enlarge for the foreseeable future. This poses profound and puzzling questions about the limits of medical knowledge and human choice.

Consider the effects of genetic information on people who, like Anne and Meghan, confront Huntington's disease. If they discover they do, in fact, have the Huntington's gene, a shadow is cast over the rest of their lives. A slight misstep becomes an omen of uncontrollable muscle movements. Feeling blue is no longer part of everyday life but a precursor of mental collapse. The person's view of life is irreversibly changed by a set of prophecies about affliction and horrifying death.

In *Mapping Fate*, Alice Wexler describes what it's like to live with this knowledge:

A dancer with Huntington's disease, in her early forties, described how, long before there were any other symptoms, she began having difficulty learning dance sequences; whereas once she had no problem memorizing complicated routines, she gradually found it more and more difficult to master a series of different steps. Later on she found it increasingly difficult to organize a meal, coordinating the different dishes so that they would all come out together. Living at risk undermines confidence, for there is no way of separating the ordinary difficulties and setbacks of life from the early symptoms of the illness. It is not like any other physical illness, where consciousness can at least continue in the knowledge that one is still oneself, despite severe pain and physical limitation. Huntington's means a loss of identity.

But long before the loss of motor control and identity, those who carry the Huntington's gene may face the loss of jobs and health coverage. Many people from families with a history of genetic disorders fear that if they are tested, the results might become public and cause employers or insurers to exclude them. Laws to prohibit such discrimination are not yet completely in place. This is the prophecy of social and medical doom that Anne is resisting.

Responsibilities to the Next Generation

But her daughter Meghan has a different set of concerns. Genetic knowledge is apt to have its greatest impact not on the lives of those who, like the stumbling dancer, are currently stricken, but on the choices to be made by those who, like Meghan, are contemplating parenthood.

If Meghan does not have the gene, then her child will not have the disease. If she does have the gene, any child she conceives has a 50 percent chance of sharing her fate.

Assuming Meghan learns that she has the Huntington's gene, what should she and her husband do? Should they take their chances with genetic roulette? Should they remain genetically childless? Should they undergo prenatal diagnosis?

Prenatal screening and diagnosis can be accomplished through methods such as amniocentesis. Sometimes genetic testing is coupled with in vitro fertilization in a technique called preimplantation genetic diagnosis (PGD). PGD is currently offered in a limited number of research facilities.

In this method, after the egg is fertilized outside the womb, the embryo is allowed to reach the eight-cell stage of development before a cell is removed. This cell is then tested for genetic components that would predispose the child to a particular disease such as Huntington's. Then, only those embryos that do not contain the disease gene are transferred to the uterus, thereby eliminating the chance of having a child with Huntington's disease.

Whatever the promise of this technique, the cost is far from trivial. It includes the fee for IVF-averaging $8,000 per cycle-plus the cost of genetic testing, which adds an estimated $2,000.

Even in the rare cases when IVF expenses are paid by health insurance, the genetic component is not covered.

Costs are also likely to be high in the even more advanced procedures now being proposed. In the future, PGD might identify candidates for emerging techniques such as constructive genetic surgery and embryonic cell cloning. Constructive genetic surgery involves removing the affected gene from an embryo and replacing it with normal genetic material. But this is risky business with a failure rate of 80 percent-far too perilous to perform on a single human embryo.

Through cell cloning, however, scientists could make multiple copies of the embryo they wish to modify, increasing the genetic surgical success rate. Indeed, cellular cloning seems to hold the key to the successful genetic engineering of humans. But to what end?

Is Meghan's wish to prune Huntington's disease from her family tree a justified use of this future technology? Suppose parents wish to eliminate the predisposition to alcoholism. What if they want to increase a child's physical stature or intellectual acumen? Would these be reasonable requests for embryonic genetic intervention?

After all, we send our children to soccer practice and tutoring after they are born; why not give them a genetic head start? Is there an ethically relevant difference between genetic therapy and genetic enhancement?

Questions and Guidelines

Reproductive and genetic technologies are opening new medical and moral frontiers, urging us to think in new ways. As the level of medical diagnosis and treatment shifts from bodies and bones to cells and chromosomes, the level of ethical consideration must do the same.

Reaching ethical conclusions about the new genetics is challenging for two reasons: First, it is inherently difficult to understand the subtleties of genetics and the wealth of data tumbling out of the HGP. Second, it is next to impossible to foresee accurately the implications and consequences-short-term, long-term, and unintended-of intervening in the genetic "stuff of life."

The following questions may help to clarify key issues as genetic medicine comes of age:

1. What is the purpose of taking a particular genetic test? Who is affected by the results?

Some people undergo genetic screening simply to know their predisposition to a particular disease. Others may hope to fix that predisposition. Currently, the diagnosis of numerous genetic diseases or predispositions is possible; in most cases, however, there is no treatment or cure. Care must be taken to ensure that patients understand this rift between diagnosis and treatment and that their expectations of the testing are realistic.

Since it became possible to test for the Huntington's gene, fewer than 15 percent of those at risk have taken the test, even when it was offered free of charge. Most would rather not know. Anne, like many of us, is reluctant to find out about an inevitable future. Perhaps, out of respect for her mother's wishes, Meghan could wait to take the test, hoping that in a few more years, scientists may make progress toward a cure. Perhaps Meghan is particularly good at keeping secrets.

Traditional notions of confidentiality are profoundly challenged by medical tests that tell patients not only about themselves but also about family members. As genetic tests become readily available, respect must be given to those who, like Anne, claim a right to ignorance.

2. Who has control of genetic information?

In this era of rapid communication and data proliferation, absolute confidentiality of medical information no longer seems realistic. In a hospital, anywhere from 60 to 200 people have access to a patient's medical records. The information is also passed along to insurance carriers and health maintenance organizations. Given that complete privacy is not possible, it is important to consider who has access to genetic information and for what purpose.

People questioned about genetic testing worry that insurers will raise rates or refuse to insure them. They express concern

that employers will not hire them. There is a general fear that
friends and family will treat them differently or abandon them
once they are "tarnished" by a deadly gene. Medicine's obligation to do no harm mandates that genetic information be used in
ways that help people, not in ways that stigmatize and marginal-
ize them.

**3. What does it mean to offer genetic testing and/or therapy
in the absence of universal access to health care?**

This is a question of justice. What counts as a fair share of
the health care pie for the poor or for those without health insurance? We live in an era of limited access to childhood immuni-
zations and routine preventive care-both of which are relatively
inexpensive and medically effective. As we pour health care
dollars into genetic research and treatment, we must also seek
to provide basic care to those who are most vulnerable to the
ravages of disease: the poor and their children.

**4. On what basis should someone undertake genetic interven-
tion such as genetic constructive surgery if and when it becomes
available?**

Two approaches to this question are possible. One is therapeutic; that is, such techniques should be used to correct particular diseases. The other is eugenic; that is, genetic intervention
is permissible to enhance specific characteristics (e.g., intellect) or to give individuals capacities they might not otherwise
have had (e.g., playing piano).

The distinction between therapy and enhancement may turn on
intention. Is the purpose of the intervention to bring a person to a state of health or to go beyond health in the design of
someone new or better?

With the fledgling capacity to alter the human genome comes
the responsibility to think carefully about what we consider a
benefit for individuals and society. Test tube racks filled with
"designer genes" hold not only the promise of molecular treatments
but also the age-old mischief of discrimination and exclusion. We
are not yet free of the specter of forced eugenics—witness reports that up until the 1970s, an estimated 60,000 people had
been sterilized in Sweden under government policies to weed out

traits such as poor eyesight and "Gypsy features." What some consider desirable traits may not be a benefit in the eyes of either
humanity as a whole or the affected individual.

5. For what kind of genetic future are we planning?

Genetics, by its very nature, embodies a concern for coming
generations. Genetic diagnosis and intervention hold great promise. However, we need to consider carefully the power conferred
on us by knowing our genetic identity and being able to alter it.

With great power comes greater responsibility, asking us to
think carefully about the dramatic impact that genetic information
and intervention might have on the future. We face not a red light
but a flashing yellow as we enter the age of genetic medicine.

◎/◎ Exercise 7.6

1. Summarize McLean's thesis in your own words. How convincingly does she support her assertions?

2. Do you agree or disagree with McLean that "We are not yet free of the specter of forced eugenics." Why or why not?

3. Discuss whether the advantages of controlling genetic information in humans outweigh the disadvantages.

4. Comment on the way McLean has formatted her argument. In what ways does it enhance the coherence and clarity of the argument?

5. Use the above four prompts in this exercise to develop a PowerPoint presentation, supporting or challenging McLean's thesis, for students in an introductory biology or bioethics course.

6. Compare McLean's use of evidence with that of Joseph Forte's essay on Shelley's "Ozymandias" or Lauren Silk's essay on aid to Africa. How do you account for the different approaches?

Strategies of Argument in Workplace Related Contexts

Writing in the professional workplace is usually undertaken for strictly utilitarian reasons: to propose a new policy or project; to convey important information to colleagues or clientele, as is the case with writing a job application letter or an instruction manual; or, from the other side of the fence, writing a recommendation for hiring a particular candidate.

Arguing Critically about a Legal Issue

The law, like medicine and health, is of great interest to the general public. Consider widely popular television shows like *Law and Order* and *Criminal Minds* and best-selling mystery writers like John Grisham, Scott Turow, and Michael Connelly (whose novel, *The Lincoln Lawyer,* was recently made into a hit motion picture). Many famous literary works are courtroom dramas: *Inherit the Wind, Twelve Angry Men,* and *To Kill a Mockingbird,* just to name a few.

Key Elements in a Critical Discussion of a Legal Issue

To risk stating the obvious, if you're going to write on a legal issue, you must thoroughly understand the law as it currently exists and then be able to translate it into nonlegalese. Arguments concerning legal issues debate not what the law is, but how the law is to be interpreted. Lawyers on either side of a case often work with the same material and facts, but they argue that readers or listeners should reach different conclusions.

What accounts for these differences? Lawyers sometimes construct theories: although an act may be indisputable (a person was shot and killed), different theories may lead to different conclusions about the accountability of the one who shot the victim. Therefore the accountability may be disputed.

One may cite previous acts of the defendant to show that the current act is one of many violent acts that have culminated in the utmost violent act, the taking of a life. But another may cite actions of the deceased prior to the shooting to indicate that in this particular incident, the act of shooting a person was justified by self-defense since the deceased also had a deadly weapon and was about to use it on the defendant. Yet another might point to the upbringing and mental health of the defendant.

Now shift that act into war: if one soldier takes the life of a soldier on the opposite side, do we use the same theories as above to determine accountability? Is accountability even a legal issue that anyone undertakes to dispute?

In general, legal theories must be consistent with prior judgments and rulings (precedents) and should yield suitable results for future judgments and rulings. Prior cases, statutes, laws, and constitutional provisions are among the bases for legal theories, but they are not the sole bases.

Example of a Short Legal Argument

Study the following news editorial that offers a new perspective on a long-standing legal issue: gun control.

GUN CONTROL DEBATE HEATS UP AGAIN

by W. E. Messamore

Tue, Apr 12th 2011

Today, the Assembly Public Safety Committee will take up AB 144, legislation introduced by Anthony Portantino (D-Pasadena) to ban the open carry of a handgun in the state of California. The controversial legislation has reinvigorated the decades-long debate over the effects of gun legislation on public safety.

Writing Monday at the *California Progress Report*, Dr. Dallas Stout, President of the California Brady Campaign to Prevent Gun Violence, argued [3] that open carry laws actually make Californians less safe. Stout cites three anecdotes to illustrate his point: a 4-year-old boy in Maryland who shot and killed himself last month; a 2-year-old in Louisiana who used a stool to retrieve a gun in his home and shot himself in the upper right chest; and a 5-year-old from Pennsylvania who grabbed his father's firearm and shot himself in the head.

These stories are all indeed very tragic, but do little in themselves to illustrate the effectiveness of gun control laws or the danger of open carry laws. The 4-year-old who tragically killed himself in Maryland did so despite that state's stringent gun control policies. Maryland does not allow open carry without a permit, and is one of the more restrictive of the nation's relatively few "May Issue" states for carry permits. Over 30 other states are less restrictive "Shall Issue" states. As Stout also acknowledges in his article, "Authorities are trying to figure out . . . how the boy was able to get access to the weapon . . ." Stout is also fair enough to report that the boy from Pennsylvania "climbed onto a chair near his parents' bedroom closet and *grabbed his part-time police officer father's duty weapon* and accidentally shot himself in the head." Stricter carry laws would not have prevented this tragedy either. Anecdotes like these are subject to endless qualifications and debate, and while emotionally powerful, do not necessarily paint a statistically sound and accurate picture of how a policy actually affects the lives of the people in a given state or jurisdiction.

256

Chapter 7   Argument across the Disciplines

A more useful argument is Dr. Stout's assertion that a "gun is 22 times more likely to be used in a homicide, suicide or unintentional shooting than to kill in self-defense." While studies have shown that a gun owner is statistically at greater risk from his or her own weapon than they are likely to use it in self-defense, that proves only that owning a gun might make the gun owner less safe, not that more permissive gun laws make society at large less safe. In fact, the overwhelming statistical evidence to the contrary shows a powerful correlation between more permissive gun laws and lower rates of violent crime.

According to a University of Chicago interview [4] with Dr. John Lott, economist and author of *More Guns, Less Crime*, data for all 3,054 counties in the United States during the 18 years from 1977 to 1994 demonstrate that:

"There is a strong negative relationship between the number of law-abiding citizens with permits and the crime rate—as more people obtain permits there is a greater decline in violent crime rates. For each additional year that a concealed handgun law is in effect the murder rate declines by 3 percent, rape by 2 percent, and robberies by over 2 percent."

So while it is statistically true that owning a gun might actually make you and your household less safe, the fact that a potential criminal knows that you have the legal right to own and carry a gun makes society more safe. It doesn't take a Ph.D. economist like Lott to understand the incentives involved. A criminal has a strong disincentive to attempt a mugging in an alley when there is any reasonable chance that his victim could be carrying a gun. That's why jurisdictions with notoriously strict gun control measures paradoxically tend to suffer from the worst rates of violent crime-- that is, places like Washington DC, Chicago, and even [5] the United Kingdom.

Will gun control make California safer? That all depends on what you mean by "safe," but if we put it down to rates of violent crime, all indications from decades of data in hundreds of cities, states, and counties seem to declare a resounding "No."

The California Independent Voter Network is published by the California Independent Voter Project. All articles, commentaries and opinions are
the sole work of the individual authors and are not directed or controlled
by CAIVP. Anyone is invited to participate. Network Editors encourage comment and debate on a broad range of issues of interest to independent
thinking voters. The Network is an issues oriented forum and as such does
not entertain or accommodate articles, commentaries or opinions which constitute personal attacks. More information on the CAIVN.org mission.
    COPYRIGHT © CAIVN, 501(c)4 organization. ALL RIGHTS RESERVED

Links:

[1] http://caivn.org/vote_up_down/node/9768/1/updown?
    destination=print/9768&token=87d9f7413f50e692f3e
    17377739a5a3e

[2] http://caivn.org/vote_up_down/node/9768/-1/updown?
    destination=print/9768&token=53a569fff3a4874b423cdbb
    31d04accd

[3] http://www.californiaprogressreport.com/site/node/8867

[4] http://www.press.uchicago.edu/Misc/Chicago/493636.html

[5] http://reason.com/archives/2002/11/01/gun-controls-
    twisted-outcome

[6] http://caivn.org/issue/public-safety-and-prison-reform

Source: "Gun Control Debate Heats Up Again" by W. E. Messamore. Published by
California Independent Voter Network (CAIVN). http://caivn.org. Used by permission.

◎/◎ Exercise 7.7

1. Summarize Messamore's stance on the gun-control debate.

2. Compare Messamore's argumentative strategies with those of Silk and
   McLean. Where are they similar? Where do they differ?

3. In view of the January 2011 shootings in Tucson, during which six
   people attending a political rally were killed by a crazed gunman, what
   modifications, if any, would you make to Messamore's point of view?

4. Does restricting or banning handguns violate the Second
   Amendment? Write a position paper supporting or defending
   the right to bear arms.

Arguing Critically about an Issue in Business

President Calvin Coolidge famously said, "The business of America is business," but we can extend that to the entire world. Business is the engine that runs every nation on earth, from the most industrialized to the most rural.

Key Elements in a critical discussion of an Issue on Business

A strong business argument often relies on case studies, statistics, surveys, or sources of evidence one does not routinely find in an argument on a painting or work of literature. Whereas aesthetic bases are appropriate to arguing the value of a painting, these are not pertinent to an argument in business.

Arguments about business-related issues often present the problem at hand before they provide background information about the field and the situation leading up to the problem. A timeline for implementation and an analysis of costs are often included as well. Some business arguments take the form of a step-by-step guide to achieving success or, like the feature presented below, a breakdown of facts from fiction when getting started in a new business venture.

Example of a Short Argument on a Business Issue

Argumentative writing can vary in level of formality, from the scholarly to the colloquial. The following piece about running an Internet business from home is an example of the latter.

THE 10 MOST POPULAR MYTHS ABOUT RUNNING A HOME-BASED BUSINESS ONLINE

Elena Fawkner

Several weeks ago I finally took the plunge into the world of network marketing. I had been running an online business for almost three years by then but knew that I would have to make the leap to network marketing at some point since it was such an obvious fit with Internet marketing. And I haven't been disappointed.

One thing did surprise me though — the number of people who approached me about my network marketing business, interested in running their businesses exclusively online, but with the mistaken belief that it would be somehow easier and less expensive than establishing and running a home-based business offline.

Well, let me tell you, there's nothing easy or inexpensive about running a home-based business - online or off. The Internet is just a different way of going about it. And that's all.

Here's my top 10 myths about running an online business (and in answer to the missing Myth#11, NO, you CANNOT run a serious online business with WebTV - get a REAL computer already).

MYTH#1 - It's Easy, Anyone Can Do It

FACT - It's not easy, by any stretch of the imagination, and no, you may not be able to do it.

Reality is, establishing an Internet business is a long, slow, frustrating process. Your first attempt at creating your own web site will be an abomination. You'll look back at it in 12 months and shudder. I know I did.

You'll feel utterly overwhelmed by the sheer amount of information you need to absorb. And the fact that six different "experts" each tell you six different things doesn't help. (There are no "experts", by the way, just a lot of people with a lot of opinions. Bottom line? Do what works. For you.)

The only way to learn is by trial and error. Some days you'll feel like you're on a roll, the next you'll feel like you're backsliding and FAST. No sooner do you manage a respectable ranking on Altavista, than your Yahoo listing disappears altogether, and where the hell did that number 5 listing with Google go?

After spending an ENTIRE DAY trying to work out what's going on with your search engine listings, giving up, going searching for yet another "expert" to tell you what you're doing wrong, finally realizing there is no such expert and you're going to have to learn how to do it all yourself after all (dammit to hell!) you suddenly realize that you've done absolutely nothing all day to promote your business and you still have to write the article for this week's ezine which has to go out tomorrow but you can't work your business tomorrow because you have to go work at your J.O.B. .... AAAARGHHHH!!!!!

Many, many people, give it up. Most, probably. It's hard work and it's frustrating. At the end of the day, most are just not prepared to do what it takes.

MYTH#2 - I Can Get Wealthy Overnight

FACT - The only way to get wealthy overnight in this world is to win the Lotto. Period. It will NOT happen on the Internet. Not these days, anyway.

MYTH#3 - Once I Build My Website I Can Relax
And Let It Do the Work For Me

FACT - Hah. See Myth #4.

MYTH#4 - Once I Build My Website The World
Will Beat A Path To My Door

FACT - No. It won't.

Merely creating a web site and uploading it to your host's server means that your web site is available for viewing by *those who know it exists*. Only problem is, you and your web host are the only ones who know. And even your web host doesn't care (at least as long as you pay your monthly hosting fees).

You now need to submit your site to the search engines (no, they will not just find it automatically and no, your web site is not just automatically added to some great universal Index once it's uploaded). Then you have to wait several weeks or months to find out whether it's been indexed. And if by some miracle it has, where and for what keywords. And then fix it.

In the meantime, you have to drive traffic to your site via other means. You'll need to submit it to directories, negotiate reciprocal links with other complementary web sites, start publishing a weekly ezine (electronic newsletter) and start promoting that to start developing your own opt-in list, start writing articles and submitting them wherever you can (including a link to your site in the resource box at the end is good free advertising) and, shudder, advertising. And not in the FFAs and free classifieds either. In other people's ezines. On other people's websites. In the classifieds section of newspapers (yes, the kind that leaves black stuff on your fingers when you read it). All of this costs money. Plenty of it. If you're running a network marketing business, you're also going to need to pay for leads during this period as well.

MYTH#5 - I Don't Have To Spend Money
To Market My Business

FACT - Yes, you do.

You wouldn't expect to be able to market an offline business without financial outlay. Well, guess what? It's just the same in your online business. See Myth #4.

Oh, and by the way, when you're re-reading Myth #4, keep this in mind. You haven't made a dime yet.

MYTH#6 - I Can Put the Whole Thing On Autopilot
And Make Money While I Sleep (Or Vacation)

FACT - True. To a point.

By automating as many of your tasks as possible you necessarily free up time to do other things. You COULD use that time to sleep or vacation and you MAY make money while you're sleeping or vacationing. THIS time. But you must sow before you can reap and if you're not continually planting and growing your business, the time will come in the not too distant future when you have nothing left to harvest. You'll wake up one morning and find that, far from filling your inbox with overnight orders, your business has bitten the dust.

So, instead of taking that freed up time and spending it sleeping or vacationing, spend it working your business.

In other words, you'll get out of your business precisely what you put into it. Just like anything else in this world. Funny about that.

MYTH#7 - I Don't Have To Deal With People,
I Can Do Everything Via Email

FACT - Email is what you use to handle routine administrative issues and a tool to get prospective customers or networking partners to contact you. Once that happens, you take the relationship OFFLINE. You get on the phone and actually TALK to these people. The Internet is not an iron curtain that protects you from having to have real life conversations and relationships with people. It's just a tool that brings you together so that the real work of establishing relationships can begin. Offline.

```
MYTH#8 - I Will Be Able to Fire My Boss And Work Where
        I Want, When I Want ... In Six Months Or Less
```

```
FACT - Don't give up your day job just yet.
```

```
MYTH#9 - When I'm Working For Myself From Home In My Online
        Business I Will Be Able To Spend As Much Time
                With My Children As I Want
```

```
FACT - When you're running a business you're running a business.
It's not a pleasant little hobby that you fit in between the
stuff of your REAL life. If you're not going to run your business
as a business, forggeddabouddit.
```

```
        MYTH#10 - The Internet Is A Magic Wand
```

```
FACT - See Myths#1 through #9.
```

```
** Reprinting of this article is welcome! **
This article may be freely reproduced provided that: (1) you include the
following resource box; and (2) you only mail to a 100% opt-in list.
    Here's the resource box to use if reprinting this article:
    Elena Fawkner is editor of Home-Based Business Online. Best business
ideas and opportunities for your home-based or online business.
```

Source: © 2004 Elena Fawkner. Elena Fawkner is editor of A Home-Based Business Online . . . practical ideas, resources and strategies for your home-based or online business. http://www.ahbbo.com

◎/◎ Exercise 7.8

1. How convincingly does Elena Fawkner distinguish between myths and facts, with regard to running an online business? How adequate is the evidence she provides?

2. How appropriate or effective is Fawker's informal diction? Identify weaknesses as well as strengths in this approach.

3. Suggest possible counterarguments to Fawkner's formulation of myths and facts about running a home-based Internet business.

4. Discuss Fawkner's argumentative strategy. For example, is her sequence of myths/facts arbitrary or purposeful? How can you tell?

5. Rework Fawkner's argument as a PowerPoint presentation. Adapt the information as you see fit—perhaps by including statistics, charts, or graphs to emphasize key points.

Arguing Critically about an Engineering Issue

Engineering students in general are surprised to discover that argumentative writing is important in their field—that engineers are responsible for procedural documents, reports, proposals, and recommendations—all of which require strategies of argumentation.

Key Features in a Critical Discussion of an Engineering Issue

The purpose of writing arguments in engineering is to convince managers or administrators to follow a particular course of action. Often a certain degree of urgency is involved. For example, following the collapse of a freeway overpass during the Loma Prieta Earthquake in Northern California in 1989, civic engineers recognized the urgent need to retrofit (reinforce) existing bridges before another strong earthquake occurred. Another example involves the Challenger and Columbia space shuttle disasters of 1986 and 2003, respectively. These tragedies prompted NASA to establish special commissions to determine the exact causes of each accident and offer recommendations for redesigning the flawed systems and revamping launch protocols.

Example of a Short Engineering Position Paper

In his Technical Writing for Engineers course, Santa Clara University professor Don Riccomini asked his students to research different reports examining the causes of the space shuttle disasters of 1986 and 2003 (students had the option of researching one or the other) and recommend to NASA which of the reports was most accurate, reliable, and thorough.

After examining the reports based on the Challenger disaster, Melissa Conlin, a student in Professor Riccomini's course, prepared the following position paper:

Date: 05/12/2010

To: Jane Doe

From: Melissa Conlin

Subject: Challenger Shuttle Disaster Recommendation

INTRODUCTION SUMMARY

You recently asked for my evaluation of three articles on the Challenger shuttle disaster. The first was the official government commission's findings, the second the personal report of

Roger Boisjoly, and the third the personal observations of Richard Feynman. I have read these reports and in this memo I have compared them under three main categories: author credibility, report content, the recommendations made. Through my analysis I have concluded that while lessons may be learned from each report, the one by Richard Feynman encapsulates the ideas of all three into one, easy to read paper and should be used for the basis of future improvements.

OVERVIEW

	Author Credibility	Report Content	Recommendations Made
Rogers Commission Report	• Fourteen members of commission • Among them: Neil Armstrong, Richard Feynman and Sally K. Ride	• Technical problems with the design of the shuttle • Analysis of the miscommunication between the managers and engineers	• Design of some parts of the shuttle must be changed • Shuttle management structure should be reviewed • Future projects such as launch abort and escape crew
Roger Boisjoly Report	• Engineer working on improvement of O-rings at time of disaster • Argued to stop the launch of the Challenger • First-hand experience	• Ethical argument of miscommunication between engineers and managers	• Focus on establishing better communication between engineers and managers
Richard Feynman Report	• Served on Presidential Rogers Commission to investigate disaster • Nobel laureate physicist from Cal Tech	• Technical and well as ethical argument of what went wrong • Focus on technical problems as well as miscommunication	• Focus on improvements to be made in solid rockets, liquid fuel engines and avionics • Argument that disparity between management and engineer understanding must be fixed

ROGERS COMMISSION REPORT ON THE CHALLENGER (OFFICIAL GOVERNMENT REPORT)
Author Credibility

The Commission was made up of fourteen members. Among the members were: Neil Armstrong, the first man to walk on the moon, Richard P. Feynman, winner of the 1965 Nobel Prize in Physics, Sally K. Ride, the first American woman in space, and two Air

Force Generals. All of the members were important people within the United States government at the time or well known within the scientific and space community. The authors' entire knowledge and experience combine into one long, very thorough report.

Report Content

The Rogers Commission Report is very long and extensively detailed. In looking at the miscommunication between managers and engineers alone there are around thirty interviews and firsthand accounts written about and included. There are also pages upon pages on the technical problems with the O-ring and what went wrong in the accident. With this report there is nothing left out, though it is informational rather than an ethical argument of what could have been done to stop the disaster. The shuttle design itself is examined, from the faulty Solid Rocket Motor joint to adding a launch abort and crew escape mechanism. The report is very formal and detailed, as the authors want nothing to be left out in their analysis. It is much too long to be read by the general public and would take anyone, regardless of their interest, a long time to get through. A manager, technician, or engineer in the specific fields discussed would find the report very informative and useful, though they would need to search through all the text to find the area related to their work.

Recommendations Made

The Rogers Commission Report offers very specific recommendations, added to the end of the analysis. The recommendations revolve around the design of the shuttle as well as the structure of the management itself. The recommendations are very specific and include fixing the faulty Solid Rocket Motor joint and seal, evaluating the Shuttle Program Management Structure, improving communications, improving landing safety, adding a launch abort and crew escape, and implementing maintenance safeguards. Even though the report itself is very long and detailed, the recommendations presented are well thought out and there are few enough of them that they can all be accomplished without changing too many things at once. Though with some of the recommendations shifting towards future projects, such as launch abort and crew escape, some of the focus could be taken off of the problems already present within the system that need fixing. It would seem preexisting problems should be fixed before shifting the spotlight to new areas. As the report claims, it was "An accident Rooted in History;" old problems must be fixed before moving onto the future.

ROGER BOISJOLY REPORT

Author Credibility

Roger Boisjoly was an engineer at Morton Thiokol who was involved in an improvement effort on the O-rings used to bring a space shuttle into orbit. Before the Challenger shuttle disaster he worked vehemently to stop the launch, claiming the O-rings would not function properly in temperatures less than fifty-three degrees. His arguments were ignored, resulting in the launch of the shuttle and the eventual disaster. Boisjoly offers a reliable, first-hand account of the events leading up to the explosion and emphasizes the lack of communication between the engineers and managers in charge at the time of the disaster.

Report Content

Boisjoly's account addresses the ethical issues within the Challenger disaster, rather than focusing on the technical aspects of what went wrong. He does spend some time discussing how tests done on the O-rings indicated problems with low temperatures, but his frustration and emotion fully come out as he discusses his attempts to stop the launch of the Challenger. He mentions the lack of management support to provide resources for testing, how he and his team received no comments back on their reports against the management leading up to the disaster, and how he felt totally helpless when the decision to launch was made. His tone is conversational and there is very little technical knowledge needed to understand his report. His goal since the disaster has been to change workplace ethics and that is exactly what he focuses on here, his report making it clear that he never wants a disaster such as the Challenger to happen again through miscommunication between engineers and their managers.

Recommendations Made

Boisjoly's recommendation is ethical rather than technical. To him the lack of communication between the engineers and the managers was much more of a problem than the O-rings and technical side of the disaster. If the communication had been better, the problem with the O-rings could have been solved or avoided. It doesn't matter if you have all of the evidence to support your claims or if you know exactly how to fix a technical problem, if you cannot communicate your knowledge to your manager nothing will come from it. According to Boisjoly, it is the professional responsibility, conduct, and accountability that require the most improvement. He sums up his thoughts and recommendation with his final statement: "All of you must now evaluate your careers and emerge with the knowledge and conviction that you have a professional and moral responsibility to yourselves and to your fellow man to defend the truth and expose any questionable practices that will lead to an unsafe product."

RICHARD FEYNMAN REPORT
Author Credibility

Richard Feynman was a Nobel laureate physicist from Cal Tech who was asked to join the Presidential Rogers Commission to investigate the Challenger disaster. Following his work for the Commission he wrote a report on his own personal observations and interpretation of what went wrong and what current problems need to be fixed. He does not offer a first-hand account of the events leading up to and during the disaster, but his experiences and interviews after provided him enough of an understanding that his report is very reliable and contains the viewpoints of those who were present. His technical knowledge as well as his outsider's view of the disparity between management and engineer understanding combine to offer a very compelling argument.

Report Content

Throughout his report, Feynman switches off between an ethical argument and a technical one. He continuously points out the disparity between management and engineers. Right from the start he

writes: "It appears that there are enormous differences of opinion as to the probability of a failure with loss of vehicle and
of human life. The estimates range from roughly 1 in 100 to 1 in
100,000. The higher figures come from the working engineers, and
the very low figures from management". As his paper continues,
he keeps pointing out the figures that the engineers have come up
with and the ones the management believes, all of them showing
just as much, if not more, of a disproportion. Though along with
the miscommunication he sees he also talks of the most important
technical improvements that he thinks need to be put into place.
He focuses on solid rockets, liquid fuel engines, and avionics.
For example, in the Avionics section he points out that there have
been no changes to computer hardware in fifteen years and that
even after sensors have failed no changes have been made to them
in eighteen months. Feynman blends both ethical and technical
problems into his argument, bringing them together seamlessly in
a conversational tone that can be understood by technicians and
the general public alike.

Recommendations Made

   Feynman recommends both technical and ethical action to improve shuttle reliability. First and foremost, managers and engineers need to be on the same page when it comes to the risks
involved. Through his analysis he shows that the managers seem to
have unrealistic visions of how safe the shuttles are. According
to the managers, if they flew a shuttle everyday for three hundred years they would only lose one. Better communication needs to
be established so that the managers know the risks as well as the
engineers. Feynman also offers three main areas to be improved in
the shuttle itself, giving details analysis of the solid rockets,
liquid fuel engineers, and the avionics. He feels the technology needs to be upgraded and offers specific places he could see
improvement being made, such as in the fifteen-year-old computer
hardware being used within the shuttles. His recommendations are
specific and detailed, though he doesn't provide so many that
too many things would be changed at once. His suggestions are
all also already existing problems, as he focuses on fixing them

before moving forward. He sums up his report with one statement, blending ethics and technology together: "For a successful technology, reality must take precedence over public relations, for nature cannot be fooled."

CONCLUSION

Richard Feynman's report should be read and reviewed, with his recommendations followed. Since Feynman was one of the authors of the Rogers Commission Report he addresses many of the same ideas, but in a much more condensed way. Instead of having to search through pages and pages of text, readers can read his shorter report and get an idea of what the Rogers Commission Report encapsulated. He also addresses some of the ethical issues that Boisjoly does in his report, pointing out the large discrepancies between managers' beliefs and the judgment of their engineers. Feynman's recommendations address these ethical issues as well as the technical ones that he found to be the most important from his work on the Rogers Commission Report. His recommendations also address current problems within the system, rather than shifting the focus to improvements that could potentially be made in the future. For these reasons, Richard Feynman's report should be used for the basis of future improvements.

◎/◎ Exercise 7.9

1. If you were evaluating the different Challenger disaster reports, what would you do differently, or conclude differently, and why?

2. Comment on the effectiveness of the format Conlin uses in this engineering proposal, including her visual (the tabulated overview).

3. What other visual aids—charts, graphs, bulleted itemizations, photographs, drawings—might be useful in reinforcing Conlin's evaluation?

4. Compare the way Conlin organizes her argument with the way Jonathan Jones organizes his argument about the Grant Wood painting *American Gothic*.

Chapter Summary

Every discipline has its own protocols for argument. The reason is that methods of research, the nature of evidence, and the manner of presenting an argument differ from one field of inquiry to another. Students writing papers on topics in the arts (e.g., painting, theater, and literature) need to become familiar with the different critical traditions and changing criteria for excellence. "Evidence" in the arts often involves documents relating to the artist's or writer's life and cultural milieu, as well as to the internal evidence of the work itself. In the natural sciences and social sciences, evidence refers to demonstrable (experimentally or mathematically verifiable) results and statistics, as well as to the interpretations and recommendations of experts who base their conclusions on demonstrable results.

Checklist

- Have I familiarized myself with the conventions of argument in the discipline I'm writing a paper in?
- Do I understand how "evidence" is defined in a given discipline?
- Do I understand what is appropriate and sufficient evidence in a given discipline?
- Have I examined the ethical implications of my thesis? (See Chapter 4.)
- Have I acknowledged challenging views and sought common ground with some of their assertions, as well as refuted other assertions? (See Chapters 3 and 5.)
- Have I collected sufficient background information to be able to argue the issue at hand?
- Did I take time to explain specialized concepts in language that laypersons can understand?

Writing Projects

For Arts Majors:
1. Study three paintings by twentieth-century artist Edward Hopper, then defend or challenge the following claim: *Hopper's city scenes attempt to negate the myth of the American dream.* Hopper's paintings are accessible online. NOTE: When cutting and pasting images such as paintings from Internet sources, be sure to acknowledge the source underneath the image and on your Works Cited page.
2. Choose one of the following poems (accessible online) and study three critical responses to it. Write an essay in which you examine these critiques

for their insightfulness and thoroughness. Call attention to aspects of the poem that were, in your opinion, misinterpreted or overlooked.

Edgar Allan Poe, "Annabel Lee"
Emily Dickinson, "I heard a fly buzz when I died"
William Butler Yeats, "The Lake Isle of Innisfree"

For Science Majors:

1. Study two or three explanations of a "black hole." First, in a short paper, decide which explanation does the best job of conveying the concept, and why. Next, convert that short paper into a PowerPoint presentation you could use to present the argument to a high school science class.

2. Some argue that we should return to the moon because of its valuable mineral resources and/or to build colonies for future human settlement. Defend or challenge one of these proposals. A good starting source is NASA's website (www.nasa.gov).

For Social Science Majors:

1. Research "social Darwinism," and then argue whether the Darwinean biological concept of "survival of the fittest" can apply to societal situations, such as warfare or workplace competition.

2. Investigate some of the challenges to *Roe* v. *Wade*. How valid are they, in your opinion?

For Business Majors:

1. Examine the advertising strategies used to market a particular product, such as a certain make of automobile or brand of shampoo. Which advertisements (print or Internet) or television ads are most effective for the product? Least effective? What recommendations can you make to improve marketability of the product? Later, expand the project to use whatever new media are at your disposal. For example, redesign the ads with your own original photographs, videos, or drawings.

2. What criteria should a person follow when preparing a résumé? Obtain recommendations from your school's career counseling service as well as from two or three employment agencies. Finally, gather information from two or three employers themselves. Study the similarities and differences in the respective guidelines and make your own recommendations.

For Engineering Majors:

1. Write a report on the feasibility of biofuels (and biofuel systems) as an automotive industry alternative for petroleum. Be sure to examine both the alleged advantages and the alleged disadvantages with equal scrutiny.

2. It has been frequently noted that a great many of America's roads are in need of repair. After surveying the streets in one particular neighborhood or area in your community, write a proposal describing in detail the kinds of repairs needed and why the repairs are urgent. Suggestion: Use Google Maps or a similar online resource to illustrate the urgent need for these repairs.

8 Researching Your Argument

> I have always come to life after coming to books.
> —Jorge Luis Borges

CONSIDERING THE DISCIPLINES

There's no law that says research has got to be tedious. The late rhetorician Ken Macrorie (1919–2009) liked to refer to researching as *searching*. It was his way of suggesting that research has an element of adventure in it: you can never fully anticipate what nuggets of information you might discover about your topic until you begin digging in the library or searching the Internet. Both the authors occasionally lose themselves in ideas and the process of researching when they write, so research can be both enjoyable and fruitful for your work. One of our colleagues who writes historical fiction loves the research phase and uses techniques such as you'll find in this chapter, so whether you are researching environmental science topics or literary topics, you will likely find yourself needing to research your topic in at least a few of the ways discussed here. In this chapter you will be introduced to the principles of academic research, along with basic research tools (print and Internet) appropriate to any field of inquiry, with emphasis on conducting research for argumentative essays.

Much of the writing you do in college—as well as beyond—requires *research*, which refers to three interconnected activities: (1) searching for and retrieving information you need for your writing project, (2) taking notes, and (3) integrating the necessary information into your paper. These activities enable you to acquire in-depth knowledge of the subject and, in turn, to strengthen the premise of your argument.

The Three Faces of Research

Research involves finding information and applying it to your own purposes. One major reason for writing an argument is to present to readers new information and insights into a topic. At the same time, however, readers need to be informed or reminded about the old information to see how the new perspective (yours) adds to the discussion of the issue and merits consideration. You therefore must learn as much as possible about your topic and know how to incorporate only the best and most relevant researched data. Sometimes students try to incorporate so much data into their papers that the papers begin to read like mere summaries of what others have written about the topic. Readers want to see your original argument *reinforced* by the findings of others.

Searching Before You Research: Taking a Mental Inventory

One of the most important steps in gathering information may seem like the least necessary: making clear to yourself how much you already know about the topic. The step is necessary because much of what you learn, if it is not used every day, ends up in the equivalent of deep storage in the brain. Some good ways for retrieving it include listing, clustering, and freewriting—predrafting strategies described in Chapter 1. These information-gathering techniques help you generate questions, ideas, and "paths" to pursue in your research.

Consider this case in point: Before Marian, a first-year composition student, sets out to research her chosen topic—possible long-term effects of secondhand cigarette smoke on children—she opens a blank document in her word-processing program and begins freewriting (rapidly recording all that she already knows or associates with the topic). Ignoring word choice, sentence correctness, or paragraph structure for the moment, Marian focuses only on content.

> My parents both smoked and I remembered coughing a lot when I was around them, and sometimes my eyes burned. I never connected my coughing and burning eyes to their smoking because I assumed that they would never do anything to undermine my health. Children can't get away from smoke. In the family, are stuck, have no choice in the matter. And then I remember that my best friend Julia's parents also smoked, even more than my parents did, and that she would cough all the time, and come down with the flu a lot. Not long afterwards (when? what year?), the Surgeon General issued a warning that ambient smoke can be just as harmful as firsthand smoke. Question: has government done studies comparing effects on children vs. adults? I also read recently that medical researchers have established a link between secondhand smoke and chronic respiratory illnesses, such as asthma. Question: I wonder if the recent upturn in asthma rates in children relates to parents' smoking? I also know that some researchers or tobacco industry people or maybe just average smokers argue that the connection is exaggerated, people's fears get overblown—Question—how to determine how real is the danger?

Marian's freewriting inventory on secondhand smoke is not extensive, but she has written down enough for questions to start occurring to her—questions that help direct and focus the research process. Also, the freewriting gets her thinking about possible opposing views as well as helps her establish a link between her personal experience with the topic and her more objective knowledge of it.

◎/◎   **Exercise 8.1**

1. Freewrite on one of the following argumentative topics:

   a. Ways to improve my local fitness center

   b. How to improve the parking situation on campus

   c. Studying to prepare for a career versus studying for the pleasure of learning

2. Write down all that you already know about a topic you enjoy reading about; then generate a list of questions about aspects of the topic you need to know more about to increase your knowledge or expertise.

Focusing Your Research for Argumentative Essays

Once you have a sense of what you need to find out about your topic, you can guide your researching activities with sets of questions to keep your information-gathering activities in focus. Once again, recall the purpose–audience–writer–subject interconnections of the rhetorical rhombus introduced in Chapter 1 (see Figure 8.1).

Generate your questions in the context of each point on the rhombus. If you are arguing against the authenticity of UFO reports, for example, you might generate sets of questions similar to those in the following four sections.

Purpose-Based Questions

Purpose-based questions are interpretive and based on values, for example:

1. What is the thesis (claim) of my essay? Is it sufficiently clear and convincing? (The next section helps you formulate a strong thesis for your papers.)

2. What values (called *warrants* in the Toulmin model) are implied by the kind of evidence I bring to the claim?

3. What larger implications are conveyed by the thesis?

4. How do I want my intended audience to think or act after reading my paper? To vote to discontinue funding of UFO research? To stop making unsubstantiated claims?

Audience-Based Questions

Audience-based questions enable you to concentrate on your readers' expectations about the subject matter, on the ways they might respond to your assertions,

FIGURE 8.1

Rhetorical Rhombus

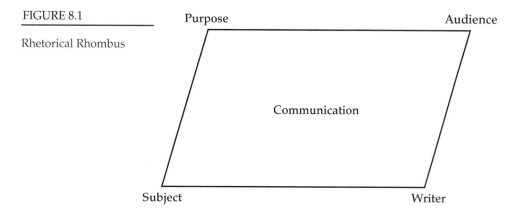

and on how you might counterrespond to their reactions. Here are some examples of audience-based questions:

1. Who are the readers I'd like to reach? Those who will support funding of future research on UFOs? Those who are writing the UFO reports to show them their bias?

2. What is my audience's opinion on the authenticity of UFOs? How strongly is that opinion held?

3. What kinds of sources are best suited to my audience? If uninformed, they need background information provided. If hostile, they need to be convinced that I understand their position fully and fairly.

4. What are my audience's main sources of information about UFOs? How reliable are these sources?

5. Exactly how does my audience benefit from reading this essay?

Writer-Based Questions

Writer-based questions enable you to concentrate on your existing knowledge in and understanding of the subject matter, and on whether you need to gather more information on it. Here are some examples of writer-based questions:

1. Why is it so important to spend time considering this anti-UFO stance?

2. Do I actually feel strongly one way or another on this issue?

3. How much do I already know about UFO reports?

Subject-Based Questions

Subject-based questions focus on the factual content of your topic. Facts are universally verifiable; that is, they can be tested or verified by anyone. They must be distinguished from interpretations, judgments, or conclusions, which are subjective responses *derived* from your analysis of the facts. Here are some examples of subject-based questions:

1. Do existing UFO reports share common elements? Do these elements reinforce authenticity or fraud?

2. What are the *scientific* data for the claims in the most notable UFO reports? How do I know those scientific data are authentic and reliable?

3. What do I need to research to discuss or refute the claims presented by the UFO reports?

4. Do I carefully consider potential challenges to my views and the best way to interpret their validity?

You can see how the answers to questions in these four areas will affect the text, from its content to its organization to its tone.

Formulating a Strong Thesis

You already know what a thesis is: It is the main point you wish to argue, the claim you are making and are trying to persuade your audience to accept, using the strongest evidence you can find. However, you may like to gain more skill in coming up with a strong, compelling thesis for your argumentative essays. Here are three steps you can take to ensure that the thesis you come up with is a good one:

1. Write down an assertion (viewpoint, claim) on a particular topic. For example, if your topic is music censorship, you might write down, "Music censorship is wrong."

2. Ask probing questions about the clarity and specificity of your assertion, making sure that you replace vague or ambiguous language with specific, precise language. If the above statement about music censorship appeared as a thesis statement, readers would have some of the following questions:

   • What is meant by *wrong?* Unethical? Illegal? Misguided?

   • What is meant by *music?* The music itself or the lyrics to songs? If songs, then what kinds of songs? Country-western? Rap? Rock? Jazz? Rhythm and blues? Hip-hop? What about the songs do some people find objectionable? Swear words? Obscenity? Political references? Actions seemingly advocated by the lyrics?

   • What is meant by *censorship?* Bleeping certain words or phrases of certain songs? Restricting sales only to those of a certain age? Banning the music altogether?

3. Turn your assertion into a well-focused, specifically worded thesis statement. For example, "Expurgating or banning rap songs because of their alleged profanity or obscenity is against the law because it violates rights guaranteed by the First Amendment."

By taking the time to examine your trial thesis statement from the point of view of its clarity and specificity, you produce effective thesis statements that in turn help you to produce more effective arguments.

◎/◎ Exercise 8.2

1. Generate three questions for each of the four elements of the rhetorical rhombus (purpose, audience, writer, subject) for an essay you have recently finished or one on which you are currently working.

2. Imagine that you are writing a paper that argues for the best ways of dealing with sexual harassment in the workplace. Generate questions in each of these categories: purpose-based, audience-based, writer-based, subject-based.

3. Revise each of the following assertions so that they can serve as strong thesis statements:

   a. Water quality needs to be improved.

   b. Males are the dominant sex because they are stronger.

   c. The university should offer more courses for minorities.

Researching Using the Internet

A late-twentieth-century invention, the Internet has become, in little more than a decade, the most revolutionary information resource since the invention of printing about 550 years ago. Its dramatic proliferation brings problems, however, as well as benefits. Some sources on the Internet are superficial, irrelevant, or unreliable. Usually, you know right away what is junk and what isn't—but sometimes it is not so easy.

You need to acquire an eye for distinguishing between documents that are substantive and relevant, and those that are not. Here are a few questions to ask about Internet documents to help you make that distinction:

1. Are the authors experts in their fields? If no biographical information about the authors is included at the site, check the library or search the Web to see whether these credentials are located elsewhere.

2. Do the authors go beyond mere generalized assertions in order to produce useful, new knowledge about the subject? For example, if you find an article that argues either for or against the use of exit tests as a condition for high school graduation, does the author back up those assertions with actual data comparing the performance of students who have prepared for such a test with those who have not?

3. Do the authors provide a scholarly context for their arguments? That is, do they relate their points of view to others who have also conducted scholarly inquiry into the subject?

4. Is the subject matter treated seriously and professionally? Be wary of an amateurish tone. For example, in debates over controversial issues such as whether the state should require creationist doctrine to be given equal standing with evolutionary theory in a high school biology class, one side might easily caricature the other side as "religious fanatics" or "radical atheists." Such pigeonholing or name-calling works against the very purpose of argument, which is to examine both sides of an issue critically, carefully, and responsibly, in order to arrive at a reasonable understanding of what really is or should be. When in doubt, weigh the tone and treatment of a questionable document with documents you know are authentic and significant.

Useful Types of Internet Resources

The most common types of information resources available on the Internet include listservers, newsgroups, databases, and online forums. The sections that follow take a closer look at each of these. *Note:* Regardless which of the below sources you consult, it is always a good idea to double-check information you access, especially when acquiring information from unknown individuals participating in a listserv, newsgroup, or forum.

Listservers

A listserver (more commonly referred to as a *listserv*) is a discussion group subscription service in which commentary and information about a given topic are exchanged with all members of the group who are all connected by email. Listserv members often participate in ongoing conversations or debates over key issues. When a great many experts and enthusiasts from all over the world argue heatedly on a given topic, a wealth of information and viewpoints is generated. For this reason, participation in such discussion groups can be an excellent way of staying informed and developing your argumentative skills at the same time.

Newsgroups

Newsgroups (also usenets or bulletin boards) are topic-based electronic discussion groups that anyone can join. Members with an interest in, say, art history can access useful information that is arranged by subtopic and posted by other members. If you are interested in Italian Renaissance art, for example, you quite likely could find, on a homepage menu, a newsgroup devoted to that area. Many of these newsgroups archive their postings, which become valuable for research.

Databases

Databases are invaluable compilations of sources in a given subject, such as a compilation of books and articles on health care, biochemistry, ancient Egyptian history, economics, or any other subject. Although many databases are accessed online, some of them, like the *Modern Language Association (MLA) International Bibliography of Language and Literature*, the *Readers Guide to Periodical Literature*, and the *Congressional Record Index* continue to be published in hard copy or put on CD-ROM. See the reference librarian at your college library when uncertain about locating a particular database for your research project.

Your college library most likely subscribes to a database company that packages electronic bibliographies. The most popular is InfoTrac, which may include newspaper bibliographies (such as those for the *Wall Street Journal*, the *New York Times*, and newspapers from your local area) as well as general reference articles across the disciplines. Your librarian will be happy to inform you of the databases to which the library subscribes, and may provide you with handouts describing each kind.

The catalogs of most academic and research libraries are available online. The Library of Congress's catalog is also available and contains more than twelve million items. The Library of Congress also has accessible special collections, such as the National Agricultural Library and the National Library of Medicine. Access any of the Library of Congress's catalogs at http://www.loc.gov.

Forums

A forum is an ongoing discussion group in real time. Forums exist for just about any subject matter and professional interest imaginable. Such forums can be an excellent way of finding highly knowledgeable people and learning from them, while enjoying interactive conversations with people all across the country or even the world. Be careful, however. The knowledge base of participants varies in these discussions, and some participants may purposefully or inadvertently give out misleading information.

Blogs [Web Logs]

Blogging is a kind of opinion-oriented journalism in which you respond to issues as they're unfolding or respond to them on your own website or the websites of others, and in which anyone else can do the same. Perhaps you have seen opportunities to respond to the thoughts of others when you have been reading newspaper columns or stories online. You may yourself have kept a blog as you travelled or worked to keep family and friends up to date on what you are doing.

If you consult blogs as research for any of your written arguments, however, you must read them through a critical lens. For example, "Shuggy," a forty-three-year-old educator in Glasgow, Scotland, chooses to air his opinions about politics and history, among other topics, and quite unashamedly lists as one of his interests "inflicting my insane thoughts on unsuspecting people via the blogosphere." Although Shuggy may be articulate and entertaining, no one has responded to him, and his ideas do not differ much from any layperson's.

Of course, the presence of responses alone does not guarantee accuracy of information. Although http://blog.createdebate.com encourages individuals to post issues that will engage others in conversation, one can see that not everyone posts useful statements that help to engage in formal argument. One extended blog that writers of arguments may wish to look at concerns a graphic that someone created to illustrate Paul Graham's article "How To Disagree" (http://blog .createdebate.com/2008/04/07/writing-strong-arguments).

Some blogs, though, may be quite informative. For example, one spot was created for law faculty: http://www.lawprofessorblogs.com. At this site, browsers can read what law professors from institutions such as Willamette have to say about environmental law. There one might see embedded photographs and links to pertinent YouTube videos, such as on the Legal Writing blog page, which has videos posted relating the history of the Legal Writing Institute, http:// lawprofessors.typepad.com/legalwriting, including an interview with some of the pioneers in teaching legal writing.

When using information from a blog, be sure to check the source's credentials, not just to use the biographical notes for your introductory comments, but also to ensure that the source is credible. Remember to credit the source on your Works Cited page.

Social Networking Sites (Facebook, MySpace, Second Life)

According to Jonathan Zimmerman ("Hooked on Facebook"), 50 to 75 percent of American teenagers have profiled themselves on one of the Internet sites dedicated to social networking, of which Facebook, MySpace, and YouTube are the most popular. Besides those, Second Life allows users to create avatars that users can modify to dress and look like themselves, or like they would prefer to present themselves. On Second Life, one can interact with individuals worldwide on different "islands" that the site provides or that institutions purchase in that virtual world.

YouTube

According to their fact sheet, YouTube "is the world's most popular online video community, allowing millions of people to discover, watch and share originally-crafted videos" (http//: www.youtube.com/t/fact_sheet). Through YouTube, it is possible to locate videos relating to current events or hobbies, and to watch scenes from a favorite television show. It is possible to insert a YouTube video into a social networking site, such as Facebook or MySpace.

You may not be surprised to learn that politicians use YouTube. One politician running for office in 2010, for example, posted a video to his blog on the minimum wage, and numerous individuals posted text responses to his comments: http://www.youtube.com/watch?v=I_IMuxMXd3E&feature5fvsr.

Twitter

Twitter, according to their fact sheet at http://twitter.com, "is a real-time short messaging service that works over multiple networks and devices." Once you sign up, you can send mini-messages ("tweets") of no more than 140 characters (including spaces) to anyone anywhere. It is the most prevalent form of instant messaging today. People tweet from war zones to major news networks, from friend to friend anywhere in the world. Because of the brevity of these messages, tweets may help a person be aware of an issue but may not provide the sort of in-depth analysis or explanation or argument that writers will find useful to include as support of their own arguments.

Searching on the Web

Searching for information on the Web is easy—almost too easy. All you do is click on a search engine icon at your Internet service provider's homepage or enter a Web address for one of the many existing search engines. Some search engines are more powerful than others, however. Among the most reliable are Google, WebCrawler, Yahoo!, AltaVista, Dogpile, *Ask,* and Lycos. Here are their URL (uniform resource locator) addresses:

http://www.google.com

http://www.webcrawler.com

http://www.yahoo.com

http://www.altavista.com

http://www.dogpile.com

http://www.ask.com

http://www.lycos.com

http://en.wikipedia.org/wiki/Main-Page

http://scholar.google.com

http://www.metacrawler.com

http://www.hotbot.com

Every search engine is different. Some, like AltaVista and Dogpile, include brief descriptions of every site called up.

The next step is to type keywords in the narrow blank rectangle provided—and here things can get a little tricky. You need to decide which three or four words come closest to the sort of information you hope to find. Use the most "official" terms you know for your subject. If you are looking for general pro–con arguments on school vouchers, for example, you might enter the keywords *school, voucher,* and *programs.* If you want to find material on vouchers relating to your state, enter the name of your state in the keyword field as well. If you wish to focus on specific concerns within the voucher system, you may need to enter an additional relevant keyword such as *curriculum, class size,* or *teaching excellence.*

Search engines usually retrieve far more sites than you can review in a reasonable time, so you have to be selective. If you're looking for substantive, scholarly commentary, look for sites from academic institutions. (You can recognize these sites by their URL extension, *.edu.*) Or look for online magazines, or *e-zines,* as they are sometimes called.

Google has a time-saving search option, an "I'm feeling lucky" button that, when clicked on, brings up far fewer hits, but those hits are likely the most relevant to the keywords you have entered.

Another problem to be aware of when searching for relevant sites is timeliness. If you require the latest information, be sure to check the dates of the sites you bring up. Some of them may be several years old.

Using Boolean Search Strategies

A Boolean search is one in which you customize your search keywords using what are called *operators.* The three most common Boolean operators are

and   ∧

not   +

or   &

Let's say you are searching the Expanded Academic Index (an international general database for source materials in the humanities, social and general sciences) for articles on logging policies or logging practices but not articles having to do with the history of logging. Instead of merely entering the keyword *logging*, you can use the Boolean operators *and* and *not* to restrict your search as follows:

```
Logging policies and practices not histories
```

Another device useful in searches is the asterisk (*), which works as a wildcard: It instructs the search engine to bring up all forms of the word attached to the word segment typed in before the asterisk. Thus, if you're looking for information about cosmology and want to bring up articles with all forms of the word *cosmology* at once instead of searching for each one separately, you would simply type in *cosm**. The search engine would then bring up database articles containing all the words bearing that segment, for example:

cosmic

cosmological

cosmologist

cosmologists

cosmology

cosmos

Of course, you would also get a lot of unwanted entries relating to words that begin with the segment *cosm* but that have nothing to do with the nature of the universe:

cosmetic

cosmetics

cosmetologist

cosmetologists

cosmetology

Useful Websites for Writers of Arguments

The list that follows gives some useful Web addresses for your research. Note, however, that websites often disappear, are updated, or change their addresses. Consider using a current *Internet Yellow Pages* (available in most bookstores and libraries) to locate sources.

For Humanities Resources
http://vos.ucsb.edu/

For Statistics from the U.S. Department of Education
http://nces.ed.gov/pubsearch/

For Resources in Religious Studies
http://www.bu.edu/sth/library/index.html

For Information about World History

http://www.hartford-hwp.com/archives (The website for the World History Archives)

For Health-Related Information from the Centers for Disease Control

http://www.cdc.gov/

For Information about Population from the U.S. Census Bureau

http://www.census.gov/

For Information about Public Policy Issues

http://www.speakout.com/activism/

Media Websites

http://www.cnn.com/	The website of the Cable News Network.
http://www.pbs.org/	The website of the Public Broadcasting Service (educational television programming).
http://www.npr.org/	The website of National Public Radio.
http://www.ecola.com/archs.php	A website directory with links to newspapers that allow back-issue searches.
http://www.nytimes.com	The website of the *New York Times*.
http://www.nytimes.com/pages/readersopinions/index.html	This website takes you to the *New York Times* forums, where you can read numerous postings on dozens of subjects by forum members. By subscribing for free, you can post your own views and responses to the postings of others.

Finally, there are websites to help you find information on the Internet as well as to think critically about available resources:

A Tutorial for Finding Information Online

http://www.lib.berkeley.edu/TeachingLib/Guides/Internet/FindInfo.html (This site introduces you to the basics of Web searching.)

Guidelines for Evaluating Websites

http://www.tucolib.info/ (A bibliography of online resources for evaluating websites)

◎/◎ Exercise 8.3

1. Compare the effectiveness of two different search engines, such as Yahoo!, Alta Vista, Dogpile, or Google. Write out a description of their respective strengths and weaknesses.

2. Enter an online forum such as Salon.com on a topic that interests you, and then report your experience orally or in an essay. What did you learn about your topic as a result of interacting with other members of the forum?

3. Compile a list of blogs that have served as sources of information for one of your research topics. Which one of these blogs has been most useful, and why?

Researching Using Print Resources

Without doubt, the Internet is a helpful, high-speed information-accessing tool, and its resources are expanding continuously. But hard-copy resources—reference books, trade books, periodicals (specialized and nonspecialized), historical documents, maps, and newspapers—continue to be indispensable. Much if not most academic scholarship continues to be published in traditional print journals, for example. Scholars often find "hard copy" easier to consult.

Locating Articles

To locate important article sources, begin with the Expanded Academic Index in your library's electronic catalog. The listing will tell you whether your library carries the periodical that the article is in. If not, you may be able to have your library obtain a fax of it for a nominal fee or obtain a book through interlibrary loan.

Other important print periodical indexes include:

Applied Sciences Index

Education Index

Environmental Index

General Science Index

Humanities Index

National Newspaper Index

Social Sciences Index

Using Additional Print Reference Works

In addition to periodical indexes, you may already be familiar with the following hard-copy reference works: encyclopedias (general and specialized), dictionaries, abstracts and digests, handbooks and sourcebooks, and atlases.

Encyclopedias   General or subject-specific encyclopedias are often a good place to begin your formal research because they offer a panoramic view of the topic with which you are working and provide references for further reading. An encyclopedia article is essentially a detailed summary of the most important facts about a topic, accompanied by a bibliography. You probably have used general encyclopedias that cover the whole spectrum of knowledge. You may not have used specialized encyclopedias, which are limited to only one subject, such as psychology or religion.

Here is just a small sampling of the kinds of encyclopedias you will find in your library's reference room:

General	Subject-Specific
Collier's Encyclopedia	Encyclopedia of Environmental Issues
The Columbia Encyclopedia	Encyclopedia of Psychoactive Drugs
Encyclopedia Britannica	Encyclopeida of Computer Science
World Book Encyclopedia	The Wellness Encyclopedia

Dictionaries   A dictionary provides more than highly concise definitions and explanations; in the case of biographical dictionaries, for example, you will find profiles of notable individuals. Most dictionaries are devoted to words in general, but there are specialized dictionaries as well. *Important dictionaries include:*

American Biographical Dictionary

A Dictionary of Biology

McGraw-Hill Dictionary of Scientific and Technical Terms

The Merriam-Webster Book of Word Histories

New Dictionary of American Slang

The Oxford English Dictionary

Who's Who

Who's Who Among African Americans

Who's Who Among America's Teachers

Who's Who Among Asian Americans

Who's Who Among Hispanic Americans

Who's Who in American History

Abstracts and Digests   An abstract is a formal summary of a scholarly or scientific paper. Virtually all disciplines publish compilations of abstracts. Digests are summaries of less formal works such as book *reviews*. Here is a sampling of abstracts and digests:

Book Review Digest

Chemical Abstracts

Dissertation Abstracts

Ecology Abstracts

Handbooks and Sourcebooks   These types of reference books provide you with guidelines and references for particular disciplines, such as English literature, philosophy, geology, economics, mathematics, and computer science. Some handbooks and sourcebooks are

> *A Field Guide to Rocks and Minerals* (similar field guides exist for most subjects in the general sciences)
>
> *A Handbook to Literature*
>
> *Opposing Viewpoints* (collections of pro–con position statements on a wide range of topics)

Atlases   Atlases are collections of maps (of countries, states, cities, the world) and may be historical, topographical (depicting landmasses of different elevations), or geographical (depicting regions in terms of population, natural resources, industries, and the like).

◎/◎   Exercise 8.4

1. At your library, consult *Opposing Viewpoints* (see listing under "Handbooks and Sourcebooks" above) and write a brief summary of each side of a particular topic that you find interesting. Decide which side is argued most convincingly and why.

2. Look up a single item in three different encyclopedias or dictionaries. Describe how the coverage differs from source to source.

3. Using *Book Review Digest* (see listing under "Abstracts and Digests" above), locate three different reviews of a single book and write a comparative evaluation of the three reviews. Which reviewer provides the most useful information about the book's subject matter? About the author?

Gathering Information from Email, Telephone Conversations, Interviews, and Surveys

As a college student, you are part of a complex community of educators, researchers, and specialists in numerous disciplines. Name your topic, and someone on your college faculty, staff, or student body will be an expert in it. But how do you contact these individuals? Very simply: by email or telephone.

Using Email or Telephone

Obtain a campus phone directory listing faculty and staff and their respective departments or offices; there you will see each person's telephone extension number and email address, along with his or her office location. You can also check your school's website to find what specialties are listed for faculty members or to learn where the various offices and departments are on campus so that you can visit them to find out who is an expert in what. Next, email or phone that person, explain who you are and what you are researching, and ask to set up a time convenient for a telephone interview or a personal interview. If the information you require is relatively complex or the person in question is too busy to be interviewed, request an email exchange.

Conducting an Interview

An interview is a focused, carefully directed conversation on a predetermined topic, usually involving the interviewee's personal involvement in the topic being discussed. Interviews can be formal or informal, depending on the nature of the topic and the relationship between interviewer and interviewee.

Information derived from interviews is valuable for two reasons:

1. It is timely (you may be getting "cutting-edge" information before it is published).

2. It provides the opportunity for obtaining personal insights into the subject matter.

Experts can also be extremely helpful in directing you to additional sources and thinking about other aspects of the topic of which you may not be aware.

When conducting the interview, keep the following suggestions in mind:

1. Always make an appointment with the person you wish to interview and be clear about what you wish to discuss and why.

2. Prepare questions to ask during the interview, but don't use them rigidly or present them in rote fashion as in an interrogation. Rather, try to work them spontaneously into your discussion. Ask specific, well-focused questions about what you need to know.

3. It is all right to engage in "ice-breaking" small talk, but once the discussion begins, try not to go off on tangents. Remember: You are there to interview the individual, not to have a casual conversation, so listen more than you talk.

4. Be alert for "spinoff" questions—unanticipated questions that occur to you in light of the way the interviewee answers a previous question. Be sure, however, that spinoff questions are relevant to the topic.

5. Avoid leading questions, whereby your manner of wording the questions reveals a bias on your part. For example, a leading question would be "Wouldn't you agree that the dangers from ozone depletion are highly exaggerated?" You want more than a *yes* or *no* response anyway.

6. Always ask for clarification of a complex idea or for definition of an unfamiliar term. Also, ask for the correct spelling of names or terms you are uncertain about.

7. If you wish to record the interview on tape, request permission to do so beforehand. But don't expect to transcribe it all. You will use the tape just to capture precise wording of an elegant or particularly apt phrase, just as when you quote a written source directly.

8. Ask the interviewee for permission to contact him or her for follow-up questions after the interview, or perhaps suggest a follow-up interview.

9. Write a thank-you note to the interviewee after the interview; acknowledge that the individual is a busy person who set aside time for you. Such common courtesy is justified and appropriate. It also makes it more likely that the individual will respond if you need any follow-up help.

Conducting a Survey

To obtain information from a large number of individuals, you can conduct a survey. The first step is to prepare a questionnaire—a set of questions with room on the sheet for answers—to distribute to individuals. These questions should be carefully worded so that (1) the respondents can answer them quickly, and (2) the survey will yield valid and useful information for your purposes.

The second step is to conduct the survey. This may be done via email, using a distribution list so it could be sent, for example, to the entire student body at once, or via personal distribution, where you simply question individuals directly or ask them to fill out your questionnaire while you wait. Also, it would be a good idea to check with your school's Human Subjects Board or Computer Center about any policies governing such actions. When you are ready to distribute the survey, you may wish to use SurveyMonkey to send it out so that you can manipulate the data into useful charts or graphs for presentation as well.

Designing a Questionnaire

A good questionnaire is a model of relevance, clarity, and concision. Word questions carefully, making sure that binary (for example, *yes-or-no*) questions do not stem from a false dichotomy (that is, where answers other than *yes* or *no* are possible). Also, do not word questions that are leading or that conceal a bias. The following is an example of a biased question:

What percentage of old-growth forest should be logged?
_____10% _____50% _____75% _____85% _____100%

This set of options is biased because (1) there is no 0% (the opposite equivalent of 100%), and (2) there is only one option below 50% but two options above 50%.

The following is an example of a leading question:

Do you agree that the sexist practices of the labor union should be stopped?
_____Yes   _____No   _____Not Sure

Sexist is judgmental and therefore risks leading the respondent to agree with that judgment. The question should describe actual documented actions that may or may not be judged as sexist, such as "Should the labor union continue to deny membership to women?"

It is usually a good idea to avoid questions that readers would not be sure how to answer or that would require long answers. Instead, choose questions that ask respondents to choose among the options you provide:

Which of the following long-term space exploration policies should NASA adopt? (Check all that apply.)

_____ Lunar colonization

_____ Robot probes of outer planets

_____ Human exploration of Mars

_____ Lunar-orbiting telescope

Finally, introduce your questionnaire in a brief, courteous paragraph that includes your name, the purpose of your research, and how much time you estimate it will take to answer the questions. Thank your readers in advance for their time.

Taking Effective Research Notes

The notes you take while reading outside sources for your argument-in-progress will come in handy when you decide which sources you need to integrate into the body of your paper. (See also "Incorporating Outside Sources into Your Argument" on pages 296–299.) The following suggestions will make your note-taking more efficient and productive.

1. Unless you have a laptop computer to take with you into the library, use index cards for taking notes (4" × 6" size is ideal): You can easily shuffle and rearrange them, as well as annotate them. Some students find that it helps to use differently colored cards for different purposes, that is, white for direct quotations, yellow for bibliography, green for the writer's own ideas. Photocopying articles and passages from books is another option, but photocopying can get expensive and can take as much time as writing out notes. Also, photocopied pages are harder to sort through and review.

2. Write out the complete bibliographic citation for every source you use; that way, you will be able to locate the source again easily if you need to and will be able to prepare your Works Cited page more quickly. Guidelines for

citing sources appear in Chapter 8, Documenting Your Sources: MLA and APA Styles.

3. Read each source straight through to get an idea of all that it includes. Then return to the beginning and copy passages that seem most useful for your needs. Always double-check to make sure you are copying the passage accurately. If you need to omit part of a passage, indicate the omission with ellipsis dots (. . .). If you need to add a word or date to make a quoted passage understandable or coherent, place it in brackets:

According to the *Cedarville Gazette*, "Last year [2003], local automobile-related fatalities numbered more than 1,500."

The Role of Serendipity in Research

Writers benefit greatly from methodical research, but not all researching is methodical. Some of it is results from good fortune, or a special kind of good fortune called *serendipity*.

Serendipity refers to the capacity for discovering important things in an unexpected manner or in an unexpected place. Serendipity seems most likely to occur when you are immersed in your work. Because your senses are on full alert, you pick up things you might not have otherwise noticed or make connections between two ideas that you would never have made in a less engaged state of mind.

Two students described the following serendipitous discoveries:

```
Student 1

While I was working on my paper on unfair hiring practices, I
happened to notice a news story on the Internet that described
how frustrating it is to follow user manuals because their in-
structions are seldom clear enough. That made a light flash in-
side my head! Perhaps hiring practices are often unfair because
the policies describing them are poorly written!
```

```
Student 2

Here I was stumped about how to develop my topic on the way stu-
dents can study effectively in groups. While I was eating lunch,
I overheard two students discussing getting together with their
Western Civilization study group to prepare for a midterm.
```

I introduced myself and asked them if they would tell me about
how they formed their group, how beneficial they thought it was,
and what sorts of pitfalls to avoid.

These examples illustrate the way in which mental alertness and engagement
can help you discover new approaches to your topic in unexpected ways.

    Exercise 8.5

1. Over the next four or five days, in addition to using methods of methodical
   researching, do the following:

    a. Browse for half an hour or so among the library stacks, in subject areas
       relevant to the topic you are working on.

    b. Listen closely for connections, however seemingly tangential, while
       talking with classmates or friends.

    c. Find some encyclopedia articles related to the topic you are working on
       and write down any ideas that might be worth incorporating into your
       essay.

    d. Review your lecture notes from other classes.

2. Report on any serendipitous discoveries that you were able to use for your
   paper. Compare your serendipity experiences with those of your classmates. If you hear of one you have not experienced, try to experience it for
   yourself.

Evaluating Your Sources

It is tempting to assume that just because information is published it is reliable.
Because that is not the case, unfortunately, you need to ensure that the sources
you incorporate into your argument are trustworthy. Evaluate every outside
source you incorporate into your paper using these five criteria:

1. *Accuracy* of information presented

2. *Relevance* to your thesis

3. *Reliability* of the author and the periodical that originally published the
   material

4. *Clarity*

5. *Thoroughness*

The sections that follow consider each criterion in turn.

Accuracy

Factual information needs to be checked for accuracy. Data, such as population trends, the latest nutritional information about a dietary supplement, academic program policies and offerings, and so on, sometimes change so frequently that the print source at your fingertips may not be the most recent information. Carefully check dates of publication, check with the campus specialist, or search the Internet for more current information.

Relevance

Does the information you plan to use in your argument truly contribute to your thesis? If you are writing about the importance of animals in medical research but use information drawn from the use of animals in cosmetic research, there may be a problem with relevance unless you can draw a medical connection to cosmetic use (for example, certain dyes in mascara can cause an allergic reaction).

Reliability

When considering the reliability of information, think about the credentials of the author presenting it. For example, if an author is conveying information about the toxins in local groundwater, that person should be a recognized authority in environmental chemistry, not just a local politician.

Clarity

Important data are sometimes presented in a way that is difficult to understand. In such cases, you may need to *paraphrase* the source material instead of quoting it directly, or to quote it directly but add your own explanation afterward. Technical information, while clear to you, might be confusing to nonspecialist readers. In such cases, you may need to provide a somewhat elaborate interpretation of the data.

Thoroughness

It is important to ensure that your data are not perfunctory bits of quotations or statistics that fail to provide sufficient grounding for your claim. The more debatable your claims, the more you need to provide sufficient data to remove any doubts from readers' minds.

Understanding and Avoiding Plagiarism

From the Latin word for "kidnapper," *plagiarism* refers to two connected acts:

1. Using someone else's work, *published* or *unpublished*, as if it were your own

2. Incorporating someone else's words or *ideas* into your own writing without explicit acknowledgment of authorship or source

You are most likely aware of the seriousness of plagiarism. Quite simply, it is a crime. People's ideas and ways of expressing them are a form of property—intellectual property—and are as worthy of protection from theft as material property. Thus, when a person plagiarizes, he or she is stealing.

Use the following guidelines to determine what kind of material should be acknowledged and what need not be.

1. Paraphrases of someone else's ideas must be acknowledged (that is, cited). Even though you are putting a passage into your own words, you are none-theless using another's ideas. Consider this original passage and the para-phrase that follows.

   Original passage: "It is too soon to know with certainty if melting polar ice taking place right now will result in coastal flooding within the next five years" (climatologist Gail Jones).

   Plagiarized paraphrase: Will the melting polar ice currently taking place lead to coastal flooding within five years? It is too early to tell.

The author of the paraphrase gives no indication that the information conveyed was taken from the article by Gail Jones. Yes, it's possible that the author simply forgot to cite the source (sometimes referred to as *accidental plagiarism*)—but it is still full-fledged plagiarism. It is every author's responsibility to remember, and properly acknowledge, all sources. The above paraphrase must be revised accordingly. For example:

   Acceptable paraphrase: Could the melting polar ice currently taking place, climatologist Gail Jones wonders, lead to coastal flooding within five years? According to Jones, it is too early to tell.

By the way, you need also to be aware of *faulty paraphrasing*. When you recast someone else's ideas into your own words, you must be careful not to distort that original idea. Consider the following paraphrase of the Gail Jones passage:

   Faulty paraphrase: It is impossible to determine whether melting polar ice will result in coastal flooding in the near future.

This is a faulty paraphrase. Jones asserted that it was too soon to know with certainty, not that it was impossible. The paraphrase also fails to capture the fact that Jones referred to melting polar ice *that is currently taking place.*

2. Any information considered common knowledge does not require ac-knowledgment. Facts such as historical dates that are readily looked up in at least three different sources constitute common knowledge. The key word is *readily.* Some factual information is clearly the product of individual research and, as such, is not readily available.

3. When you need to quote verbatim (using the author's exact words), be mindful of these pointers:

   a. Quote only what is necessary to convey the author's ideas. Too many or too lengthy quotations can make a paper difficult to read.

b. Do not rely on quoted material to carry your argument forward. This is a common pitfall of beginning writers. You want your paper to represent *your* way of thinking, not that of the experts you are quoting.

c. Besides quoting, *comment* on a quotation of one to two sentences or longer. Do not drop a quotation in if your reason for quoting someone else is not patently clear.

d. Use quotation marks around all material quoted verbatim. If the passage you are quoting runs more than four lines, place the passage, without quotation marks, in a separate paragraph, indented ten spaces from the main text.

☯⦿ Exercise 8.6

1. Label each of the following statements as common knowledge (not requiring acknowledgment) or not common knowledge (requiring acknowledgment).

   a. Some books should be savored slowly, others devoured ravenously.

   b. Like the 1995 flooding of the Rhine, the inundation of the upper Mississippi and Missouri Rivers in 1993 provided a dramatic and costly lesson on the effects of treating the natural flow of rivers as a pathological condition (Janet Abramovitz, *Imperiled Waters, Impoverished Future* 16).

   c. The Battle of Hastings took place in 1066 C.E.

   d. Many educators these days tend to regard the Internet as a cure-all for getting students to read.

2. Choose any one of the arguments from Part 2, Reading Clusters, and evaluate in writing its evidence in terms of the five criteria: accuracy, relevance, reliability, clarity, and thoroughness.

3. Study the following passage and the paraphrases that follow. Determine which of the paraphrases (if any) are acceptable and which are unacceptable. If unacceptable, explain why (that is, faulty, plagiarized).

The market forces of globalization are invading the Amazon, hastening the demise of the forest and thwarting its most committed stewards. In the past three decades, hundreds of people have died in land wars; countless others endure fear and uncertainty, their lives threatened by those who profit from the theft of timber and land. —Scott Wallace, "Last of the Amazon," *National Geographic*, Jan. 2007: 43.

   a. **Paraphrase A:** The forces of globalization are destroying the Amazon forests. In the past thirty years, hundreds of people have died in the land wars there; many others experience fear, their lives threatened by timber profiteers.

b. **Paraphrase B:** Worldwide market forces, notes Scott Wallace, are contributing to the rapid destruction of the Amazon forests. According to Wallace, land wars are endangering the lives of hundreds (*National Geographic* 43).

c. **Paraphrase C:** According to Scott Wallace, timber barons have all but destroyed the remaining Amazon forests and are murdering anyone who gets in their way (*National Geographic* 43).

Incorporating Outside Sources into Your Argument

The purpose of bringing outside sources into your argument is to add depth and authority to your own original insights. Make sure, then, when incorporating these sources into your paper, that you do not bury your thread of discussion, that your own voice prevails. You may be tempted to relinquish your voice to those of scholars who are recognized experts in their fields, but keep in mind that experts become so as a result of doing what you are beginning to do seriously as a writer: developing an original thesis so that other scholars will learn from you.

Notice, in the following passage, how the writer's voice becomes obscured by the voice of the authority she quotes:

Academic integrity is taken seriously at Santa Clara University. "The University is committed to a pursuit of truth and knowledge that requires both personal honesty and intellectual integrity as fundamental to teaching, learning, scholarship, and service. Therefore, all members of the University community are expected to be honest in their academic endeavors, whether they are working independently or collaboratively, especially by distinguishing clearly between their own original work and ideas, and those of others, whether published or not" (*Undergraduate Bulletin*, 2003–05: 2). This should be a clear sign to students that academic integrity is part of the learning experience.

In that last sentence, the writer makes an important, original contribution to the conversation about academic integrity, but it is all but lost in the excessively long quotation that precedes it. It's as if the writer is saying to her audience, "Don't listen to me—I'm just a lowly student; listen to what the university administration says!" But that defeats the very reason for writing, which is to contribute new knowledge or new ways of thinking about old knowledge. Seeing her mistake, the student revised the passage as follows:

Academic integrity at Santa Clara University is taken seriously, mainly because such integrity is part of the learning experience. That explains why the new SCU *Undergraduate Bulletin* for 2003–05 goes into elaborate detail about the issue. Administrators emphasize that the "pursuit of truth" to which the University is committed *"requires* [emphasis mine] both personal honesty and intellectual integrity" (2). In other words, you cannot truly become an educated person if you are unable or unwilling to make a clear, explicit distinction between what you know and what others know, between what you can contribute to an area of study and what others have contributed.

With this revision, the student asserts herself as a worthy contributor to the conversation on academic integrity. She has earned her stripes as an authority in her own right.

Also, all writing needs to "flow" for the points to unfold logically and smoothly for the reader. An important element in a smoothly developed argument is a clear link between each general point and the specific reference to outside sources. The writer's text should lead into the quoted material not just with a reference to who made the statement but also with the credentials of the source.

When you are incorporating others' ideas into your argument, you will want to lead into the borrowed material with signals that you are about to use a source to support your claim and that your source is a reliable one for your claim.

Finally, check to make sure that you have fully *synthesized* the material from outside sources with the new information that you have contributed. Synthesis occurs when you show that the outside (pre-existing) information together with the new information that you bring to the discussion results in new understanding: A + B = C. Returning to our endangered Amazon forests example in Exercise 8.6, assume that the new information you want to bring into the discussion is your own sense of the global disaster that could arise if Amazon forests are depleted. That insight, combined with the factual information from Scott Wallace, might lead you to the following synthesis.

> Preserving the South American forests represents our planet's greatest hope for an environmentally sound future. If, through application of aggressive international policies, we can find a way to stop the destruction in the Amazon, we will have opened a new chapter in twenty-first-century forest stewardship that will prevent not one environmental disaster but many.

To quote or paraphrase? Generally, you should quote another's exact words when one of the following three reasons is true:

1. The precise phrasing is so elegant or apt that you wish to reproduce it intact.

2. You are going to focus on the wording itself (or some part of it).

3. You could not rephrase it without significantly changing the meaning or coming close to plagiarizing.

If none of those three reasons applies, you probably should paraphrase the source, remembering still to lead into the paraphrased material as you would a direct quotation and to provide appropriate documentation at the end of the paraphrase. Your readers should be able to tell precisely where another's ideas begin and end and where yours begin anew.

Consider the following passage:

> We may be a lot more creative than we realize. "Although we each have nearly limitless potential to live creatively, most people use only a small percentage of their creative gifts" (John Chaffee, *Critical Thinking, Thoughtful Writing*, 1st ed. 64). Therefore, we should work harder to cultivate these gifts.

Does it seem awkward or clunky to you? Can you tell what causes the awkwardness? Now read the following revision:

> We may be more creative than we realize. As John Chaffee points out in his book, *Critical Thinking, Thoughtful Writing*, "[M]ost people use only a small percentage of their creative gifts" (64). Taking the time to cultivate our creativity thus sounds like a wise investment.

This revised version makes the link between general comment and specific reference smoother and more coherent. Note that the writer trims back some of the original quotation, using only what is essential. The reader is thus able to process the information more efficiently.

Another important principle to keep in mind when you quote from outside sources is not to overquote. Use only that portion of a passage essential to making your point. Remember that you can leave out parts of a passage that seem irrelevant by using an ellipsis (. . .) to let readers know that words, phrases, or sentences are being omitted. Always make certain, however, that in choosing words to delete you do not distort the meaning of the original passage. In cases where you need to convey a lot of information from a source, consider combining direct quotation with paraphrase, or simply rely entirely on paraphrase (making sure your paraphrase remains faithful to the essential point of the source).

◎/◎   **Exercise 8.7**

Examine the following passage to determine how well the writer has incorporated outside sources. Revise the passage where necessary to make it more coherent. In class, compare your revision with those of other students. You will need to consult the book being quoted to make your determination.

> Libraries that receive public money should as a condition of funding be required to publish monthly lists of discards on their websites, "so that the public has some way of determining which of them are acting on behalf of

their collections," recommends Nicholson Baker in his book about the way libraries have been destroying or selling off their hard-copy newspaper collections, *Double Fold: Libraries and the Assault on Paper* (New York: Random, 2001) 270. His other recommendations are that "The Library of Congress should lease or build a large building" in which to store any print materials they don't have room for; that several libraries around the country should work together to save the nation's newspapers in bound form; and that the N.E.H. should ban the current U.S. newspaper program in which newspapers are destroyed after they are microfilmed (270).

Chapter Summary

Argumentative writing often requires research, which is a dynamic, multitask process that involves searching for background information and integrating that information effectively into your paper. The research process can include many activities: searching databases to which your college library subscribes; using online search engines to search for material on the Internet; conducting surveys; interviewing specialists, such as the faculty and staff members in your university community; and using the many kinds of print sources (abstracts, atlases, bibliographies, books, government documents, indexes, and so on) available in your library. While most of your research activities should be planned and well-organized, allow for serendipitous discovery—stumbling on unexpected sources as a result of being immersed in your planned research. By acquiring a thorough knowledge of their topics supported by careful research, writers argue their claims more authoritatively. Good research begins with taking a mental inventory and generating questions (writer-based, audience-based, subject-based, and purpose-based) about the topic that need answering. Purpose-based questions lead to formulating a strong thesis. A strong thesis, in turn, helps keep writers on track as they conduct research on the Internet, in the library, and with experts through well-prepared interviews.

Checklist

1. Do I take a thorough mental inventory of my topic?

2. Do I ask myself good purpose-, audience-, writer-, and subject-based questions about my topic?

3. Is my thesis strong and well-focused?

4. Do I screen my Internet and print sources to make sure they meet the criteria for accuracy, relevance, reliability, clarity, and thoroughness?

5. Do I cite sources where necessary? Use proper documentation format?

6. Do I interview experts on campus or elsewhere about my topic?

7. Do I integrate researched information into my argument smoothly and clearly?

8. Do I check to ensure that I have paraphrased accurately?

9. Do I properly acknowledge the source of paraphrased as well as verbatim-quoted information?

10. Am I certain not to overlook acknowledging a source of outside information?

Writing Projects

1. Keep a detailed log of all your research-based activities for your upcoming writing assignment. Include idea-generating; initial outlining; initial searches through various print and online reference works (list search engines used); and more methodical and focused research, interviews, and surveys. Describe your method of preparing the drafts—rough draft, first draft, and subsequent revisions.

2. Write a critical commentary on the usefulness of the Internet as a research tool. Comment on degrees of usefulness of various websites and different search engines, as well as the timeliness, reliability, and thoroughness of the information found in selected sites.

3. Write a comparative evaluation of print resources (as housed in your college library) versus Internet resources. Are both resources equally valuable? One more valuable than the other? Defend your assertions as fully as possible using specific examples.

4. Prepare a set of ten interview questions based on the topic you are currently researching or are planning to research. Next, search through your college's faculty directory or bulletin to locate faculty or staff members who might serve as good interview subjects for your research.

Documenting Your Sources: MLA and APA Styles

> I quote others only the better to express myself.
> —Montaigne

Citation of Source Material: A Rationale

You must acknowledge information and ideas taken from sources not your own (commonly referred to as *outside sources*). There are two main reasons for doing so:

1. **Original ideas are a form of property known as *intellectual property.*** Published material is protected from theft by copyright law. Plagiarism, which means to pass off someone else's ideas or writings as your own, is, quite simply, against the law. Thus, by acknowledging your sources explicitly, you protect yourself from being accused of and prosecuted for copyright violation (see "Understanding and Avoiding Plagiarism" in Chapter 7, pages 293–296).

2. **Acknowledging your sources provides an important service to other scholars.** People who read your essays are often interested in consulting the sources you consult to obtain more detailed information.

Which Documentation Style to Use?

The MLA style is commonly used to document sources in writing done within the humanities disciplines (for example, English and the foreign languages). The APA style is commonly used to document sources in writing done within the social sciences (for example, psychology and sociology). Clarify with your instructor whether you should follow the MLA style (see page 302), APA style (see page 321), or some other system. (For example, *Chicago* style, based on *The Chicago Manual of Style*, 15th edition, is commonly used to document sources in writing done within history and sometimes other humanities disciplines.)

No one expects you to memorize all the details of any particular system of documentation, but you are expected to know how to look up and apply these details each time you write a paper that includes references to other sources. You are expected to know how to follow the instructions and examples given in documentation manuals and to make your citations complete and consistent with the recommendations of an established documentation style. Therefore, get into the habit of checking the proper format either in this chapter or in the other MLA or APA reference manuals listed in this chapter.

A Guide to MLA Documentation Style

The following guide presents the system for documenting sources established by the Modern Language Association (MLA). For more detailed information on how to document a wide variety of both print and electronic sources with the MLA style, see *MLA Handbook for Writers of Research Papers*, 7th ed., New York: MLA, 2009; *MLA Style Manual and Guide to Scholarly Publishing*, 3rd ed., New York: MLA, 2008; and the MLA website at http://www.mla.org.

Remember the following about the MLA documentation system:

1. In the body of your paper, you must (a) inform readers of the last name of the author or authors for each source as you use it in your paper, and (b) give the page number where each source appears originally in a larger work. These elements of the MLA system together form what is called the *author/page in-text citation*. Note that no page numbers are needed if your source is an online one or if it is less than a page long.

2. At the end of your paper, beginning on a new numbered page, you must list in alphabetical order by authors' last names, doubled-spaced, all the sources you refer to within your paper. This list is called *Works Cited*.

Before we look at the details of how to cite various types of sources in your text and the way to list them in your Works Cited, let us look at how to present quoted material and how to paraphrase.

Presenting Quoted Material

When quoting or paraphrasing in MLA style, mention the author's surname and indicate the page number of the passage parenthetically. List the page number (or numbers) without the "page" or "pages" abbreviation. If you are citing more than one page number, indicate them in the following way: 15–16; 140–42; 201–04; 390–401.

Using Quotation Marks and Block-Style Quotation Format

Use double quotation marks around the words quoted if the passage is no more than four lines.

> According to Charles Lamb, Shakespeare's plays "are grounded deep in nature, so deep that the depth of them lies out of the reach of most of us" (7).

Lamb's name (last name first) and the title of the essay, "On the Tragedies of Shakespeare," appear in the Works Cited, along with more information about the publisher and date of the essay.

Because you are already using double quotation marks to indicate another author's work, substitute single quotation marks for any double quotations that appear in the original author's material.

```
The distinguished teacher of creative writing, Brenda Ueland,
insists that taking long walks is a good way to generate
thoughts: "If I do not walk one day, I seem to have on the
next what Van Gogh calls 'the meagerness'" (42).
```

The end punctuation should be placed as follows: close inner quotation, close outer quotation, insert page number of quotation in parentheses, period.

If the passage is four lines or longer, use block-style quotation. Set the passage off as a separate paragraph and indent each line ten spaces from the margin. If you are quoting two or more paragraphs in the block quotation, indent the first line of each an additional three spaces (that is, thirteen spaces from the left margin). Quotation marks are not used with block-style quotations: Consider indentation to take the place of quotation marks.

```
Commenting on Shakespeare's villains, Charles Lamb notes that
while we are reading any of his great criminal characters—
Macbeth, Richard, even Iago—we think not so much of the crimes
which they commit, as of the ambition, the aspiring spirit,
the intellectual activity, which prompts them to over-leap
those moral fences. (12)
```

The period at the end of a block quotation precedes the parenthetical information.

Quoting Verbatim

Do not change punctuation or spelling (for example, changing the British spelling of "colour" to color"). In rare cases in which the author or printer makes a spelling or grammatical error, follow the error with the Latin word *sic* (meaning "thus") in brackets to indicate that the word appears this way in the original source. Whereas the Latin word *sic* is italicized, the brackets surrounding it are not.

Using an Ellipsis

Indicate omission of any *unnecessary* portion of the passage with an ellipsis—three dots separated from each other by a single space.

Original passage: "The timing, as I mentioned earlier, had to be precise."

Quoted passage, using ellipsis: "The timing . . . had to be precise."

Be certain that the words you omit from a passage do not alter its essential meaning.

Paraphrasing

A paraphrase is a rewording of an author's idea that presents it more concisely or clearly. By paraphrasing instead of quoting directly, you can more clearly and efficiently integrate the author's thoughts with your own. Of course, you must thoroughly understand the material you wish to paraphrase to avoid distorting it. You must also cite the author's name and a page number as if the paraphrase were a direct quotation. A paraphrase of the Charles Lamb passage quoted previously might be worded like this:

```
Lamb claims that we regard Macbeth, Richard III, and Iago less
as criminals than as high-reaching spirits marked by great in-
telligence (12).
```

Make sure your readers will be able to tell which ideas are yours and which are the paraphrased ideas of another author. Do not, for example, merely list a name and page number at the end of a long paragraph. Readers will not be able to tell whether the paraphrase is the last sentence only or the entire paragraph being paraphrased, as in the following example:

```
Revenge takes many forms. Most often it is a hot-tempered re-
action to a perceived injustice. But sometimes it is cool and
calculated, like Iago's revenge against Othello. Either kind,
though, can be thought of as a kind of wild justice which, the
more we are tempted by it, the more urgently we must weed it
out (Bacon 72).
```

The writer of the above passage does not make it clear whether the entire paragraph is a paraphrase of Francis Bacon's essay, just the last sentence, or even one portion of the last sentence. A simple revision clarifies the matter:

```
Revenge takes many forms. Sometimes it is cool and calculated,
like Iago's revenge against Othello. Other times it is what
Francis Bacon, Shakespeare's contemporary, once defined as
wild justice. As Bacon put it, the more we are tempted to run
to it, the more urgently we should weed it out (72).
```

Index for Citing Sources: MLA Style

Author/Page In-Text Citations

See the following pages for instruction and examples.

List of Works Cited

See the following pages for instruction and examples.

Using Author/Page In-Text Citations

As you write the body of your paper, you will weave in references to the work of others to support or amplify the points you are making. Make sure that your readers can easily distinguish between your words and ideas, and the words and ideas of others. To create this clear distinction, refer by name to whomever you are quoting or paraphrasing. You can either include the author's name in a lead-in remark:

author's full name mentioned in lead-in remark

As Eliot Asinof describes the reaction to the 1919 baseball scandal, "The American people were at first shocked, then sickened" (197).

or you can include the author's last name in parentheses with the page number after the quotation or paraphrasing:

In reacting to the 1919 baseball scandal, "[t]he American people were at first shocked, then sickened" (Asinof 197).

author's last name mentioned in parentheses   no comma   page number

The preferable style is to use the author's name in your lead-in.

Note the following variations on this pattern, depending on the type of source you are citing and whether you are including the author's name in a lead-in remark.

1. Author Named in Lead-In Remarks. As long as you mention the author's last name in your lead-in remarks, the only information needed in parentheses is the page number, because the full citation will appear in the Works Cited at the end of your paper.

author

According to John Jones a colony on Mars would rapidly pay for itself (15).

page number   period

author

In her biography of Alice James, Jean Strouse writes that the James children "learned to see and not see, say and not say, reveal and conceal, all at the same time" (xii).

quotation   page number   period

When citing a piece from an anthology or edited volume, cite the name of the author of the piece to which you are referring, not the editor or editors of the anthology.

2. Author Not Named in Lead-In Remarks.   If you do not name the author as you lead into a quotation or paraphrase, place the author's name in parentheses along with the page number of the source.

> No one person in 1919 knew all of the factors that contributed
> to the Black Sox Scandal or could tell the whole story
> (Asinof 11).

author's last name no comma page number

3. Two or More Authors.   If you are citing a work that has two or three authors, mention all their names in your lead-in remarks or in parentheses after the reference.

> Critical reading involves going beyond simple decoding of the
> literal meanings of the written word (Cooley and Powell 3).

authors' last names   no comma   page number

If you are citing a work with four or more authors, state the first author's last name and then write "et al." (a Latin phrase meaning "and others"; "al." always has a period since it is an abbreviation for *alia*).

4. Multiple Works by the Same Author.   If you are referring to more than one work by the same author, refer to the work's title in your lead-in remarks.

> In *Teaching a Stone to Talk*, Dillard describes the drama of
> the moon blocking the sun during a total eclipse by saying,
> "It did not look like the moon. It was enormous and black. . . .
> It looked like a lens cover, or the lid of a pot. It
> materialized out of thin air—black, and flat, and sliding,
> outlined in flame" (94).

page number

Alternately, you can include a short form of the title in parentheses, along with the page number.

> One observer described the mystery of the eclipse by saying,
> "If I had not read that it was the moon, I could have seen
> the sight a hundred times and never thought of the moon once"
> (Dillard, *Teaching* 94).

author   comma   abbreviated title   page number

5. Works with Anonymous or Corporate Authorship.   Cite works that name no author or editor as follows:

> According to the Consumer Protection Agency, the number of
> car owners who report being cheated by dishonest mechanics has
> dropped by 15 percent in 2000 (7).

6. Internet Sources.   For most electronic sources, it is not possible to provide a page number in the in-text citation. Instead, check to see if an author's name is given and if there are numbered paragraphs or other text divisions. If so, use these pieces of information in place of page numbers in your in-text citation.

```
Some universities have been questioning their use of
Aztec signs and symbols and the use of mascots like "Monty
Montezuma" (Weber, par. 6).
```
                          author comma numbered paragraph

Preparing the MLA List of Works Cited

Definition.   The list of Works Cited is an alphabetical listing of all the sources cited, paraphrased, or referred to in a paper. The list of Works Cited does not include additional readings, no matter how relevant; however, your instructor may ask you to prepare a separate list of additional readings and to head it Works Consulted.

Purpose.   The main purpose of the list of Works Cited is to assist readers who wish to obtain more information about the topic by consulting the same sources you have. A secondary purpose is to give readers an opportunity to double-check the accuracy and appropriateness of your quotations and paraphrases. It is possible to quote someone accurately but in a way that misrepresents that author's original intentions—of course, not something you intend to do but may accidentally do.

General Procedure

1. Begin the list of Works Cited on a separate page.

2. Title the page *Works Cited* and center the heading.

3. List everything alphabetically by author's surname. List the author's surname first. If a work has more than one author, alphabetize the entry according to the surname of the author listed first. If no author is listed, enter the title alphabetically. Titles of books and pamphlets are underlined. Include the city of publication, the abbreviated name of the publisher, and the date of publication.

4. Begin each entry at the left margin. If an entry runs longer than one line, those subsequent lines are indented five spaces.

In the following examples and in the sample student paper beginning on page 313, note the MLA style for citing various types of sources in the list of Works Cited.

Citing Print Sources

1. Single-author Book or Pamphlet

```
Jones, John. Colonizing Mars. New York: Far Out, 2002. Print.
```

2. Book with More than One Author

```
Witt, Linda, Karen M. Paget, and Glenna Matthews. Running as a
     Woman: Gender and Power in American Politics. New York:
     Free, 1994. Print.
```

When more than three authors, use the name of the first author and follow it with "et al."

```
Johnson, Eric, et al. Smart Shopping. Boston: Lifestyle, 1999.
     Print.
```

3. Chapter from a Book

```
Blair, John. "The Anglo-Saxon Period." The Oxford History of
     Britain. Ed. Kenneth O. Morgan. New York: Oxford UP,
     1988. 60-119. Print.
```

4. Government Document

Author Byline Given:

```
Elkouri, Frank, and Edna Asper. Resolving Drug Issues.
     Washington: Bureau of National Affairs, 1993. Print.
```

No Author Byline Given:

```
United States. Department of Health and Human Services. Summary
     Report of the Graduate Medical Educational National
     Advisory Committee. Washington: GPO, 1980. Print.
```

5. Article from a Periodical

Magazine:

```
Singer, Mark. "God and Football." New Yorker 25 Sept. 2000:
     38-42. Print.
```

Academic Journal:

```
Gibson, Ann. "Universality and Difference in Women's Abstract
     Painting." Yale Journal of Criticism 8 (Spring 1995):
     103-32. Print.
```

Newspaper:

```
Revkin, Andrew C. "A West African Monkey Is Extinct,
     Scientists Say." New York Times 12 Sept. 2000: A20.
     Print.
```

Letter to the Editor:

> Kenny, Shirley Strum. Letter. *New York Times* 19 Mar. 2001:
>   A22. Print.

Unsigned Editorial:

> "Flawed Election in Uganda." Editorial. *New York Times* 16 Mar.
>   2001: A20. Print.

6. Book Review

Titled Review of a Work:

> Dowd, Maureen. "The Man in White." Rev. of *Hooking Up*, by Tom
>   Wolfe. *New York Times Book Review* 5 Nov. 2000: 6. Print.

Untitled Review of a Work:

> Warren, Charles. Rev. of *The Material Ghost: Films and Their
>   Medium*, by Gilberto Perez. *Georgia Review* 54 Spring 2000:
>   170-74. Print.

Citing Nonprint Sources

7. Interview

Personal Interview:

> Sanders, Julia. Personal interview. 15 Oct. 2006.

Telephone Interview:

> Ellis, Mark. Telephone interview. 17 Oct. 2006.

8. Correspondence

Paper Letter:

> Beaumont, Clyde. Letter to the author. 10 Jan. 2007.

Email Letter

> Beaumont, Clyde. E-mail to the author. 10 Jan. 2007.

If a paper letter is not dated, use the date of the postmark. Email messages are dated automatically.

9. Web page When your source is a web page—an electronic document from an Internet site—include in your citation (1) the author's name; (2) the title of the document in quotation marks; (3) information about a print version of the same document (if any is given on the website); and (4) information about the document's electronic publication. MLA no longer recommends providing Web addresses (URLs). If an Internet source is used, indicate simply with the word "Web." Rationale: it is simpler to locate the article via a search engine such as Google; URLs are cumbersome to use and it is easy to make mistakes when entering it; URLs will sometimes change. If you cannot locate within your electronic source all of these four categories of information, include as much in your citation as possible, always with the goal of allowing your reader to find your source.

Document from an Internet Newspaper or Journal Site:

author   title

Stein, Charles. "After the Last Whistle: Some Workers, Towns

Have Rebounded Amid the Loss of Factory Jobs. Others Won't

information about print publication   information about electronic publication

Make It." *Boston Globe*. Boston Globe, 23 Oct. 2003. Web. 23 Oct. 2003.

date of access

Fredman, Allen. "To the Point: The Adapted Landscape of a Former Baltimore Factory Stays True to its Sudsy Past." *Landscape Architecture*. American Society of Landscape Architects, Nov. 2003. Web. 29 Oct. 2003.

Document from an Article in a Reference Database:

Heitz, Thomas R. "Babe Ruth." *Encarta*. MSN Learning and Research, 2003. Web. 13 Oct. 2003.

Article from an Online Posting:

Online posting. "NASA Chief Predicts Scientific Tsunami." 11 Oct. 2000. Web. 21 Oct. 2000.

Rather than citing a posting, the writer should try to locate any article cited therein at its proper Web address, so readers will be able to find it. Thus, for instance, though the article "NASA Chief Predicts Scientific Tsunami" was originally discovered on the Metanews listserv, it should be cited as follows:

David, Leonard. Online posting. "NASA Chief Predicts Scientific Tsunami." *SPACE.com*. Space.com, 11 Oct. 2000. Web. 21 Oct. 2000.

Article from a Magazine:

Norton, Amy. "Video Games May Do the Aging Brain Good." *Psychology and Aging*. Reuters, 19 Dec. 2008. Web. 24 Aug. 2009.

10. Television or Radio Program

"Senators Battle Over Judicial Nominee." Narr. Jim Lehrer. *Newshour*. PBS. WGBH, Boston, 23 Oct. 2003. Radio.

11. Recording

Audiocassette:

Churchill, Winston S. *The Great Republic*. Random House Audiobooks, 1998. Audiocassette.

Compact Disc (CD):

Von Bingen, Hildegard. Canticles of Ecstasy. Perf. Sequentia. Deutsche Harmonia Mundi, 1994.

Videocassette (VCR):

Witness. Dir. Peter Weir. Perf. Harrison Ford and Kelly McGillis. Paramount, 1985. Videocassette.

Digital Video Disc (DVD):

Rodgers & Hammerstein's "South Pacific" in Concert from Carnegie Hall. Dir. Walter Bobbie. Perf. Reba McEntire, Brian Stokes Mitchell, Alec Baldwin. PBS, 2005. DVD.

12. Film

The Queen. Dir. Stephen Frears. Perf. Helen Mirren, James Cromwell, Alex Jennings. Miramax, 2006. Film.

13. Lecture

Chaudhuri, Haridas. "The Philosophy of History." Cultural Integration Fellowship, San Francisco. 7 Jan. 2007. Lecture.

14. Work of Art (Painting, Sculpture, or Photograph)

Munch, Edvard. *The Scream*. 1893. Oil, tempera, and pastel on cardboard. National Gallery, Oslo.

Note: If you are referring to a reproduction of the work in a book, cite the book instead of the location of the work, as follows:

Munch, Edvard. *The Scream*. 1893. *Edvard Munch*. Dr. Ulrich Bischoff. Germany: Benedikt Taschen Verlag, 1988.

15. Figure (Published Chart, Graph, Table)

Note: Citation must appear directly underneath the figure (following the caption, and prefaced by the word "Source") as well as in the Works Cited page.

```
United Nations, World Population Prospects, the 1998 Revision.
     Population Reference Bureau.
```

16. Map

```
"Central Asia." Map. Hammond Odyssey Atlas of the World.
     Hammond World Atlas Corporation, 1994. 31. Print.
```

17. Advertisement

```
Cannon HD Camcorder. Advertisement. National Geographic
     Jan. 2007: 12-13. Print.
```

18. Email Message

```
Frost, Gary. Message to the author. September 10, 2009. E-mail.
```

Sample Student Paper: MLA Documentation Format

1 inch margins — 1/2 inch from top of page — ½"

Gibson 1 — Running head: student name + number on every page

Daniela Gibson

Argumentation

Professor Billings

May 16, 2009

Why We Should Punish

The caning of a young American in Singapore in 1994 for minor vandalism has added new fuel to a centuries-old debate about proper forms of punishment. Logic demands, however, that prior to the decision of the proper form of punishment, we must decide on the proper aim or purpose of punishment. The views on the proper aim of punishment seem to vary widely. Writers such as Barbara Wootton and H. L. A. Hart believe that the proper aim of punishment is the rehabilitation of the criminal. Others, in contrast, argue for retribution as the proper aim of punishment. Criminal Justice professor Graeme Newman, for example, writes, "Punishment must, above all else, be painful" (40).

Notes (margin): Name, course, instructor, date — Famous case serves as attention-grabbing opening — Double-space paper throughout — Title, centered, not underlined — No extra space between title and first line of text — Paraphrased sources; quotation marks not used — Page number reference all that is needed since author mentioned in the discussion

Gibson 2

Summary
of source

A third view of the proper purpose of punishment is
deterrence, "removing the criminal from activity and

Scope of the
question of
punishment
described

serving as a caution to would-be-criminals" (Rottenberg
41). One recently profiled advocate of punishment as
deterrence is Joe Arpaio, sheriff of Maricopa County,
Arizona (Phoenix area). According to Arpaio, "Jail
should be about punishment and the punishment should be
so unpleasant that no one who experienced it would ever
want to go through it again" (Graham 61).

The overall function of punishment is to enforce
and protect the moral values of a society, a function Statement
of thesis
that appears to be incompatible with the idea of
retribution and only partly compatible with the ideas
of deterrence and rehabilitation. Punishment
linked to society
score values

The punishment and the moral values of a society
are inseparably linked by the laws of that society.
Our laws always reflect and are based on our core
values. Most societies recognize the right to life
as a core value. In the case of our American society,
core values are also the ownership of property and the
freedom of speech. Consequently, America has laws that
protect private property and the freedom of speech.
Theft is against the law and so is violation of the
freedom of speech. Furthermore, since these laws are
based on values, and values always imply a right
and wrong, a trespassing of these laws must have
consequences that reflect and uphold these moral
judgments. Walter Berns addresses this interdependence

Block-style
quotation
indented ten
spaces from
margin; dou-
ble-spaced;
no quotation
marks used,
except for
those that
appear in
the original
source

between morality and punishment when he writes the
following about the death penalty:

> [It] serves to remind us of the majesty of the
> moral order that is embodied in our law and of
> the terrible consequences of its breach. . . .
> The criminal law must be made awful, by which
> I mean awe-inspiring, or commanding "profound
> respect or reverential fear." It must remind us

of the moral order by which alone we can live as human beings. (12)

Although I do not necessarily agree with the need for the death penalty and "reverential fear," Berns's observation is significant: Punishment, indeed, must always "remind us of the moral order" by which we live, for if the breaking of the law would have no consequences, our moral values would be void (85). If, for example, the violation of the freedom of speech had no consequences, such a violation could take place again and again. But then, it could hardly be called a value since we would not seem to care about it and would not protect it.

Those in favor of retribution as the aim of punishment agree that a criminal act must have legal consequences for the criminal. Despite this very broad similarity between retribution and the protection of moral values, retribution appears impractical and morally wrong in the context of the American value system. Advocates of retribution often refer to Kant, who writes that the principle for legal justice is "[n]one other than the principle of equality . . . any undeserved evil that you inflict on someone else among the people is one that you do to yourself. . . . Only the law of retribution can determine exactly the kind and degree of punishment" (qtd. in Berns 18). Such a view, however, is impracticable, for who would rape a rapist (and how) for retribution of the crime? In addition to these questions, it seems hardly possible that the loss of one individual can truly be retributed by the execution of the murderer.

Yet retribution is precisely the major motive behind capital punishment. The danger with this extreme form of punishment is irreversible miscarriage of justice, as when an innocent man or woman is sentenced to death (Berlow) or when racist lawyers eliminate Blacks, Hispanics, and other racial minorities

Why one scholar's view of punishment makes sense

Author presents challenging view

Reference to a source quoted by another author

Author refutes challenging view

Gibson 4

as potential jurors during jury selection—which was
shown to be the case with Nevada death-row inmate
Thomas Nevius (Amnesty International).

References
to Internet
sources

    But more importantly, retribution as the goal of
punishment is immoral, at least in the context of our
value system. Mark Costanzo, chair of the Department
of Social Psychology at Claremont McKenna College, correctly identifies that "[o]ur efforts to mitigate pun-
ishments arise out of the recognition that we must
not sink to the level of the criminal; raping a rapist would debase us, weaken our moral solidarity, and
undermine the moral authority of the state" (23). If
we punish via retribution, the danger is that we would
focus too narrowly on one crime and in doing so would
lose sight of the moral code that makes the crime a
crime. In other words, the crime would move to the
foreground and would overshadow the moral authority
that it violates. For example, if someone hits my car,
I could exercise the punishment of retribution by
hitting that person's car in return. However, doing so
fails not only to fix my car but also to ensure me that
there is a moral code and its representative law that
will protect me from similar instances in the future.
Hence, retribution undermines the very same moral law
that punishment is supposed to uphold.

    In contrast to retribution, which must be
rejected as the proper aim of punishment on moral
and practical grounds, deterrence appears to be
partly compatible with the upholding of moral values.

Deterrence vs.
retribution
as a basis for
punishment

Ernest van den Haag, a retired professor of Jurispru-
dence, expresses the views of deterrence advocates when
he writes that "[h]arsher penalties are more deterrent
than milder ones" (114). In his explanation, he draws
an analogy to everyday life situations:

        All other things equal, we penalize our
        children, our friends, or our business partners
        the more harshly the more we feel we must deter

them and others in the future from a wrong
they have done. Social life would not be
possible if we did not believe that we
can attract people to actions we desire
by giving them incentives, and deter
them from actions we do not desire by
disincentives. (115)

Van den Haag's analogy works—up to a certain point.
Clearly, if we care about our values, we need to protect them, and one way of doing so is to punish offend-
ers as a means of deterrence. And in some
situations, deterrence might be the only way of
communicating what is right and wrong. I remember, for
example, when I was three years old, I took doll clothing home from preschool. I did so because I
liked to play with it more at home, and I did not understand that it was not mine. When my parents found
out, they did the right thing: They told me if I ever
did that again, I could no longer play with my dolls.
In that situation deterrence was necessary since I
was too young to understand the concept of private
property and its proper relationship to right and
wrong; I understood, however, that I wanted to play
with my dolls and that I could no longer do so if I
would take doll clothing home again.

There is a danger, however, in viewing deterrence
as the only proper aim of punishment: it could
disconnect that what is feared from what is
morally bad, what is desired from what is morally
good. The *Oxford English Dictionary* defines
deterrence as "deterring or preventing by fear."
If I, when I was old enough to grasp the meaning
of right and wrong beyond immediate desires,
would have not been taught why it is wrong to take
what is not mine, but instead would have been
continuously motivated by fear, I could have never
developed a deep respect for moral values. Rather, I

Author addresses punishment as rehabilitation

Author qualifies her preceding claim

Gibson 6

would have learned to associate fear with my parents'
knowledge of my "wrongdoing," but not with the
wrongdoing itself. Thus, I would have most likely
sought to avoid my parents' knowledge or that of any
other authority but not to avoid the deed itself. I
believe that this example is generally applicable to
deterrence as the main purpose of punishment: Criminals

Why rehabili-
tation cannot
be the sole
basis for
punishment

and potential criminals would be caught not that their
acts were wrong on moral grounds, but that they should
seek to avoid conflicts with authority. But such an attitude would instill in them a distrust for the laws
rather than an understanding and respect for the values
that they represent.

Another view of punishment is rehabilitation.
Rehabilitation in the sense of education seems compatible with and even part of our value system. However, we
need to ensure that rehabilitation qua education is not
conflicting with other essential values. Costanzo points
to the importance that background and circumstances can
play in a crime (27). For example, it would seem naïve
to expect from a young man proper law-abiding behavior
if that man had suffered from "routine beatings from an
abusive father" and "grew up in a poverty-ridden, gang-
infested neighborhood and received very little in the
way of parental guidance or supervision" (31). If that
man had committed a crime, rehabilitation that includes
a positive alternative to the values or lack thereof of
his childhood upbringing seems appropriate. It might not
only protect our societal values by preventing further
criminal acts by this young man, if the rehabilitation
was successful, but it would also reinforce our values,
for the effort of rehabilitation shows that we are taking
these values seriously and are deeply caring about them.

Yet, as commendable as such rehabilitation efforts
are, we cannot allow them to replace other important

values such as responsibility and justice. By rationalizing a criminal behavior with the criminal's disadvantageous upbringing, we are in danger of denying individual responsibility, a core value of our society. Further, by granting college loans and "grants," books, "compassion and understanding," to criminals, as one former prisoner demands, we would also commit injustice (Stratton 67). For how could we explain this special treatment to all those who have abided by the law, some even despite their background, but do not enjoy grants, loans, etc.? Because these aims are potentially in conflict with each other and because our highest responsibility is to defend the values of our society, rehabilitation can be an integral part of punishment, but it should never replace punishment.

Concluding
reflections

The discourse about the proper aim of punishment is indeed complex. But exactly because of this complexity, we need to approach the question of punishment step by step. It would be fatal to jump to the question of the proper forms of punishment before the question of the proper aim of punishment has been settled. It is absolutely mandatory that the question of the proper aim of punishment is addressed a priori. With respect to its answer, if the upholding of the moral values of a society is any indicator, we should dismiss retribution, and very cautiously consider deterrence and rehabilitation—but by no means should we draw any hasty conclusions.

No extra
space
between
title and
first line
of text

Second
and
subse-
quent lines
indented

Sources
listed in
alphabeti-
cal order

Gibson 8

Works Cited

Amnesty International. "Serious Allegations of Racism and
    Injustice in Nevada Death Penalty Case." 6 Apr. 2001. Web.
    30 Apr. 2001.

Berlow, Alan. "The Wrong Man." Atlantic Monthly. Nov. 1999. Web.
    6 Apr. 2001

Berns, Walter. For Capital Punishment. New York: Basic, 1991.
    Print.

Costanzo, Mark. Just Revenge. New York: St. Martin's, 1997.
    Print.

"Deterrence." Oxford English Dictionary. 2nd ed. CD. Vers. 1.13
    Oxford: Oxford UP, 1994.

Graham, Barry. "Star of Justice: On the Job with America's
    Toughest Sheriff." Harper's Magazine Apr. 2001: 59–68.
    Print.

Hart, H. L. A. Law, Liberty, and Morality. Stanford: Stanford
    UP, 1963. Print.

Newman, Graeme R. Just and Painful: A Case for Corporeal
    Punishment of Criminals. London: Macmillan, 1983. Print

Rottenberg, Annette T., ed. Elements of Argument. 6th ed. New
    York: Bedford, 2000. 569. Print.

Stratton, Richard. "Even Prisoners Must Hope." Newsweek, 17 Oct.
    1994: 67. Print.

van den Haag, Ernest. The Death Penalty Pro and Con: A Debate.
    New York: Plenum, 1983. Print.

Wootton, Barbara. Crime and Penal Policy. London: Allen, 1978.
    Print.

A Guide to APA Documentation Style

The following guide presents the system for documenting sources established by the American Psychological Association (APA). For more detailed information on how to document a wide variety of sources, both print and electronic, see the *Publication Manual of the American Psychological Association*, 5th ed. (Washington, D.C.: APA, 2001) and the APA *Publication Manual* at http://www.apastyle.org. Remember the following about the APA documentation system:

1. In the body of your paper, you must (a) inform readers of the last name of the author or authors for each source as you use it in your paper, and (b) give the year of publication. These elements of the APA system together form what is called the *author/year in-text citation.*

2. At the end of your paper, beginning on a new numbered page, you must list in alphabetical order by authors' last names, double-spaced, all the sources you refer to within your paper. This list is called *References.* Before we look at the details of how to cite the various types of sources in your text and how to list them in your References, let us look at how to present quoted material and how to paraphrase.

Presenting Quoted Material

When quoting or paraphrasing in APA style, indicate the surnames of each author, together with the year the source was published.

```
According to Freud (1900) . . .
```

At the end of the quoted or paraphrased passage, indicate the page number. (*Note:* The abbreviations for page(s)—page and pages—are no longer used.)

Using Quotation Marks and Block-Style Quotation Format

Use double quotation marks around the words quoted if the passage has fewer than forty words.

```
Freud (1900) notes that "in the psychic life there exist
repressed wishes" (288).
```

This passage is from *The Interpretation of Dreams,* but it is not necessary to put that information at the end of the quotation because it will appear in the References, along with other relevant publication information. Because you are already using double quotation marks to indicate another author's work, substitute single quotation marks for double quotations that appear in the original author's material.

```
Henry Petroski (1992) reports that in 1900 "an American patent
was issued to Cornelius Brosnan...for a 'paper clip' which
has been regarded in the industry as the 'first successful
bent wire paper clip'" (62-63).
```

If the passage is forty or more words long, use block-style quotation. Set the passage off as a separate paragraph and indent each line five spaces from the margin. If you are quoting two or more paragraphs in the block quotation, indent the first line of each new paragraph an additional five spaces (that is, ten spaces from the left margin). Quotation marks are not used with block-style quotations.

```
What we recollect of the dream, and what we subject to our
methods of interpretation, is, in the first place, mutilated by
the unfaithfulness of our memory, which seems quite peculiarly
incapable of retaining dreams, and which may have omitted pre-
cisely the most significant parts of their content. (470)
```

This passage is also from *The Interpretation of Dreams.*

Quoting from Internet Sources

If the pages of document from which you are quoting are not numbered, refer parenthetically to the number of the paragraph(s) immediately after the quotation; use the abbreviation "para."

> According to Norton (2008), adults in their 60s and 70s "who learn to play a strategy-heavy video game" improved their scores on a number of tests of cognitive function" (para. 2).

For Internet documents that are paginated, indicate the page number (s) of the quoted passage, as with print documents. *Note:* The abbreviations for page(s)—page and pages—are no longer used.

> von Hippel, F. N. (2008, May). Rethinking nuclear fuel recycling. *Scientific American*, 88–93.

Quoting Verbatim

Always double-check to ensure that you have quoted the passage accurately. Do not change punctuation or spelling (for example, changing the British spelling of "colour" to "color"). In rare cases in which the author or printer makes a spelling error, follow the word with the Latin word *sic* (meaning "thus") in brackets to indicate that the word appears this way in the original source.

Using an Ellipsis

Indicate omission of any *unnecessary* portion of the passage with an ellipsis— three dots separated from each other by a single space.

Original passage: According to Clifford Geertz (1973), "We are, in sum, incomplete or unfinished animals who complete or finish ourselves through culture" (49).

Quoted passage, using ellipsis: According to Clifford Geertz (1973), "We are … incomplete or unfinished animals who complete or finish ourselves through culture" (49).

Always check to make sure that the ellipsis does not distort the original intention of the author.

Paraphrasing

A paraphrase is a rewording of an author's idea that presents it more concisely or clearly. You must cite the author's name and the year of publication as if the paraphrase were a direct quotation. Although APA style does not require that a page number be given with a paraphrase, it suggests that you do so. A paraphrase of the Clifford Geertz passage quoted previously might be worded like this:

```
According to Geertz (1973), humans are incomplete animals who
reach completeness through culture (49).
```

Make sure your readers will be able to tell which ideas are your own and which are the paraphrased ideas of another author. Do not, for example, merely list a name and page number at the end of a long paragraph. Readers will not be able to tell whether the paraphrase is the last sentence only or the entire paragraph.

Index for Citing Sources: APA Style

Author/Page In-Text Citations

See the following pages for instructions and examples.

List of References

See the following pages for instructions and examples.

Using Author/Year In-Text Citations

Introduce outside information smoothly and explicitly so that readers will be able to distinguish between your ideas and the outside source authors' ideas. You provide this clear distinction by referring by name to whomever you are quoting or paraphrasing, as in the following examples.

1. Author Named in Lead-In Remarks

author's full name mentioned in lead-in remark

```
According to Carolyn Heilbrun (1979), womanhood must be
reinvented (29).
```

So long as you mention the author's last name, the only other necessary information is the page number because the full citation will appear in the References.

2. Author Not Named in Lead-In Remarks

One feminist scholar asserts that womanhood must be invented (Heilbrun, 1979, 29).

author's last name   date   page number
              comma

3. Two or More Authors

authors listed alphabetically separated by commas date in parentheses

Colombo, Cullen, and Lisle (2001) emphasize that critical thinking involves cultivating the ability to imagine and the curiosity to question one's own point of view (2).

4. Multiple Works by the Same Author

date followed by letter to indicate the different works

Jones (1998b, 130) considers colonization of space a vital step in human evolution. He even argues that our survivability as a species depends on it (1998a, 47-51).

date followed by letter to indicate the different works

The letters *a* and *b* following the date are assigned according to the alphabetized order of the publications' titles. Thus, in the list of references, Jones's 1998a publication appears alphabetically before her 1998b publication, even if the 1998b reference is cited first in the text. Works by the same author published in different years are indicated with one instance of the surname, followed by dates: (Jones, 1999, 2001). When citing two or more different authors sharing the same surname, be sure to include each author's initials: (A. Jones, 1957; C. Jones, 2001).

5. Works with Anonymous or Corporate Authorship

corporate authorship

According to the Consumer Protection Agency (2001), the number of car owners reported being cheated by dishonest mechanics dropped 15 percent in 2000 (7).

6. Internet Sources

Page from a Website:

According to the Coalition for Affordable and Reliable Energy (2001), coal fuels more than half the country's electricity.

Article from an Online Periodical:

author of online article
┌──┴──┐
```
Farmer (2001) envisions a memory chip that, when implanted,
will give humans the ability to process information one
hundred times faster and more efficiently.
```

Posting from an Online Forum:

```
Dr. Charles Taylor (2001), a biologist, claims in an online
forum that human cloning will pose no dangers to cloned per-
son's senses of selfhood because "the mind and personality can
never be cloned."
```

Note that you do not need to include more than the author's name and the date when citing online sources. Information such as Web addresses will appear in the References.

Preparing the APA List of References

Definition.   The list of References is an alphabetical listing of all the sources cited or paraphrased or referred to in a paper. The list of References does not include additional or recommended readings, no matter how relevant; however, your instructor may ask you to prepare a separate list of supplemental readings.

Purpose.   The main purpose of the list of References is to assist readers who wish to obtain more information about the topic by consulting the same sources you have. A secondary purpose is to give readers an opportunity to double-check the accuracy and appropriateness of your quotations and paraphrases. It is possible to quote someone accurately but in a way that misrepresents that author's original intentions—of course, not something you intend to do but may accidentally do.

General Procedure

1. Begin the list of References on a separate page.

2. Title the page *References* and center the heading.

3. List everything alphabetically by author surname. List the author's surname first, followed by initials. Authors' or editors' full names are not given in APA format. If the work has more than one author, alphabetize according to the surname of the author listed first. If no author is listed, enter the title alphabetically. List the year of publication in parentheses after the authors' names. Titles of books or names of periodicals are italicized; titles of articles use neither italics nor quotation marks. Capitalize only the first

word of book titles and article titles, but not of journal titles. Also, the first word after a colon, whether it is part of the title of a book, journal, or article, should be capitalized.

4. Begin the first line of each entry flush with the left margin; turnover lines are indented five spaces.

In the following examples and in the sample student paper beginning on page 330, note the APA style for citing various types of sources in the list of References.

Citing Print Sources

1. Single-author Book or Pamphlet

Boorstin, D. J. (1987). *Hidden history*. New York: Harper & Row.

2. Book with More than One Author

Witt, L., Paget, K., & Matthews, G. (1994). *Running as a woman: Gender and power in American politics*. New York: Free Press.

3. Chapter from a Book

Blair, J. (1988). "The Anglo-Saxon period." In K. O. Morgan (Ed.), *The Oxford history of Britain* (pages 60–119). New York: Oxford University Press.

4. Article from a Periodical

Magazine:

Singer, M. (2000, September 25). God and football. *The New Yorker*, 76, 38–42.

Academic Journal:

Gibson, A. (1995, Spring). Universality and difference in women's abstract painting. *The Yale Journal of Criticism*, 8, 103–132.

Newspaper:

Revkin, A. C. (2000, September 12). A West African monkey is extinct, scientists say. *The New York Times*, page A20.

Letter to the Editor:

Kenny, S. S. (2001, March 19). The useless SAT [Letter to the editor]. *The New York Times*, page A22.

Unsigned Editorial:

> Flawed election in Uganda. (2001, March 16). Editorial. *The New York Times*, page A20.

In APA format, if a journal article has more than six authors, after the sixth author's name and initial, use "et al." to indicate the remaining authors of the article.

5. Book Review

Titled Review of Work:

> Dowd, M. (2000, November 5). The man in white [Review of the book *Hooking up*]. *The New York Times Book Review*, page 6.

Untitled Review of Work:

> Warren, C. (2000, Spring). [Review of the book The material ghost: Films and their medium]. *The Georgia Review*, 54, 170–174.

6.   Government Document

Author Byline Given:

> Elkouri, F., & Asper, E. (1993). *Resolving drug issues*. Washington, D.C.: Bureau of National Affairs.

No Author Byline Given:

> U.S. Department of Health and Human Services. (1980, April). *Summary report of the Graduate Medical Educational National Advisory Committee*. Washington, D.C.: U.S. Government Printing Office.

Citing Nonprint Sources

7. Web pages.   Treat sources from the Internet just as you do print sources. Cite the author and the title of the work, publication data such as journal names and volume or issue numbers, and the publication date. In addition, however, you need to give the date the site was last updated (if different from the publication date), the date you accessed the site, and the Web address. The reason for the latter information is that websites sometimes disappear or the addresses change.

Periodical Article from Web page:

Sharlet, J. (2000, September 15). A philosopher's call to
    end all paradigms. *The Chronicle of Higher Education*.
    Retrieved from http://chronicle.com/article/
    A-Philosophers-Call-to-End/34622/

Original Web page Article:

Williams, A. D. (1994). Jigsaw puzzles: Not just for children
    anymore. Retrieved from http://www.gamesmuseum.uwaterloo.
    ca/VirtualExhibits/puzzles/jigsaw/essay.html

Message Posted to an Electronic Mailing List or Newsgroup:

NASA chief predicts scientific tsunami. (2000, October 20).
    Message posted to http://metanews@meta-list.org

8. Television Program

Turner Broadcasting. (2000, November 8). *CNN evening news*
    [Television broadcast]. Atlanta: Cable News Network.

9. Recording

Audiocassette:

Churchill, W. S. (Speaker). (1998). *The great republic*
    [Audiocassette]. New York: Random House Audiobooks.

Videocassette:

Weir, P. (Director). (1985). *Witness* [Motion picture]. Los
    Angeles: Paramount Pictures.

Compact Disc:

Von Bingen, H. (1994). O choruscans stellarum [Recorded by
    Sequentia]. On *Canticles of Ecstasy* [CD]. Arles: Deutsche
    Harmonia Mundi.

10. Film

Nimoy, L. (Director). (1984). *Star trek IV: The voyage home*.
    [Motion picture]. United States: Paramount Pictures.

11. Email Message

Frost, G. (2009, Feb. 10). Message to the author. [Email].

12. Do not include nonprint sources such as interviews or correspondence in references

Sample Student Paper: APA Documentation Format

1 inch
margins
left and
right

Child Molestation 1

Jarrett Green

Argumentation

Professor Billings

May 16, 2009

Abstract

Concisely
states the
problem, the-
sis, and how
the problem
can be solved.

Child molestation has been established as a disease in both the physiological and psychological sense of the word. For this reason, prison sentences fail to cure the molester, as researchers have demonstrated. Once out of prison, molesters easily reestablish their concealed identities. Clearly, alternative measures are needed, such as forcing released molesters to publicly identify themselves as such and having the media warn the public of molesters' reestablished presence in the community.

Running head:
short title +
page number

Name, course,
instructor,
date; double,
spaced

Title, centered

Quotation works as a concrete lead-in to the topic

Child Molestation: Anything but Your Typical Crime

"I've got these urges, and I can't control myself"
(Friedman, 1991, page 2). Although these words come from the
mouth of one particular child molester, they easily could
have been uttered by thousands of others. Child molesters
come in all shapes and sizes, and live in all types of communities—from small farming towns to large metropolitan cities. All child molesters, however, have one very important
trait in common: They have an intense sexual fixation with or
attraction to children. What makes this trait so dangerous is
that it causes immense damage and, at times, destruction to
the lives of countless innocent children. Child molestation,
unlike any other illegal or stigmatized act, directly attacks
our nation's youth—our nation's future. Most states continue
to simply imprison child molesters. Some states, on the other
hand, have implemented minimal publicity programs that give
communities access to information on released child molesters.

Give author's name, year, page number if author not mentioned in the sentence

The question of how to punish or deal with child molesters
is not an easy one. I, however, believe that attaining a proper
understanding of the nature of this crime makes its solution
crystal clear. Child molestation is unlike any other crime[1] for
two reasons: (1) It has been established to be a physiological
and psychological disease, and (2) it requires secrecy and
identity concealment. This exceptional combination requires
that we treat molesters differently than we treat burglars
and car-jackers. More specifically, it requires that we *publicize*[2] child molesters, not to *shame* or *embarrass* them, but
to *disable* them.

Explanation of uniqueness of the problem

Child molestation is anything but a typical crime.
In fact, it has been established as a physiological and
psychological disease. Doctor Kieran Sullivan, Ph.D.,

Child Molestation 3

an Associate Professor in the Santa Clara University
Psychology Department, explains that pedophilia (or the
disorder from which child molesters suffer) "is officially
recognized as a diagnostic mental disorder by the DSM IV,
the psychiatrist's bible" (K. Sullivan, personal interview,
March 10, 2001). More importantly, Sullivan explains that
child molestation is

Block style
quotations
(of more than
40 words) are
indented
5 spaces from
margin and
double-spaced

> the only crime that is actually a
> psychological disorder. Although we consider
> serial killers to be "insane," their crime
> is not a direct manifestation of a
> physiological/psychological disease. Child
> molesters, on the other hand, have an
> overwhelming inner compulsion to engage in
> sexual interaction with children. It is
> an ever-present disease that drives them
> and controls them. This is what makes
> child molesters so unique. (K. Sullivan,
> personal interview, April 10, 2001)

Sharon Rice is a psychiatric nurse who
currently works in the Ohio Veteran's
Administration Outpatient Child Clinic. She has
counseled hundreds of child molesters throughout
her career, both in one-on-one and group settings.
Rice claims that child molesters are

Expert
description of
psychopathology

> inflicted with a horrible disease. Nearly all
> of the child molesters claim that if they are
> released, they will be unable to not molest
> again. Most of them think that pedophilia should
> be legalized, as they believe that they are
> just giving children love and care. The others,
> though, believe their behavior is destructive
> and harmful toward children—and they feel

Child Molestation 4

incredible guilt and depression for what they
have done. When asked whether or not they believe
they could overcome their feelings if released,
most believed that they could not. They believed
their yearning would eventually be too powerful
for them to control. Child molestation is really
a disease that overpowers the will of the
individual. (S. Rice, telephone interview,
April 16, 2001)

Child molestation is obviously a unique crime.
The child molester suffers from a disease that
overpowers any and all restrictions (such as society's
ethical standards or the molester's personal guilt).
His[3] external acts are dominated by a physiological and
psychological disorder.

Because child molestation is a physiological
and psychological disease, even the harshest prison

Explanation
of why
current strat-
egies have
failed

time usually fails in deterring the molester from
recidivating. The overall rates of recidivism, although
very difficult to determine, are extremely high. One
examination, which studied 197 convicted male child
molesters, found that 42% of the men were reconvicted
within the next 31 years (Hanson, Steffy, & Gauthier,
1993, page 646). The study offers the following important
clarification:

Although reconviction rates were used as
the recidivism criteria in this study, it is
likely that reconviction rates underestimate the
rate of reoffending. It is widely recognized that
only a fraction of the sexual offenses against
children result in the offender being convicted.
Consequently, it is possible that all of the
men in our study could have reoffended but that
only about one half got caught. (page 650)

Mary Sue Barone is the Assistant Prosecuting Attorney for the Criminal Division of the Wood County District in the state of Ohio. During her years as a prosecuting attorney she has prosecuted nearly every offense in the book, including numerous child molestation cases. Barone (telephone interview, April 16, 2001) claims that "recidivism rates of child molestation are consistently the highest of any crime, including drug abuse. It is a disease that plagues a child molester for his entire life." When asked whether prison is the proper solution for such a "disease," she replied, "We live in a society of politics. Families and society want to see the child molester locked up. Unfortunately, prison time doesn't seem to do much good the moment the child molester is released." I cannot stress this point enough: Child molestation is a disease—it is a sickness. Locking someone up for six to eight months is not going to suppress the disease. Even if the prison time is harsh, the child molester reenters society with a physiological and psychological urge that remains unimpeded. Thus, the prison's lesson goes in one ear, and the disease throws it out the other. Child molestation is not a typical crime.

The second reason child molestation is an atypical crime is due to the fact that it is inherently dependent on secrecy and identity concealment. Rarely are child molesters strangers who abuse random children at the playground. In nearly all cases, the child molester is the little league coach, the day-care assistant, the family friend, or the next-door neighbor. Everybody assumes that he is a harmless, good person. The child molester conceals his true self. He hides his destructive fantasies and intentions so that he can earn the trust of the child's parents. Having gained the trust of others, he

Child Molestation 6

commits the crime. But his crime is dependent on secrecy and concealment of his true identity.

Our current system of throwing child molesters in prison only makes the process by which they conceal their identities easier. We catch child molesters after they have *secretly* damaged or ruined the lives of countless children. Next we *hide* them in prison cells for the length of their terms and then toss them back *without warning* into the world of children. Although mere prison time is undoubtedly a "feel-good" solution, it is really no authentic solution at all. Child molesters come out of prison and are far too easily able to reestablish their concealed identities. They once again hide their molesting selves and, once again, use this concealment to poison and destroy the lives of innocent children.

Because child molestation is a truly unique crime (since it is a *disease* that undermines prison's function as a deterrent and it is inherently dependent on identity concealment), it screams for alternative state reaction, namely, publicity. Because child molestation is a disease that plagues child molesters, we cannot release them with the expectation that they will never molest again. Consequently, we must do all that we can to decrease the ease by which the disease controls child molesters' lives and damages children's lives. Publicity is this road block. It will make it difficult for child molesters to act on hidden dangerous impulses, since others will be aware of their disease. It will prevent them from succeeding in manipulatively gaining parents' trust and children's friendships so as to satisfy their harmful desires.

Emotional appeal

If we care about the lives of our children, we must make it as difficult as possible for child molesters

Child Molestation 7

to satisfy their harmful impulses through identity concealment. We must prevent them from deceiving the world
into trusting them. We must rob them of the tools used
to molest children: secrecy and identity concealment. As
I explained before, child molesters do not just molest
random kids while in line for the movies. We can and must

Explanation
of a poten-
tial solution

obstruct such development of loyalty and trust by *publicizing* child molesters. Each child molester, on release
from prison, should be publicized by a combination of
four "awareness" tactics. First, newspapers should publish the names and photographs of child molesters as they
reenter society. Second, local television news programs
should warn communities of the release of child molesters.
News programs frequently display the names and snapshots
of so-called "dangerous" citizens (such as people who are
currently wanted by the police). Released child molesters are at least as dangerous and arguably more dangerous than on-the-run convicts or prison escapees (depending
on the crime, of course). Third, child molesters should
be forced under supervision to go door-to-door throughout their entire neighborhood (if not further) and inform
people of their danger to children. Fourth, and last,
child molesters should be forced to hold up signs (such
as "I am a child molester and have recently been released
from prison") in popular public locations (such as inside shopping malls or outside movie theatres) in their
communities.

The combination of these four "awareness"
tactics makes it far more difficult for the child molester
reentering society simultaneously to reenter the lives
of children. Because the child molester so desperately
needs his disease covered up if he is successfully to
form new relationships with children, *publicizing* his

Child Molestation 8

disease will make it far more difficult for him to dupe
parents and children into thinking that he is harmless.
Thus, publicity does far more than shame the child molester
(which it may or may not actually succeed in doing); it
disables him by depriving him of the one tool that he needs
in order to molest more children: identity concealment.

Disabling child molesters by depriving them of their
necessary tool (i.e., identity concealment) is not much
different than the ancient punishment of depriving pick-
pocketers and thieves of their necessary tool (i.e., their
fingers). Pick-pocketers and thieves obviously depended
on their fingers in order to commit their crimes. Cutting
off their fingers was a simple way of preventing them from
repeating their crimes. Similarly, child molesters depend on
the concealment of their identities in order to commit their
crimes. Depriving them of their concealment via *publicity*
is really the only way we can save countless children from
being sexually molested. Child molestation is possibly the
only crime that fully depends on (which is to say—is impossible without) the concealment of identity. For this reason,
crimes such as assault and robbery (which do not depend on
the secrecy and deception of identity) should not be coun-
tered by publicity. Child molestation is a unique crime. It
requires a unique punishment.

My opponents, at this time, would claim that such
a punishment is unjustifiably excessive. They would argue
that although publicity would disable a molester from molesting, it would also disable him from successfully seeking
and holding a job. Additionally, because the child molester
has already served his time, he now ought to be permitted
to reestablish a normal life, which necessarily involves
getting a job so that he may feed, clothe and house himself.
Some, such as Judith Shepphard (1997), a journalism professor

*Acknowledge-
ment of
challenging
view*

Child Molestation 9

at Auburn University, argue that publicizing child molesters is indefensible because it constitutes double punishment (page 37).

Refutation of challenging view

I respond by arguing that we must use publicity against child molesters *in place* of full prison terms. I am advocating a decrease in (but not elimination of) prison sentences so that publicity becomes a normal part of "serving one's time." Thus, my opponents' argument that publicity is unfair because child molesters have *already served* their time is moot. The publicity with which they will be forced to deal is not *in addition* to their time; it *is* their time. A typical "punishment" for child molestation should be two-pronged: It should begin with a (shortened, according to today's norms) prison sentence, and conclude with a powerful dosage of public exposure. This public exposure is obviously not going to help child molesters get jobs (of course, our current system requires that molesters admit in their job applications that they were convicted of child molestation, which doesn't help this cause much either).

Melvin Watt, the Democratic senator from North Carolina, claims that "our Constitution says to us that a criminal defendant is presumed innocent until he or she is proven guilty. . . . The underlying assumption of this [argument] is that once you have committed one crime of this kind, you are presumed guilty for the rest of your life" (Tougher "Megan's law," 1996). Senator Watt's point demonstrates a blatant misunderstanding of the nature of child molestation. As we established earlier in the paper, child molestation is a physiological and psychological disease from which child molesters suffer. It is not as if they were only *suffering* from the disease the moment they committed the act that led to their

When authorship is not given, state title; in this case, no page number is given since the source is from a website

convictions. In reality, molesters continuously *suffer* from the disease—it is a mental disorder that they cannot escape. Child molesters are not "presumed guilty" for the rest of their lives; they are, however, presumed dangerous for the rest of their lives. This presumption, due to the nature of molestation, seems fair to make.

The final rebuttal that my opponents make is that publicity violates the convicted child molester's right to privacy. Although at an initial glance this argument appears persuasive, a proper understanding of government-enforced punishment defeats it. If a person assaults another, he is put in prison. Every individual in America has an inalienable right to liberty. We believe, however, that an individual can sacrifice this right by behaving in certain ways (such as by assaulting an innocent other). If we so easily accept that the state can violate an individual's right to liberty, why is it so shocking for me to suggest a punishment in which the state violates the individual's right to privacy? We are simply accustomed to the violation of liberty (which, by the way, is a truly sacred right). The fact that the right to privacy is not regularly violated by the government (in response to illegal behavior) does not entail that it is unjustifiable. In the case of the child molester, the violation of this right is perfectly justifiable.

Thus, I do not support the publicity of child molesters so that we might slowly eliminate individual rights or eventually revert back to our days of public shaming. I support publicity because it can *disable* and *handicap* people who leave prison prepared, due to their controlling disease, to molest more children. Although it will not put an end to the molestation of children, it will make it far more difficult for child

Restatement of thesis and concluding remarks

Child Molestation 11

molesters to reenter society and effortlessly start up where they left off.

Footnotes

[1] If a crime exists that I am presently unaware of that satisfies each of the two stated criteria, it would also be subject to *publicity* as a "punishment."

Note use of footnotes for informational purposes

[2] I acknowledge that this use of *publicize* is atypical; however, the need for such a use will become clear later in this paper. Also later in this paper, I will specify the exact manner in which child molesters will be publicized.

[3] Throughout this paper, I intentionally use the male pronoun in referring to child molesters since the great majority of child molesters are male.

Child Molestation 12

References

Friedman, S. (1991). *Outpatient treatment of child molesters*. Sarasota, FL: Professional Resource Exchange.

Hansen, K. R., Steffy, R. A., & Gauthier, R. (1993). Long-term recidivism of child molesters. *Journal of Consulting and Clinical Psychology, 61*(4), 646–652.

Shepphard, J. (1997). Double punishment?: Megan's law on child molesters. *American Journalism Review, 19*(9), 37–41.

Tougher "Megan's law" would require notification. (1996). Retrieved from http://www.cgi.cnn.com/ALLPOLITICS/1996/news/9605/08/sexoffenders/index.shtml

Title is centered

Indent second and successive lines of each entry 5 spaces

Entries are listed in alphabetical order by author surname (or by title if no author listed)

Ampersand used before name of last author listed

First word in article title and journal title capitalized; journal title and volume number italicized

Glossary of Rhetorical Terms

Active reading.   A form of critical reading, conducted in groups, for the purpose of determining the rhetorical techniques, strengths, and weaknesses of a given selection.

Ad hominem fallacy.   Literally, argument directed against the person. An error of reasoning in which the arguer attacks an individual's character or person as a way of attacking his or her ideas or performance, as in "Adam Stone does not deserve an Oscar for Best Film Editing; he has been diagnosed as psychotic."

Affirming the consequent fallacy.   In order for the outcome of a hypothetical statement ("If x, then y") to be valid, the antecedent (the "if" clause) must be affirmed or the consequent (the "then" clause) denied. It is a fallacy, however, to say that if the consequent is affirmed, then the antecedent must be denied. Consider this hypothetical statement: "If taxes are raised, the economy will prosper." To affirm the consequent—that is, to say "the economy is indeed prospering; therefore, taxes were raised"—is a fallacy (the economy, given the framework of the statement, could have prospered for other reasons). One can only deny the consequent: "The economy did not prosper; therefore, taxes were not raised."

Analogy.   Comparison made, for purpose of clarification, between two ideas sharing similar characteristics.

Analysis.   Breakdown of an idea into its constituent elements to facilitate comprehension.

Appeals.   The three means of persuasion described by Aristotle: *ethos* (referring to persuasion through character, ethics, values); *pathos* (referring to persuasion through emotions, feelings); and *logos* (referring to persuasion through logical reasoning). The three appeals often overlap in an argument.

Apples and oranges.   An error of reasoning in which a comparison is made between two things that are not comparable (because they are not part of the same category).

Argument.   A discussion in which a claim is challenged or supported with evidence. *See also* Persuasion.

Backing.   In Toulmin argument, support for the *warrant*, which is not, in itself, self-validating. The more substantial the backing, the more compelling the warrant.

Bandwagon fallacy.   The assumption that if an opinion is shared by a majority, the opinion must be correct.

Begging the question fallacy.   (1) An error of reasoning in which the "evidence" used to support a claim is merely a rephrasing of the problem, as in "Imprisonment does not deter crime because it does nothing to discourage criminal activity"; (2) Presenting a disputable claim in a manner that suggests it is beyond dispute, as in "Her whimsical ideas should not be taken seriously."

Brainstorming.   A form of prewriting in which one spontaneously records or utters ideas for a topic.

Categorization.   Arrangement or classification according to shared similarities.

Claim.   The idea or thesis that forms the basis of an argument.

Classical (or Aristotelian) argument.   A model of argument that follows a preestablished structure consisting of an introduction to the problem, a statement of the thesis or claim, a discussion of the evidence in support of the thesis, a refutation of opposing views, and a conclusion.

Clustering.   A form of prewriting in which one spontaneously writes down similar ideas and examples in circled groupings or clusters, in order to generate content for an essay.

Common ground.   In Rogerian argument, determining which points or values writer and audience agree upon despite the larger difference of opinion. *See also* Redundancy.

Composing process.   A reference to the multiple (but not necessarily sequential or otherwise orderly) activities of a writer in the act of completing a writing task. These activities typically involve such prewriting activities as brainstorming, freewriting, listing, and clustering; drafting activities such as preparing a first draft, revising, re-revising, and copyediting; and proofreading.

Concision.   Using as few words as possible without losing clarity or readability. In fact, concision improves clarity and readability. Example: "The article titled 'On Improving Memory,' which was written by Sam Smith, was published in today's *Oakville Gazette*," can be made more concise as follows: "Sam Smith's article, 'On Improving Memory,' appears in today's *Oakland Gazette*"—eleven words instead of eighteen.

Data.   Another word for *evidence*. It can also refer to statistical evidence as opposed to testimonial, mathematical, or observational evidence.

Database.   An electronic list of references grouped by subject matter.

Deduction.   A mode of reasoning that begins with what is known to be true, and seeks to determine the elements or premises that demonstrate the validity of that truth. *See also* Induction.

Definition.   In argumentative writing, definitions of technical terms are often necessary when the claim involves a specialized topic in law, the sciences, technology, business, and industry. A definition often includes reference to a word or expression's origin (etymology), and usage history, as well as a standard lexical meaning.

Denying the antecedent fallacy.   *See* Affirming the consequent fallacy.

Development.   Examining an idea in depth, using illustrations, cases in point, analysis, statistics, and other means of supporting assertions.

Discourse.   Sustained communication through oral or written language. There are three modes of discourse: (1) expository (or referential), which refers to explanation and analysis; (2) expressive, which refers to descriptive and dramatic writing; and (3) persuasive, which refers to the use of the Aristotelian appeals to change readers' minds about something. *See also* Appeals.

Either/or fallacy.   An error of reasoning in which a many-sided argument is presented as having only two sides. Also known as the *false dichotomy.*

Enthymeme.   In deductive reasoning, a syllogism in which one of the premises goes unstated because it is assumed to be understood. In the enthymeme, "Socrates is mortal because he is a human being," the omitted-because understood premise is "All human beings are mortal." *See also* Syllogism.

Ethos.   *See* Appeals.

Evidence.   Support for a claim. Evidence may be direct (data from surveys, experiments, research studies, and so on) or indirect (mathematical or logical reasoning). *See also* Proof.

Fallacy.   An error or flaw in logical reasoning.

False analogy or faulty analogy.   An error of reasoning that assumes the accuracy of an inaccurate (false) or inappropriate (faulty) comparison.

False dichotomy.   *See* Either/or fallacy.

Fourth-term fallacy.   An error of reasoning in which one term is carelessly or deceptively substituted for another in order to force the assumption that both terms mean the same thing (thereby adding a "fourth term" to a syllogism, which can contain only three terms in their respective premises: major, middle, and minor). *See also* Syllogism.

Freewriting.   A form of prewriting in which one writes spontaneously and swiftly without regard to organization, development, usage, or mechanics.

Generalization.   A nonspecific, summative statement about an idea or situation. If a generalization does not account for some situations it is said to be *hasty* or *premature.* If a generalization is not accompanied by particular examples, it is said to be *unsupported.*

Glosses.   Notes, such as comments or cross-references, in the margins of texts that enhance understanding as well as help to develop a critical stance on the ideas presented.

Hasty generalization.   *See* Generalization.

In-depth reading.   In critical reading, the stage of reading involving close attention to complexities of the topic, to subtle meanings and inferences; follows Previewing. *See also* Previewing.

Induction.   Form of reasoning whereby one attempts a generalization or hypothesis after considering particular cases or samples, not before. *See also* Deduction.

Linking.   In critical reading, the connecting of one part of a sentence with another in order to determine meaning and continuity of idea.

Listserv.   An online discussion group, acquired through subscription.

Mediation.   A form of argument that attempts to fairly present an objective discussion of opposing views before attempting to reach a conclusion.

Misreading the evidence fallacy.   Accidental or deliberate misinterpretation or misrepresentation of data as part of an effort to discredit a challenging view.

Newsgroup.   An electronic bulletin board or forum. Also known as *usenet*.

Non sequitur fallacy.   Error in reasoning in which an assertion cannot logically be tied to the premise it attempts to demonstrate.

Paraphrase.   *See* Quotation.

Peer critiquing.   A draft workshopping activity whereby the participating writers share similar backgrounds; e.g., they are all first-year college students.

Persuasion.   A form of argument that relies on using emotional appeals more than logical analysis to get readers or listeners to change their minds about something.

Plagiarism.   The use of others' ideas as if they were one's own. Plagiarism is a violation of international copyright law and therefore illegal.

Poisoning the well fallacy.   Attempting to corrupt an argument before the argument begins.

Post hoc fallacy.   Shortened form of *post hoc ergo propter hoc* ("after the fact, therefore because of the fact"). An error of reasoning in which one attaches a causal relationship to a sequential one.

Premature conclusion.   *See* Generalization.

Previewing.   The initial stage of critical reading consisting of prereading, skim-reading, and postreading. *See also* In-depth reading.

Prove.   To provide evidence involving mathematical deduction or the presentation of indisputable facts.

Proofreading.   Reading semifinal draft copy for errors in grammar, spelling, punctuation, capitalization, and the like.

Qualifier.   In Toulmin argument, a limitation imposed on a claim that makes it valid only under some or most circumstances, but not all. *See also* Toulmin argument.

Quotation.   The words of an authority used in argumentative writing to reinforce one's own views on a given topic. Direct quotation refers to verbatim citation of the author's words, which are placed in quotation marks. Indirect quotation or paraphrase refers to the author's idea without quoting verbatim. Both forms of quotation must be properly documented.

Red herring fallacy.   An error of reasoning in which one throws in an unrelated but similar seeming bit of information to throw one off the track of the issue being argued.

Redundancy. Words that unnecessarily repeat a thought already conveyed by other words in the passage. Examples: "She spoke in a soft whisper" instead of "She whispered"; "The tiles were gray in color and had rectangular shapes" instead of "The tiles were gray and rectangular.

Refutation. The technique of representing fairly and then demonstrating the shortcomings of assertions that challenge your own.

Research. The process of searching, retrieving, and integrating information from outside sources to authenticate or reinforce one's argument.

Review. A critical evaluation of an artistic work, a new product, or a restaurant.

Revising. Substantive development or restructuring of a draft. *Cf.* Proofreading.

Rhetoric. The art of or the techniques used in writing or speaking effectively. Aristotle defined rhetoric as the art of finding the best available means of persuasion in a given case.

Rhetorical rhombus. A schematic for showing the elements involved in written or oral communication: Purpose, Audience, Writer, Subject.

Rogerian argument. A mode of argument established by Carl Rogers in which arguers are urged to cooperate, to seek a common ground on which to negotiate their differences.

Serendipity. In research, a fortunate coming-together of ideas through unexpected discovery.

Slighting the opposition fallacy. An unfair downplaying of a challenger's claim, despite its potential validity.

Slippery slope fallacy. An error of reasoning in which one alludes to a sequence of highly unlikely consequences resulting from an observed or proposed situation.

Summary. A highly condensed version of a work using or paraphrasing only the work's key points.

Suspect authority. An error of authorization in which an authority's credentials do not prove his or her expertise on the topic.

Syllogism. A form of logical argument consisting of a major premise ("All stars are suns"), a minor premise ("Sirius is a star"), and a conclusion ("Therefore, Sirius is a sun").

Thesis. The claim or main idea or premise of an argument.

Topic. The specific subject of a paper.

Toulmin argument. A strategy of argument developed by philosopher Stephen A. Toulmin, in which it is understood that any claim is arguable because it is based on personal ethical values or warrants as well as on outside evidence or data.

Tracking. In critical reading, shifting the perspective of meaning from sentence to word or from sentence to paragraph or from paragraph to whole essay.

Tu quoque **fallacy.**   Literally "you too." An error of reasoning whereby one asserts that an action (or refusal to take action) is validated by the fact that the other person acted or refused to act. "Why should I obey the rules when you're always breaking them?"

Tweet: An ultra-short typed cell phone message of no more than 140 characters, including spaces, typically making use of code-like truncations such as Gr8 for "great."

Unsupported generalization.   *See* Generalization.

Vague authority.   An error of authorization in which an ambiguous entity, such as a concept or discipline, is cited as a figure of authority.

Visual aids.   Images such as charts, diagrams, or photographs, used for illustrating and reinforcing a claim.

Warrant.   *See* Toulmin argument.

Index of Authors and Titles

Index of Terms